Comparative Perspectives on the Development of Memory

COMPARATIVE PERSPECTIVES ON THE DEVELOPMENT OF MEMORY

Edited by

ROBERT KAIL
Purdue University
NORMAN E. SPEAR
State University of New York at Binghamton

LAWRENCE ERLBAUM ASSOCIATES, PUBLISHERS
1984   Hillsdale, New Jersey   London

Lawrence Erlbaum Associates, Inc., Publishers
365 Broadway
Hillsdale, New Jersey 07642

Library of Congress Cataloging in Publication Data
Main entry under title:

Comparative perspectives on the development of memory.

Based on a conference held at Purdue University, May
19–21, 1982.
Includes bibliographical references and indexes.
1. Memory—Congresses.   2. Memory in children—
Congresses.   3. Psychology, Comparative—Congresses.
I. Kail, Robert V.   II. Spear, Norman E.
BF371.C717   156'.312   83-20507
ISBN 0-89859-317-4

Printed in the United States of America
10   9   8   7   6   5   4   3   2   1

Contents

Preface

In May of 1972 a paper by Byron Campbell and one of the editors of this volume (NS) appeared in the *Psychological Review*. The other editor (RK) remembers the appearance of that paper very well: He was finishing his first year of graduate study and was hard at work mastering the literature on memory development in children. A paper entitled ''Ontogeny of memory'' appearing in the *Psychological Review* would undoubtedly provide the synthesis of the literature he needed. Unfortunately, it did not, because RK soon saw that NS and Campbell talked almost exclusively about the development of memory in rats and mice, so he read no further.

RK's graduate student response was typical of most psychologists studying the development of memory then and today. The developmental literature is divided along species lines, and researchers typically know little about the work of those who study the same phenomena in other species. Let us mention one esoteric bit of evidence to document this lack of communication between the two groups of psychologists. In 1977 a volume appeared that RK edited with John Hagen, entitled *Perspectives on the development of memory and cognition*. In 1979, a volume edited by NS and Campbell was published entitled *Ontogeny of learning and memory*. Both books include chapters by some of the leading researchers studying the development of memory, but the Kail and Hagen volume concerns exclusively memory in humans, while the Spear and Campbell book focuses entirely on learning and memory in infrahuman organisms. Now, if one defines a regular contributor to either of these literatures as an individual taking more than a single line in the author index (admittedly an arbitrary criterion, but not a totally irrational one), then there are 145 such contributors in Kail and Hagen (1977) and 85 in Spear and Campbell (1979), but only *one* who is common to both volumes, B. J. Underwood.

Other less esoteric forms of evidence could be cited to make the same point. The two groups of psychologists belong to different professional organizations, and they typically publish in different journals. Hence, the editors of this volume organized a conference, held 19–21 May 1982 at Purdue University, to bring these two groups of investigators together to discuss their common research interests. The talks and discussions were relatively informal. The chapters included in this volume were prepared afterward and have been organized in three sections. The first section includes chapters that provide historical overviews of the two research literatures. The second section consists of chapters by developmental psychologists and developmental psychobiologists that consider developmental constraints on memory as well as the development of various components of memory. The chapters in the final section identify points of contact between development of memory in humans and the development of memory in infrahumans, and suggest useful research strategies for increasing such contacts in the future. We think that the authors have skillfully laid a foundation for a comparative psychology of memory development, and have, reflecting our optimism, so named the volume.

Several individuals helped us to organize and conduct the conference and to assemble this book. Terry Powley first heard the general plans for the conference and encouraged us to pursue it together. Catherine Hale assisted us in many ways to ensure that the conference ran smoothly. Support of and funding for the conference came from F. Robert Brush, Head of the Department of Psychological Sciences at Purdue, Robert L. Ringel, Dean of Purdue's School of Humanities, Social Sciences and Education, and Lawrence Erlbaum, our publisher. To all of these individuals, many thanks.

Robert Kail
Norman E. Spear

HISTORICAL OVERVIEWS

1 The Development of Human Memory: An Historical Overview

Robert Kail
Purdue University

Mark S. Strauss
University of Pittsburgh

The purpose of this chapter is to provide a broad overview of current theoretical and empirical work on memory in infants and children. Detailed reviews of this work abound (Brown, 1975, 1979, 1982; Brown, Bransford, Ferrara, & Campione, in press; Hagen, Jongeward, & Kail, 1975; Kail & Hagen, 1977, 1982; Ornstein, 1978; Reese, 1976). Hence, we see little value in describing the database yet again. Instead, our approach will be historical, tracing the evolution of the research literature. We begin with the 1940s, when the prevailing framework for the study of children's learning was derived from studies of animal learning, and describe the literature up to the present, when artificial intelligence, linguistics, and Piagetian theory are the dominant theoretical forces in the analysis of the development of learning and memory.

The literature dealing with infants and toddlers (defined roughly as from birth to 2 years of age) has evolved separately from comparable research dealing with preschoolers and school-age children. This dissociation of research by the age of the individual stems, in part, from the fact that pressing theoretical questions have differed for the very young versus the somewhat older child. It is also borne of the limited response repertoire of the young child who cannot produce and has limited understanding of human speech. We consider the course of these research literatures separately, then point to some of their common themes.

RESEARCH WITH PRESCHOOL AND SCHOOL-AGE CHILDREN

Little work on children's learning during the first four decades of the twentieth century has had direct impact on current theorizing. The number of relevant studies during the period is small, and most were of a descriptive or normative rather than theoretical bent. (For an exception, see early work described by Cornell, this volume). However, beginning with a study by Kuenne (1946) described by many observers (e.g., Stevenson, 1972) as the beginning of the "modern era" of research on children's learning, one can trace a continued progression of research and theory up to the present time.

Kuenne's (1946) research concerned young children's performance on transposition problems of the following type. Children first learned to select the smaller of two otherwise identical squares to receive a toy. Two transfer tasks then followed in which one square was approximately twice the size of the other. On a *near* test, the smaller of the original squares was paired with an even smaller square. On a *far* test, the two squares were both novel and were considerably smaller than those presented during original learning.

Animals such as rats and monkeys would consistently select the smaller of the two squares on a near test (i.e., they would transpose), but would chose squares indiscriminately on a far test (Spence, 1937). Spence's account of these findings was that learning the original discrimination establishes excitatory and inhibitory tendencies towards the rewarded and nonrewarded stimuli. These excitatory and inhibitory potentials generalize to other stimuli. Summing the excitatory and inhibitory potentials for a stimulus yields the net or effective excitatory tendency. On near tests, the animal selects the smaller stimulus because of its greater excitatory potential. On far tests, generalization of excitatory and inhibitory potential is negligible because of the distance from the original training stimuli; lacking a systematic basis for distinguishing stimuli, the animal chooses randomly.

Kuenne (1946) hypothesized that young preverbal children would solve transposition problems in the manner described by Spence. Hence, they should transpose on near tests but not far tests. Kuenne suggested that older children's learning would be directed not by the net excitatory potentials. Older children would, instead, verbalize the relation between the stimuli and respond on the basis of that verbalized relation (e.g., "pick the smaller one"). These verbalizations should transfer as readily to much larger and much smaller squares as to similar sized ones. Hence, older children should solve near and far tests with equal skill. In fact, no 3-year-olds consistently selected the smaller square on far tests, while 27%, 50%, and 100% of the 4-, 5-, and 6-year-olds, respectively, did so. Thus, Kuenne's data were consistent with her hypothesis that learning was more likely to be controlled by verbal responses as children developed.

This hypothesis of verbally mediated learning in older but not younger children motivated much of the research on children's learning for the ensuing 20 years. This was a vital period of research during which investigators carefully probed all facets of the mediational theory of children's learning. Among the key theoretical questions addressed were the following: (1) Are there simply two developmental phases, as described above, or is there an additional intermediate phase in which appropriate verbal responses are available but do not direct learning (Maccoby, 1964)? (2) Do later, mediated forms of learning displace the earlier nonmediated variety, or are both mediated and unmediated learning present in older children and adolescents (White, 1965)? (3) Is the mediator necessarily verbal, or is it conceptual or attentional in nature (Kendler & Kendler, 1962; Zeaman & House, 1963)?

Throughout this period, *neobehaviorism,* or as it is sometimes called *theoretical behaviorism,* provided the overarching theoretical framework. This framework, while not monolithic (Kendler & Kendler, 1975) does entail a set of claims about the nature of the organism, its development, and the theoretical tools needed to explain the organism's development (Bolles, 1975; Kendler & Kendler, 1975; White, 1970). Theoretical behaviorism is derived from the *mechanistic* worldview in which the organism is viewed as inherently at rest. Like a machine, this passive organism shows activity only in response to external forces. It was assumed that the concepts of stimulus, response, and associations among stimuli and responses provided sufficient theoretical machinery to explain the behavioral development of this fundamentally passive organism.

Beginning in the 1960s, the limitations of S-R concepts became apparent to many investigators. White (1976), for example, argued that

> The great plague of learning experiments in their heyday was the plethora of odd effects which could not be handled in the conventional S-R terminology and which therefore had to be handled in discussion sections of papers. People kept discovering untoward set effects, expectancy effects, orienting effects; they kept inventing new terminology for odd, non-S-R transfer mechanisms. Nothing so much forced the rediscovery of the active organism as the recalcitrance of learning experiments designed on the premise of a passive organism. (pp. 105–106)

A study by Flavell, Beach, and Chinsky (1966) illustrates the phenomenon described by White (1976). These investigators used a serial recall task to determine if there is a stage in learning during which children can name stimuli (and hence have available an appropriate verbal mediator), but they do not do so spontaneously in the course of a learning task. Children of ages 5, 7, and 10 years were shown seven pictures. Then the experimenter pointed to a subset of two to five pictures for the children to remember on that trial. Children's spontaneous verbalizations were observed by an experimenter trained as a lip reader, a feasible procedure because pictures had been chosen so that their names would be quite discriminable from one another. Only 10% of the 5-year-olds verbalized the names of the pictures during the memory task, while 60% of the 7-year-olds and 85% of the 10-year-olds did so. Subsequently, children were asked to name all of the pictures, which proved to be a trivial task for all. Thus, a large number of 5-year-olds and some 7-year-olds seemed to be in the hypothesized intermediate stage in which appropriate verbal mediators were available but not used.

The intriguing question, of course, is why the younger children did not use the available and beneficial mediators. Flavell et al. discussed two possible explanations. In the first, representing their attempt to stay within the confines of theoretical behaviorism, they proposed that only gradually do children learn to use language beyond its original communicative context. The memorization task used by Flavell et al. represented one of those contexts to which language had not yet been extended by the younger children.

The second explanation goes far beyond the bounds of S-R constructs. Flavell et al. argued that

> Verbal coding and rehearsal on a task such as ours could be construed as reflecting or embodying certain intellectual competencies which have nothing intrinsically verbal about them. An S who codes and rehearses is, first of all, responding to the task in an intellectually active fashion . . . coding and rehearsal represents a systematic plan for coping effectively with the task requirements; it is, as such, a kind of problem-solving "algorithm" of the S's own devising. And finally, it represents a time-binding, goal-directed effort on his part . . . Viewed in this way, our kindergarten Ss may have failed to talk to themselves for reasons having nothing whatever to do with their level of linguistic development. That is, they may simply have been too young to engage in the kinds of intellectual activities which assume the guise in this particular task, of verbal coding and rehearsal. (pp. 297–298)

Obviously this explanation represents a complete abandonment of neobehaviorism. The organism is now actively interpreting the task instead of acting only in response to external forces. Goals, plans, and strategies are the key theoretical constructs, replacing stimuli, responses, and associations.

Use of Mnemonic Strategies

Flavell et al.'s second explanation spawned an entire decade of research, beginning in the late 1960s, concerning developmental change in children's use of strategies for learning and remembering (Brown et al., in press, Kail & Hagen, 1982). This work revealed that by 8 or 9 years of age, children would use numerous strategies as aids in their efforts to remember. They would rehearse the names of stimuli and organize stimuli in terms of various semantic properties (Hagen & Kail, 1973; Neimark, Slotnick & Urich, 1971; Ornstein, Naus, & Liberty, 1975). Children younger than 7 or 8 years would rarely use these or any of a number of other potentially helpful memory strategies. These children often seemed to be conspicuously inactive in response to instructions to remember, a marked contrast to the elaborate memorization schemes of older children.

The foregoing essentially derogatory characterization of the young child was, for several reasons, unsatisfactory. First, it was primarily a description of mnemonic shortcomings rather than a positive portrayal of competencies. Because most developmental psychologists assume that later competencies emerge (at least in part) from earlier ones, a "description by deficit" is of little help in suggesting how children develop greater expertise. Second, the unflattering description of preschoolers' memory skills was a discordant note in a period replete with demonstrations of competence in preschool children (Gelman, 1978). Third, the inept characterization of young children did not jibe well with parents' reports that their young children often remember quite accurately.

The cumulative impact of these criticisms was to focus research in the late 1970s on the memory skills of preschoolers and young children. One line of research was designed to identify those factors governing the development of effective memory in these children. Much of this work has been done by Marion Perlmutter and her colleagues (Myers & Perlmutter, 1978; Perlmutter, 1980) and is described in Chapter 11 of this volume. A second line of research has addressed the reasons for young children's failure to use mnemonic strategies. It was proposed (e.g., Flavell & Wellman, 1977) that the emergence of strategic behavior may be partly attributable to the growing child's acquisition of the many mnemonic facts that implicitly govern the behavior of a more mature individual. For example, consider the concept of "forgetting" and the consequences of incomplete or inaccurate understanding of this concept. Because memory strategies are used to avoid or at least minimize forgetting, use of memory strategies would seem to presuppose some rudimentary understanding of forgetting.

In fact, it is now well established that these kinds of metamnemonic knowledge increase in an orderly fashion as children develop. Preschool children do have rudimentary understanding of the terms "remember," "forget," "know," and "guess" (Johnson & Wellman, 1980; Wellman & Johnson, 1979) and they typically behave differently when told to remember stimuli than when given nonmnemonic instructions regarding stimuli (Appel, Cooper, McCarrel, Sims-Knight, Yussen, & Flavell, 1972; Wellman, Ritter, & Flavell, 1975). At the same time, preschoolers consistently overpredict the number of items they will recall in a memory-span task; not until the middle elementary years do children's predictions of their recall approximate actual recall (Flavell, Friedrichs, & Hoyt, 1970; Yussen & Levy, 1975). To cite another example of preschoolers' lack of mnemonic awareness, not until approximately 9 or 10 years of age do children understand that sematically related material is easier to remember that unrelated material (Kreutzer, Leonard, & Flavell, 1975).

There has been less success in demonstrating that the lack of task-relevant knowledge is the cause of young children's failure to use strategies. On the one hand, there are many correlational studies in which investigators have assessed children's knowledge of some mnemonic fact (e.g., retention is aided by forming groups of similar items during study) with their tendency to behave accordingly. Generally, these relationships have been weak (e.g., Salatas & Flavell, 1976; Yussen, Levin, Berman, & Palm, 1979). On the other hand, training young children to use strategies is more likely to be successful—in the sense that training persists over time—if the training regimen includes a metamnemonic component. That is, young children can readily be taught to use many mnemonic strategies (e.g., Keeney, Cannizzo, & Flavell, 1967), but children will typically *not* continue to use the newly acquired strategies unless the link between their improved retention and their use of the strategy is made explicit (Kennedy & Miller, 1976; Paris, Newman, & McVey, 1982; Ringel & Springer, 1980).

The upshot of these findings has been rethinking of the notion that relevant metamnemonic knowledge is necessary and sufficient for the appearance of the appropriate mnemonic behavior. One suggestion is methodological: In most of the aforementioned correlational studies, the task-relevant knowledge was assumed rather than verified directly; thus, ephemeral memory-metamemory relationships may reflect errors in the presumed task-relevant knowledge (Cavanaugh & Perlmutter, 1982). A second suggestion is that current views of metacognition are too "static" and ignore the fact that much of what we call metamemory (e.g., knowledge of, goals for, and the effort allocated to a task) may evolve over the course of task performance (Paris & Cross, 1983). Yet another idea is that the term metamemory (and, more generally, metacognition) is too all-encompassing. Greater understanding would occur if we abandoned the study of metamemory-memory relations and looked instead at relations between memory and the various component skills (e.g., planning ahead, monitoring current performance) that are now lumped together.

In sum, there is considerable agreement that the original conceptions of metamemory (and of its relation to memory) were ambiguous and too simple. At the same time, there is at least as much agreement that the various phenomena studied thus far under the twin rubrics of metamemory and metacognition are central to our understanding of cognitive development and that they certainly warrant additional empirical and theoretical scrutiny (Brown, 1978; Brown et al., in press; Flavell & Wellman, 1977; Paris & Cross, 1983).

Constructive Memory Processes

Research on memory strategies and metamemory—like much memory work in experimental psychology—is a part of the Ebbinghaus tradition in memory experimentation. Children are asked to remember relatively meaningless stimuli for brief periods of time. Investigators often go to great lengths to ensure that stimuli are equally familiar to all children so that older children do not have an "unfair" advantage over young children. There is, however, another tradition of memory research, that traced to Bartlett (1932), which has had growing impact on empirical and theoretical efforts in developmental psychology. According to this *constructive* view of memory, people use their knowledge to embellish and elaborate information they store in memory. A consequence of this tendency is that verbatim recall of complex, meaningful stimuli is often poor, but rarely is the meaning or gist of information lost. The interesting developmental corollary to this view is that, as children acquire more knowledge in a particular domain, they should construct increasingly more complex and elaborate mnemonic representations of information in that domain.

Developmental work in this tradition is recent, dating from the early to mid-1970s. Developmental psychologists have typically followed Bartlett's (1932) lead methodologically in using recall of prose to study constructive memory processes. By manipulating the content and organization of stories, one can determine if memory for the story is mediated by story-relevant knowledge. Some specific manipulations have included the following: (1) Test "recognition" of information that was not presented but that is consistent with information actually presented (Liben & Posnansky, 1977; Paris & Carter, 1973; Small & Butterworth, 1981); (2) include information in a story that is presumed to be inconsistent with most children's knowledge, then determine if children omit such information in recall or distort it to make it more consistent with their story-relevant knowledge (Koblinsky & Cruse, 1981; Koblinsky, Cruse, & Sugawara, 1978; Liben & Signorella, 1980); (3) include passages in a story that are vague, then determine how recall of such passages is influenced by the presence of disambiguating information such as a title (Brown, Smiley, Day, Townsend, & Lawton, 1977; Harris, Mandias, Terwogt, & Tjintjelaar, 1980; Omanson, Warren, & Trabasso, 1978).

Despite the diversity of paradigms, research of this sort typically points to a common conclusion of *quantitative* rather than *qualitative* differences in constructive memory processes. Beginning in the late preschool years, children are likely to elaborate their memory for a story with pertinent knowledge, derive relevant inferences, and so on, but typically their constructive activities are not as extensive as those of older individuals. In some cases this may be because young children do not have as much story-relevant knowledge to bring to bear as older children. In other cases the story-relevant knowledge may be available but is not activated. At this point, there is insufficient evidence to be able to decide between these (and other) explanations of quantitative differences in constructive memory.

Developmental Invariance

In virtually all of the research described thus far, developmental differences in memory performance are assumed; it is the question of developmental differences in memory processes that attracts attention. Yet it would be inaccurate to imply that the advantage of older individuals over younger ones extends to all memory tasks. To the contrary, when memory tasks minimize the use of strategies or minimize the potential mnemonic role of task-relevant knowledge, developmental differences in performance are likely to be minimized.

One task that fits this description is recognition memory, and in fact, preschoolers have exceptionally accurate recognition memory. For example, 4-year-olds shown a series of 100 pictures recognized those pictures with 84% accuracy 1 day later and with 75% accuracy 1 week later (Brown & Scott, 1971). This high level of recognition accuracy was maintained even when the recognition foils consisted of a figure seen previously but depicted in a different pose (Brown & Campione, 1972). However, when recognition is made dependent upon conceptual development (e.g., Mandler & Robinson, 1978) or sustained attention (e.g., Hoffman & Dick, 1976), younger children's performance will usually be poorer than that of older children and adults.

Similar to recognition memory is the judgment of recency task. As in recognition memory tasks, children are shown a series of pictures. Later they are shown a pair of pictures from the series and are asked to judge which of the pair was presented later (i.e., more recently) in the list. When relatively long series (i.e., 20+) of pictures are used (thereby reducing the impact of age-related differences in rehearsal or other mnemonics), there is consistent developmental similarity in performance (Brown, 1973; Brown, Campione, & Gilliard, 1974).

A final case of minimal developmental differences comes from the Sternberg (1966) paradigm. When adults are shown a subspan set of stimuli and immediately thereafter are asked if a particular stimulus was a member of that set, response time is typically a linear-increasing function of the number of stimuli in the set. The slope of this function, typically approximately 35 to 40 milliseconds for adults, reflects the amount of time to scan memory for each additional stimulus in the set.

The pertinent development literature seems, at first glance, full of contradictory evidence. For example, estimates of scanning rates for 7- and 8-year-olds range from 223 milliseconds per digit (Herrmann & Landis, 1977) to approximately 40 milliseconds per digit (Harris & Fleer, 1974), a greater than fivefold difference. However, the studies in this area differ considerably in the amount of practice that children received prior to the trails used to estimate scanning speed. Salthouse and Kail (1983) showed that when studies are distinguished in terms of the amount of practice, the findings become much more consistent. When subjects had at least moderate practice (i.e., 48+ practice trials), age was unrelated to scanning rate (Dugas & Kellas, 1974; Harris & Fleer, 1974; Naus & Ornstein, 1977). All age groups scanned at approximately 40 millisceonds per digit, a value approximating Sternberg's (1966) estimate of the scanning rate of young adults. Further, the standard deviation of the six means associated with these studies is less than 6 milliseconds, an astonishingly small figure considering the varied sources of the means.

RESEARCH ON MEMORY IN HUMAN INFANTS

Given the long history of psychological research concerned with understanding the human memory system, it is perhaps surprising that basic cognitive research with infants has been conducted only within the last 20 to 30 years. To understand why this is the case requires some discussion of the historical antecendents that have led to the current field of infant cognitive psychology.

For the major part of history, infancy has been considered a relatively unimportant portion of the human lifespan. To a large extent this may have been the result of the high mortality rates typically associated with infants, and parents consequently did not become overly invested in the relatively fragile child. Indeed, by as late as the 1750s, the odds were 3 to 1 against a child reaching the fifth birthday. And as recently as 1890, 25% of the population did not survive to their fifth birthday (Kessen, 1965). By the early to mid-1900s, not only had mortality rates during infancy decreased dramatically, but there was a growing influence in psychology of the psychoanalytic theory of personality development. Freud and his followers stressed how development during the first years of life could have lasting impact on both childhood and adulthood. Concurrent with the growing influence of psychoanalytic theory was an increasing concern with the educational system and the extent to which social class differences in academic skill might have their origins in infancy and the preschool period (Kagan, 1971).

As a result of these and other developments, there was a proliferation of infancy research in the 1930s to 1950s. However, most of this research consisted of the collection of detailed descriptive data (e.g., Dennis & Dennis, 1937; Leopold, 1939; Valentine, 1930) and norms of development (e.g., Bayley, 1933; Cattell, 1940; Gesell, 1925; Shirley, 1931). While the classic work of Gesell, Bayley, and others made an important contribution to our knowledge of infant development, most of this work was not experimental in nature, being concerned instead with documenting observable physiological changes and the course of motor development. Thus, before a true discipline of research on infant cognitive development could emerge, there had to be (1) a shift in interest from research concerned almost exclusively with motor and physiological development to one concerned with sensory and cognitive development, and (2) a shift from descriptive and purely normative research to experimentally based research.

Both of these shifts began to take place by the end of the 1950s and during the 1960s. They were prompted by two primary forces. First, early work of Robert Fantz demonstrated how simple procedures such as recording the infant's visual attention could be used to explore a number of basic processes including visual acuity (Fantz, Ordy, & Udelf, 1962), perception (Fantz & Nevis, 1967), and memory (Fantz, 1964). Second, a number of researchers began to investigate whether the infant could be conditioned classically (e.g., Kaye, 1967; Lipsitt & Kaye, 1964) or operantly (e.g., Siqueland & Lipsitt, 1966; Papousek, 1967; Watson, 1966).

This research of the 1960s had a major impact in establishing an experimentally based field of infant cognitive research. In restrospect, however, it also had some important limitations. First, as mentioned previously, much of this work was focused on cataloging what basic psychological skills infants possessed. Little concern was given to how these processes operate or develop. Second, this research was limited as a result of it having grown directly out of the neobehaviorist approach that was still the dominant force in experimental psychology. In line with this approach, many of the infant studies were limited to observations of how overt behavior of the infant could be changed as a result of experimental manipulations; little concern was given to what internal processes could account for these changes. Also, there was a tendency to "operationally define" the independent variables of an experiment, with little thought being given to whether these variables had any construct validity. For example, a number of studies were conducted to explore whether, with development, infants tend to "prefer" increasingly "complex" stimuli. Typically, complexity was operationally defined as "number of checkerboards," with a 2 × 2 considered less complex than a 4 × 4 or 8 × 8, and so on. Indeed, based on a number of studies, it was concluded that as infants develop they do prefer stimuli of increasing complexity. Unfortunately, most researchers were satisfied with the "number of checks" as an operational definition, and little thought was given as to whether this really represented a scale of cognitive complexity to the infant. Indeed, later work by Karmel and Maisel (1975) and by Miranda and Fantz (1971) demonstrated how such "preferences" were actually due to the infant's developing visual abilities and did not reflect what could be called "cognitive preferences."

A third limitation of much of the research of the 1960s was the existence of a strong predisposition to consider the infant overly "competent" and to some extent fully developed at birth. The research demonstrated that infants had a number of behaviors which many interpreted as evidence that even newborns were relatively complex cognitive organisms. For example, many interpreted the early work of Fantz et al. (1962) as demonstrating that even newborn infants possessed clearly "cognitive preferences" with respect to what types of stimuli they "wanted" to observe. A large literature also suggested that infants had innate "cognitive preferences" for facelike stimuli. In retrospect, we realize that much of this data was overly interpreted and that adequate controls were often not used (for example, see the discussion of face perception by Cohen, DeLoache, & Strauss, 1979).

Nevertheless, the term "competent infant" became very popular. Consider the introductory chapter of a book entitled *The Competent Infant* (Stone, Smith, & Murphy, 1973). In this chapter, the authors quoted some stances that they considered so embarrassing that they would not reveal the authors of the quotations. Three of these quotations are cited here:

> The newborn's eye is incapable of form or pattern discrimination. (1942)

> Consciousness, as we think of it, probably does not exist in the newborn, but the sense of pain does, and the baby is also sensitive to touch and pressure . . . The responses to all of these sensations, however, are of purely reflex character and are mediated . . . below the level of the cerebral cortex. (1964)

> The human infant at birth, and for a varying period of time thereafter, has been seen as functionally decorticate, since the cortex does not exhibit its full functioning until later. Therefore, the newborn has been considered as largely a reflex organism, primarily controlled by his internal environment and organic processes, but responsive to a number of external impacts. (1966)

Interestingly, most current researchers, while perhaps not totally agreeing with these statements, certainly would not find them embarrassing, and would probably consider them accurate, at least generally. Thus, another historical shift which needed to occur for the development of our current state of infant cognitive research was the separation of carefully controlled empirical findings from a strong predisposition concerning the competency of newborns and infants.

The First Decade of Research

The direct historical antecedents of current research on infant memory were summarized by Cohen (1976).

> Interest in infant habituation originated primarily from two sources. In the 1950s investigators of animal behavior were becoming increasingly disenchanted with traditional drive reduction theories such as those of Hull (1943) and Spence (1956), and were discovering that a wide variety of organisms would approach or explore a stimulus for no reason other than that it was novel (Welker, 1961) . . . New motivational theories were proposed which put the reinforcing effects of novelty or stimulus change on a par with other more primary reinforcers such as food, water, and sex . . . The second source of interest in infant habituation stemmed from the work of Sokolov (1963, 1969) on the orienting reflex . . . According to Sokolov, the orienting reflex is not simply a reaction to current stimulation. Rather, it is a product of the discrepancy between current inputs and the neuronal trace or memory of prior ones. He assumed that within certain limits, the magnitude of the OR was proportional to the difference between the trace and the stimulus operating at a given moment. Since the discrepancy should be greatest when a novel stimulus is first presented, the largest OR should also occur. Repeated presentation of the same stimulus should lead to a buildup of the trace of that stimulus, reducing the discrepancy and thereby producing habituation of the OR.

The trends described by Cohen coincided, as noted above, with the emergence of an experimental tradition among psychologists studying infants and specifically with Fantz's (1958) description of a procedure for measuring visual attention based on corneal reflection. The result was a number of studies designed to examine infants' attention and habituation to visual stimuli (for reviews see Cohen, 1976; Cohen et al., 1979; Fantz, Fagan, & Miranda, 1975; Jeffrey & Cohen, 1971). Fantz (1964), for example, presented 10 pairs of pictures to 1- to 6-month-olds, for 1 minute per pair. One picture was the same for all 10 pairs, while the other picture in the pair was always novel. Before 2 months of age, infants attended to the two pictures equally; beyond this age infants looked less at the picture that was common to all pairs. The Fantz (1964) data imply, then, that by 2 to 3 months of age, infants are capable of discriminating the patterns (in this case, pictures taken from magazines) and remembering them for (minimally) the duration of the intertrial interval. Subsequently, it was demonstrated that even newborns apparently are capable of such immediate recognition of previously seen stimuli (Friedman, 1972 a, b; Friedman & Carpenter, 1971; Friedman, Bruno, & Vietze, 1974).

Given that immediate recognition was apparent from birth, researchers soon began to investigate other characteristics of infants' retention. For example, "long-term" retention was studied by varying the time between habituation to a stimulus and the presentation of that stimulus with a novel stimulus. Work by Fagan (1970, 1973) is illustrative. In one experiment checkerboard patterns were shown to 6-month-olds for 2 minutes. Either immediately or after delays of 24 or 48 hours, this checkerboard was shown for 20 seconds with a novel pattern. Infants looked consistently longer at the novel stimulus, regardless of the length of time between initial viewing of the stimulus and the "memory test." In a second experiment, the stimuli were photographs of human faces. Retention was tested after intervals ranging from less than 1 day to 2 weeks; in every case, 6-month-olds looked reliably longer at the novel stimuli, prompting Fagan (1973, p. 448) to conclude "that long-term recognition memory for pictorial stimuli is a very basic ability occurring . . . in the early months of life."

Subsequently, the habituation paradigm and other derivative paradigms have been used with infants to study a long list of classic memory phenomena. Included would be (a) the influence of amount and distribution of familiarization time on infants' recognition (Cornell, 1980; Fagan, 1974); (b) the manner in which multidimensional stimuli are encoded in memory (Cornell & Strauss, 1973; Fagan, 1977; Miller, 1972; Strauss & Cohen, 1978); (c) interference phenomena (Bornstein, 1976; Martin, 1975; Olson, 1976; and (d) cues that improve infants' recognition (Fagan, 1978).

The Current State

It is obvious that habituation paradigms have been and will continue to be important tools in the study of infant memory. Yet extensive use of these paradigms has made their limitations evident as well (Sophian, 1980). One potential problem is that preferential looking at a familiar stimulus actually reflects two phenomena: memory of the familiar stimulus and a bias towards looking at novel stimuli rather than familiar ones (Sophian, 1980, 1981). Hence, one must be able to eliminate novelty preference as an explanation for differential looking in order to make conclusions about memory (Sophian, 1980, 1981). This has not been a serious problem in most of the existing work (Carter & Strauss, 1981) but could be more problematic as investigators attempt to address more subtle questions using habituation procedures, particularly when differences in degree of differential looking (rather than its mere presence or absence) is the key datum.

Another drawback to the habituation procedure is that it yields data only about recognition (Sophian, 1980). And to some, it is an odd brand of recognition memory at that. Rovee-Collier and Fagen (1981), for example, characterized the habituation paradigm in the following way:

> A retention test, administered after one or more exposures of a given stimulus (S_1) involves the simultaneous (paired-comparison paradigm) or successive (habituation/discrimination paradigm) presentation of a novel stimulus (S_2). Retention ("recognition") of S_1 is *inferred* from the relatively greater attention allocated to S_2, i.e., from the extent to which the infant does *not* attend to S_1. Paradoxically, this analysis terminates with response to S_2; it provides no mechanism by which to measure whether the infant can use the information "recognized" in S_1. When carried to a logical conclusion, this model describes the processing and storage of stimulus attributes to which an infant will systematically *not* attend in the future. It is difficult to conceptualize the evolutionary advantage of such a memory system. (p. 226)

(For other criticisms and related discussion, see Carter & Strauss, 1981; Clifton & Nelson, 1976; Sophian, 1980, 1981; Werner & Perlmutter, 1979).

The cumulative impact of these criticisms is an emerging awareness that habituation paradigms be supplemented with other procedures. Sophian (1980), for instance, suggests that object permanence tasks could be a potentially fruitful source of data. However, by far the most extensive and systematic body of experimental work on infant memory outside of the habituation tradition is the research of Rovee-Collier and her colleagues (Fagen & Rovee-Collier, 1982; Rovee-Collier, this volume; Rovee-Collier & Fagen, 1981). They have used a conjugate reinforcement procedure to study a variety of memory phenomena in 8- to 12-weeks-olds. Their research represents an important broadening of the data base on infant memory. Other, comparably powerful methodologies are needed for a complete account of infant memory and represent an important part of the current agenda for psychologists studying infant memory.

CONCLUDING REMARKS

The two bodies of research summarized here have two common aims. The first is a precise description of the development of memory skill from birth to adulthood. That is, we wish to know the shape of the developmental function for various memory skills. The second objective is a theory that can explain the observed developmental function of at least one and preferably several memory processes. These general objectives are shared by scientists studying the development of learning and memory in animals (e.g., Campbell & Coulter, 1976). Hence, a few summary comments may be useful regarding developmental psychologists' success in achieving these goals.

Consider the first of these goals—characterizing the developmental function. Most of the published studies of infant memory involve infants of just one age group. Developmental studies are the exception and even the small number of developmental studies typically involve a comparison of only two age groups. The reason, of course, for this paucity of developmental data is that infancy is a period of such rapid and dramatic ontogenetic change that most paradigms used with 3-month-olds are completely unsuitable for 9-month-olds. As a consequence, for the foreseeable future, accounts of memory development during infancy are likely to be extrapolations based on performance from different tasks that ostensibly tap the same memory processes.

One might expect that developmental psychologists studying verbal children would have made better headway, for many tasks can be administered—in essentially the same form—to 2- and 3-year-olds and to adults. This is not the case. The "modal memory experiment" (Brown & DeLoache, 1978) with children involves two age groups, usually selected from the extremes of the elementary school grades. While such experiments can be useful in highlighting developmental differences in mnemonic phenomenon, they provide few insights into the manner in which children acquire progressively greater mnemonic skill. Instead, research of this type often reads like a comparison of the "haves" versus the "have nots"; older children are competent with regard to the process under study while younger children are not. The result is that our description of memory development beyond infancy remains, to a large extent, a patchwork of findings derived from different paradigms. We are simply not close to developmental timetables of the type described in work with infrahumans for sensory development (Alberts, this volume) or learning (Rudy, Vogt, & Hyson, this volume).

With this limited progress in the descriptive domain, it is not surprising that there has been only modest success in formulating *theories* of human memory development. Some theories have been proposed regarding the role of processing capacity in producing change in memory (e.g., Case, 1978) and theories regarding specific environmental influences on memory have also been proposed (Cole & Scribner, 1977; Wachs, this volume; D. A. Wagner, 1978; Wagner & Paris, 1981). The primary shortcoming of these theories is that they typically address relatively circumscribed aspects of memory and deal with an equally circumscribed portion of the lifespan. For example, much of the theoretical work on memory-relevant environmental factors has concerned ways in which formal schooling may result in the emergence of memory strategies in children after 5 or 6 years of age. Hence, a more comprehensive, integrative theoretical account of human memory development remains a major objective of future work.

A final comment on memory theory in developmental psychology may be helpful. Current views of human memory development have been influenced by a number of sources including work in cognitive psychology, artificial intelligence, linguistics, and Piagetian theory. Notable by their absence from this list are theories of conditioning (Rescorla & Holland, 1976; A. R. Wagner, 1976, 1978) and a biological/evolutionary/ecological perspective (Bolles, 1975; Spear, this volume). As noted earlier in this chapter, neobehaviorism, with its emphasis on the study of conditioning and other varieties of learning, was the dominant perspective in "experimental child psychology" until it was displaced in the late 1960s and early 1970s by the cognitive tradition. This seems to be a case of the proverbial "throwing out the baby with the bath water," for with the demise of neobehaviorism the study of learning per se was also virtually eliminated from the scientific agenda for psychologists studying preschoolers and older children (Bisanz, Bisanz, & Kail, 1983; Brown et al., 1983). This shift was not as pervasive for researchers studying infants. It is the case, however, that with the exception of work by Watson (this volume) and Rovee-Collier (this volume), conditioning theories have had negligible impact on theorizing about infant memory. In like manner, the evolutionary/ecological perspective has been ignored by most developmental psychologists interested in memory. How various memory processes might be adaptive (or maladaptive) for development are questions that are only beginning to be raised in the developmental literature (Brown, 1982; Brown et al., 1983; Rovee-Collier & Fagen, 1981).

REFERENCES

Appel, L. F., Cooper, R. G., McCarrell, N., Sims-Knight, J., Yussen, S. R., & Flavell, J. H. The development of the distinction between perceiving and memorizing. *Child Development*, 1972, *43*, 1365–1381.

Bartlett, F. C. *Remembering*. Cambridge, England: Cambridge University Press, 1932.

Bayley, N. *The California first-year mental scale*. Berkeley: University of California Press, 1933.

Bisanz, J. H., Bisanz, G. L., & Kail, R. (Eds.). *Progress in cognitive development research* (Vol. 4): *Learning in children*. New York: Springer-Verlag, 1983.

Bolles, R. C. Learning, motivation, and cognition. In W. K. Estes (Ed.), *Handbook of learning and cognitive processes* (Vol. 1). Hillsdale, N.J.: Lawrence Erlbaum Associates, 1975.

Bornstein, M. H. Infants' recognition memory for hue. *Developmental Psychology*, 1976, *12*, 185–191.

Brown, A. L. Judgment of recency for long sequences of pictures: The absence of a developmental trend. *Journal of Experimental Child Psychology*, 1973, *15*, 473–480.

Brown, A. L. The development of memory: Knowing, knowing about knowing, and knowing how to know. In H. W. Reese (Ed.), *Advances in child development and behavior* (Vol. 10). New York: Academic Press, 1975.

Brown, A. L. Knowing when, where, and how to remember: A problem of metacognition. In R. Glaser (Ed.), *Advances in instructional psychology* (Vol. 1). Hillsdale, N.J.: Lawrence Erlbaum Associates, 1978.

Brown, A. L. Theories of memory and the problems of development: Activity, growth, and knowledge. In L. S. Cermak & F. I. M. Craik (Eds.), *Levels of processing in human memory*. Hillsdale, N.J.: Lawrence Erlbaum Associates, 1979.

Brown, A. L. Learning and development: The problem of compatibility, access, and induction. *Human Development*, 1982, *25*, 89–115.

Brown, A. L., & Campione, J. C. Recognition memory for perceptually similar pictures in preschool children. *Journal of Experimental Psychology*, 1972, *95*, 55–62.

Brown, A. L., & DeLoache, J. S. Skills, plans, and self-regulation. In R. Siegler (Ed.), *Children's thinking: What develops?* Hillsdale, N.J.: Lawrence Erlbaum Associates, 1978.

Brown, A. L., & Scott, M. S. Recognition memory for pictures in preschool children. *Journal of Experimental Child Psychology*, 1971, *11*, 401–412.

Brown, A. L., Campione, J. C., & Gilliard, D. M. Recency judgments in children: A production deficiency in the use of redundant background cues. *Developmental Psychology*, 1974, *10*, 404.

Brown, A. L., Bransford, J. D., Ferrara, R. A., & Campione, J. C. Learning, remembering, and understanding. In P. Mussen (Ed.), *Carmichael's manual of child psychology* (Vol. 1). New York: Wiley, 1983, in press.

Brown, A. L., Smiley, S. S., Day, J. D., Townsend, M. A. R., & Lawton, S. C. Intrusion of a thematic idea in children's comprehension and retention of stores. *Child Development*, 1977, *48*, 1454–1466.

Campbell, B. A., & Coulter, X. Neural and psychological processes underlying the development of learning and memory. In T. J. Tighe & R. N. Leaton (Eds.), *Habituation: Perspectives from child development, animal behavior, and neurophsyiology*. Hillsdale, N.J.: Lawrence Erlbaum Associates, 1976.

Carter, P., & Strauss, M. S. Habituation is not enough, but it's not a bad start—A reply to Sophian. *Merrill-Palmer Quarterly*, 1981, *27*, 333–337.

Case, R. Intellectual development from birth to adulthood: A neo-Piagetian interpretation. In R. S. Siegler (Ed.), *Children's thinking: What develops?* Hillsdale, N.J.: Lawrence Erlbaum Associates, 1978.

Cattell, P. *The measurement of intelligence of infants and young children*. New York: Psychological Corporation, 1940.

Cavanaugh, J. C., & Perlmutter, M. Metamemory: A critical examination. *Child Development*, 1982, *53*, 11–28.

Clifton, R. K., & Nelson, M. N. Developmental study of habituation in infants: The importance of paradigm, response system, and state. In T. J. Tighe & R. N. Leaton (Eds.), *Habituation: Perspectives from child development, animal behavior, and neurophysiology*. Hillsdale, N.J.: Lawrence Erlbaum Associates, 1976.

Cohen, L. B. Habituation of visual attention. In T. J. Tighe & R. N. Leaton (Eds.), *Habituation: Perspectives from child development, animal behavior, and neurophysiology*. Hillsdale, N.J.: Lawrence Erlbaum Associates, 1976.

Cohen, L. B., DeLoache, J. S., & Strauss, M. S. Infant visual perception. In J. Osofsky (Ed.), *Handbook of infant development*. New York: Wiley, 1979.

Cole, M., & Scribner, S. Cross-cultural studies of memory and cognition. In R. V. Kail & J. W. Hagen (Eds.), *Perspectives on the development of memory and cognition*. Hillsdale, N.J.: Lawrence Erlbaum Associates, 1977.

Cornell, E. H. Distributed study facilitates infants' delayed recognition memory. *Memory & Cognition*, 1980, *8*, 539–542.

Cornell, E. H., & Strauss, M. S. Infants' responsiveness to compounds of habituated visual stimuli. *Developmental Psychology*, 1973, *9*, 73–78.

Dennis, W., & Dennis, M. G. Behavioral development in the first year of life as shown by forty biographies. *Psychological Record*, 1937, *1*, 349–361.

Dugas, J., & Kellas, G. Encoding and retrieval processes in normal children and retarded adolescents. *Journal of Experimental Child Psychology*, 1974, *17*, 177–185.

Fagan, J. F. Memory in the infant. *Journal of Experimental Child Psychology*, 1970, *9*, 217–226.

Fagan, J. F. Infants' delayed recognition memory and forgetting. *Journal of Experimental Child Psychology*, 1973, *16*, 424–450.

Fagan, J. F. Facilitation of infants' recognition memory. *Child Development*, 1978, *49*, 1066–1075.

Fagan, J. F. Infant recognition memory: The effects of length of familiarization and type of discrimination task. *Child Development*, 1974, *45*, 351–356.

Fagan, J. F. An attention model of infant recognition. *Child Development*, 1977, *48*, 68–78.

Fagen, J. W., & Rovee-Collier, C. K. A conditioning analysis of infant memory: How do we know that they know what we know they knew? In N. E. Spear & R. L. Isaacson (Eds.), *The expression of knowledge*. New York: Plenum, 1982.

Fantz, R. L. Pattern vision in young infants. *Psychological Record*, 1958, *8*, 43–49.

Fantz, R. L. Visual experience in infants: Decreased attention to familiar patterns relative to novel ones. *Science*, 1964, *146*, 668–670.

Fantz, R. L., & Nevis, S. Pattern preferences and perceptual-cognitive development in early infancy. *Merrill-Palmer Quarterly*, 1967, *13*, 77–108.

Fantz, R. L., Ordy, J. M., & Udelf, M. S. Maturation of pattern vision in infants during the first 6 months. *Journal of Comparative and Physiological Psychology*, 1962, *55*, 907–917.

Fantz, R. L., Fagan, J. F., & Miranda, S. B. Early visual selectivity. In L. B. Cohen & P. Salapatek (Eds.), *Infant perception: From sensation to cognition* (Vol. 1). New York: Academic Press, 1975.

Flavell, J. H., & Wellman, H. M. Metamemory. In R. V. Kail & J. W. Hagen (Eds.), *Perspectives on the development of memory and cognition*. Hillsdale, N.J.: Lawrence Erlbaum Associates, 1977.

Flavell. J. H., Beach, D. R., & Chinsky, J. M. Spontaneous verbal rehearsal in a memory task as a function of age. *Child Development*, 1966, *37*, 283–299.

Flavell, J. H., Friedrichs, A. G., & Hoyt, J. D. Developmental changes in memorization processes. *Cognitive Psychology*, 1970, *1*, 324–340.

Friedman, S. Habituation and recovery of visual response in the alert human newborn. *Journal of Experimental Child Psychology*, 1972, *13*, 339–349. (a)

Friedman, S. Newborn visual attention to repeated exposure of redundant versus "novel" targets. *Perception & Psychophysics*, 1972, *12*, 291–294. (b)

Friedman, S., & Carpenter, C. S. Visual response decrement as a function of age of human newborn. *Child Development*, 1971, *42*, 1967–1973.

Friedman, S., Bruno, L. A., & Vietze, P. Newborn habituation to visual stimuli: A sex difference in novelty detection. *Journal of Experimental Child Psychology*, 1974, *18*, 242–251.

Gelman, R. Cognitive development. *Annual Review of Psychology*, 1978, *29*, 297–332.

Gesell, A. L. *The mental growth of the preschool child: A psychological outline of normal development from birth to the sixth year. including a system of developmental diagnosis*. New York: Macmillan, 1925.

Hagen, J. W., Jongeward, R. H., & Kail, R. V. Cognitive perspectives on the development of memory. In H. W. Reese (Ed.), *Advances in child development and behavior* (Vol. 10). New York: Academic, 1975.

Hagen, J. W., & Kail, R. V. Facilitation and distraction in short-term memory. *Child Development*, 1973, *44*, 831–836.

Harris, G. J., & Fleer, R. E. High speed memory scanning in mental retardates: Evidence for a central processing deficit. *Journal of Experimental Child Psychology*, 1974, *17*, 452–459.

Harris, P. L., Mandias, F., Terwogt, M. M., & Tjintjelaar, J. The influence of context on story recall and feelings of comprehension. *International Journal of Behavioral Development*, 1980, *3*, 159–172.

Herrmann, D. J., & Landis, T. Y. Differences in the search rate of children and adults in short-term memory. *Journal of Experimental Child Psychology*, 1977, *23*, 151–161.

Hoffman, C. D., & Dick, S. A. A developmental investigation of recognition memory. *Child Development*, 1976, *47*, 794–799.

Hull, C. L. *Principles of behavior*. New York: Appleton-Century-Crofts, 1943.

Jeffrey, W. E., & Cohen, L. B. Habituation in the human infant. In H. W. Reese (Ed.), *Advances in child development and behavior* (Vol. 6). New York: Academic Press, 1971.

Johnson, C. N., & Wellman, H. M. Children's developing understanding of mental verbs: Remember, know, and guess. *Child Development*, 1980, *51*, 1095–1102.

Kagan, J. *Change and continuity in infancy*. New York: Wiley, 1971.

Kail, R. V., & Hagen, J. W. (Eds.). *Perspectives on the development of memory and cognition*. Hillsdale, N.J.: Lawrence Erlbaum Associates, 1977.

Kail, R., & Hagen, J. W. Memory in childhood. In B. B. Wolman (Ed.), *Handbook of developmental psychology*. Englewood Cliffs, N.J.: Prentice-Hall, 1982.

Keeney, T. J., Cannizzo, S. R., & Flavell, J. H. Spontaneous and induced verbal rehearsal in a recall task. *Child Development*, 1967, *38*, 953–966.

Karmel, B. Z., & Maisel, E. B. A neuronal activity model for infant visual attention. In L. B. Cohen & P. Salapatek (Eds.), *Infant perception: From sensation to cognition* (Vol. 1). New York: Academic Press, 1975.

Kaye, H. Infant sucking behavior and its modification. In L. P. Lipsitt & C. C. Spiker (Eds.), *Advances in child development and behavior* (Vol. 3). New York: Academic Press, 1967.

Kendler, H. H., & Kendler, T. S. Vertical and horizontal processes in problem solving. *Psychological Review*, 1962, *69*, 1–16.

Kendler, H. H., & Kendler, T. S. From discrimination learning to cognitive development: A neobehavioristic odyssey. In W. K. Estes (Ed.), *Handbook of learning and cognitive processes* (Vol. 1). Hillsdale, N.J.: Lawrence Erlbaum Associates, 1975.

Kennedy, B. A., & Miller, D. J. Persistent use of verbal rehearsal as a function of information about its value. *Child Development*, 1976, *47*, 566–569.

Kessen, W. *The child*. New York: John Wiley, 1965.

Koblinsky, S. A., & Cruse, D. F. The role of frameworks in children's retention of sex-related story content. *Journal of Experimental Child Psychology*, 1981, *31*, 321–331.

Koblinsky, S. A., Cruse, D. F., & Sugawara, A. I. Sex role stereotypes and children's memory for story content. *Child Development*, 1978, *49*, 452–458.

Kreutzer, M. A., Leonard, C., & Flavell, J. H. An interview study of children's knowledge about memory. *Monographs of the Society for Research in Child Development*, 1975, *40*(1, Whole No. 159).

Kuenne, M. R. Experimental investigation of the relation of language to transposition behavior in young children. *Journal of Experimental Psychology*, 1946, *36*, 471–490.

Leopold, W. F. *Speech development of a bilingual child*. Evanston: Northwestern University Press, 1939.

Liben, L. S., & Posnansky, C. J. Inferences on inference: The effects of age, transitive ability, memory load, and lexical factors. *Child Development*, 1977, *48*, 1490–1497.

Liben, L. S., & Signorella, M. L. Gender-related schemata and constructive memory in children. *Child Development*, 1980, *51*, 11–18.

Lipsitt, L. P., & Kaye, H. Conditioned sucking in the human newborn. *Psychonomic Science*, 1964, *34*, 371–376.

Maccoby, E. E. Developmental psychology. *Annual Review of Psychology*, 1964, *15*, 203–250.

Mandler, J. M., & Robinson, C. A. Developmental changes in picture recognition. *Journal of Experimental Child Psychology*, 1978, *26*, 122–136.

Martin, R. M. Effects of familiar and complex stimuli on infant attention. *Developmental Psychology*, 1975, *11* 178–185.

Miller, D. J. Visual habituation in the human infant. *Child Development*, 1972, *43*, 483–493.

Miranda, S. B., & Fantz, R. L. *Distribution of visual attention of newborn infants among patterns varying in size and number of details.* Presented at the annual meeting of the American Psychological Association, Washington, D.C., 1971.

Myers, N. A., & Perlmutter, M. Memory in the years from two to five. In P. A. Ornstein (Ed.), *Memory development in children.* Hillsdale, N.J.: Lawrence Erlbaum Associates, 1978.

Naus, M. J., & Ornstein, P. A. Developmental differences in the memory search of categorized lists. *Developmental Psychology,* 1977, *13,* 60–68.

Neimark, E., Slotnick, N. S., & Ulrich, T. Development of memorization strategies. *Developmental Psychology,* 1971, *5,* 427–432.

Olson, G. M. An information-processing analysis of visual memory and habituation in infants. In T. J. Tighe & R. N. Leaton (Eds.), *Habituation: Perspectives from child development, animal behavior, and neurophysiology.* Hillsdale, N.J.: Lawrence Erlbaum Associates, 1976.

Omanson, R. C., Warren, W. H., & Trabasso, T. Goals, inferential comprehension, and recall of stories by children. *Discourse Processes,* 1978, *1,* 337–354.

Ornstein, P. A. (Ed.). *Memory development in children.* Hillsdale, N.J.: Lawrence Erlbaum Associates, 1978.

Ornstein, P. A., Naus, M. J., & Liberty, C. Rehearsal and organizational processes in children's memory. *Child Development,* 1975, *46,* 818–830.

Pancrantz, C. N., & Cohen, L. B. Recovery of habituation in infants. *Journal of Experimental Child Psychology,* 1970, *9,* 208–216.

Papousek, H. Conditioning during postnatal development. In Y. Brackbill & G. G. Thompson (Eds.), *Behavior in infancy and early childhood: A book of readings.* New York: Free Press, 1967.

Paris, S. G., & Carter, A. Y. Semantic and constructive aspects of sentence memory in children. *Developmental Psychology,* 1973, *9,* 109–113.

Paris, S. G., & Cross, D. R. Ordinary learning: Pragmatic connections among children's beliefs, motives, and actions. In J. H. Bisanz, G. L. Bisanz, & R. Kail (Eds.), *Progress in cognitive development research* (Vol. 4). Learning in Children. New York: Springer-Verlag, 1983.

Paris, S. G., Newman, R. S., & McVey, K. A. Learning the functional significance of mnemonic actions: A microgenetic study of strategy acquisition. *Journal of Experimental Child Psychology,* 1982, *34,* 490–509.

Perlmutter, M. (Ed.). *New directions in child development: Children's memory.* San Francisco: Jossey Bass, 1980.

Reese, H. W. Models of memory development. *Human Development,* 1976, *19,* 291–303.

Rescorla, R. A., & Holland, P. C. Some behavioral approaches to the study of learning. In. M. R. Rozensweig & E. L. Bennett (Eds.), *Neural mechanisms of learning and memory.* Cambridge, Mass.: MIT Press, 1976.

Rovee-Collier, C. K., & Fagen, J. W. The retrieval of memory in early infancy. In L. P. Lipsitt (Ed.), *Advances in infancy research* (Vol. 1). Norwood, N.J.: Ablex, 1981.

Ringel, B. A., & Springer, C. On knowing how well one is remembering: The persistence of strategy use during transfer. *Journal of Experimental Child Psychology,* 1980, *29,* 322–333.

Salatas, H., & Flavell, J. H. Behavioral and metamnemonic indicators of strategic behaviors under remember instructions in first grade. *Child Development,* 1976, *47* 81–89.

Salthouse, T. A., & Kail, R. Memory development throughout the life span: The role of processing rate. In P. B. Baltes & O. G. Brim (Eds.), *Lifespan development and behavior* (Vol. 5). New York: Academic, 1983, in press.

Shirley, M. M. *The first two years. A study of twenty-five babies.* Minneapolis: University of Minnesota Press, 1931.

Siqueland, E. R., & Lipsitt, L. P. Conditioned headturning in human newborns. *Journal of Experimental Child Psychology,* 1966, *3,* 356–376.

Small, M. Y., & Butterworth, J. Semantic integration and the development of memory for logical inferences. *Child Development,* 1981, *52,* 732–735.

Sokolov, E. N. *Perception and the conditioned reflex.* New York: Macmillan, 1963.

Sokolov, E. N. The modeling properties of the nervous system. In M. Cole & I. Maltzman (Eds.), *A handbook of contemporary Soviet psychology.* New York: Basic Books, 1969.

Sophian, C. Habituation is not enough: Novelty preferences, search and memory in infancy. *Merrill-Palmer Quarterly,* 1980, *26,* 239–257.

Sophian, C. Reply: Habituation may not be a bad start, but it's time to expand our horizons. *Merrill-Palmer Quarterly,* 1981, *27,* 339–344.

Spence, K. W. The differential response in animals to stimuli varying within a single dimension. *Psychological Review,* 1937, *44,* 430–444.

Spence, K. *Behavior theory and conditioning.* New Haven: Yale University Press, 1956.

Sternberg, S. High-speed scanning in human memory. *Science,* 1966, *153,* 652–654.

Stevenson, H. W. *Children's learning.* Englewood Cliffs, N.J.: Prentice-Hall, 1972.

Stone, L. S., Smith, H. T., & Murphy, L. B. *The competent infant.* New York: Basic Books, 1973.

Strauss, M. S., & Cohen, L. B. *Infant immediate and delayed memory for perceptual dimensions.* Unpublished manuscript, 1978.

Valentine, C. W. The innate basis of fear. *Journal of Genetic Psychology,* 1930, *37,* 394–420.

Wagner, A. R. Priming in STM: An information-processing mechanism for self-generated or retrieval-generated depression in performance. In T. J. Tighe & R. N. Leaton (Eds.), *Habituation: Perspectives from child development, animal behavior, and neurophysiology.* Hillsdale, N.J.: Lawrence Erlbaum Associates, 1976.

Wagner, A. R. Expectancies and the priming of STM. In S. H. Hulse, H. Fowler, & W. K. Honig (Eds.), *Cognitive processes in animal behavior.* Hillsdale, N.J.: Lawrence Erlbaum Associates, 1978.

Wagner, D. A. Memories of Morocco: The influence of age, schooling and environment on memory. *Cognitive Psychology,* 1978, *10,* 1–28.

Wagner, D. A., & Paris, S. G. Problems and prospects in comparative studies of memory. *Human Development,* 1981, *24,* 412–424.

Watson, J. The development and generalization of contingency awareness in early infancy: Some hypotheses. *Merrill-Palmer Quarterly,* 1966, *12,* 123–136.

Welker, W. I. An analysis of exploratory and play behavior in animals. In D. Fiske & S. Maddi (Eds.), *Functions of varied experience.* Homewood, Ill.: Dorsey Press, 1961.

Wellman, H. M., & Johnson, C. N. Understanding of mental processes: A developmental study of "remember" and "forget." *Child Development,* 1979, *50,* 79–88.

Wellman, H. M., Ritter, K., & Flavell, J. H. Deliberate memory behavior in the delayed reactions of very young children. *Developmental Psychology,* 1975, *11,* 780–787.

Werner, J. S., & Perlmutter, M. Development of visual memory in infants. In H. W. Reese & L. P. Lipsitt (Eds.), *Advances in child development and behavior* (Vol. 14). New York: Academic Press, 1979.

White, S. H. Evidence for a hierarchical arrangement of learning processes. In L. P. Lipsitt & C. C. Spiker (Eds.), *Advances in child development and behavior* (Vol. 2). New York: Academic, 1965.

White, S. H. The learning theory tradition in child psychology. In P. H. Mussen (Ed.), *Carmichael's manual of child psychology* (Vol. 1). New York: Wiley, 1970.

White, S. H. The active organism in theoretical behaviorism. *Human Development,* 1976, *19,* 99–107.

Yussen, S. R., Levin, J. R., Berman, L., & Palm, J. Developmental changes in the awareness of memory benefits associated with different types of picture organization. *Developmental Psychology,* 1979, *15,* 447–449.

Yussen, S. R., & Levy, V. M. Developmental changes in predicting one's own span of short-term memory. *Journal of Experimental Child Psychology,* 1975, *19,* 502–508.

Zeaman, D., & House, B. J. The role of attention in retardate discrimination learning. In N. R. Ellis (Ed.), *Handbook of mental deficiency.* New York: McGraw-Hill, 1963.

2 Reflections on the Ontogeny of Learning and Memory

Byron A. Campbell
Princeton University

In the 25 years or so since I first embarked on the study of learning and memory in infant animals much has transpired. In the 1950s and early sixties there was tremendous interest and emphasis on the lasting effects of certain types of experiences occurring early in development. J. P. Scott was in the midst of publishing his studies on the critical period for socialization in the puppy, Harry Harlow was describing the profound effects of early isolation on the rhesus monkey, and Mark Rosenzweig was touting the enduring effects of enriched environment on brain morphology. Simultaneously the impact of the European ethologists with their emphasis on the significance of imprinting was finally beginning to be felt on this continent. Not surprisingly, my early work showing the transient effects of early learning in the infant—the infantile amnesia syndrome—was considered by developmental psychobiologists to be about as interesting as leprosy before the days of antibiotics. At that time every one was convinced that any event occurring during infancy had a much more pronounced and longer lasting effect than a similar occurrence during adulthood. Any evidence to the contrary was overlooked or rejected.

An interesting example of this can be seen in Harriet Rheingold's concluding comments in *Early Behavior: Comparative and Developmental Approaches* (Stevenson, Hess, & Rheingold, 1967), a book based on a two-session conference sponsored by the Social Science Research Council. In her summary chapter she catalogued the ways in which infant mammals respond to various stimuli and the manner in which such stimulation can modify early behavior as reported by the conference attendees. Emphasis was placed on how early in development infant behavior could be altered by stimulation or training and on the long-lasting effects of early experience. No mention was made of the studies I reported showing poor memory in infancy nor was any comment made about my first description of the reinstatement phenomenon. When my work was mentioned it was to note that rate of learning was the same across animals of different ages and to commend me for my efforts to equate motivation.

The conference itself was quite similar. Without question my presentations evoked more critical reactions and looks of disbelief than any other. In fact, one focus of the conference was on the discrepancy between my emphasis of the transient effects of some early experiences and the long-lasting effects of other early experience such as imprinting. Eckhardt Hess, as one of the organizers of the conference, was particularly disbelieving that any early experience could be less long lasting than one occurring in adulthood.

Obviously, as this conference attests to, there is a striking difference in attitudes today. Infantile amnesia in animals is now a widely accepted and well-documented phenomenon, and reinstatement is so well established as a principle that it has become a laboratory tool for studying basic information storage and retrieval processes. I am, of course, delighted with this turn of events, and it is a pleasure to share some of my reflections on the ontogeny of this field with you. At the request of the organizers of this conference I am going to review briefly some of the mileposts in my career in developmental psychobiology.

My fascination with the developmental process began during my graduate school years at Yale in the early 1950s. At that time there was immense interest in distilling psychoanalytic theory into a few basic S-R principles. As a result there was much discussion and reading of the Freudian literature, and I became fascinated with the paradox posed by infantile amnesia on the one hand and the extreme emphasis placed upon the importance of early childhood experiences on the other. Freud's deft attempt to attribute infantile amnesia to repression seemed suspect because no memories of infancy, regardless of the emotional tone surrounding the event, persisted into adulthood. Moreover, even the most ardent of Freudians quailed at Rank's attempt to attribute significance to the birth trauma.

Given this setting, my initial inclination was to undertake a dissertation on the development of learning and memory in laboratory rats, but the practical concerns raised by both myself and my advisers of devising appropriate tasks, equating motivation, and reinforcement, and so forth, led me to postpone that effort and focus first on developing techniques for measuring and equating aversive motivation in rats of different ages. That goal led me astray for several years during which time I published a goodly number of papers on the psychophysics of motivation and reinforcement. It was not until 1962 that I published my first paper (Campbell & Campbell, 1962) on the ontogeny of learning and memory in developing rats. That paper, because of the significance and clarity of the findings obtained, marked a major transition in my research career and from that time on I considered myself primarily a developmental psychobiologist. With that paper as a starting point I would like to review with you what I consider some of the major steps in that career. To simplify this presentation I have chosen eight

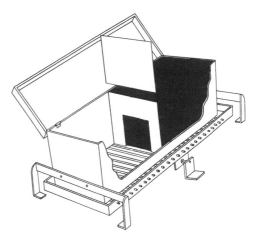

FIG. 2.1. Apparatus used for studying retention of conditioned fear in animals of different ages.

illustrations from previous papers to structure my recollections. The first of these (Fig. 2.1) depicts the two-compartment black and white apparatus used to condition fear in the developing rat in that first experiment. The drawing is idealized as one might expect. In actuality, the initial apparatus was somewhat shabbily constructed and was housed in an ancient, non-functional refrigerator painted a gaudy orange and black to celebrate my recent arrival at Princeton. The laboratory itself was equally inelegantly housed in a 3 by 100-yard-long, heavily reinforced concrete tunnel-like structure built during World War II to test artillery shells.

The data obtained in this primitive setting were remarkable in their consistency as shown in Fig. 2.2. The basic procedure used to obtain these data consisted of confining the animal in the black section of the apparatus using a solid door to separate the two chambers. We then administered a series of brief inescapable

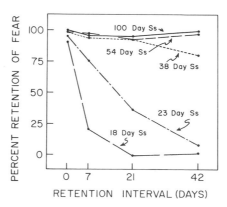

FIG. 2.2. Retention of conditioned fear as a function of age and retention interval.

shocks. This was followed by an equivalent period of time in the white compartment without shock. The whole procedure was repeated a second time. During the test trials the solid door separating the two compartments was removed and the animal was allowed to move back and forth between the two compartments. Animals that had been shocked in the black compartment showed strong (nearly 100%) avoidance of that side, which in control (unshocked) animals was the preferred side. Young rats (18 days of age) appeared to acquire the conditioned fear with ease but to forget it with great rapidity compared to older animals. This finding was, of course, similar to the infantile amnesia syndrome so commonly observed in human development. What was particularly puzzling to me at the time was the widespread reluctance of many developmental psychobiologists to accept these findings when, as humans, we are so unable to recall anything of our first few years of life. As Tolstoy put it so eloquently in his "Recollections": "from the day I was born until I was three years old, all the time I was nursing and being weaned, beginning to crawl and walk and talk, however, I rack my brains, I can remember nothing. . . . From the child of five to me is only a step. From the newborn babe to the child of five is a great leap. From the embryo to the newborn child is an abyss" (from Jacobson, 1970, p. 344). To me, the question both then and now is, why are the memories of infancy beyond recall? Even though we have learned a great deal about the development of the central nervous system in recent years, there is still no answer to this intriguing question.

The first order of business was to show that the poor memory of infancy was not due to some obvious difference between infant and adult rats in motivation or in the incentive properties of reinforcers. This issue provoked a substantial amount of research which, in retrospect, was probably of relatively little significance. Yet some of the developmental phenomena observed were so systematic that they compelled exhaustive analysis.

In the first of these methodological papers we (Campbell, Teghtsoonian, & Williams, 1961) studied the effects of food deprivation on spontaneous locomotor activity and survival time in rats of different ages. Not surprisingly, the smaller, younger animals lost weight more rapidly, became active much sooner, and survived for a much shorter period of time. Those data are reproduced in Fig. 2.3. They serve to emphasize the vast differences in severity of motivation that are produced by simple deprivation procedures in animals of different ages.

To further clarify this point we showed in a companion paper (Williams & Campbell, 1961) that percentage weight loss rather than hours of deprivation determined the amount of quinine-adulterated milk that animals of different ages would consume. In Fig. 2.4, it is worth noting that at the 25% weight-loss point the 23-day-old animals had been deprived for 2½ days and the 100-day-old subjects had been deprived 8½ days. Clear-cut as these data are, they did not suggest a procedure for maintaining equal levels of motivation over several days since other work (unpublished) showed that maintaining young animals at some percentage of their starting weight or some percentage of ad libitum-fed control

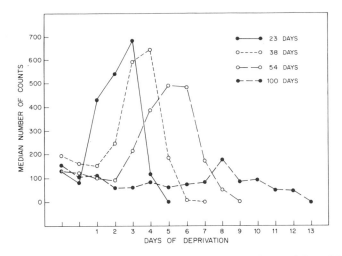

FIG. 2.3.   Spontaneous locomotor activity as a function of age and days of food deprivation.

animals led either to stunted growth or gradual loss of motivation. As a result we concluded that an easy and effective way to equate motivation in animals of different ages would be to allow them ad libitum access to food but to impose an instrumental response requirement on food delivery.

Some years later we utilized this technique to demonstrate once again the phenomenon of infantile amnesia in the developing rat. In this experiment (Campbell, Jaynes, & Misanin, 1968), young and adult rats were housed continuously in operant cages and food was available only on a variable interval light-dark discrimination schedule. The results of this experiment are shown in Fig. 2.5. These data show that young animals acquire a light-dark discrimination at more or less the same rate over a 5-day training period and reach the same or higher asymptote as older animals, yet over a prolonged retention interval show much greater forgetting. It is worth noting that the young animals were 28–31

FIG. 2.4.   Ingestion of quinine-in-milk solution expressed as a proportion of total milk consumed by control animals at the same deprivation level plotted as a function of percentage of weight loss.

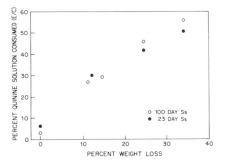

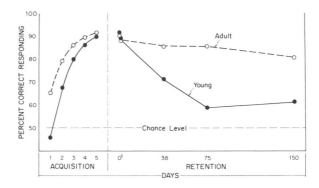

FIG. 2.5.   Acquisition and retention of the light-dark discrimination in young and adult rats.

days of age at the end of training, which is relatively old compared to animals showing poorer retention in other studies.

The other side of the motivational picture concerned the relative sensitivity of young animals to electric shock, the stimulus of choice for most aversively motivated behavior. While it was intuitively unlikely, there was always the possibility that young animals were less sensitive to electric shock and thereby less motivated by it than older animals. To assess this possibility we used procedures developed in earlier research (Campbell & Teghtsoonian, 1958) to determine aversion thresholds and aversion difference limens for electric shock in young and adult rats.

The *aversion threshold* was defined as the intensity of electric shock that produced 75% avoidance in a spatial preference situation. No differences in aversion thresholds were found between 25-, 50-, and 100-day-old rats indicating that there were no developmental differences in sensitivity to low intensities of electric shock. We (Stehouwer & Campbell, 1978) recently extended this general finding to rats of younger ages using leg flexion as the criterion response. With a fixed electrode attached to the forelimb of rats ranging in age from 3 to 15 days of age there were no substantial differences in the shock intensity required to elicit leg flexion.

The absence of a difference in sensitivity to low intensities of electric shock does not guarantee, however, the absence of differences in reactivity to higher intensities. Younger rats, for example, could be either more or less behaviorally impaired by high shock intensities. To investigate this possibility, we measured the reactions of young (25-day-old) and adult (100-day-old) rats to inescapable shock (Campbell, 1967). The amount of locomotor activity elicited by inescapable shock was almost identical in the two ages up to the point where tetanization occurred. Younger rats, however, became immobile (tetanized) at somewhat lower shock intensities than adult rats.

Perhaps the more crucial question is whether or not young animals can discriminate between different levels of shock as well as older animals. In short, can young animals detect differences in shock intensity and respond to those differences with the same accuracy as adult animals? To answer this question we determined shock *aversion difference limens* for young (25 day) and adult (100 day) rats. The *aversion difference limen* was a term we concocted as part of a concurrent effort to scale motivation and reinforcement using conventional psychophysical procedures. Although those techniques have been largely overlooked by the scientific community, I still believe that they are particularly useful when comparing animals of different ages or of different species. By shock *aversion difference limen* is meant the change in shock intensity from any preset intensity necessary to produce a 25% shift in preference: Either 25% preference for a lower shock intensity or 75% avoidance of a higher intensity. In practice, we selected five standard voltages delivered from a fixed impedance (150K ohm) shock source and determined that average change in voltage required to produce a 75% avoidance of the higher intensity (Campbell, 1967). These data are shown in Fig. 2.6. As is readily apparent, the aversion difference limen increases sharply with shock intensity just as detectability difference limens increase in all the sensory dimensions. Equally remarkable is the similarity between young and adults. These findings suggest that different shock intensities are perceived and responded to in the same fashion by young and adult rats.

The next, and perhaps most important paper in this series, was the one in which we first demonstrated the phenomenon of reinstatement. The impetus for this research stemmed from the frequently expressed view that early learning experiences were much more important than my data suggested. To counter this argument we demonstrated that learned behaviors which were normally forgotten rapidly by infant animals could be maintained if they were given periodic partial repetitions of the initial experience that were not in themselves sufficient to induce learning. To remind everyone of the simplicity of this phenomenon, I have reproduced the original findings in Fig. 2.7. In that experiment, two groups

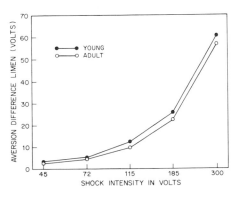

FIG. 2.6. Aversion difference limens in young and adult rats as a function of shock intensity.

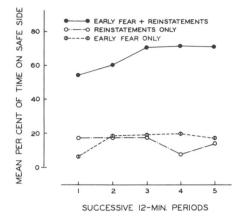

FIG. 2.7. The effect of reinstatement on retention of conditioned fear.

of animals were trained in the apparatus shown in Fig. 2.1 using the same classical conditioning procedures. Thirty shocks were administered to the animals while confined in the black compartment, and no shocks given to the animals while in the white compartment over an equal period of time. Then, during a subsequent 4-week retention interval, one group was returned once per week to the original situation where they received a single brief shock on the fear side. The other group received no interpolated training. In addition, a third group received the interpolated training of one shock per week in order to determine whether the abbreviated "reinstatement" training was sufficient to condition fear to the black compartment. At the end of the four-week retention period, the three groups were tested for their avoidance of the black compartment. The amount of time spent in the "safe" white compartment during the 60-minute test trial is shown in Fig. 2.7. These data show, as demonstrated earlier (Fig. 2.2), that an early fear experience is rapidly forgotten by young animals, *but* that the fear is easily maintained by a single CS-US pairing administered only once a week during the four-week retention interval. The group receiving only the interpolated fear conditioning showed no evidence of acquiring the conditioned fear. This finding led us to formulate the principle of reinstatement and to define it as the "periodic partial repetition of an experience such that it maintains the effects of that experience through time" (Campbell & Jaynes, 1966, p. 478).

What has been particularly pleasing about this finding is the ease with which it has been replicated, analyzed, and extended. To name a few of those developments, I have been particularly delighted with the advances made by David Riccio, Skip Spear, and Carolyn Rovee-Collier in recent years. Skip Spear (Spear & Parsons, 1976), as you all know, has been enormously effective in identifying the components of memory that are restored or maintained by reinstatement (reminder, in his terms) mechanisms. David Riccio (Riccio & Concannon, 1981) has been ingenious in showing that memory can be maintained through only partial replication of the original training conditions and has used that finding to show that in many instances consolidation of memory is dependent upon reinstatement mechanisms. Finally, Carolyn Rovee-Collier (Chapter 5, this volume) has shown in a series of elegant experiments that memory can be maintained for extended periods in very young human infants using reinstatement procedures.

In the next phase of this research saga, I began to speculate about the possible causes of the poor memory in infancy. It was obvious that two broad classes of possible determinants could be identified: environmental and physiological. To help untangle the various possibilities within these two categories, I enlisted the assistance of Skip Spear who had dual expertise in human and animal learning through his graduate training at Northwestern. Together we tried to identify the major hypothetical mechanisms that might underly infantile amnesia and published those conjectures in 1972 (Campbell & Spear, 1972). On the environmental side, we listed stimulus generalization decrement, differentiation, retroactive and proactive interference, response generalization and immature language skills as possible causes of rapid forgetting in infancy. On the physiological side, we postulated either central nervous system immaturity at the time of original learning or growth of the central nervous system following original learning as potential determinants of infantile amnesia.

While it is quite possible, if not highly likely, that all of these and perhaps many other mechanisms contribute to the poor memory of infancy, my own guess is that the major causes of infantile amnesia are neurological in nature. Part of this belief stems from one of the most tortuous series of experiments we ever performed in my laboratory. The intent of the research was to compare the emergence of long-term memory in precocial guinea pigs with that of the rat, the assumption being that the nervous system of the guinea pig is more fully developed at parturition than that of the rat. If infantile amnesia is, indeed, dependent on neurological immaturity at the time of original learning, then the neonatal guinea pig should show little or no forgetting relative to the rapid memory loss shown by the neurologically immature rat. These experiments were spread over several years and exhausted a number of graduate students and technicians. We tried an incredible variety of experimental procedures before settling on those we completed and published. My favorite failure was our effort to measure retention of learned fear using the conditioned suppression technique. We turned to this procedure because our efforts to use the black-white conditioned fear apparatus (shown in Fig. 2.1) led to total frustration due to the animals' tendency to stand motionless in any unfamiliar place for hours on end regardless of whether they received shock. Because of this tendency to freeze, we decided to train guinea pigs for food and, after pairing a tone with shock, measure the amount that tone would suppress bar-pressing for food. Little did we know that the CS alone, unpaired with shock, would totally suppress bar-pressing ad infinitum. Every time the tone sounded the guinea pig would stop responding. Nor could this tendency be eliminated by literally hundreds of prior habituation trials. Conversely, when we tried to use a light stimulus as the CS we found little consistent evidence of conditioning even after repeated CS-US pairings. As a result of this and many other negative experiences including the guinea pigs' tendency to spill endless quantities of water into increasingly soggy excreta pans, I vowed never to use guinea pigs again in my research. We did, however, persevere long enough to complete two studies, one of which is shown in Fig. 2.8. In this study we trained young (3-day-old) and adult guinea pigs to run in a T-maze using escape from shock as the reinforcer. To assess the effects of degree of original learning on retention, we gave different groups at each age either 0, 20, 40, or 100 training trials and then tested for retention of the discriminated escape response 75 days later. As can be seen in Fig. 2.8, there were no substantive differences between young and adult guinea pigs during either acquisition or retention. This finding, along with similar findings from a lick-suppression study, led us to conclude that neurological maturity and not chronological age at the time of original learning was the major determinant of infantile amnesia. This finding also minimizes the potential effects of experiences occurring either before or after original learning as major determinants of infantile amnesia.

Unfortunately, this interesting and potentially important finding started me off on a series of fruitless and unsuccessful experiments. The research focused on the question: "Is rate of forgetting in the developing rat proportional to rate of central nervous system maturation after original learning?" To provide an answer, all we had to show was that rate of forgetting increased if neural growth was accelerated and decreased if growth was retarded. At that time this did not seem like a particularly preposterous series of experiments. Relatively recent research had shown that thyroid hormone agonists and antagonists accelerated and retarded growth respectively, that undernutrition retarded growth, and that some neurotoxins selectively inhibited growth of various regions of the forebrain. In addition, we reasoned that lesioning the neonatal neocortex might leave

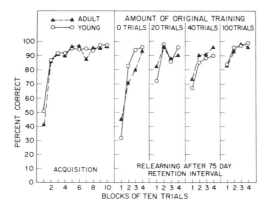

FIG. 2.8. Acquisition and retention of a shock-motivated T-maze escape response in young and adult guinea pigs.

some memories intact that would ordinarily be lost when that structure matured. Needless to say, none of these experiments proved successful. Although I cannot claim that we pursued any of these notions with either great diligence or skill, we certainly did not obtain any evidence suggesting that rate of forgetting could be slowed or accelerated by altering maturation of the central nervous system. Instead we found, if anything, that long-term memory was impaired in animals receiving those treatments. This observation was later confirmed, at least when growth was slowed by undernutrition (Nagy, Porada, & Monsour, 1980).

While these unsuccessful studies were being undertaken, my interests shifted to the changes in neural control of behavioral arousal that occur during development, and for the next 10 years or so my major efforts were in that area. During that time there was a dramatic resurgence of interest in the development of learning, beginning with the technological breakthroughs introduced by Ted Hall in the mid-seventies. Clear evidence of learning was observed earlier and earlier in development until Johanson and Hall (1979) finally demonstrated that even the 1-day-old rat pup could acquire a discriminated instrumental response for food reinforcement.

During this same period however, remarkably little work was done on the ontogeny of long-term memory. Skip Spear and his students described in detail the nature of the memory loss that occurs at different stages of development, while other investigators documented the age at which long-term memory emerged for stimuli presented in the various sensory dimensions. Jeff Alberts and I (Campbell & Alberts, 1979), for example, showed that long-term memory for taste stimuli approached the adult level of competence somewhere between 12 and 15 days of age, long before it occurred for either auditory or visual stimuli. Incidentally, this finding was just recently confirmed in an excellently designed and executed study by Schweitzer and Green (1982). Similarly, although there is no definitive parametric study on the subject, it now appears that long-term memory for olfactory stimuli reaches adult levels even earlier in development (Rudy & Cheatle, 1979).

The impact of these studies on my thinking and that of others in the field has been substantial. In the early seventies when Skip and I were writing our review paper, we implicitly conceived of the emergence of long-term memory as a unitary process mediated by some cluster of central late-maturing cortical structures. It is now obvious that as each sensory system develops it is able to encode and store information independently of the maturity of other sensory and central systems. Thus, the olfactory system is able to encode long-term memories at a developmental stage when other sensory systems and much of the brain appear to be incredibly immature and nonfunctional.

These observations have dramatically shaped the course of ongoing research. Now instead of analyzing the emergence of learning and memory in complex environments that stimulate multiple sensory channels, investigators are beginning to focus on single sensory systems. The best example of this is Jerry Rudy's

(Chapter 8, this volume) analysis of the emergence of associative learning mediated by the auditory system of the rat. By using conditioned stimuli confined to this one sensory dimension, he has been able to show that the rat's capacity to acquire sensory information progresses from simple CS-US associations to the ability to encode, store, and retrieve increasingly complex information. Moreover, there is considerable indirect evidence suggesting that this capacity is linked to the sequential maturation of brain stem to cortical auditory pathways.

Given these experimental and theoretical advances it seems clear that the path of future research in this area will be to analyze in much greater detail maturation of the sensory and perceptual capacities of developing animals and to relate those findings to the ontogeny of learning and memory in each sensory channel. Similarly, there may be a sequential development of response repertoires also paralleling maturation of the central nervous system that will expand the spectrum of behaviors that can be acquired. Delineation of these sequential sensory, central, and motor capacities and their interrelation to learning and memory should lead to an exciting decade of research in developmental psychobiology.

ACKNOWLEDGMENT

This work has been supported by National Institute of Mental Health grant MH01562, now in its 26th year.

REFERENCES

Campbell, B. A. Developmental studies of learning and motivation in infra-primate mammals. In H. W. Stevenson, E. H. Hess, & H. L. Rheingold (Eds.), *Early behavior: Comparative and developmental approaches.* New York: John Wiley & Sons, 1967.

Campbell, B. A., & Alberts, J. R. Ontogeny of long-term memory for learned taste aversions. *Behavioral and Neural Biology,* 1979, *25,* 139–156.

Campbell, B. A., & Campbell, E. H. Retention and extinction of learned fear in infant and adult rats. *Journal of Comparative and Physiological Psychology,* 1962, *55,* 1–8.

Campbell, B. A., & Jaynes, J. Reinstatement. *Psychological Review,* 1966, *73,* 478–480.

Campbell, B. A., Jaynes, J., & Misanin, J. R. Retention of a light-dark discrimination in rats of different ages. *Journal of Comparative and Physiological Psychology,* 1968, *66,* 467–472.

Campbell, B. A., & Spear, N. E. Ontogeny of memory. *Psychological Review,* 1972, *79,* 215–236.

Campbell, B. A., & Teghtsoonian, R. Electrical and behavioral effects of different types of shock stimuli on the rat. *Journal of Comparative and Physiological Psychology,* 1958, *51,* 185–192.

Campbell, B. A., Teghtsoonian, R., & Williams, R. A. Activity, weight loss and survival time of food-deprived rats as a function of age. *Journal of Comparative and Physiological Psychology,* 1961, *54,* 592–596.

Jacobson, M. *Developmental neurobiology.* New York: Holt, Rinehart & Winston, 1970.

Johanson, I. B., & Hall, W. G. Appetitive learning in 1-day-old rat pups. *Science,* 1979, *205,* 419–421.

Nagy, Z. M., Porada, K. J., & Monsour, A. P. Ontogeny of short- and long-term memory capacities for passive avoidance training in undernourished rats. *Developmental Psychobiology,* 1980, *13,* 373–384.

Riccio, D. C., & Concannon, J. T. ACTH and the reminder phenomenon. In J. L. Martinez, R. A. Jensen, R. B. Messing, H. Rigter, & J. L. McGaugh (Eds.), *Endogenous peptides and learning and memory processes.* New York: Academic Press, 1981.

Rudy, J. W. & Cheatle, M. D. The ontogeny of associative learning: Acquisition of odor aversions in neonatal rats. In N. E. Spear & B. A. Campbell (Eds.), *Ontogeny of learning and memory.* Hillsdale, N.J.: Lawrence Erlbaum Associates, 1979.

Schweitzer, L., & Green, L. Acquisition and extended retention of a conditioned taste aversion in preweanling rats. *Journal of Comparative and Physiological Psychology,* 1982, *96,* 791–806.

Spear, N. E., & Parsons, P. J. Analysis of reactivation treatment: Ontogenetic determinants of alleviated forgetting. In D. Medin, W. Roberts, & R. Davis (Eds.), *Processes in animal memory.* Hillsdale, N.J.: Lawrence Erlbaum Associates, 1976.

Stehouwer, D. J., & Campbell, B. A. Habituation of the forelimb flexor reflex in neonatal rats. *Journal of Experimental Psychology: Animal Behavior Processes,* 1978, *4,* 104–119.

Stevenson, H. W., Hess, E. H., & Rheingold, H. L. (Eds.), *Early behavior: Comparative and developmental approaches.* New York: John Wiley & Sons, 1967.

Williams, R. A., & Campbell, B. A. Weight loss and quinine-milk ingestion as measures of "hunger" in infant and adult rats. *Journal of Comparative and Physiological Psychology,* 1961, *54,* 220–222.

II ONTOGENY OF MEMORY AND ITS PREREQUISITES

3 Sensory and Perceptual Constraints on Memory in Human Infants

Richard N. Aslin
Indiana University

Contemporary views of adult memory typically deal with the flow of information through a series of levels, including sensory transduction and encoding, short- and long-term storage, and search and retrieval (see, for example, Shiffrin, 1976). Similarly, contemporary views of memory in young children typically trace the *development* of these encoding, storage, and retrieval mechanisms (see, for example, Kail & Hagen, 1977). Perhaps as a result of the assumption that the initial stage of sensory transduction is adultlike in early childhood, researchers have tended to focus on top-down explanations of memory development. That is, the primary concern is with how various types of encoding and retrieval strategies are utilized by the child to maximize the veridicality of stored information. A particularly popular term used to describe this top-down model of memory development is *metamemory;* that is, the knowledge of one's own memorial strategies and capacities.

In contrast to these theoretical and empirical studies of memory in children and adults, investigations of memory abilities in human infants must take into account the enormous changes in sensory and perceptual capabilities that occur during the first postnatal year. These relatively low-level mechanisms involved in the acquisition and preliminary analysis of sensory inputs may place severe constraints on the quality of information actually available for subsequent storage and retrieval. Thus, to provide an account of the basis for developmental improvements in memory performance during infancy, one must clarify what information is processed by the sensory and perceptual systems of the infant at different ages. In short, studies of infant memory may require a focus on *antememory;* that is, the processing of stimulus information prior to its entrance into short- or long-term storage.

In this chapter, a wide range of topics on sensory and perceptual development in infancy is reviewed. In the interest of brevity, and because the vast majority of infant memory studies have employed visual stimuli, only the visual system is discussed. Within the visual modality, the following topics are covered: retinal anatomy and eyeball size, acuity and contrast sensitivity, optics and accommodation, pattern perception and scanning, eye movement control, binocular fixation and depth perception, and color vision. In addition, the methodological techniques that are used to assess sensory and perceptual development in infants are evaluated, particularly since many of these techniques are nearly identical to those used in assessing infant memory. In general, this review makes three points: (1) there are significant constraints on sensory and perceptual development during the first 6 postnatal months, (2) these constraints will certainly influence the quality of information that is actually available to the infant's memory system for storage, and (3) these sensory and perceptual constraints must be ruled out as possible explanations of memory failure in infants before concluding that storage and retrieval mechanisms are involved.

ANATOMICAL CONSTRAINTS

The human visual system undergoes a number of remarkable changes during the first postnatal year. These include the migration of cell layers in the retina to form the foveal depression (Mann, 1964), the growth of cells in the different layers of the lateral geniculate nucleus (Hickey, 1977), and the dendritic branching of pyramidal cells in the layers of the visual cortex (Conel, 1939, 1941, 1947, 1951). As a result of these anatomical changes, several structural alterations occur in the young infant's visual system that may constrain visual processing. For example, the spatial location of individual photoreceptors on the retina appears to change as the eyeball grows. In addition, the separation of the two eyes in the skull increases greatly during the first postnatal year, resulting in a changing relation between object distance and retinal coordinates. To illustrate the potential relation between structural anatomy and visual processing, I will now consider these last two examples: retinal photoreceptor loci and interocular separation.

The early research on retinal anatomy in humans, summarized by Mann (1964), revealed that the foveal depression was not fully developed at birth. As shown in Fig. 3.1, a number of cell layers are located between the photoreceptors and the optical path of the retinal image. During the course of early postnatal development, these cell layers recede to form the photoreceptor-midget bipolar-ganglion cell configuration of the mature adult fovea. These anatomical observations have recently been replicated in a study by Abramov, Gordon, Hendrickson, Hainline, Dobson, and LaBossierre (1982). An 8-day-old neonate retina was found to have very rudimentary foveal photoreceptors, as well as the charac-

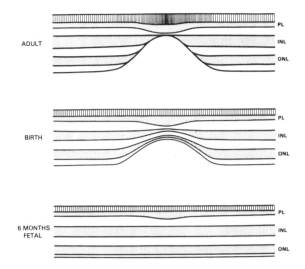

FIG. 3.1.   Cross-sections of the human retina at different ages during fetal and postnatal development illustrating the formation of the foveal depression. PL = photoreceptor layer; INL = inner nuclear layer; ONL = outer nuclear layer. (Redrawn from Mann, 1964)

teristic overlay of other cell layers noted by Mann (1964). Thus, it would appear that the newborn does not possess the anatomical structure which, at least in adults, is necessary for fine visual resolution and color vision. Of course, it is impossible to say with certainty that all newborns are incapable of adultlike vision simply because their retinal anatomy is not adultlike. However, on the basis of these findings, it would seem likely that young infants require a certain amount of postnatal development before adultlike vision is possible.

Another interesting aspect of retinal anatomy in the newborn is the suggestion, based on research with infant monkeys, that the individual photoreceptors migrate across the retina during development. Hendrickson and Kupfer (1976) reported that photoreceptors within the foveal region of the macaque increase in density during postnatal development as extrafoveal photoreceptors migrate toward the foveal depression. Given the fact that the total number of photoreceptors remains constant during postnatal development, the relation between a given photoreceptor and its corresponding locus in space must change during this period of neural migration. If a similar developmental sequence holds for the human infant, then some reorganization must occur in the spatial coordinate system that specifies visual direction based on the locus of retinal stimulation. In short, a particular object in the world viewed at a constant distance might stimulate a different configuration of retinal photoreceptors at different postnatal ages. Thus, in an infant memory task that spanned several days or weeks prior to retrieval, an identical stimulus presented for encoding and retrieval might act as *two* effectively different stimuli for the developing infant.

The perception of object distance based on binocular information may also be subject to postnatal anatomical changes. In the first two postnatal years the eyeballs undergo a 50% increase in their separation within the skull (see Aslin & Dumais, 1980). As a result, the amount that the two eyes must converge to binocularly fixate an object at a given distance increases considerably. In adults, judgments of object distance are closely tied to the angle of vergence (Owens & Leibowitz, 1976). Thus, it is possible that infants also use vergence angle as a means of calibrating the judged distance of an object. In fact, von Hofsten (1977) has reported that infants, viewing an object through wedge prisms that alter the angle of vergence, reach (incorrectly) to different distances.

Another aspect of binocular vision that is affected by differences in interocular separation is the magnitude of binocular parallax. Binocular parallax refers to the slightly different views that are obtained by the two eyes while viewing a near object. The quantitative measure of binocular parallax, called retinal disparity, is dependent upon interocular separation. Thus, the perception of object distance and depth (solidity) is directly related to this gross anatomical parameter (interocular separation) that changes quite dramatically in the first two postnatal years. It is possible that distance and depth information, if it were a critical aspect of the stimulus to be encoded in an infant memory task, may be perceived by the infant's visual system as *different* information. In summary, if identical stimulus information is presented at two different times during development, the perceptual information actually received by the encoding and retrieval levels of the memory system may be quite different.

ACUITY AND CONTRAST SENSITIVITY

Perhaps the most obvious constraint on the acquisition of visual information during infancy is the ability to resolve the stimulus presented for encoding or retrieval. During the past decade, a number of techniques have been developed to assess the young infant's ability to detect and discriminate fine details in visual patterns. A fundamental aspect of visual resolution is acuity: the limit of resolution. In adults and verbal children acuity can be measured by presenting smaller and smaller pattern elements and asking the subject to indicate those details that are just above threshold. In infants, however, acuity must be estimated with nonverbal techniques. Three such techniques have been used successfully with infants: (1) preferential looking, (2) optokinetic nystagmus (OKN), and (3) visual evoked potentials (VEP).

The preferential looking technique was originally developed by Fantz (1958) and later applied by Fantz, Ordy, and Udelf (1962) to assess infant acuity. The essential aspects of the technique consist of a visual pattern, typically containing black and white stripes or checks, presented simultaneously with a nonpatterned region whose average luminance is equal to the patterned stimulus. An observer judges whether the infant looked at the patterned or patternless stimulus more frequently or for a longer duration. If the observer's judgments indicate that the infant looked longer at the patterned stimulus, then one can conclude that the infant detected the stimulus. The patterned stimulus with the smallest checks or narrowest stripes that is reliably preferred by the infant provides an estimate of acuity.

Recently, this preferential looking technique has been incorporated into traditional psychophysical procedures to provide an extremely reliable measure of infant acuity (see Teller, 1979). As shown in Fig. 3.2, the infant is presented with a series of trials during which vertically oriented black and white stripes varying in stripe width are paired with a gray patternless stimulus. On each trial the right-left locations of the two stimuli are randomized and the observer, blind as to the side of the patterned stimulus, makes a forced-choice judgment based on the infant's looking responses as to the side which contains the patterned stimulus. The percentage correct of the observer's judgments is plotted as a function of stripe width. Since the observer could obtain a score of 50% correct by guessing, a value significantly above 50% is chosen as the threshold, and the interpolated stripe width corresponding to this threshold criterion provides an estimate of the infant's acuity.

The OKN and VEP measures of infant acuity follow the same rationale as preferential looking. OKN consists of an involuntary repetitive eye movement response to vertically oriented stripes that are swept laterally across the subject's visual field. Typically, one stripe is fixated and tracked as it moves left or right.

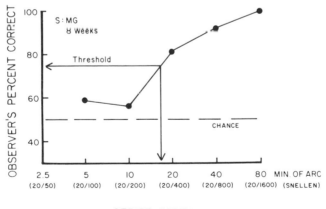

STRIPE WIDTH

FIG. 3.2.   A psychometric function from an infant viewing stripes of different widths in the preferential looking technique. The observer's percentage correct in judging the side of the display containing the striped pattern is plotted as a function of stripe width. The 75% threshold estimate of acuity is approximately 16 minutes of arc or 20/320. (Reprinted from Teller, 1979)

When the eye has reached its maximum horizontal excursion, a rapid refixation back toward the center of the array of stripes is made to fixate a different stripe. As the width of the stripes is decreased, a point is reached when OKN is not present. The smallest stripe width which leads to reliable OKN is an estimate of the infant's acuity. VEP relies on the fact that the onset of a patterned stimulus elicits a change in the spontaneous brain wave activity recorded from scalp electrodes. By repeatedly presenting a pattern containing stripes or checks of a given size, an average evoked signal is obtained. The amplitude or latency of this averaged signal is proportional to the size of the pattern. As the pattern size is decreased, the amplitude drops to zero and the latency of the peaks in the waveform becomes extremely long. Thus, some amplitude (e.g., Sokol, 1978) or latency (e.g., Sokol & Jones, 1979) criterion can be used to estimate the infant's acuity.

Despite the differences in these three techniques for assessing infant acuity, the resultant developmental acuity functions are remarkably similar (see Dobson & Teller, 1978). As shown in Fig. 3.3, acuity is approximately 20/400 at birth; that is, newborns can resolve at 20 feet what a normal adult can resolve at 400 feet. During the subsequent 6 to 9 months, infant acuity improves to approximately 20/50. In fact, it is possible that by 12 months of age acuity is 20/20 (adultlike) but underestimated by the fact that infants are not highly motivated and/or attentive during lengthy testing sessions. Nevertheless, it is clear that acuity undergoes a threefold improvement in the first 6 months of life. Thus, if a visual stimulus is presented for encoding to a very young infant, it is likely that a

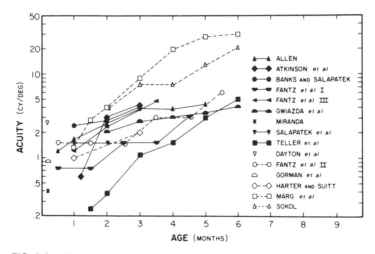

FIG. 3.3. Visual acuity in infancy as a function of age. Solid symbols and lines indicate data collected with preferential looking and open symbols and dashed lines indicate data collected with OKN or VEP. [Reprinted from Banks & Salapatek, 1981]

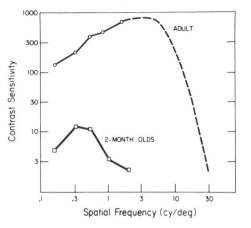

FIG. 3.4. Contrast sensitivity function obtained from adults and 2-month-old infants. Contrast sensitivity (the reciprocal of stimulus contrast) is plotted as a function of spatial frequency (the number of black stripes per unit of visual angle; 30 cyc/deg = stripes 1 minute of arc wide). (Reprinted from Banks & Salapatek, 1981)

few short weeks later the same stimulus may appear quite different to the more mature infant visual system.

The acuity data shown in Fig. 3.3 are for stimuli composed of high contrast stripes; that is, bar patterns with a large luminance difference between the black of the bars and the white of the background. Another very important aspect of visual resolution is the ability to detect small differences in stimulus contrast. For example, if the luminance of the black bars was increased and the luminance of the white background was decreased, the contrast of the overall stimulus (i.e., the luminance *difference*) would be reduced. Several investigators (Atkinson, Braddick, & Moar, 1977; Banks & Salapatek, 1978) have used preferential looking to assess infant contrast sensitivity for stripes of varying widths. As shown in Fig. 3.4, adults can detect a contrast of less than 1% for medium-width stripes, whereas infants appear quite poor at detecting contrasts less than 10%. Thus, many of the subtle differences in contrast that are contained in visual patterns (e.g., the shading differences that define the characteristics of a face) may not be discriminable by young infants.

A related aspect of visual resolution is the ability to detect small changes in luminance between a target and its background. Not only are adults very sensitive to small luminance increments, but the ratio of the luminance of a just-detectable target increment to its background remains constant throughout a large range of background luminances. As a result of this constant ratio, adults perceive the relative brightness of an object as invariant despite sudden changes in overall luminance (e.g., leaving a darkened movie theater). Dannemiller and Banks (1983) have recently shown that infants up to 3 months of age do not exhibit this constant ratio of luminances between a target and its background across a wide range of background luminances. They tested infants with the preferential looking technique by presenting a small region of light of variable luminance on the right or left of a background of constant luminance. The difference between the target luminance and the background luminance that is reliably detected by the infant provides a measure of the infant's increment threshold. The increment thresholds at a number of different background luminances (adaptation levels) were not a constant proportion of the background luminance. Thus, for infants up to 3 months of age, a change in background luminance is likely to lead to the perception of a different appearance for an object (e.g., stimulus contrast may change). In summary, acuity, contrast sensitivity, and light adaptation change substantially during the first 3 to 6 months after birth. If we assume that all the visual information present in a stimulus is available to the infant's visual system for encoding, when in fact only some degraded representation of the stimulus is available, then a failure by the infant to show evidence of memory for the stimulus may be attributed inappropriately to immature memory abilities rather than to deficient spatial resolving powers.

OPTICS AND ACCOMMODATION

It has long been assumed that a large portion of the young infant's poor spatial resolution results from the poor quality of the retinal image. For adults, this assumption is quite correct: Degradation in retinal image quality results in a loss of spatial resolution (acuity and constrast sensitivity). However, in infants the basis for poor spatial resolution is less straightforward. Even if the retinal image is in perfect focus for the infant, acuity is poorer than in adults. Thus, at best, infants have poorer spatial resolution than adults because of a *neural* immaturity rather than a simple optical error.

There are, however, optical and motor control factors that could degrade the infant's spatial resolution even further. For example, the presence of an in-focus retinal image is largely the result of the refraction (bending) of light by the front or corneal surface of the eyeball. If the eyeball is too short in comparison to the refractive power of the cornea, then the retinal image will be in focus behind the retina. To overcome this insufficient refractive power, the lens in the eyeball can accommodate to bring the image of the object coincident with the retina. This example of a too-short eyeball corresponds to a person with hyperopia or farsightedness. For distant objects, the person can accommodate and bring the retinal image into sharp focus. However, for near objects the ability to accommodate reaches a limit, and clear focus cannot be attained. Fortunately, placement of a convex lens in front of the eye can compensate for this refractive error. In a similar manner, if the eyeball is too long, the image of a distant object is focused in front of the retina because the cornea has too much refractive power. Near objects are brought into clear focus by relaxing accommodation, but far objects remain out of focus because accommodation cannot be relaxed sufficiently. In this case of myopia or nearsightedness, a concave lens placed in front of the eye can compensate for the refractive error.

If infants have large refractive errors and/or inaccurate control over accommodation, it would seem obvious that acuity and contrast sensitivity would be reduced. A number of investigators have shown that newborns are generally farsighted (see review by Banks, 1980a). However, the magnitude of this hyperopia is relatively small (2 diopters), particularly since their accommodative range of approximately 10 diopters can usually overcome this refractive error except for extremely near objects. There is also evidence that the measurement of refractive errors in infants overestimates the magnitude of hyperopia (see Green, Powers, & Banks, 1980). In contrast, if infants were myopic, then only near objects could be brought into clear focus. Thus, unless the infant's refractive error is myopic or grossly hyperopic (greater than 2 diopters), its effect on acuity and constrast sensitivity may be minimal.

Haynes, White, and Held (1965) provided the first detailed study of accommodation in young infants. They found that infants under 2 months of age exhibited a fixed focal distance of approximately 20 cm regardless of object distance. During the next 2 or 3 months, accommodation became quite accurate, suggesting that by 4 months of age objects at all distances were brought into clear focus. Two findings have raised several questions concerning this early interpretation by Haynes et al. First, Salapatek, Bechtold, and Bushnell (1976) reported that 1- and 2-month-olds did not show differences in acuity as the distance of a striped pattern was varied. Because the stimuli were presented both near the 20 cm fixed focal distance reported by Haynes et al. and farther than this optimal distance, one would expect a fall off in acuity at the far-viewing distances. One aspect of their stimuli hinted at a partial answer to this apparent inconsistency. Haynes et al. had used a small visual stimulus whose retinal size became smaller at the farther viewing distances. Salapatek et al., however, kept the retinal size of the striped patterns constant at the different viewing distances. Thus, the failure of young infants in the Haynes et al. study to accommodate accurately to the far target distances may have been the result of the target dropping below the infants' acuity threshold. Subsequently, Braddick, Atkinson, French, and Howland (1979), Banks (1980b), and Brookman (1980) have shown that young infants rarely have a fixed focal distance unless they are drowsy. Nevertheless, these studies have indicated that young infants often exhibit errors in accommodation, even though their accommodative accuracy is slightly better than that reported by Haynes et al. Thus, it is puzzling that Salapatek et al. did not find acuity differences as a function of viewing distance.

Although the details need not concern us here, Green and Campbell (1965) demonstrated that, for large patterns (wide stripes), the adult's visual system is not very sensitive to blurring. However, for narrow stripes, even a small amount of blurring can lead to a large loss in resolution. Because the young infant's acuity is poor even when the retinal image is in optimal focus, only wide stripes are visible at any time. The blurring introduced by errors in accommodation does not result in a significant acuity loss given this already poor spatial resolution.

Powers and Dobson (1982) have verified this minimal influence of accommodative error on infant acuity by showing that acuity is not greatly affected by blurring the retinal image with lenses. In fact, the inability to detect changes in stimulus clarity (blur insensitivity) may account for the inaccuracy in accommodation among young infants (see review and model in Banks, 1980b).

In summary, infants until at least 6 months of age have poor spatial resolution compared to adults. The postnatal improvement in acuity and contrast sensitivity indicates that the fine details present in many visual stimuli are not processed by the young infant's visual system. Thus, encoding of visual information in early infancy may be degraded compared to encoding in later infancy, and retrieval of earlier encoded information may be biased toward gross rather than fine details. Finally, although refractive errors may limit the amount of visual information available for encoding by the young infant's visual system, errors of accommodation do not appear to be a severe constraint on visual processing until after 3 months of age when accommodative control is adultlike.

PATTERN PERCEPTION

An issue of great concern to studies of visual memory in infants is whether the stimulus to be encoded is actually stored in memory for subsequent retrieval. Even if we assume that anatomical factors and spatial resolution are not serious constraints on encoding, it is possible that the visual stimulus is not represented in memory in a manner similar to an adult representation. The primary technique that has been used to address this pattern perception question is preferential looking. In contrast to the acuity procedure, *two* suprathreshold patterns are presented simultaneously for inspection by the infant. If one of the patterns is fixated preferentially, then discrimination can be inferred. If neither pattern is fixated preferentially, then either the infant had no preference (although discrimination may have occurred) or the infant was incapable of discriminating the difference between the two patterns.

Over the past 20 years a wide array of pattern pairings has been presented to infants (see Fantz, Fagan, & Miranda, 1975). Although it is tempting to draw general conclusions from these many studies, it is also nearly impossible to do so. First, there is an infinite number of possible stimulus pairings. No single set of stimulus features, attributes, or dimensions has been successful in characterizing pattern preferences in infants. Second, the presence of pattern discrimination based on preferential looking does not clarify *what* aspects of the patterns were encoded. For example, it seems straightforward to conclude that a preference for one of two faces is evidence for facial perception. But it is possible that the infant simply fixated a limited region of the facial stimuli and preferred one face because of a local difference in contour density or luminance. We would not consider this example of pattern discrimination to be evidence of facial perception. An infant who at a young age showed evidence of facial discrimination might perceive the facial stimuli as regions of contour, whereas the older infant might perceive the facial stimuli as faces (i.e., as integrated configurations of features).

Two general strategies have been adopted to clarify this interpretive problem associated with the preference technique. First, a scheme for characterizing all visual stimuli according to a few simple parameters has been developed. This scheme, based on the application of linear systems analysis to vision (see Banks & Salapatek, 1981), combines a mathematical treatment of the distribution of contrast in a stimulus with the contrast sensitivity function of the infant's visual system. In this way, all of the possible complex features, attributes, and dimensions of two-dimensional visual stimuli can be described by a limited set of parameters (spatial frequency, orientation, and phase), and the discriminability of visual stimuli can be estimated by filtering out information to which the infant's visual system is insensitive. At the present time, this approach has proven successful in accounting for many of the preferential looking results obtained with a variety of visual stimuli in infants younger than 4 months of age (see Banks & Salapatek, 1981). However, in later infancy there are a number of more complex stimulus variables (e.g., the configuration of contour elements) that cannot be accounted for solely by the linear systems approach.

A second strategy used to clarify preferential looking data involves detailed measurements of the specific locations on a visual stimulus which the infant fixates. In this way one can gain information about which subregions of the pattern the infant attends to most closely. The early use of these scanning measures (e.g., Salapatek & Kessen, 1966) provided evidence that newborns consistently fixate contours. An unfortunate outgrowth of this scanning technique, however, was the implicit assumption that the direction of gaze was coincident with the retinal region that performed visual processing. This assumption, of course, ignores the possibility that stimuli falling on the peripheral retina may also be processed. Given the earlier discussion of developments in foveal anatomy, it is possible that the line of sight is only a precursor of a retinal region that will eventually have superior processing powers. Scanning data alone do not provide evidence of stimulus encoding since visual processing may not occur during each individual fixation.

In summary, if infants fail to discriminate two patterns as indicated by the preference technique, then scanning measures can determine if the infant's line of sight was limited to one subregion of the patterns (perhaps a subregion that did not carry distinctive information). A limited scanpath would provide suggestive evidence for concluding that attention was not deployed to fixate the appropriate regions of the two patterns. Thus, discrimination failure could be the result of an inefficient encoding strategy. In contrast, if infants discriminate two patterns, then the basis for this discrimination may be local or global. To clarify this possibility, scanning data can determine if a limited subregion of the stimulus was fixated. If so, then it is likely that this subregion provided sufficient information for a preference to be exhibited. Caution must be used in reaching this conclusion, however, since peripheral processing may occur despite a restricted scanpath.

Given this interpretive problem associated with scanning as a measure of pattern perception, other techniques have been used to supplement measures of visual fixation. Milewski (1976) conducted a study in which high amplitude sucking (HAS) was used to assess pattern discrimination in 1- and 4-month-olds. In the HAS technique the infant sucks on a nipple connected to a pressure transducer that monitors the occurrence of high amplitude sucks. After an initial baseline period, the presentation of a visual stimulus is made contingent upon the occurrence of a suck. Infants quickly learn that sucking leads to the presentation of the visual stimulus, and this conjugate reinforcement results in an increase in the frequency of sucks. After several minutes of this contingency, most infants show a decline in sucking, presumably as a result of satiation to the reinforcing properties of the stimulus-response contingency. At this point in the testing session, infants receive either a change in the visual stimulus (experimental group) or no change in the initial stimulus (control group). If the experimental group receiving the changed stimulus shows an increase in sucking while the control group shows no increase in sucking, then discrimination of the two stimuli can be inferred.

Milewski's (1976) study was based on an earlier finding by Salapatek (1975) that infants under 2 months of age fail to fixate a small pattern element when it is embedded in a larger, surrounding pattern element. Infants older than 2 months, however, direct nearly all of their fixations to the internal element. If the direction of gaze is correlated with visual processing, then the younger infants should not discriminate a change in the shape of the internal pattern element. Both 1- and 4-month-olds received a change in either the internal pattern element or the external pattern element. While the 4-month-olds showed evidence of discriminating a change in either the internal or external pattern element, the 1-month-olds discriminated only the change in the external pattern element.

Recall that previous scanning data indicated that 1-month-olds fixate predominantly the external elements of a complex pattern. Hence, Milewski's results suggest that the subregion of a pattern that is predominantly fixated is the subregion that is encoded for later comparison in a HAS discrimination task. This conclusion is further supported by Milewski's finding that 1-month-olds discriminate a change in the shape of the internal element when it is presented in isolation (without a surrounding external element). Thus, acuity alone cannot explain the younger infants' failure to discriminate the smaller internal element embedded in the larger external element. Subsequently, Milewski (1978) and Bushnell (1979) have shown that the internal aspect of these complex visual patterns is not unique because a small pattern element located *adjacent* to a larger pattern element is also not discriminated by younger infants. To date, no scanning data have been gathered on this type of adjacent-element stimulus.

These findings on pattern perception for geometric stimuli are also relevant to facial perception. As discussed above, evidence of facial discrimination based on preference data does not indicate whether this discrimination was made via global or local stimulus characteristics. It now seems likely that young infants are constrained to fixate only certain subregions of a complex pattern. Moreover, this restricted scanning is associated with the absence of processing and/or encoding of nonscanned subregions. Scanning data from infants presented with facial stimuli (Hainline, 1978; Haith, Bergman, & Moore, 1977; Maurer & Salapatek, 1976) demonstrate that younger infants limit their fixations to external attributes (hairline, chin), whereas older infants fixate all attributes, but especially the eyes (internal elements). Thus, ecologically relevant stimuli such as faces seem to follow the same developmental trend in scanning that is found for geometric patterns. Unfortunately, to date we have no HAS data on the discrimination of facial stimuli, and we do not know the size of the retinal region surrounding the line of sight that is involved in visual processing. In addition, current technologies allow for the recording of scanning movements only to the nearest 4 or 5 degrees. Thus, it is possible that visual processing occurs within a fairly large region of the retina.

EYE MOVEMENT CONTROL

Both the preferential looking and scanning techniques rely on the fact that infants spontaneously direct their gaze to fixate certain select visual stimuli. If there is a significant developmental change in the strategic use or ability to control the sequence of visual fixations, then different types of visual information may be encoded at different ages. The studies of scanning in newborns raised an interesting question: Is the scanpath initially guided toward stimulus contours or does the line of sight move randomly until a contour is located on the fovea? This issue of controlled eye movements versus a random walk could not be settled by scanning studies alone because a complex visual stimulus offers many individual contour elements that compete for the infant's attention. Thus, several investigators have attempted to examine the young infant's ability to move the line of sight toward a single target initially located in the peripheral visual field.

In the first studies in this area (e.g., Tronick, 1972), a target appeared in the infant's periphery, and investigators asked whether the line of sight eventually was attracted to this extrafoveal location. Although infants between birth and 3 months of age showed an increasing area of the visual field within which localization responses would be made, it was clear that many of these presumed target localization responses occurred by chance. In subsequent studies a more sophisticated question was asked: Is the *first* eye movement after introduction of a peripheral target directed toward the target's location? Both Harris and Mac-Farlane (1974) and Aslin and Salapatek (1975) reported that in newborns and 1- and 2-month-olds, respectively, the initial eye movement was directed toward the location of a peripheral target. Thus, the ability to detect and localize a single stimulus that is initially presented to the peripheral retina is apparently built in to the visual-motor system. In both of these studies, however, the probability of making a localization response was greatly reduced if the fixation stimulus presented prior to the introduction of the peripheral target remained in the infant's visual field. For example, at a 10 degree eccentricity the probability of directing the first eye movement toward the target hemi-field was over .8 whether or not the central stimulus remained present. However, at increasing eccentricities, the continued presence of the central stimulus greatly reduced the probability of directing the first eye movement toward the peripheral target. Thus, young infants tend to remain fixated on contours that currently occupy their attention rather than employ a rapid sequence of searching eye movements. This same trend toward restricted scanpaths in young infants has been noted by several researchers studying the scanning of complex visual stimuli (Leahy, 1976; Salapatek, 1975).

Another interesting aspect of the research on peripheral target localization is the finding by Aslin and Salapatek (1975) that 1- and 2-month-olds employ a very inefficient means of moving the line of sight toward a peripheral target. Despite the fact that the first eye movement is reliably directed toward the target, the form of the movement is not adultlike. Adults typically use a single rapid eye movement, called a saccade, to bring the image of the peripheral target on the fovea. Infants, however, use a series of small saccades of nearly equivalent amplitude to localize the target. Despite their ability to make large saccades in the dark, young infants do not program magnitude-appropriate saccades to bring a peripheral target onto the fovea. There are many potential explanations of this phenomenon. First, saccades are ballistic in nature. That is, once the neural command is directed to the extraocular muscles, the resultant saccade cannot be cancelled or modified. Thus, the muscular contraction required to move the eyeball a specific angular amount must be specified prior to the movement. Given the changing mass of the infant eyeball and the increase in extraocular muscle strength during early postnatal development, visual-motor experience in making saccades may be required to calibrate this localization system. Second, the migration of photoreceptors (described in an earlier section of this chapter) may demand a recalibration of the link between the locus of retinal stimulation and the required oculomotor command. Whatever the eventual explanation, however, it is likely that the presence of grossly inaccurate saccadic eye movements disrupts the processing of visual information in young infants. Pilot work in my laboratory and a study of eye-head coordination by Regal and Salapatek

(1982) suggest that by 6 months of age the frequency of multiple saccades is diminished as the localization system becomes more adultlike.

Another approach to determining if infants' scanning is controlled or random consists of changing a portion of a complex visual stimulus during an episode of scanning. Bronson (1982) reported that 2- to 5-month-olds will direct their fixations immediately toward a small pattern element within a multi-element pattern when the small element undergoes a change in shape. Interestingly, the change in fixation to detect this changed pattern element occurred only if the small element was located 5 degrees from the current line of sight and not if it was located 15 degrees away. This finding implies that the detection of pattern changes in the peripheral visual field is limited to a near-foveal region of the retina. Alternatively, the infants may have detected this peripheral pattern change but failed to fixate the element in the farther periphery because they chose not to exert the effort (motor or attentional) to do so. Without another measure of peripheral visual processing, it is impossible to say with certainty that pattern changes in the far periphery are not discriminated. This methodological problem, of course, is precisely the one mentioned earlier in interpreting scanning data; that is, the size of the region surrounding the line of sight which is involved in pattern processing is unknown.

So far I have considered only saccadic eye movements directed toward stationary visual stimuli. Another important aspect of eye movement control is the ability to move the line of sight to follow a moving visual stimulus. In adults, if the fovea does not closely match the velocity of the moving stimulus, then some of the pattern details of the stimulus are degraded because the stimulus is located on less acute peripheral retinal areas. In infants, there were several early reports that smooth pursuit eye movements were not present until approximately 2 months of age (Dayton & Jones, 1964; McGinnis, 1930). Recently, Kremenitzer, Vaughan, Kurtzberg, and Dowling (1979) reported that newborns show brief segments of smooth pursuit, but they employed a very large (12 degree) target, raising the possibility that peripheral retinal areas were mediating this response. In a more recent study, I (Aslin, 1981) used a small (2 degree) target and a more accurate corneal reflection technique to record the tracking movements of 3- to 13-week-olds. Examples of pursuit movements in these infants are illustrated in Fig. 3.5. Notice that until at least 6 weeks of age the pursuit movements are totally saccadic. By 8 weeks of age some small segments of smooth pursuit are evident, and by 12 weeks of age smooth pursuit predominates, with a few saccadic interruptions. Thus, the early reports on pursuit in infants have been replicated in this more recent study.

There are a number of potential explanations for the failure of young infants to show smooth pursuit. Because these explanations are relevant to a variety of visual abilities in young infants, they have been listed in Table 3.1. Note that four general classes of explanations are proposed: (1) attentional/motivational,

6-WEEK-OLD

10-WEEK-OLD

ADULT

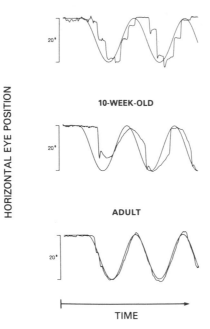

HORIZONTAL EYE POSITION

TIME

FIG. 3.5. Pursuit eye movements in infants viewing a small target that moved back and forth through a 20-degree horizontal excursion. The solid sinusoidal line indicates the position of the moving target. (Reprinted from Aslin, 1981)

(2) anatomical/neuromuscular, (3) sensory, and (4) sensory-motor. Although none of these explanations can be definitely ruled out, the sensory-motor class is the most relevant to perceptual phenomena and infant memory. First, young infants may have accurate information about the velocity of the moving target but be unable to program the extraocular muscles to move the eyeball appropriately. As a result, the fovea falls behind the moving target and the ability to extract detailed information from the moving stimulus may be degraded. Second, young infants are known to show poor evidence of appropriate binocular alignment (see next section). As a result, there is the possibility that a single visual target is seen as double (diplopia), and the young infant's visual system may become confused as to which of the "two" images should be foveated and followed during stimulus movement. Third, the background upon which a moving target is presented creates a stimulus that is *not* moving. Infants and adults must suppress this peripheral visual information during eye movements because a rightward eye movement creates a leftward movement of the image of the background. If infants do not suppress this counter-movement of the background, the visual system may program an eye movement in the direction opposite to the eye movement that is induced by the movement of the target. Fourth, infants may not be able to discriminate between movements of the image across the retina due to actual target movement and those due to spontaneous movements of the eyeball.

The perception of target motion requires the visual system to differentiate translations of the retinal image due to target movement from translations due to head
and eye movements. If young infants ignore small translations of the retinal
image, they may fail to program a smooth pursuit movement until the target is
quite distant from the fovea. As a result, a saccade may be used to bring the
target's image back on the fovea and smooth pursuit movements may never be
initiated.

In summary, the control of eye movements in young infants is less accurate
than in adults, and these inaccuracies may place constraints on the efficiency
with which information is extracted from visual stimuli. The fovea in infants is
frequently directed to nonoptimum locations for visual processing (assuming that
visual processing is better via the fovea), and the perceptual implications of
poorly controlled eye movements (e.g., disjointed views of complex visual stimuli, both moving and stationary) are potentially significant. If young infants
receive a degraded view of a to-be-encoded stimulus in a memory task, they may
perceive the re-presentation of that same stimulus as a novel stimulus at a later
age, even though storage and retrieval of the encoded stimulus was accurate. In
short, invariant encoding at different ages is likely to depend on similar strategies
for fixating the visual stimulus.

BINOCULAR FIXATION AND DEPTH PERCEPTION

An important aspect of visual processing is the ability to discriminate the distance and depth relations among objects. This ability is mediated by two general
classes of visual stimuli: monocular information and binocular information.

TABLE 3.1
Possible Explanations for the
Absence of Smooth Pursuit in Early
Infancy

A. Attentional/Motivational Factors
B. Anatomical and Neuromuscular Factors
   1. Damping Characteristics
   2. Frequency Response
C. Sensory Mechanisms
   1. Acuity and Contrast Sensitivity
   2. Temporal Resolution
   3. Velocity Analysis
D. Sensory-Motor Control Mechanisms
   1. Muscle Programming Based on Velocity Information
   2. Binocular Interference (Diplopia)
   3. Peripheral Field Interference
   4. Motion Perception

Monocular information is provided by visual cues available to a single eye, including the pictorial cues to depth (e.g., shading, perspective, occlusion) and motion parallax (the relative velocity of retinal image movement). The pioneering work in this area was done by Walk and Gibson (1961) using the visual cliff. However, it was not clear from this work whether monocular or binocular information typically mediated the infants' avoidance of the so-called "deep" side. Monocular information was sufficient, as evidenced by avoidance while wearing a single eyepatch, but a definitive test of the use of binocular information was not available until recently.

Prior to the recent work on binocular depth perception, a number of more elementary issues were addressed (see review by Aslin & Dumais, 1980). For example, one requirement of accurate binocular depth perception is the presence of appropriately aligned eyes. That is, to extract accurate depth relations among an array of objects, it is necessary to align the two eyes to simultaneously fixate a single target. Failure to do so results in either the perception of double images (diplopia) or the suppression (without eye closure) of the input to one eye. In either case, the accuracy of depth perception is greatly reduced. Thus, it was of some interest to determine if young infants appropriately align the two lines of sight to binocularly fixate a single target.

In two studies (Aslin, 1977; Slater & Findlay, 1975) newborns and 1-month-olds did not maintain consistent binocular fixation of near targets (less than 10 inches away), even though the initiation of vergence movements (convergence to near targets and divergence to far targets) was appropriate. Thus, it appeared that young infants may experience diplopia or suppression. However, a second experiment by Aslin (1977) raised the possibility that diplopia is *not* present in young infants. A series of wedge prisms were placed in front of one eye while the infant viewed a target. The prisms had the effect of misaligning the eyes slightly. Not until nearly 6 months of age did the infants show an eye movement response indicating that the misalignment was corrected. Thus, when an object is moved large distances creating large misalignments, infants by 2 or 3 months of age generally realign their eyes. However, when a prism is used to create a small eye misalignment, the eyes are apparently not realigned until almost 6 months of age. Although it is possible that infants under 6 months of age experience double images as a result of both large and small eye misalignments, it is also possible that these findings can be accounted for by a developmental improvement in the resolution of small differences in binocular correspondence. That is, specific locations on each retina are paired in the visual system to result in the perception of a single object despite stimulation of two different retinal loci (one in each eye). This phenomenon of single vision is called fusion. In adults, fusion breaks down (i.e., leads to diplopia) whenever even the slightest misalignment of the eyes occurs because the paired retinal loci are not stimulated simultaneously by the same target. In infants, however, just as in adults under conditions of low illumination, the effective requirement of eye alignment may be relaxed, allowing for a broader tolerance for fusion. This potential explanation of inaccuracies in binocular fixation in young infants is supported by several studies of binocular depth resolution.

The resolution of differences in distance is called stereoacuity. Stereoacuity is a quantitative measure of a more general phenomenon called stereopsis: the perception of relative object distance based solely on retinal disparity. As shown in Fig. 3.6, retinal disparity is created by binocularly fixating a stimulus that contains a subregion viewed separately by each eye. A small lateral offset of these subregions creates retinal disparity because noncorresponding retinal loci are stimulated. When this stereogram is viewed by normal adults, the subregion appears fused and located at a different distance from the background. Also shown in Fig. 3.6 is a recent development in stereogram displays called the random-element stereogram. This display has the advantage of camouflaging the motion parallax and other monocular cues typically present in traditional line stereograms.

NON-STEREOSCOPIC APPEARANCE

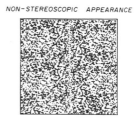

INPUT TO LEFT EYE   INPUT TO RIGHT EYE

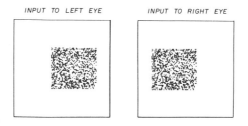

FIG. 3.6. The configuration of a random-element stereogram illustrating the lateral offset of two subregions that are viewed separately by the two eyes. The angular equivalent of the lateral offset is a measure of retinal disparity. Note that in the middle and bottom portions of the figure the background elements are removed to provide a clearer illustration of the lateral offset. (Reprinted from Aslin & Dumais, 1980)

STEREOSCOPIC APPEARANCE

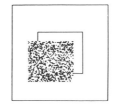

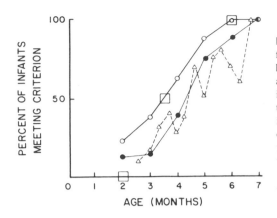

FIG. 3.7. Summary of the results from three studies of stereopsis in human infants showing the percentage of infants tested that provided evidence of stereopsis as a function of their age at testing. ○ crossed disparity of 58 minutes of arc and ● crossed disparity of 1 minute of arc from Birch et al. (1982); □ from Petrig et al. (1981); △ from Fox et al. (1980) and additional data from Shea et al. (1980). (Reprinted from Teller, 1982)

In two recent studies using random-element stereograms there is evidence that infants by 3 months of age have stereopsis (Fox, Aslin, Shea, & Dumais, 1980; Petrig, Julesz, Kropfl, Baumgartner, & Anliker, 1981). In two other studies using line stereograms, steroacuity has been shown to improve dramatically between 3 and 5 months of age (Birch, Gwiazda, & Held, 1982; Held Birch, & Gwiazda, 1980). Thus, as shown in Fig. 3.7, infants under 3 months of age may not perceive the binocular depth relations in visual stimuli presented for encoding. As a result, depth information contained in a stimulus to be encoded by a young infant may not be recognized as similar by this same infant at a later age.

With regard to monocular cues to depth, Yonas and his colleagues have recently reported that infants older than 5 months of age reach differentially to pictorial stimuli containing the cues of linear perspective (Yonas, Cleaves, & Pettersen, 1978) and familiar size (Yonas, Pettersen, & Granrud, 1982). Thus, by the age when accurate reaching emerges, many monocular cues to depth appear to be effective in guiding the infant's spatial behavior. It will remain unclear whether these cues to depth are processed at an earlier age until other methodologies are developed for use with younger infants.

COLOR VISION

Many of the stimuli used in studies of infant memory contain chromatic information. Thus, if infants are being asked to store this type of information, it seems relevant to ask whether they possess the sensory ability to discriminate differences in wavelength. Ironically, wavelength discrimination per se may *not* be a critical factor in studies of color memory because most chromatic stimuli are presented in a very crude manner to infants. That is, the perception of color is dependent on three major variables: hue, saturation, and luminance. The color of a stimulus can be altered by changing its luminance (intensity) or its saturation (percentage of white) without changing its hue (wavelength). Consequently, until quite recently hue discrimination had not been conclusively demonstrated in young infants. Peeples and Teller (1975) used preferential looking to show that a red stimulus could be discriminated from a white background by 2 months of age. To ensure that the discrimination was based solely on hue, they systematically varied the luminance of the target relative to the background. In this way, they guaranteed that one of the target luminances was matched to the background luminance. Previous investigators had assumed that the sensitivity of the infant's visual system to different hues was identical to the adult norm. This assumption was incorrect, particularly at long wavelengths (the blue end of the spectrum; see Dobson, 1976; Moskowitz-Cook, 1979). In the absence of this luminance control, therefore, infants might have been colorblind but detected the "red" target based solely on its luminance difference compared to the background.

As shown in Fig. 3.8, a wide variety of wavelengths have been paired with white to test the young infant's hue discrimination. Teller, Peeples, and Sekel (1978) have shown that by 2 months of age nearly all wavelengths are discriminated from white. However, there are a few discrimination failures that do not fully support the presence of trichromacy (three photopigments as in color-normal adults). Studies of wavelength discrimination with nonwhite backgrounds (Hamer, Alexander, & Teller, 1982) and spectral sensitivity following chromatic adaptation (Pulos, Teller, & Buck, 1980) suggest that until 3 months of age the three cone types may not be functional. However, in other respects very young infants and adults are similar, as demonstrated by the close correspondence between the dark-adapted spectral sensitivity functions in 1-month-olds, 3-month-olds, and adults (Powers, Schneck, & Teller, 1981). In summary, although rod-mediated vision is similar in infants and adults, the fine sensitivity to different wavelengths characteristic of the normal adult does not appear to be present in infants until at least 3 months of age.

Another aspect of color vision is the manner in which different wavelengths are grouped into color categories. If infants perceived the spectrum as a large number of discrete hues rather than a few color categories (e.g., blue, green, yellow, and red), the task of encoding wavelength information would be very difficult. Bornstein and his colleagues (see review in Bornstein, 1981) have argued that infants by 4 months of age perceive the spectrum as a small number of hue categories, and that the infant's categories are quite similar to those of adults. The evidence in support of this claim consists of differential rates of habituation of looking time to hues from the center of a wavelength category versus hues from the boundaries of a hue category. In addition, infants dishabituated to between-category changes in wavelength but not to within-category changes, despite the fact that the magnitude of all changes in wavelength were equivalent. It is important to note that these categorization effects are not simply

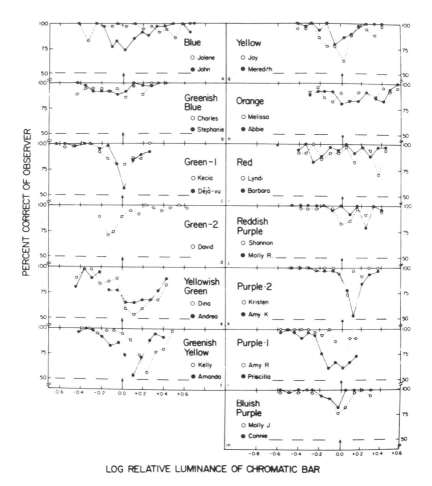

FIG. 3.8. Preferential looking detection functions for 2-month-old infants presented with a chromatic target on a white background. The observer's percentage correct is plotted as a function of the luminance of the target relative to the fixed luminance background. Functions that dip to chance indicate the failure to discriminate the color from the background when the perceived brightnesses of the target and background are equivalent. (Reprinted from Teller, Peeples, & Sekel, 1978)

the result of a failure to discriminate within-category differences in wavelength or to an effect of perceptual learning via reinforcement or linguistic labeling. In summary, although there are significant changes in hue discrimination during the first 3 months of life, many of the encoding mechanisms used by adults to store chromatic information appear to be present in infants by 4 months of age.

SUMMARY AND CONCLUSIONS

The development in the past two decades of a number of powerful measurement techniques has enabled researchers to assess the development of visual abilities in early infancy. In this chapter a variety of sensory and perceptual abilities in young infants have been summarized. In general, infants until at least 3 months of age do not appear to have many of the basic sensory abilities present in adults. The retina undergoes a number of structural changes that suggest visual resolution and color vision may be deficient. Behavioral and electrophysiological assessments of acuity and contrast sensitivity have shown that visual resolution is in fact quite poor at birth and continues to improve throughout the first postnatal year. The presence of refractive errors in early infancy is quite common, and the control of accommodation is somewhat limited until 3 months of age. Pattern vision remains largely a mystery despite a great number of preference studies. Discriminations are made in early infancy, but their basis has remained unclear despite attempts to simplify the description of stimuli and to use detailed measures of visual scanning. The control of eye movements is inefficient until at least 2 months of age for smooth pursuit and vergence and until 6 months for saccades. Binocular fusion has not been conclusively demonstrated in young infants, but it appears likely that at least some of the time very young infants experience diplopia or suppression. Stereopsis appears to emerge in the 4th postnatal month and stereoacuity shows a very rapid development between 3 and 5 months of age. Finally, color vision in infants younger than 3 months of age appears to lack at least some of the properties that characterize normal adult color vision.

The implication of these sensory and perceptual developments for studies of infant memory is that the quality of information that can be processed by infants at different ages changes quite dramatically. Thus, if the infant is faced with a recognition task after visual information has been stored at some earlier age, the same visual stimulus that was encoded earlier may appear different to the more mature visual system. As a result, the failure to show recognition may be the result of a mismatch between the stored representation of the stimulus, which contained "degraded" information, and the perceptual information contained in the current recognition memory stimulus. Careful attention to these sensory and perceptual constraints on visual information processing may clarify the basis for memory failures in young infants.

ACKNOWLEDGMENT

Preparation of this chapter was made possible by a Research Career Development Award from NIH (HD–00309) and research grants from NSF (80–13075) and NICHHD (HD–11915–05).

REFERENCES

Abramov, I., Gordon, J., Hendrickson, A., Hainline, L., Dobson, V., & LaBossierre, E. The retina of the newborn human infant. *Science*, 1982, *217*, 265–267.

Aslin, R. N. Development of binocular fixation in human infants. *Journal of Experimental Child Psychology*, 1977, *23*, 133–150.

Aslin, R. N. Development of smooth pursuit in human infants. In D. F. Fisher, R. A. Monty, & J. W. Senders (Eds.), *Eye movements: Cognition and visual perception*. Hillsdale, N.J.: Lawrence Erlbaum Associates, 1981.

Aslin, R. N., & Dumais, S. T. Binocular vision in infants: A review and a theoretical framework. In H. W. Reese & L. P. Lipsitt (Eds.), *Advances in child development and behavior* (Vol. 15). New York: Academic Press, 1980.

Aslin, R. N., & Salapatek P. Saccadic localization of visual targets by the very young human infant. *Perception and Psychophysics*, 1975, *17*, 293–302.

Atkinson, J., Braddick, O., & Moar, K. Development of contrast sensitivity over the first 3 months of life in the human infant. *Vision Research*, 1977, *17*, 1037–1044.

Banks, M. S. Infant refraction and accommodation. *International Ophthalmology Clinics*, 1980, *20*, 205–232. (a)

Banks, M. S. The development of visual accommodation during early infancy. *Child Development*, 1980, *51*, 646–666. (b)

Banks, M. S., & Salapatek, P. Acuity and contrast sensitivity in 1-, 2-, and 3-month-old human infants. *Investigative Ophthalmology and Visual Science*, 1978, *17*, 361–365.

Banks, M. S., & Salapatek, P. Infant pattern vision: A new approach based on the contrast sensitivity function. *Journal of Experimental Child Psychology*, 1981, *31*, 1–45.

Birch, E., Gwiazda, J., & Held, R. Stereoacuity development for crossed and uncrossed disparities in human infants. *Vision Research*, 1982, *22*, 507–514.

Bornstein, M. H. Psychological studies of color perception in human infants: Habituation, discrimination and categorization, recognition, and conceptualization In L. P. Lipsitt (Ed.), *Advances in infancy research* (Vol. 1). Norwood, N.J.: Ablex, 1981.

Braddick, O., Atkinson, J., French, J., & Howland, H. C. A photorefractive study of infant accommodation. *Vision Research*, 1979, *19*, 1319–1330.

Bronson, G. The scanning patterns of human infants: Implications for visual learning. *Monographs on Infancy*, No. 2. Norwood, N.J.: Ablex, 1982.

Brookman, K. E. *Ocular accommodation in the human infant*. Unpublished doctoral dissertation, Indiana University, 1980.

Bushnell, I. W. R. Modification of the externality effect in young infants. *Journal of Experimental Child Psychology*, 1979, *28*, 211–229.

Conel, J. L. *The postnatal development of the human cerebral cortex* (Vol. 1): The cortex of the newborn. Cambridge, Mass.: Harvard University Press, 1939.

Conel, J. L. *The postnatal development of the human cerebral cortex* (Vol. 2): The cortex of the one-month infant. Cambridge, Mass.: Harvard University Press, 1941.

Conel, J. L. *The postnatal development of the human cerebral cortex* (Vol. 3): The cortex of the three-month infant. Cambridge, Mass.: Harvard University Press, 1947.

Conel, J. L. *The postnatal development of the human cerebral cortex* (Vol. 4): The cortex of the six-month infant. Cambridge, Mass.: Harvard University Press, 1951.

Dannemiller, J. L., & Banks, M. S. The development of light adaptation in human infants. *Vision Research*, 1983, *23*, 599–609.

Dayton, G. O. & Jones, M. H. Analysis of characteristics of fixation reflexes by use of direct current electrooculography. *Neurology*, 1964, *14*, 1152–1156.

Dobson, V. Spectral sensitivity of the 2-month infant as measured by the visually evoked potential. *Vision Research*, 1976, *16*, 75–81.

Dobson, V., & Teller, D. Y. Visual acuity in human infants: A review and comparison of behavioral and electrophysiological studies. *Vision Research*, 1978, *18*, 1469–1483.

Fantz, R. L. Pattern vision in young infants. *Psychological Record*, 1958, *8*, 43–47.

Fantz, R. L., Fagen, J. F., & Miranda, S. B. Early visual selectivity as a function of pattern variables, previous exposure, age from birth and conception, and expected cognitive deficit. In L. B. Cohen & P. Salapatek (Eds.), *Infant perception: From sensation to cognition*. New York: Academic Press, 1975.

Fantz, R. L., Ordy, J. M., & Udelf, M. S. Maturation of pattern vision in infants during the first six months. *Journal of Comparative and Physiological Psychology*, 1962, *55*, 907–917.

Fox, R., Aslin, R. N., Shea, S. L., & Dumais, S. T. Stereopsis in human infants. *Science*, 1980, *207*, 323–324.

Green, D. G., & Campbell, F. W. Effect of focus on the visual response to a sinusoidally modulated spatial stimulus. *Journal of the Optical Society of America*, 1965, *55*, 1154–1157.

Green, D. G., Powers, M. K., & Banks, M. S. Depth of focus, eye size, and visual acuity. *Vision Research*, 1980, *20*, 827–836.

Hainline, L. Developmental changes in visual scanning of face and nonface patterns by infants. *Journal of Experimental Child Psychology*, 1978, *25*, 90–115.

Haith, M. M., Bergman, T., & Moore, M. J. Eye contact and face scanning in early infancy. *Science*, 1977, *198*, 853–855.

Hamer, R. D., Alexander, K., & Teller, D. Y. Rayleigh discriminations in young human infants. *Vision Research*, 1982, *22*, 575–587.

Harris, P., & MacFarlane, A. The growth of the effective visual field from birth to seven weeks. *Journal of Experimental Child Psychology*, 1974, *18*, 340–348.

Haynes, H., White, B. L., & Held, R. Visual accommodation in human infants. *Science*, 1965, *148*, 528–530.

Held, R., Birch, E., & Gwiazda, J. Stereoacuity of human infants. *Proceedings of the National Academy of Science*, 1980, *77*, 5572–5574.

Hendrickson, A., & Kupfer, C. The histogenesis of the fovea in the macaque monkey. *Investigative Ophthalmology*, 1976, *15*, 746–756.

Hickey, T. L. Postnatal development of the human lateral geniculate nucleus: Relationship to a critical period for the visual system. *Science*, 1977, *198*, 836–838.

Kail, R., & Hagen, J. W. *Perspectives on the development of memory and cognition*. Hillsdale, N.J.: Lawrence Erlbaum Associates, 1977.

Kremenitzer, J. P., Vaughan, H. G., Kurtzberg, D., & Dowling, K. Smooth-pursuit eye movements in the newborn infant. *Child Development*, 1979, *50*, 442–448.

Leahy, R. L. Development of preferences and processes of visual scanning in the human infant during the first three months of life. *Developmental Psychology*, 1976, *12*, 250–254.

Mann, I. *The development of the human eye*. London: British Medical Association, 1964.

Maurer, D., & Salapatek, P. Developmental changes in the scanning of faces by young infants. *Child Development*, 1976, *47*, 523–527.

McGinnis, J. M. Eye movements and optic nystagmus in early infancy. *Genetic Psychology Monographs*, 1930, *8*, 321–430.

Milewski, A. Infant's discrimination of internal and external pattern elements. *Journal of Experimental Child Psychology*, 1976, *22*, 229–246.

Milewski, A. Young infants' visual processing of internal and adjacent shapes. *Infant Behavior and Development*, 1978, *1*, 359–371.

Moskowitz-Cook, A. The development of photopic spectral sensitivity in human infants. *Vision Research*, 1979, *19*, 1133–1142.

Owens, D. A., & Leibowitz, H. W. Oculomotor adjustments in darkness and the specific distance tendency. *Perception and Psychophysics*, 1976, *20*, 2–9.

Peeples, D., & Teller, D. Y. Color vision and brightness discrimination in two-month-old human infants. *Science*, 1975, *189*, 1102–1103.

Petrig, B., Julesz, B., Kropfl, W., Baumgartner, G., & Anliker, M. Development of stereopsis and cortical binocularity in human infants: Electrophysiological evidence. *Science*, 1981, *213*, 1402–1405.

Powers, M. K., & Dobson, V. Effect of focus on visual acuity of human infants. *Vision Research*, 1982, *22*, 521–528.

Powers, M. K., Schneck, M., & Teller, D. Y. Spectral sensitivity of human infants at absolute threshold. *Vision Research*, 1981, *21*, 1005–1016.

Pulos, E., Teller, D. Y., & Buck, S. L. Infant color vision: A search for short-wavelength-sensitive mechanisms by means of chromatic adaptation. *Vision Research*, 1980, *20*, 485–493.

Regal, D., & Salapatek, P. Eye and head coordination in human infants. *Supplement to Investigative Ophthalmology and Visual Science*, 1982, *22*, 85.

Salapatek, P. Pattern perception in early infancy. In L. B. Cohen and P. Salapatek (Eds.), *Infant perception: From sensation to cognition*. New York: Academic Press, 1975.

Salapatek, P., Bechtold, A. G., & Bushnell, E. W. Infant visual acuity as a function of viewing distance. *Child Development*, 1976, *47*, 860–863.

Salapatek, P., & Kessen, W. Visual scanning of triangles by the human newborn. *Journal of Experimental Child Psychology*, 1966, *3*, 155–167.

Shea, S. L., Fox, R., Aslin, R. N., & Dumais, S. T. Assessment of stereopsis in human infants. *Investigative Ophthalmology and Visual Science*, 1980, *19*, 1400–1404.

Shiffrin, R. M. Capacity limitations in information processing, attention, and memory. In W. K. Estes (Ed.), *Handbook of learning and cognitive processes* (Vol. 4): *Attention and memory*. Hillsdale, N.J.: Lawrence Erlbaum Associates, 1976.

Slater, A. M., & Findlay, J. M. Binocular fixation in the newborn baby. *Journal of Experimental Child Psychology*, 1975, *20*, 248–273.

Sokol, S. Measurement of infant visual acuity from pattern reversal evoked potentials. *Vision Research*, 1978, *18*, 33–39.

Sokol, S., & Jones, K. Implicit time of pattern evoked potentials in infants: An index of maturation of spatial vision. *Vision Research*, 1979, *19*, 747–755.

Teller, D. Y. The forced-choice preferential looking procedure: A psychophysical technique for use with human infants. *Infant Behavior and Development*, 1979, *2*, 135–153.

Teller, D. Y. Scotopic vision, color vision, and stereopsis in infants. *Current Eye Research*, 1982, *2*, 199–210.

Teller, D. Y., Peeples, D., & Sekel, M. Discrimination of chromatic from white light in two-month-old human infants. *Vision Research*, 1978, *18*, 41–48.

Tronick, E. Stimulus control and the growth of the infant's effective visual field. *Perception and Psychophysics*, 1972, *11*, 373–375.

von Hofsten, C. Binocular convergence as a determinant of reaching behavior in infancy. *Perception*, 1977, *6*, 139–144.

Walk, R. D., & Gibson, E. J. A comparative and analytical study of visual depth perception. *Psychological Monographs*, 1961, *75* (15 Whole No. 519).

Yonas, A., Cleaves, W., & Pettersen, L. Development of sensitivity to pictorial depth. *Science*, 1978, *200*, 77–79.

Yonas, A., Pettersen, L., & Granrud, C. E. Infants' sensitivity to familiar size as information for distance. *Child Development*, 1982, *53*, 1285–1290.

4 Sensory-Perceptual Development in the Norway Rat: A View Toward Comparative Studies

Jeffrey R. Alberts
Indiana University

INTRODUCTION

One essential key to understanding an organism's behavior is knowledge of the sensory information it receives from the world. Our ability to appreciate the diversity of behavior displayed by animals is enhanced by learning about the perceptual world (*umwelt*) of each species. Similarly, the analysis of behavioral development and its underlying processes is enhanced by learning about sensory-perceptual function at each stage of maturation.

In 1899 Willard Small published his diary of observations on the development of behavior, as seen in a litter of domesticated rats. In many respects, Small's paper, "Notes on the Psychic Development of the Albino Rat," still stands as the "best" unified overview of sensory and behavioral development in *Rattus norvegicus*. Nevertheless, over the intervening 80 or so years, considerable ontogenetic data for the rat has accumulated on these topics. Such data, and the research that has produced it, warrants review.

But my goal for the present chapter is more limited than a comprehensive review. In the present chapter I attempted to extract from the literature a sample of behavioral studies, with some correlative anatomical and physiological data, that pertain to the ontogeny of sensory-perceptual function in the rat; to integrate this chapter with present volume, particular efforts were made to identify issues relevant to the design, conduct, and interpretation of research on memory development.

Similarly, in the spirit of the important comparative theme of the present volume, I attempt to put the data on *R. norvegicus* into a comparative framework and in the section immediately following this one I discuss comparative perspec-

65

tives on development in particular. There are still practical reasons to review data on "the rat" in the context of "comparative" analyses: The majority of research on psychological processes conducted on nonhuman subjects is conducted on Norway rats. I hope this will not always be the case. The spirit of comparative analysis is to appreciate evolutionary variation and diversity of adaptation. Single species can be appreciated in such frameworks, but the highest goals are to be realized with broadly comparative studies. In theory, comparative research will yield general principles. With this aim in mind, I have included in several themes that appear to have some general utility, and treat them, tentatively, as principles of sensory ontogenesis.

Comparative Perspectives on Development

One general goal of comparative studies is to discern and to describe commonalities shared by life forms that are otherwise dissimilar. Such cross-species commonalities can then be used as clues for further analyses in which the shared features are used to determine shared ancestries. Hodos and Campbell (1969) have discussed this aspect of comparative work. They emphasized the important differences between making comparisons of extant forms to determine common ancestry, *versus* the less defensible approach of making such comparisons for the purpose of revealing evolutionary continua across current phylogenetic lines.

Developmental analyses have always played an important role in comparative research, but recent appraisals and applications of ontogenetic concepts have further enhanced the recognized importance of development as a central issue. There are several ways in which developmental processes are highlighted in comparative thinking. In one, developmental phenomena provide data that are used to judge questions of analogy and homology in phylogenetic patterns (Ghiselin, 1966; Smith, 1967). Careful comparative analyses of development patterns can reveal cross-species similarities in ontogenesis. When two or more species share common early features but differ in adult phenotype, we can examine their developmental courses more fully to identify the ontogenetic events which result in divergent outcomes. What is the theme that is elaborated upon by alterations in ontogenesis? That is, what common elements have been used as the basis for the subsequent variety seen in the world?

The second way in which developmental concepts have become prominent is through recognition of ontogeny as a mechanism of phylogenetic change. Organisms can be viewed as developmental cycles that reproduce (e.g., Bonner, 1974). Organismic (phylogenetic) variation is therefore a reflection of differences in developmental cycles. Thus, the comparative method becomes a means of recognizing crucial similarities and differences that mediate the diversity in the world and provides some insight into historical/evolutionary roots of such differences. Gould (1977) is one of the most eloquent and prolific contemporary spokesmen on such issues.

Another way in which comparative perspectives are useful is as a means of providing larger frameworks for appreciation. Processes that are hidden in some systems are vividly apparent in others. To focus on just one species, even the human, often leads to a narrow view of *biological* issues. The present chapter is, in fact, only a meager tribute to the comparative approach, since its content is based almost entirely on Norway rats and some closely related murid rodents. There is much to be gained from broader and more comparative studies.

Finally, it is worth noting that the "comparative perspective," even in its most limited sense, that is, with reference to studies of nonhuman animals, has a special, pragmatic relevance to developmental studies. Investigations of human infants and nonhuman animal subjects both require methods suitable to nonverbal organisms. Thus, methodological, procedural, and interpretive problems (and solutions) can often be shared between two "camps" that are too often separated by traditional boundaries. Even in situations where particular data are not directly applicable from one species to the next, an *approach* that was useful in one setting may be similarly applicable in another. Endeavors such as the present volume will contribute to creative and productive interchanges and mutual enhancement of research and understanding.

PRINCIPLES OF SENSORY ONTOGENESIS

Principle 1: Sequential Onsets of Function

Gottlieb (1971) has surveyed decades of empirical investigations and, based on a skillfully integrated appraisal of electrophysiological, histological, and behavioral data, he derived a schedule for the *onset* of function of the vestibular, tactile, auditory, and visual systems in a wide variety of species. These four sensory systems provided the most complete database at the time. The use of studies conducted over many years in many laboratories for as many different purposes undoubtedly added variance to the results of Gottlieb's inquiry. In this light, the outcome is even more impressive. Rather than review his thorough analysis in detail, I will merely summarize some of the more stunning findings and elaborate upon them with some more recent additions. The interested reader can and should consult his essays.

Onset of function for these four sensory systems was the same in each of the species that was analyzed. In every case, onset of sensory function proceeded in the following order: vestibular, tactile, auditory, visual. I have created a graphic representation of the results of part of Gottlieb's survey, shown here as Fig. 4.1. Only a subset of the range of species surveyed is shown, but I attempted to maximize available taxonomic differences by including species representing birds, rodents, lagomorphs, carnivores, ungulates, and primates. It is the stability of the sequence across these divergent taxa that is most impressive. The temporal sequence of onsets of function appears to transcend the myriad ecologi-

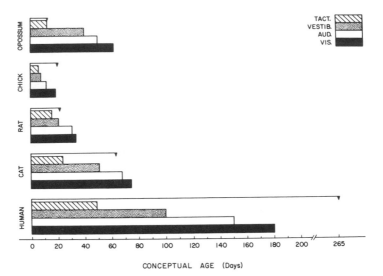

FIG. 4.1. Sequential onsets of function in four sensory systems of a species of marsupial (opossum, *Didelphis viginiana*), bird (domestic chicken, *Gallus gallus*), rodent (Norway rat, *Rattus norvegicus*), carnivore (domestic cat, *Felis catus*) and primate (human, *Homo sapien*), in relation to conceptual age and the event of birth or hatching. The small marker above each set of histograms depicts the organism's birthdate. For each species the bar graphs represent (top to bottom), onset of function for tactile, vestibular, aduitory and vestibular sensitivity. The values shown were based on interpretive reviews and discussions of Gottlieb (1967, 1971).

cal and social facets of each species that might have been expected to have produced difference. Indeed, other timed events, such as birth or hatching (shown by the small arrows beneath each set of histograms) display a great cross-species range of occurrence. Nevertheless, whether onset is prenatal, postnatal, or distributed across both periods, the basic sequential template has endured.

Figure 4.2 is provided to lend a more evolutionary view to this consideration. The reader will find a similar depiction in Gottlieb (1971), who initially borrowed this type of phylogenetic tree from one of Romer's classic treatises (1966). Stretched across the contemporary (i.e., uppermost) branches of this tree are the same five extant species that comprise the data for Fig. 4.1. Shown in the lower branches and along the trunk of the phylogenetic tree are the most likely common ancestors. An approximate timeline is provided along the side as well. It is important to emphasize that the range of extant organisms shown along the top, despite their apparently increasing complexities, are *not* to be interpreted as ancestors of one another. Ancestry is to be seen in the vertical relations in Fig. 4.2. The major point to be derived from this presentation is that the species depicted in these figures have been evolutionarily independent for 70–100 million years, or even 150 million years including the avian representative. This suggests that the most recent common ancestor that was shared by all the species in this survey was a therapsid, or possibly even a thecodont. Such phylogenetic stability stands as an impressive principle of development with regard to the onset of function in these sensory systems.

At the time Gottlieb assembled these data, there was insufficient information on other sensory systems to include them in the sequence. Similarly, Gottlieb bemoaned the absence of parallel data from reptilian representatives; confirmation from that organismic group would further buttress the principle seen here. In the coming sections of the present chapter, when I focus more exclusively on

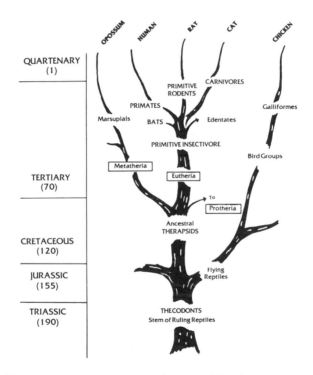

FIG. 4.2. A phylogentic "tree" depicting relationships of common ancestries for the five species shown in Figure 1. A timeline, expressed in millions of years past, runs vertically. According to such depictions, the present time is seen as a horizontal slice across the top of the tree. Horizontal "relationships" among extant species are not revealed by such a view, and for this reason the branches were arranged to avoid the kinds of hierarchical arrangements that can give the impression of graded complexity across extant phyla. This figure is based on one shown by Gottlieb (1971) and discussions of Romer (1966).

sensory ontogenesis in the Norway rat (*Rattus norvegicus*), I insert the olfactory, gustatory and thermal modalities into this ontogenetic sequence. I do so with the hope that such information, if available in other species, would again echo the same pattern found in *R. norvegicus*. All indications are, to my knowledge, affirmative.

Principle 2: Function Prior to Functional Maturation

In every sensory system in every species that has been studied, psychophysical operating characteristics of sensory-perceptual function undergo changes following onset of function. These are typically in the form of improved sensitivity, specificity, the ability to discriminate among increasingly similar stimuli, and the like. When such operating characteristics stabilize, we view the system as "functionally mature." This is clearly an oversimplification, but it serves to focus our attention on the period around and following onset of function.

Onset of function is surprisingly tricky to define precisely. For example, in many altricial animals (altricial means, literally, "nest-sitting" and is used to refer to animals born in an immature stage of development, such as that of most mammals, in which a period of maternal care is usually provided), the ears are still sealed shut at birth and remain closed for days or even weeks. It is common and appropriate to consider the time of ear-opening as a landmark in the onset of auditory function. Indeed, when the external meatus opens, there is a vast increase in the amount and force of sound energy that can reach the auditory receptors; behaviorally, animals show an immediate change in the range of acoustic cues to which they can respond. Nevertheless, it can be shown that auditory function begins prior to ear-opening and to ignore this is to fail to appreciate the degree to which receptor and sensory system maturation has progressed. Similarly, to consider the auditory sensory system as functionally complete once the ears have unsealed and responsivity broadens is to miss important processes of further development, some of which may be experience- (i.e. function) dependent.

Figure 4.3 is an idealized view of possible relationships between onset of function and the attainment of a "final" or "mature" level of function. In Fig. 4.3, the line representing System A depicts a sensory modality in which onset of function occurs prenatally. Function in System A gradually improves during postnatal life and reaches an asymptotic level or plateau that is considered to represent "functional maturation." In contrast, System B only begins to function postnatally. According to this depiction, however, System B is more rapidly maturing than A and reaches its level of functional maturity before A, even though onset of function was earlier for A. Arnold (1980) has noted the possible interpretive complexities related to comparisons of level of function during ontogenesis. He warned that it is often crucially important to define specific points

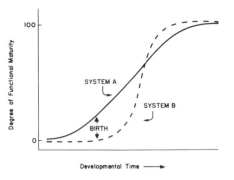

FIG. 4.3. Developmental rates for two hypothetical sensory systems, drawn to depict achievement of functional maturation in relation to their status at birth.

in development for comparative evaluations because the ontogenetic *stability* of a phenotypic character can vary dramatically. Only by making systematic comparisons can develpmental level be accurately defined.

Principle 3: Heterochrony

It is important to reiterate that the developmental sequence to be recognized for sensory maturation refers specifically to *onset of function*. Subsequent attainment of functional maturation is another, separate issue. Sensory development proceeds at different rates within and between individuals—and even more dramatically between species. Thus, although Sensory System A may procede System B for onset of function, B may nevertheless attain functional maturity before A, and after Sensory System C, which initiated function after both A and B. Anokhin (1964) elaborated upon the idea of differences in timing (heterochrony) in sensory maturation, and based on his concept "systemogenesis" as a regulating principle of neural maturation on heterochronous development of functional sensory systems.

Systemogenesis is a concept that emphasizes the integrated maturation of functional systems which serve proximate, adaptive roles during early life. From a systemogenic point of view, natural selection has acted not so much to regulate the development of particular sensory systems that are needed at various stages of early life as to coordinate the rates of development of functional systems, groups of nerves that might otherwise be classified as parts of different groups, except that they work together during infancy to serve some functional role. One of Anokhin's examples is the maturation of nerve groups that together form the afferent and efferent pathways for nursing. These portions of the nervous system attain early function and support the life of the suckling infant. Other branches of nerves that are closely aligned in the adult may remain incompletely developed until later in life since, presumably, they are not part of the nursing system and have therefore not been subjected to the same selection pressures. It is this principle of heterochrony that has been incorporated into evolutionary thinking as a significant ontogenetic mechanism that can result in phenotypic divergence and speciation (deBeer, 1958; Gould, 1977).

DEVELOPMENT OF FUNCTION AND FUNCTION DURING DEVELOPMENT

In a previous essay (Alberts, 1981), I discussed the implications of the similar-sounding but distinctly different ideas of *development of function* and *function during development*. I incorporate some of the concepts used in that interpretive discussion of olfactory ontogenesis into the present consideration of sensory development and its relationship to studying development of memory in young animals.

Development of function refers to changes over ontogenetic time in the *operating characteristics* of sensory systems. These operating characteristics are the psychophysical parameters and more general perceptual capacities that influence the processing of sensory input. The bulk of the present chapter is devoted to a review of the development of the operating characteristics of the various sensory modalities in the Norway rat.

Development of function is vitally important to the conduct and interpretation of studies of memory development, particularly in infants. Altricial species (which include many birds and nearly all mammals and constitute the basic subject population of developmental studies of memory) present onerous risks of confound to systematic analyses of memory. The immature subject often learns a task or some aspect of stimulus relations at a stage when the operating characteristics of its crucial sensory-perceptual systems are different than they are later, when memory is assessed. Thus, the "same" stimulus may be perceived quite differently, due to maturational changes in the operating characteristics of the sensory inputs. The ability to demonstrate memory of a cue may be confounded by alterations in the sensory input associated with the same physical stimulus. Such maturational effects vary enormously, of course, depending on species, stage of maturation, and the sensory system involved. Detailed awareness of the ontogenetic parameters of function can help to identify such effects when they exist or to avoid them by the judicious selection of stimuli and tasks.

Function during development raises a different dimension of interpretive concern with respect to sensory function and developmental studies of learning and memory. In this context, "function" is used in its *adaptive* meanings to indicate that during early life, as in later stages, certain stimuli are functionally important, sometimes vital, in relation to survival and eventual reproductive success. The ability of an infant to "adapt" to its neonatal environment is often dependent on its capacity to perceive and respond to a very narrow subset of available stimuli. Infant rats, for instance, find nipples and suckle by responding to specific chemical cues. Without the presence of the appropriate cue or without the propensity to respond, the pup will die of inanition.

Awareness of such functional roles of specific stimuli during development is valuable for several reasons. First, it alerts the researcher to the fact that all stimuli, even those with seemingly similar characteristics, are not necessarily equal. The "meaning," or the salience, or the ease with which a stimulus is processed by the organism may be significantly different when the cue is part of an adaptive specialization of sensory function. Second, such awareness also alerts us to the (likely) possibility that such specializations of function will change with maturational stage. Stimuli that were functionally crucial at one stage may no longer be special at a later stage. Stimuli that were once "neutral" may acquire special status later in life. Third, there is the related, but more general issue that in many animals the sensory controls of behavior change during the course of their development. Rosenblatt (1976), in particular, has provided some thoughtful discussions on this issue. He has suggested that behavioral organization in numerous mammalian species undergoes sequential change in terms of the stimulus modalities used by the developing organism to accomplish particular tasks such as orienting to the nest or to conspecifics. Thus the "same" behavior may be accomplished on the basis of thermotactile stimuli at one stage whereas olfactory cues may dominate the act one week later (see Alberts & Brunjes, 1978 for an example of this). Rosenblatt (1979) posits some striking interrelations between such sequential changes in behavioral organization and the development and expression of motivational systems.

With these considerations in mind, it is possible to see the ways in which interpretive difficulties may lurk in the shadows of seemingly straightforward retention paradigms. The developing animal is a potential carrier of specialized functions and general processes that undergo ontogenetic modifications that can seriously confound interpretation of memory and its expression.

The remainder of the chapter is composed of discussions of development of the vestibular, thermal, tactile, olfactory, gustatory, auditory, and visual senses in the Norway rat (*Rattus norvegicus*). The sequence of presentation is semiarbitrary. Gottlieb's original order is preserved though I have inserted the thermal and chemical senses. It is clear that onset of function for these additional modalities precedes that of vision and audition, but it is premature to assert that olfaction precedes taste, or that either of these necessarily follow the thermal or tactile senses. Further research can provide the answers and, if done on a comparative scale could create a database that would support an exciting consideration of evolutionary relationships between sensory function and behavior.

Vestibular Function

The mammalian vestibular system, with its end-organs located in the inner ear, provides information derived from forces such as gravity, and those of angular and accelerative movements. Components of the vestibular apparatus, such as the utricles and the canals are sometimes discussed as subsystems that are separately responsive to static and to dynamic forces, respectively. Such distinctions, however, cannot be made precisely. First, it is not possible to dissociate these stimulus classes. Gravity, accelerative movement, and centrifugal force are not mutually exclusive stimuli. Moreover, both vestibular receptors are responsive to both static and dynamic forces.

Vestibular perceptions contribute to the maintenance of orientation of the head and body and are important integrative cues that combine with sensory-motor and visual inputs to coordinate various kinds of compensatory adjustments of the body in relation to itself and to the environment.

The vestibular system is among the first, if not the first, sensory system to become functional. Onset of vestibular function begins prenatally in every species that has been studied (Gottlieb, 1971). These prenatal origins present formidable technical problems to systematic analysis, and there are too few empirical studies to be reviewed on the topic of early vestibular function (cf. Gottlieb, 1971).

Altman and Sudarshan (1975) have presented a detailed and thoughtful evaluation of postural and locomotor skills in developing rats. Observations of dynamic postural adjustments are interpreted as evidence for perception and integration of vestibular information. Pups placed on their backs "right" themselves and reestablish a normal, quadrapedal orientation on a surface. Even newborn rats can accomplish this, although they may require 50 seconds or more to respond successfully. By 2 weeks of age they react in less than 2 seconds. The differences can be explained in terms of motor competence. By the time of birth the rat detects such gross vestibular perturbations. Righting in midair, a task that requires short response latencies and fine motor coordination, is not evidenced until Days 16–17 in the rat.

Negative Geotaxis.   Evidence of early vestibular function can also be derived from observations of responses to surface inclination (Crozier & Pincus, 1926). Rat pups show reliable "negative geotaxis" in response to surface inclination: They turn and orient so that their head faces against the angle, that is, away from gravity. This is an unlearned and reliable reaction. Pups placed on an incline, with their heads facing down, make a postural adjustment of 180°. The motoric acts and latency of this response vary with age. The geotactic stimulus appears sufficiently potent that it stimulates momentary quadraped walking several days sooner than seen in open-field tests (Altman & Sudarshan, 1975).

In my laboratory we have begun to use a test of vestibular sensitivity which probably requires somewhat finer abilities of detection. Rat pups are placed on a small horizontal stage with their body axes parallel to an axle on which the platform can be tipped. The stage is tipped gradually to one side, at about 2 degrees/second and the pups' responses are videotaped with an arrangement of mirrors that provides simultaneous views from above, head-on, and the side (Alberts, 1982, unpublished). Rat pups show reliable responses to vestibular changes of 10° at 2 days of age.

Although little is known about the pups' vestibular "acuity," or discrimination, such data could be applied profitably to studies of early learning and memory, particularly at early ages before other sensory modalities are functional. For instance, vestibular cues could be used as conditional or as discriminative stimuli.

Development of Thermal Responsivity

Thermal stimuli are among the most behaviorally potent cues for young mammals in general and for rat pups in particular. The importance of thermal cues and the impressive strength of temperature-determined aspects of behavior have long been acknowledged. It is therefore surprising that thermal stimuli have not played a larger role in the history of developmental studies of learning and memory.

A review of the literature on thermal perception would be scanty and of limited relevance to the issues most germane to the present chapter and book. Instead, I briefly survey various aspects of thermal-behavior relations in developing animals, for here we find some of the data most pertinent to interpretation of past results and helpful for future studies.

Thermal responsivity appears to have prenatal onset since newborn mammals are immediately responsive to stimuli that vary in temperature characteristics. Temperature-sensitive receptors located in the snout region of adult cats have been evaluated electrophysiologically (e.g., Hensel & Kenshalo, 1969; Kenshalo, Hensel, Graziadei, & Fruhstorfer, 1971). Their location in the facial and perioral regions where they intermingle with a well-developed field of tactile-sensitive receptors suggests that thermal receptivity in this locale may be part of an early functional system used to coordinate the rooting and probing movements of newborns that maintain contact with the mother and littermates (Alberts, 1978b; Cosnier, 1965; Rosenblatt, 1976).

Leonard (1974) has described a dramatic, stereotyped temperature response in neonatal hamsters (*Mesocricetus auratus*). When a hamster pup is placed on a surface across which there is a temperature gradient, the altricial infant makes a few scanning movements, orients toward the warmer region of the gradient and then, with wriggling and swimming movements, propels itself into warmer regions of the temperature gradient. Leonard terms this response "thermotaxis."

Similar tendencies are also seen in young rats, cats, and rabbits. Under natural conditions in the nest environment, this response bias may be sufficient to ensure the elicitation and maintenance of contact with the mother and littermates. Thermotaxis is present during infancy and gradually wanes before weaning.

The behavioral effects of generalized ambient warmth are different than those described for localized sources of heat, but not less profound. In conditions of warm ambience, infant rats can be induced to display behavioral propensities that would otherwise be totally hidden or displaced by different classes of behavioral reactions. One of the most striking examples is the recent finding that 5-day-old rat pups, infants that normally ingest *only* by nursing from their mothers, will independently lap milk from the floor of a warm, 37°C incubator. Such precocious, independent ingestive behavior appears to be sensitive to internal signals that typically regulate feeding, as opposed to suckling behavior (Blass & Cramer, 1982; Hall & Rosenblatt, 1977). Under identical conditions, but in a cooler environment, infant rats would fail to display their ability to ingest independently and would die of inanition. Johanson and Hall (1980) argued that this effect was based not on the pups' body temperatures in the warmer environments, but on their cutaneous perception of the ambient warmth. Their conclusion was based on the results of experiments in which core body temperatures of hungry pups were lowered by cooling prior to their introduction to the warm incubator where food was available. Cooled pups also displayed rapid and robust independent ingestion, before the warmth of the test chamber had raised their body temperatures.

Learning by neonatal rodents can also be facilitated by ambient warmth. Rat pups presented with an odor that was paired with an infusion of milk through an oral cannula acquired preference for the milk-paired scent when they were trained under warm conditions but not under room temperature conditions (Johanson & Hall, this volume; Johanson & Teicher, 1980).

In addition, warmth can be an effective reinforcer for young animals. Chicks will acquire color preferences on the basis of paired presentations with the warmth of a heat lamp (Taylor, Sluckin, & Hewitt, 1969). Similarly, rat pups acquire odor preferences following various kinds of odor-heat associations (Alberts, 1981). Conversely, cool temperatures can be a useful negative stimulus in learning situations. In my laboratory, we found that infant rats will show acceleratory cardiac responses to odors that have been paired with injection of an illness-producing drug and deceleratory patterns to control odors. The same type of "negative" acceleratory reaction is acquired to odors paired with brief, 10-minute exposures to severe cold (Martin & Alberts, 1982).

The infant rat's sensitivity and responsivity to the thermal characteristics of stimuli and to the thermal conditions of environment can be understood in terms of the fragility of its ability to defend itself against thermal challenges from the environment and the physiological necessity of a relatively constant and warm body temperature for efficient function and development. These issues have been discussed from several different perspectives (e.g., Barnett & Mount, 1971; Hull, 1973). Readers interested in the design and interpretation of learning studies in neonatal rodents would probably benefit from a general familiarity with the basic thermobiology of the infant mammal.

Tactile Responsivity

Tactile perception is another sensory avenue that is functional at birth in the altricial animal. Cutaneous cues have largely escaped use by experimenters in learning studies. Responsivity to punctate tactile stimulation has been mapped topographically across different body regions in the developing rat. Tactile sensitivity begins *in utero*, so these studies have involved elegant methods of externalizing and maintaining living fetuses for controlled, acute studies (e.g., Narayanan, Fox, & Hamburger, 1971). Motor responses to localized, light forms of tactile stimulation were used to assess detection. In a small proportion of the fetuses, tactile stimuli elicited generalized motor responses on embryonic Day 16 (about 6 days before birth). The effective sites, however, were limited to the vibrissal area of the snout and the palmar surface of the forepaw. Thus, it was the facial and more anterior regions of stimulation that were initially responsive. By embryonic Day 19, all rostral and caudal loci were responsive in 50% of the fetuses tested. This rostral-to-caudal topographic trend in tactile responsivity appears to be echoed postnatally in the overall pattern of sensitivity, which seems to increase over at least the first week of life. Unfortunately, there exist little systematic and precise data on this topic.

It is worth noting that, in practice, many forms of tactile stimulation also bear some thermal component. The "contact comfort" associated with soft, furry surfaces usually attracts young mammals and can have powerful calming and/or reinforcing properties (Harlow & Suomi, 1970). Soft, furry surfaces trap air which is warmed, particularly during prolonged contact involving one or more thermogenic masses. Thus, contact comfort probably involves *thermotactile* stimulation, as do many other instances of stimulation that are casually and improperly referred to as being either "thermal" or "tactile." It is surprising that the nature of the stimulation underlying "contact comfort" has escaped further analysis. The information derived from a fuller, empirically based understanding of contact comfort would undoubtedly clarify the roles of tactile and thermal cues and their possible interactions. Such information could be useful in the design of studies of early learning. In this regard it would be particularly important to assess developmental differences in the action of comfort cues so that memory tests that spanned different ontogenetic stages could be interpreted accurately.

Vibrissae: The Tactile Hairs.   The newborn rat, like its adult counterpart, is equipped with an organized field of "tactile hairs," the vibrissae or whiskers.

Each vibrissa arises from a hair follicle that is equipped with several mechanoreceptor endings (Andres & von During, 1973; Woolsey, Durham, Harris, Simons, & Valentino, 1981). Each follicle is innervated with as many as 200 myelinated nerve fibers derived from the maxillary branch of the trigeminal nerve (CN V). In rats and related rodents the larger vibrissae are arranged in five distinct rows along the upper lip. Each row contains between four and seven hairs. Together they comprise the mystacial or moustache vibrissae. The mystacial vibrissae are vibrated in a stereotyped back-and-forth manner, at regular rates (Welker, 1964). The perfect coordination of the vibrissal "whisking" and sniffing has been documented and considered as a functional system for exploration (Komisaruk, 1970; Welker, 1964).

The central projections of trigeminal afferents and their central projections derived from the vibrissae have attracted a good deal of recent attention, especially since neurobiologists discovered the clear topographic representation of the mystacial pad at various levels of the CNS (see Woolsey, et al., 1981). In rat, Layer IV of sensorimotor cortex receives third-order projections via the thalamus. The Layer IV cells are organized into three-dimensional "barrels." These cortical barrels display topographic isomorphism with the peripheral pad and are uniquely linked to individual mystacial vibrissae.

Modern developmental neurobiologists have described the ontogeny of the vibrissal somatosensory system. It is an early-developing system, as might be predicted by the brain-stem neural groups and rostral receptor populations that comprise it. To review a few highlights: Studies with ^{3}H-thymidine autoradiography reveal that final mitosis of the neurons that form the somatosensory system is complete before birth. These cellular birthdays begin by embryonic Day 12 (E12). Vibrissal follicles are present on Day E12 and small emergent hairs are visible as early as Day E13. Nevertheless, the associated mechanoreceptors are not seen for several days (English, Burgess, & Kavka-Van Norman, 1980). The overall sequence of neuronal birthdays follows an outside-to-inside sequence through the central somatosensory pathways. Similarly, there is a parallel pattern in the sequence in which the various neural substations achieve adultlike appearances. Trigeminal and brain-stem nuclei appear to resemble their adult form in the newborn (Waite & Cragg, 1979). The thalamic elements do not appear adultlike until postnatal Day 5 and the barrels in Layer IV of the somatosensory cortex are not complete in appearance until Day 7. Unfortunately, the functional meaning of these neurobiological landmarks are not known, but they serve as an enticement for future correlative studies. The vibrissal pathway has, however, been used for detailed analyses of experimental disruption during development. Again, there is great potential for parallel, functional studies.

Until we have a fuller appreciation of the development of function in the vibrissal somatosensory system, it will not be possible to exploit this tactile pathway in research on memory or learning. I therefore presented the information above with the goal of alerting the interested reader to the availability and potential usefulness of this early-developing sensory system. Presently its role in the early life of the rat is not well understood.

It is likely that vibrissal cues as well as tactile inputs from other body regions contribute to the rat's well-known tendency to contact and move along walls and similar vertical surfaces (Patrick & Laughlin, 1934). This response is usually called *thigmotaxis* and is present in the infant rat (Alberts, 1978b) as in the adult. Thigmotaxis in infant rats is probably a significant component of their huddling behavior as well as contact reactions involved in suckling and other early adaptive responses. Because thigmotaxis is maintained throughout the organism's life, it may prove to be a useful response or mode of stimulus presentation for workers interested in memory studies that involve protracted developmental periods.

Olfaction

Beginning in the first hour of postnatal life, the rat pup is dependent for its survival on the perception of olfactory cues. Recall that the newborn rat lives in a sightless, silent world. The salience of olfactory inputs may be even higher in early postnatal life than later, when additional modalities of sensory stimulation are added ontogenetically.

Rat pups are dependent on olfactory input for suckling. Without normal input the anosmic rat pup does not nurse and may die in inanition (Alberts, 1976; Singh & Hofer, 1976; Tobach, Rouger, & Schneirla, 1967). Volatile molecules, possibly dimethyl disulfide (DMDS) that are deposited on and around the dam's nipples are recognized by rat pups and excite their approach to and apprehension of nipples. Young rats also form and maintain adaptive aggregates, or huddles, on the basis of olfactory inputs (Alberts, 1978a,b; 1981; Alberts & Brunjes, 1978). Odors of the home nest keep pups within its safe confines, while later in early life, odors guide pups to feed upon safe foods.

These statements clearly indicate that the sense of smell in the newborn rat is operable. Indeed, one might reasonably predict that, due to its crucial importance to survival, this sensory-perceptual system would be particularly *well developed* in early life. This reasonable inference is wrong. The rodent olfactory system, though functional at birth and necessary for survival, is markedly undeveloped, and major developmental changes occur during the first 2–3 weeks of life. In order to appreciate the development of function in the olfactory system, it is important to consider the architecture of the system itself and I review it briefly, below.

1. The Olfactory System and its Development.   We usually speak of "the sense of smell" as a singular channel or modality. Anatomically speaking, the sense of smell is not singular at all. The olfactory system is more accurately characterized as a multiple-channel system, composed of separate subsystems. Each subsystem consists of distinct populations of receptor cells that project into the CNS via nonoverlapping, but sometimes parallel projections. The targets of these projections in the central nervous system are also separate. For our purposes, there are three chemosensitive afferent subsystems to consider. These are (a) the olfactory nerve (CN I) and its central connections in the olfactory bulb and telencephalon, (b) the vomeronasal system and its projection in the brain via the accessory olfactory bulb, and (c) some chemosensitive branches of the trigeminal (CN V) nerve that innervates the snout and portions of the nasal epithelium. The anatomical distinctions among these three components subsystems of olfaction are supported by ontogenetic data. The main, vomeronasal, and trigeminal chemosensitive pathways each have distinct developmental timecourses.

The development of the olfactory receptors of the I nerve has been described in more detail for the laboratory mouse (*Mus musculus*) than for the Norway rat, but their embryology and phylogeny are close enough to permit the following general characterizations. Receptor development begins early in embryogenesis—around Day E9. By Day E17, 4 days before birth, receptors in the olfactory mucosa display the characteristic features of functional, adult receptors (Cuscheri & Bannister, 1975b). Receptor development continues throughout life, however, as olfactory receptors are regularly replaced (Moulton, 1975). The axons of receptor neurons gather into bundles and penetrate the cribiform plate in the posterior recesses of the nasal cavity to contact the anterior forebrain. In the rat, fasiculi of the olfactory nerve reach the olfactory bulbs by Day E16 (Singh, 1977) and form recognizable glomeruli by birth.

The receptors of the accessory olfactory system are contained within the vomeronasal organ, a specialized tube-shaped structure, located bilaterally on the floor of the nasal cavity. The organ differentiates prenatally. In the mouse, it achieves its tubular form by Day E12 and nerve fibers are differentiating and migrating out toward the brain.

The early development of chemosensitive branches of the rodent trigeminus has not been specifically described. The V nerve, however, is one of the earliest cranial nerves to develop. The functional precocity of cranial nerve innervation to the facial region of the fetal rat has already been noted (Narayanan, Fox, & Hamburger, 1971).

2. Central Development.   The olfactory bulbs actually contain at least two anatomically distinct nuclear structures. The main olfactory bulb, as its name implies, makes up most of the volume of this part of the brain and it exclusively receives the projections of the I nerve axons (probably more than 10^6 in the adult). The accessory olfactory bulb occupies the dorsomedial portion of the mass, and it receives exclusively the first-order projections from the vomeronasal organ. Both "bulbs" are actually cortical layers that together form the anterior protuberances of the brain, referred to as the olfactory bulbs. Pedersen and Shepard have recently noted a glomerulir population in the main bulb that is precociously active. It preferentially takes up radioactive 2-deoxyglucose *in utero*. This unique precocious metabolic activity has led to the suggestion that this "modified glomerular complex" might be an additional subsystem of the main olfactory system. The prenatal activity of these olfactory neurons implicates them in the dramatic phenomena associated with prenatal chemosensory experiences (Pedersen & Shepard, 1982).

The early development of the main and accessory olfactory bulbs provides a fine example of heterochrony in sensory system maturation. The two systems are well suited for comparison, for each is comprised of the same three neuronal elements—mitral, tufted, and granule cells. Time-of-origin studies with H^3-thymidine reveal that the mitral cells arise first, followed by tufted and then granule cells, as would be predicted by the general rule that neuroblasts arise in order according to decreasing final size (Fujita, 1964).

The main and accessory olfactory bulbs contain homologous populations of mitral, tufted, and granule cells. Within each structure there occurs the same sequence of mitotic activity and morphological development, but the two structures develop on different schedules. Neuronal birthdays are earlier for cells in the accessory olfactory bulb than for their counterparts in the main bulb. Smith (1938) noted that the relative size of the accessory bulb was greatly advanced relative to the main bulb in the newborn rat. Final size (volume) of the accessory structure was attained by the third postnatal week, whereas the growth of the main bulb continued into adulthood (see Alberts, 1976, 1981, for more detailed reviews).

3. Stimulus Sampling: Development of Nasal Respiration.   Rats are obligate nose breathers, which is to say that normal respiration provides continuous nasal sampling of air-borne molecules. Olfactory perception depends on the active transport of molecules across the nasal epithelium. The normal inhalation-exhalation cycle of the rat thus provides continuous "nasal sampling epochs." In rats as in many other organisms, sudden changes in the environment are responded to with an increase in the average rate of nasal sampling epochs: *sniffing* is said to occur. Sniffing is a means of more closely examining or exploring the olfactory environment, and it is a highly invariant, habituation-resistant response to stimulus change, particularly olfactory-based changes.

We have studied the development of nasal respiration and rapid, stereotyped sniffing (polypnea) in the rat pup (Alberts & May, 1981a). Rapid sniffing was relatively rare and poorly maintained in pups less than 1 week old. With age, however, there was a marked increase in the baseline rate of respiration, concommitant with more frequent episodes of regular and rhythmic "spontaneous" accelerations. Figure 4.4 is a composite graph showing several developmental dimensions of nasal respiration.

The development of nasal respiration and sniffing correlates with a marked increase in sensitivity to odor stimuli in the rat pup (Alberts & May, 1980b). Nasal respiration may also play a determinative role in olfactory coding (cf. Moulton, 1967; Mozell, 1971). Thus, to some extent the neuromuscular developments that underly the pups' ability to generate and maintain trains or episodes of polypnea may be an indirect, ontogenetic limitation on the sensory-perceptual ability of the animal, independent of the receptor or central processing characteristics, per se.

4. Sensitivity.   Although it is clear that the newborn rat is capable of detecting olfactory cues in its environment and responding to them behaviorally, virtually nothing was known about the functional parameters of the sense of smell during infancy and possible changes with subsequent development. We therefore undertook a cross-sectional, olfactometric study of the early development of odor sensitivity in rat pups (Alberts & May, 1980b). Detection of a controlled olfactory cue by rat pups was measured by strain gauge plethysmography (Alberts & May, 1980b). Controlled quantities of amyl acetate, a broadspectrum olfactant, were delivered via a dilution olfactometer to rat pups, 1- to

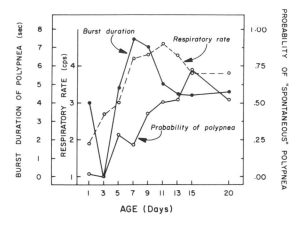

FIG. 4.4.   Various developmental parameters of nasal repiration and sniffing in Norway rat pups. Pups were placed in a clean, glass container for 30 sec. Respiratory movements were recorded by strain gage plethysmography. The solid line connecting open circles shows the probability of pups exhibiting "spontaneous" polypnea or sniffing (5–7 cps). The average durations of such bursts of sniffing are shown by the solid circles. The broken line with open circles shows the overall, average "baseline" respiratory rate, computed for seconds. (From Alberts & May, 1981.)

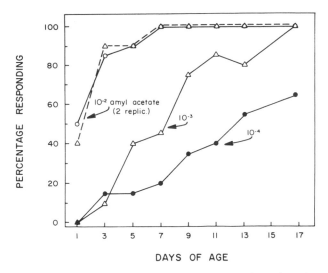

FIG. 4.5 Development of sensitivity to controlled dilutions of amyl acetate. Unconditioned changes in respiratory rate by rat pups were used to determine whether the odor stimulus was detected. Respiration was monitored with a strain gage plethysmograph. (From Alberts & May, 1981b).

17-days of age. Figure 4.5 shows that nasal chemosensitivity of rat pups improves dramatically and steadily during the first few postnatal weeks.

We also inquired into the possibility that the development of olfactory sensitivity may be different for different olfactory stimuli. For instance, it seemed possible that infant pups might be predisposed to detect *biological* odorants with greater acuity than they exhibited toward the "arbitrary" chemical olfactant, amyl acetate. We therefore developed a simple scaling procedure whereby the strength of a biological odor (female rat urine) was equated operationally to the strength of amyl acetate. The development of chemosensitivity to the biological and reagent olfactants appeared identical (Alberts & May, 1980a).

The development of chemosensitivity is also related to the effects of thyroid hormones. Pups administered exogenous thyroxine on postnatal Days 1–4 showed greater olfactory sensitivity than their littermate controls during the first 2 weeks of life. By 19 days of age, however, experimental and control pups were equivalently sensitive to amyl acetate (Brunjes & Alberts, 1981).

5. Discrimination and Recognition of Odors. In addition to detecting the presence of olfactory stimuli, newborn rats can discriminate among a variety of odors and recognize certain scents that they have experienced previously. One particular dramatic instance of early olfactory discrimination by a newborn is the finding that 1-day-old rats learned to push either of two scented overhead paddles to deliver a milk reward via an oral cannula. The discriminative stimuli that labeled the rewarding and nonrewarding paddles were the odors of lemon and cloves (Johanson & Hall, 1979, this volume).

It is known that rodent pups display "home orientation" responses, which are usually measured in terms of spatial preferences. In a typical test, individual pups are placed on a screen floor, below which are two equal areas that contain soiled bedding materials from their home cage or clean shavings. "Home orientation" refers to the pup's tendency to spend more time above the bedding that contains the odors of home, relative to the clean area. Neonatal pups are not differentially attracted to the odors of their *own home* versus the odors of some *other home*. Around Days 9–12, however, rats begin to show preferences for the familiar odors of their own home in a two-choice test between own and other home shavings. This is an impressive discrimination, given that the 2-week-old pup is reacting to odors derived from same inbred strain, maintained on the same diet, under identical conditions.

Home cage odors have also been implicated as powerful contextual cues that significantly affect learning and performance of young rats (Smith & Spear, 1978). Sixteen-day-old rat pups are usually found to learn only with great difficulty tasks that involve passive avoidance or similar kinds of "withholding" responses. Smith and Spear (1978) found that the presence of home cage cues ameliorated many of the age-related "deficits" of the young animal in several learning and performance situations. This is a potentially important phenomenon, perhaps related to some of the effects of ambient warmth discussed earlier. It warrants careful consideration and further study.

The ability of the rat pup to learn and to later recognize specific odors is a remarkable feature of its olfactory system and memory capabilities (Campbell & Alberts, 1979; Martin & Alberts, 1979; Rudy & Cheatle, 1977). Recently, it has been suggested that *fetal* rats can learn odor aversions—by experiencing LiCl-induced illness after a novel chemical is injected into the amniotic fluid on Day 20 of gestation (Smotherman, 1982). Such pairings were remembered at 10 days of age (postpartum) in a retention test. Pups were trained to approach and suckle from an anesthetized dam. When the odor of the prenatal stimulus (apple juice) was introduced into the alley, running speeds were depressed in the LiCl-injected pups, but not in the animals that had been injected with saline as fetuses. Control pups that had received only LiCl, or prenatal exposure to the CS without illness, continued to approach the dam with normal rapidity. No other parameters of this striking effect are presently known.

Taste

The rat's sense of taste has only begun to be exploited in studies of early learning and memory. The oral chemosensory system is the site of important early stimulation. Rat pups nurse avidly and engage in considerable amounts of nonnutritive suckling. They explore with their mouths the dam's body, often focusing their activities around her mouth, ears, and anogenital region. In addition, it is common to observe pups in the huddle mouthing their paws and nearby appendages of their littermates, as well as inanimate objects in the nest environment. The perception of flavors is usually based on combined gustatory and olfactory stimulation. This is almost certainly the case in rat pups, though too little is known to make even a preliminary assessment of the relative contribution of each type of input at any ontogenetic stage. Nevertheless, for our present purposes we will deal with the taste system as if it operated separately.

1. The Taste System and its Early Development.   Taste buds are the chemosensory receptors that mediate gustation. Most, but not all taste buds are located on the tongue and are therefore termed lingual taste buds. Taste buds are contained within *papillae*. They are gustatory papillae and consist of three populations, fungiform, circumvallate, and foliate. The spatial distribution of these papillae have cross-species generality, but there are some significant differences in the substructure of the papillae between species. Figure 4.6 is an abstraction of a rat tongue, drawn to illustrate the distribution of the gustatory papillae. As can be seen in the figure, the three types of papillae are distributed in an orderly manner across the surface of the tongue. *Fungiform* papillae contain one taste bud each, and occupy the anterior two-thirds of the tongue. In contrast, the *foliate* group which resides on the rear one-third of the tongue, each contain about 200 taste

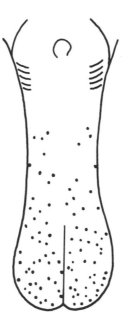

FIG. 4.6 Distribution of gustatory papillae on the surface of a rat tongue. The dots represent fungiform papillae, distributed across the anterior two-thirds of the surface. The rat's single circumvallate papilla is shown in the posterior midline, and sets of folliate papillae are shown by diagonal lines on the lateral borders (Adapted from Mistretta 1981.)

buds. The tongue of the rat has a single *circumvallate* papilla that contains 400 taste buds, located medially toward the caudal region. These three types of gustatory papillae are arranged among a larger oral field of *filiform* papillae which contain no taste buds. The filiforms are mechanoreceptors, providing sensory-motor and tactile information from the oral region.

Regardless of the papilla in which it resides, each taste bud contains microvilli, which are believed to be the anatomical transducers of taste stimuli. The anatomical arrangement of the microvilli is compatible with this functional view: Above the microvilli are discrete openings called *taste pores* which are appropriately structured to permit stimuli to reach the sensoria. Mistretta (cf. 1981) uses the taste pore as an anatomical index of maturity in the taste system. Figure 4.7 shows some of her developmental results. At 2 days of age in the rat, only about 2% of the fungiform papillae have pores. By Day 12 there are pores in about 70% of the papillae.

Neural projections from the tongue to the brain are separable in a manner that is reminiscent of the situation described for the olfactory system, except that the major afferent pathways for taste do not reach cortical tissue in the brain until numerous synapses have been crossed. In contrast, the olfactory receptors enjoy a uniquely direct route to the brain. The afferent channels of olfaction and taste are similar, however, in the neat separation of contributions from the various receptor populations. Thus, inputs to the nervous system from fungiform papillae on the anterior tongue are carried by the chorda tympani (CN VII), circumvallate contributions travel via a branch of the glossopharyngeal nerve (CN IX), and taste buds of the foliate population are distributed across both of these cranial nerve afferents. Taste input initially projects to the brain stem, to the nucleus solitarius, on to pontine taste areas and then fans out to the amygdala and on to gustatory cortex, via thalamic relays. At all levels of the taste system, neurons

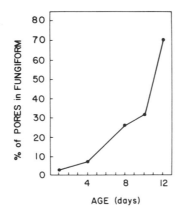

FIG. 4.7.   The development of taste pores in fungiform papillae on the tongue of the Norway rat pup. The number of pores is expressed as a percentage of the total number of papillae examined on each tongue. (Redrawn from Mistretta 1972.)

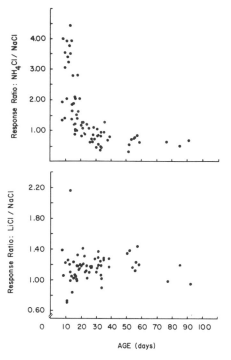

FIG. 4.8. Response ratios computed for discharges of the chorda tympani nerve in response to stimulation of the tongue by NH4Cl (upper graph) and LiCl (lower graph) *relative* to discharges in response to NaCl. The response ratios are plotted as a function of postnatal age for the Norway rat. The LiCl–NaCl ratios remain relatively constant throughout development whereas the NH4Cl response ratios decrease. (Based on Ferrell, et al., 1981).

appear to be nonspecific in their response properties to different taste stimuli. The gustatory code, like that of olfaction, remains to be cracked.

Despite persistent ignorance concerning the coding of taste stimuli, researchers have devised ways to study and to describe functional development in the taste system that successfully reveals orderly developmental characteristics. Electrophysiological techniques have been used to measure responses of the chorda tympani nerve to taste stimuli applied to the tongues of rat pups at different ages. Discharges of the chorda tympani in response to various taste stimuli were compared to a "standard" discharge pattern shown by the same animals in response to 0.1M NaCl. Figure 4.8 shows an example of the results of this type of analysis. The graphs in the figure illustrate gradual changes with age in the relative effectiveness of the various taste stimuli. These scatterplots show that in preweanling rats, NH4Cl elicits greater responses than equimolar NaCl, but after Days, 20–30, both NaCl and LiCl are more effective stimuli. This developmental pattern of chorda tympani responses was discovered independently in two laboratories (Ferrell, Bradley, Mistretta, & Miklossy, 1979; Hill & Almli, 1979). It is even more impressive that similar changes in taste responsivity have also been described for sheep, a species that has a much longer developmental schedule than that of rats (see Mistretta, 1981).

2. Behavioral Indices of Taste Development.   There has long been uncertainty and confusion surrounding the range and acuity of gustatory function in the rat pup. Small (1899) placed small amounts of taste substances in the mouths of the pups in his subject litter. He reported facial expressions of disgust in the neonates to nearly all flavors, with a gradual development of more appropriately discriminating affective expressions. Decades later a similar approach to evaluating taste responsivity was used (Jacobs & Sharma, 1969).

More recently, Hall and Bryan (1981) studied behavioral reactivity to taste stimuli delivered directly to the mouth via a tongue cannula, constructed with narrow polyethelene tubing. The cannula opened onto the posterior of the pup's tongue, and controlled amounts of solutions could be infused into the mouth. The behavioral reactions of the pups to taste stimuli, changes in activity and ingestion, were compared to response levels exhibited to oral infusions of milk alone. It was therefore possible to examine taste responsivity in sated and hungry (deprived) infants using a similar metric and to evaluate possible, nonspecific changes in baseline reactivity associated with privation and maturation. Pups, 3 days old and older, displayed the ability to discriminate sucrose (5% and 10% solutions) from water. The discrimination was enhanced by deprivation, particularly in terms of the magnitude of the activity responses. These experiments were not designed to examine thresholds or sensory changes with deprivation. Responsiveness to quinine appeared to develop more slowly. Ingestion of cannulated quinine solution (.025%) and water did not differ until Day 9. Mouthing and ingestion were both decreased by the bitter stimulus. The ability of 3-day-old pups to reject a solution was tested by infusing strong solutions of saline (5%, .85 M NaCl) into their mouths. These infants showed clear signs of detection and suppressed their intake of the strong, salty stimulus. Hall and Bryan (1981) were primarily concerned with the ability of taste stimulation to alter the ingestive behavior of infant rats, rather than in the development of psychophysical or hedonic aspects of the gustatory system. They noted, however, the possibility that infant rats might perceive water as unpleasant, a suggestion that has been made for the response of human infants to water (Desor, Maller, & Andrews, 1975). Although baseline acceptance rates for water were low, infants nevertheless displayed the ability to suppress their intake further, in response to the strong saline solutions, for example. These interpretative points are useful reminders that the gustatory system can change along both sensory and affective dimensions.

To what extent does suckling provide gustatory experiences to the infant? Do taste experiences associated with nursing affect taste perception or behavior later in life? The answers to these fundamental questions have only begun to be clarified. The teats of a lactating rat are remarkably elastic. The suckling pup draws deep into its mouth the distendible teat (see Martin & Alberts, 1979, Fig. 6). Mother's milk is delivered from the nipple via discrete pulses or "let-downs" (Lincoln, Hill, & Wakerly, 1973); it is thought that the milk is "shot" directly down the pup's throat by the continuous negative pressure established by the saliva seal around the nipple and pre-ejection suckling. The suckling situation presents a surprising combination of poorly understood variables: receptor populations are unevenly distributed in the mouth, particularly with respect to the lumen of the nipple; the receptors and the taste system are maturing during most of the suckling stage of life; milk cues follow a dubious time course on the receptor surface; and the milk itself is a relatively unknown stimulus.

Despite this formidable array of mysteries, it is possible to make some useful assertions about the pup's taste experiences during suckling and the influences of these perceptions on subsequent behavior. (It is admittedly arbitrary to deal with chemical perception during suckling as simply gustatory. There is almost certainly olfactory involvement in the perception of milk cues. The present scheme is used only for convenience.) Milk derived from suckling is perceived. Upon ejection, pups display an invariant "stretch reflex" that is a completely reliable index of milk delivery from the nipple (Lincoln et al., 1973). In addition, milk is not only detected, but qualitative aspects of the milk stimulus are perceived by the pups. Taste cues derived from the mother's diet are passed into her milk and the suckling pups can perceive these cues. Taste experiences derived from suckling determine the pups' initial selection of solid food and enhance the preferences shown by pups for the diet their mother had been eating during lactation (Galef & Henderson, 1972). Thus, taste experiences occur in pups during nursing and significantly affect later taste perception. It is not known whether taste experiences derived from early versus late phases of the nursing stage are differentially important. Indeed, it is not known if early suckling provides similar types of gustatory perceptions as those experienced closer to weaning. Prenatal taste experiences also deserve consideration. Swallowing by the fetus is enhanced by the addition of taste cues to the amniotic fluid (Bradley & Mistretta, 1973).

It should be noted, therefore, that there are a variety of genetic, prenatal, and early postnatal experiences, including social experiences, that contribute to the establishment of preferences and aversions for taste stimuli (Galef, 1981a). Memory tests can therefore follow retention intervals during which various determinative factors can alter taste perception and/or preferences. Such variables should be carefully examined. It is even possible that they could be used productively as independent variables in novel paradigms to study development of memory.

Audition

Infant rats emit both humanly audible (c 20 kHz) and high-frequency sounds. The so-called "ultrasonic" vocalizations of the rat pups, the frequencies of which range up to about 40 kHz, have been interpreted to be important communication signals in rats. The pups' high-frequency calls lie within the peak hearing range of adult conspecifics. Nevertheless, there have been few definitive demonstrations of clear or specific behavioral roles of ultrasonic vocalizations in rat pups. Adult rats rely on auditory cues for a variety of purposes, including predator avoidance and both amicable and agonistic social interactions.

1. Development of the Auditory Apparatus.   In the adult, auditory stimulation is initiated by vibrational waves that pass through the external auditory meatus (ear canal) to impinge upon the tympanic membrane. Tympanic vibrations are, in turn, transferred via the ossicles of the middle ear to the oval window, at the base of the cochlea. At the cochlea, vibrational energy is converted into the electrochemical energy of the neural action potentials by the hair cells of the organ of Corti.

Synapses at the base of each hair cell constitute afferent input to the auditory nerve (CN VIII). The auditory nerve projects to the dorsal and ventral cochlear nuclei in the brain stem and fibers go on to synapse directly or indirectly in the inferior colliculus, the medial geniculate nucleus of the thalamus, and finally in auditory cortex.

At birth, the rat's external auditory apparatus is discernible only as a tiny fold of skin on the side of the head. Internally, the auditory system is correspondingly unformed. By Postnatal Day 8 or 9 (P8–P9) an endo-choclear potential (a DC resting potential of the fluid of the cochlear duct) can be recorded (Bosher, 1975; Bosher & Warren, 1971; Saunders & Bock, 1978).

The cochlear microphonic, an evoked response to auditory stimulation, can be recorded at the same ontogenetic stage at which the endo-cochlear potential appears. Crowley and Hepp-Raymond (1966) characterized the development of the cochlear microphonic in the rat by determining the minimal signal necessary to generate a standard 1uV, electrical response. Initially, the effective bandwidth was narrow, in the range of .2-2 kHz. By Day P14, however, the effective range expanded to .1–60 kHz with a correspondingly dramatic increase in sensitivity (as great as 125 dB).

Synapses between hair cells and the VIII nerve become operable on postnatal Days 0–12. Auditory nerve development appears to proceed in relative independence from that of the more peripheral structures. The relative timing of ontogenesis of the receptor apparatus and the VIII nerve is such that on Day P10−P12, when the synapses between the hair cells and the neurons of the VIII nerve become operable, it is possible to evoke auditory nerve potentials (Alford & Ruben, 1963). Following these and other events of internal maturation is the opening of the external ear on Days P12 or P13. By this point, the ear canal is surrounded by a detached, movable pinna.

Broadly speaking, these are the events that presage and mark the *onset* of auditory function in the rat. The functional range and levels of sensitivity of the rat pup's auditory system are markedly limited at the onset of function. The processing abilities of the auditory system show gradual and systematic improvement over the subsequent weeks. Figure 4.9, for instance, shows frequency-intensity coordinates for tone bursts that are just sufficient to elicit spiking above levels for unstimulated or spontaneous activity in single cells of rodent brain stem. Looking from top to bottom, it can be seen that absolute sensitivity of single neurons increased developmentally, in conjunction with increased frequency sensitivity.

The normal occlusion of external ear significantly attenuates auditory inputs, at least for the final days before the ears open. Removal of the pinna and external auditory meatus prior to normal ear-opening produced significant potentiation of cochlear responsivity. In contrast, the same experimental manipulation after normal ear-opening had only slight effects (Crowley & Hepp-Raymond, 1966). It is clear that the auditory system of the rat and other altricial mammals is functional prior to the opening of the ear canal. Patency of the external auditory meatus, however, constitutes such a significant reduction in the attenuation of acoustic inputs that many workers consider ear-opening to be the onset of auditory function.

2. Behavioral Responsivity to Auditory Stimulation.   Although it is common for human observers to consider onset of auditory function to be coincident with ear-opening, the first behavioral responses to acoustic stimulation in rats coincide developmentally with the formation of functional synapses between the cochlea and the VIII nerve (Alford & Ruben, 1963; Pujol & Hilding, 1973; Saunders & Bock, 1978), that is, around Day P10–P12 and therefore prior to ear-opening. Salas and Shapiro (1970) reported the existence of auditory-evoked responses in younger rats, but these were not accompanied by behavioral measures.

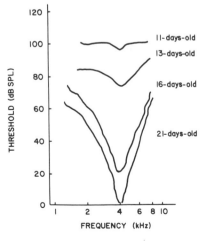

FIG. 4.9. Frequency-intensity coordinates for tones that elicit discharges just above non-stimulated levels from single units in rodent brainstem. These tuning curves were centered at 4 kHz to illustrate the age-related decrease in minimal threshold seen from Days 11 to 21. (Redrawn from Clopton, 1981).

Considering the sizeable literature on auditory development at the anatomical and physiological levels, there is a surprising shortage of corresponding psychophysical studies of the development of behavioral responses to acoustic cues. In general, the methods used in the past have been relatively crude: detection of auditory stimuli by rats has been measured by some form of "startle" response. Sometimes the so-called "Preyer reflex" (twitch response of the pinna of the ear to sound) is used as a similar dependent measure. Production of acoustic cues has been poorly controlled. Handclaps and whistles are often the sources of acoustic stimuli.

Figure 4.10 shows the results of the first parametric study of behavioral responses of rat pups to controlled acoustic stimuli (Brunjes & Alberts, 1981). Tones of 1, 4, 16, and 40 kHz were presented to rat pups beginning before ear-opening and after. As can be seen in Fig. 4.10, pups began responding behaviorally, as measured by Startle and Preyer reflexes, to the 1 and 4 kHz cues shortly before their ears were opened. Responses to the high, 40 kHz tones were not fully expressed until about Day 15, two days after the ears opened. These behavioral data nicely parallel the physiological evidence reviewed earlier. Both types of measures emphasize that onset of function in the auditory system precedes the point of opening of the external receptor apparatus. Furthermore, behavioral and physiological data both indicate that low frequencies are perceived earlier than higher frequency cues.

Haroutunian and Campbell (1981) recently assessed developmental changes in auditory perception of rat pups by recording unconditioned heartrate (HR) changes to various acoustic stimuli. Generally speaking, increases in HR are

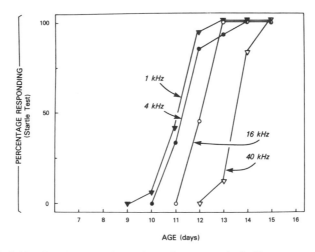

FIG. 4.10.   Development of acoustic startle responses in the Norway rat to tones of various frequencies. (Based on Brunjes & Alberts, 1981).

initially seen in response to acoustic stimulation. However, with age a deceleratory component emerged in the HR reaction. Campbell and Haroutunian (in press) also noted a general trend toward termed "perceptual sharpening." Pups habituated to a constant acoustic stimulus showed discrimination of a subsequent cue with a HR response. This discriminatory ability became significantly more precise with age, reflecting a "sharpening" of perception. This relatively innovative approach has produced a set of data that is generally superior to that typical of many past efforts. The current investigations of Rudy and his associates (this volume) is another example of research that is yielding new insights into the development of sensory function in altricial laboratory animals. The results from these studies are already raising new issues that are important to analyses of learning and memory. They portend well for the future.

Vision

The eyelids of the newborn rat are sealed shut. The obvious landmark event of eye-opening on Day 14 or 15 is usually taken to mark the onset of visual function in the rat, but it is possible to consider more precisely the ontogenesis of visual function in the rat. It is difficult to evaluate early vision in the Norway rat, particularly from an adaptive-functional perspective, because the species tends to deliver and rear the young in burrows, into which very little light penetrates. The young remain in the natal burrow for several weeks after eye-opening and then adopt the nocturnal or crepuscular habits of the adults. Thus it seems unlikely that the species relies extensively on fine visual information for many of its daily activities. On the other hand, the retina of the Norway rat is adapted to its poorly illuminated habits; all of the photoreceptors are rods (Braekevelt & Hollenberg, 1970). The lateral and slightly dorsal location of the eyes of the rat result in limited binocularity, but such ocular placement is usually considered efficient for panoramic vision and predator detection. The presence of bright, cyclic illumination in the early environment of the laboratory rat is thus atypical for the feral rat, but the current discussion is concerned with the course of visual development found in the laboratory environment, for this is most germane to our concerns in the present volume—and nearly the only kind of information available in the literature. Tees (1976) has, however, studied the development of vision in young rats that have been exposed to various amounts of visual stimulation at different times in their lives.

Morphological development of the visual system begins prenatally, as early as embryonic Day 10 (E10) when the forebrain evaginates to form the optic vesicles. Proliferation of cells that comprise neuronal structures and pathways of the visual system begins by Days E12–14 for the superior colliculus (Bruckner, Mares, & Biesold, 1976) and lateral geniculate (Lund & Mustari, 1977).

Despite these early beginnings, significant landmarks in the development of the visual system are not achieved until well into the *post*natal period. For instance, basic retinal lamination is not achieved until Days P8–10 (Weidman & Kuwabara, 1968) and synapses in visual cortex cannot be classified until after the first postnatal week (Juraska & Fifkova, 1979). Synaptogenesis in portions of the visual system continues in stagelike waves throughout early postnatal life and until as late as Day P40 (Lund & Lund, 1972).

Cortical evoked responses to photic stimulation can be recorded as early as postnatal Day 10 (Rose, 1968), which is several days before eye-opening. The earliest evoked responses are rudimentary, but mature-looking evoked waves are present at the time of eye-opening.

Behavioral indices of visual function in the rat are known from a limited number of studies, and only the crudest accounts of function can be given. Walk and Gibson (1961) placed young rats over a "visual cliff." Adultlike cliff-avoidance was demonstrated by pups 27–30 days of age. Performance of albino rats was inferior to that of their pigmented counterparts.

Vestal and King (1968, 1971; Vestal, 1973) introduced the use of optokinetic responses to a moving array of vertical lines as a means of testing visual acuity in two species of wild mice (*Peromyscus*). We have adopted their methods for a developmental study of visual acuity in laboratory rats (Brunjes & Alberts, 1981).

Visual acuity is assessed by measurements of a pup's body movements with respect to a moving visual array. Individual pups were placed in a small, transparent container that was suspended within a concentric vertical cylinder. The inside wall of the cylinder was completely lined with vertical black-and-white stripes which could be varied in spatial frequency (from 1°, 21' to 12°, 36' of visual angle). Rat pups, like adult *Peromyscus,* show an optokinetic response to the moving stripes when the outer drum is rotated. Under our conditions, pups responded with rotational body movements to movement of a visual array, but not to movement of the drum when the stripes were removed and the wall was visually homogenous. Acuity was assessed by increasing the visual frequency of the striped array until it surpassed the acuity of the pup and the optokinetic response disappeared, presumably because the stripes were not seen and the field appeared homogenous.

Visual acuity during the first week after eye-opening was also evaluated in normal laboratory rat pups and hyperthyroid littermates that had been given daily injections of exogenous thyroxine on postnatal Days 1–4 (Brunjes & Alberts, 1981). Early hyperthyroidism is associated with early eye-opening and therefore accelerated onset of visual function. We were also interested in the commonly made assumption that the morphological event of eye-opening is directly linked to other morphological and functional events in visual development.

The eyes of hyperthyroid pups opened 2 days earlier than those of their normal littermate controls. The results of the visual acuity tests, administered on the day of eye-opening, are shown in Fig. 4.11. Responses to the "blank," a moving homogenous field were negligible and did not differ from baseline.

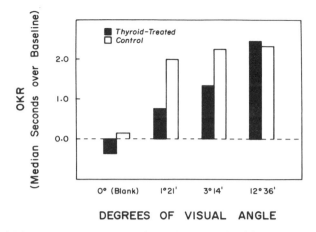

FIG. 4.11.   Optokinetic responses of normal and hyperthyroid rat pups to various arrays of moving vertical stripes. Pups were tested one day after eye-opening. (From Brunjes & Alberts, 1981.)

Control pups detected and responded reliably to each array. The performance of hyperthyroid pups was inferior to control pups when they confronted the finer arrays on the day of eye-opening (about 2 days earlier than normal). Performance of hyperthyroid and control pups was comparable with the least challenging stimulus. Thus, we were able to assess levels of acuity in rat pups and to show that the developmental achievements of eyelid separation and the development of acuity are *not* tightly linked. Hyperthyroidism was associated with precocious eye-opening but not with precocious development of acuity. The results of the studies suggested that vision was not impaired in the hyperthyroid animals; it simply was not accelerated along with the external morphology. The lesson is to avoid sole reliance on external markers of sensory function. The development of morphological landmarks and early function can be dissociated hormonally in both auditory and visual development in rats (Brunjes & Alberts, 1981) and genetically for vision in *Peromyscus* (Vestal, 1973).

It is appropriate to add an additional caveat to the interpretation of such optokinetic data, particularly with respect to implications of the results to studies of learning. Optokinetic responses can be mediated in some instances by noncortical neural mechanisms. Massive areas of neural tissue can be removed without eliminating optokinetic reactions. Apparently, it is possible for relatively peripheral networks of the sensory motor systems to mediate the response and the most conservative conclusion to be drawn from the presence of an optokinetic reaction is that the lens and retina can resolve the array and affect a sensory-motor response. It is possible that an animal could display clear optokinetic responses but fail to show learned responses to the same stimulus because the visual information is not reaching relevant portions of the nervous system.

Important information pertinent to such questions of sensory and perceptual function can be attacked with the application of learning paradigms to psychophysical tests.

CONCLUDING REMARKS

The 4-week period beginning with the final trimester of uterine life and extending to the early weaning period (about 21 days postpartum) contains numerous stages of sensory-perceptual development for the Norway rat. Although the rat is an extreme altricial species, quite embryonic at birth, onset of function is prenatal for the vestibular, tactile, thermal, and chemical senses. Audition and vision begin to function postnatally. Some stages of sensory maturation are readily apparent (e.g., eye-opening) but most maturational stages require systematic analyses to be revealed.

I have discussed sensory maturation in the Norway rat from a comparative perspective, seeking to describe some maturational principles that are repeated phylogenetically, while attempting to acknowledge specializations that reflect adaptive features of the species.

Empirical research on memory development involves the exploitation of sensory systems. Typically, information is entered (training), sometime later (retention intervals) the same stimulus is presented and we observe the extent to which the responses of previously trained subjects are the same (memory). When subsequent reactions are different, we usually infer loss of information (forgetting).

The data and discussions in this chapter indicate that sensory-perceptual processing is dynamic during early life. Constant stimuli may not be perceived as such at different stages of maturation. Indeed, the extent to which developing rats successfully remember stimuli and responses is most remarkable. This aspect of functional continuity during periods of maturational discontinuity represents, to me, a major problem worthy of consideration.

It is surprising to discover the extent of our ignorance of basic sensory development in the Norway rat, considering its predominance as a research animal. Nevertheless, on the basis of the information surveyed here, it appears that we have neglected some types of sensory input that are sufficiently understood to be useful in developmental studies of memory. In particular, I think that we have failed to take advantage of heat cues, thermotactile stimuli, and vestibular cues. Each of these is salient and behaviorally potent, particularly in the neonates. Older animals detect and can also respond to these stimuli. Such cues appear useful as discriminative stimuli, possibly as reinforcers, and might be applied in ways to study maturational and memorial changes in response topography.

Development of function (the ''operating characteristics'' of sensory processing) and the function of sensory processes during development (the adaptational aspects of ontogeny) are both essential for an understanding of development and its underlying processes. Behavioral development involves sequential changes organized in relation to sequential ontogenetic "niches" which represent different types of environmental demands (cf. Galef, 1981b; Oppenheim, 1981). Studies of memory development often encompass several such stages of ontogenesis, and it is therefore imperative to include these organismic factors in our experimental designs and interpretation. Stage-typical characteristics can be used to enhance our analyses by applying stimuli and responses that are relevant to the subjects at various distinct ontogenetic stages. Basic knowledge of sensory and behavioral development is necessary for these approaches to be realized.

ACKNOWLEDGMENTS

Research from the author's laboratory described in this chapter was supported by Grant #28355 from the National Institute of Mental Health and by Grant BNS 15116 from the National Science Foundation. Preparation of the chapter and portions of the research effort were supported by Research Scientist Development Award #00222, also from the NIMH, to J. R. Alberts. The support of these organizations is gratefully acknowledged.

I also thank the editors of this book for their efforts and initiative in organizing the Purdue Symposium and producing the present volume. This chapter benefited from their editorial comments. The scope and content of this chapter was also enhanced by the research and scholarship of Dr. Peter C. Brunjes, whose dissertation was a valuable resource.

REFERENCES

Alberts, J. R. Olfactory contributions to behavioral development in rodents. In: R. L. Doty (Ed.), *Mammalian olfaction, reproductive processes and behavior.* New York: Academic Press, 1976.

Alberts, J. R. Huddling by rat pups: Group behavioral mechanisms of temperature regulation and energy conservation. *Journal of Comparative and Physiological Psychology,* 1978, *92,* 231–240. (a)

Alberts, J. R. Huddling by rat pups: Multisensory control of contact behavior. *Journal of Comparative and Physiological Psychology,* 1978, *92,* 220–230. (b)

Alberts, J. R. Ontogeny of olfaction: Reciprocal roles of sensation and behavior in the development of perception. In R. N. Aslin, J. R. Alberts, & M. R. Petersen (Eds.), *Development of perception: Psychobiological perspectives* (Vol. 1). New York: Academic Press, 1981.

Alberts, J. R., & Brunjes, P. C. Ontogeny of thermal and olfactory determinants of huddling in the rat. *Journal of Comparative and Physiological Psychology,* 1978, *92,* 897–906.

Alberts, J. R., & May B. Development of nasal respiration and sniffing in the rat. *Physiology and Behavior,* 1980, *24,* 957–963. (a)

Alberts, J. R., & May, B. Ontogeny of olfaction: Development of the rat's sensitivity to urine and amyl acetate. *Physiology and Behavior,* 1980, *24,* 965–970. (b)

Alford, B. R., & Ruben, R. J. Physiological, behavioral, and anatomical correlates of the development of hearing in the mouse. *Annals of Otology, Rhinology and Laryngology,* 1963, *72,* 237–247.

Altman, J., & Sudarshan, K. Postnatal development of locomotion in the laboratory rat. *Animal Behaviour*, 1975, *23*, 896–920.

Andres, K. H., & von During, M. Morphology of cutaneous receptors. In A. Iggo (Ed.), *Handbook of sensory physiology II. Somatosensory system*. New York: Springer-Verlag, 1973.

Arnold, S. J. The microevolution of feeding behavior. In A Kamil & T. Sargent (Eds.), *Foraging behavior: Ecological, ethological and physiological approaches*. New York: Garland Press, 1980.

Anokhin, P. K. Systemogenesis as a general regulator of brain development. *Progress in Brain Research*, 1964, *90*, 54–86.

Barnett, S. A., & Mount, S. E. Resistance to cold in mammals. In A. H. Rose, *Thermobiology*. New York: Academic Press, 1971.

Blass, E. M., & Cramer, C. P. Analogy and homology in the development of ingestive behavior. In *Changing concepts of the nervous system*. New York: Academic Press, 1982.

Bonner, J. T. *On development*. Cambridge, Mass.: Harvard University Press, 1974.

Bosher, S. K. Morphological and functional changes in the cochlea associated with the inception of hearing. *Symposia of the Zoological Society of London*, 1975, *37*, 11–22.

Bosher, S. K., & Warren, R. L. A study of the electrochemistry and osmotic relationships of the cochlear fluids in the neonatal rat at the time of the development of the endocochlear potential. *Journal of Physiology*, 1971, *212*, 739–761.

Bradley, R. M., & Mistretta, C. M. Swallowing in fetal sleep. *Science*, 1973, *179*, 1016–1017.

Braekevelt, C. R., & Hollenberg, M. J. The development of the retina of the albino. *American Journal of Anatomy*, 1970, *127*, 281–302.

Bruckner, G., Mares, V., & Biesold, D. Neurogenesis in the visual system of the rat. An autoradiographic investigation. *Journal of Comparative Neurology*, 1976, *166*, 245–256.

Brunjes, P. C., & Alberts, J. R. Olfactory stimulation induces filial huddling preferences in rat pups. *Journal of Comparative and Physiological Psychology*, 1979, *93*, 548–555.

Brunjes, P. C., & Alberts, J. R. Early auditory and visual function in normal and hyperthyroid rats. *Behavioral and Neural Biology*, 1981, *31*, 393–412.

Campbell, C. B. G., & Hodos, W. The concept of homology and the evolution of the nervous system. *Brain, Behavior and Evolution*, 1970, *3*, 353–367.

Cosnier, J. *Le comportement du rat d'elevage*. Unpublished doctoral dissertation, University of Lyon, France, 1965.

Crowley, D. E., & Hepp-Raymond, M. C. Development of cochlear function in the ear of the infant rat. *Journal of Comparative and Physiological Psychology*, 1966, *62*, 427–432.

Crozier, W. J., & Pincus, G. The geotropic conduct of young rats. *Journal of Genetic Psychology*, 1926, *10*, 257–269.

Cuscheri, A., & Bannister, L. H. The development of the olfactory mucosa in the mouse: Electron microscopy. *Journal of Anatomy*, 1975, *119*, 471–478.

de Beer, G. R. *Embryos and ancestors*. Oxford: Claredon Press, 1958.

Desor, J. A., Maller, O., & Andrews, K. Ingestive responses of human newborns to salty, sour, and bitter stimuli. *Journal of Comparative and Physiological Psychology*, 1975, *89*, 966–971.

English, K. B., Burgess, P. R., & Kavka-van, N.D. Development of rat Merkel cells. *Journal of Comparative Neurology*, 1980, *194*, 475–496.

Ferrell, M. F., Bradley, R. M., Mistretta, C. M., & Miklossy, K. Developmental changes in neural taste responses in postnatal rats. *Neuroscience Abstracts*, 1979, *5*, 127.

Ferrell, M. F., Mistretta, C. M., & Bradley, R. M. Chorda tympani taste responses during development in the rat. *Journal of Comparative Neurology*, 1981, *198*, 37–44.

Fujita, S. Analysis of neuron differentiation in the central nervous system by tritiated thymidine autoradiography. *Journal of Comparative Neurology*, 1964, *122*, 311–327.

Galef, B. G., Jr. Development of flavor preference in man and animals: The role of social and nonsocial factors. In R. N. Aslin, J. R. Alberts, & M. R. Petersen (Eds.), *Development of perception: Psychobiological perspectives* (Vol. 1). New York: Academic Press, 1981. (a)

Galef, B. G., Jr. The ecology of weaning: Parasitism and the achievement of independence by altricial mammals. In D. J. Gubernick & P. H. Klopfer (Eds.), *Parental care in mammals*. New York: Plenum Press, 1981. (b)

Galef, B. G., Jr., & Henderson, P. Mother's milk: A determinant of the feeding preferences of weaning rat pups. *Journal of Comparative and Physiological Psychology*, 1972, *78*, 213–219.

Ghiselin, M. T. An application of the theory of definitions to systematic principles. *Systematic Zoology*, 1966, *15*, 127–130.

Gottlieb, G. Prenatal behavior of birds. *Quarterly Review of Biology*, 1968, *48*, 148–174.

Gottlieb, G. Ontogenesis of sensory function in birds and mammals. In E. Tobach, L. R. Aronson, & E. Shaw (Eds.), *The biopsychology of development*. New York: Academic Press, 1971.

Gould, S. J. *Ontogeny and phylogeny*. Cambridge, Mass.: Belknap Press, 1977.

Hall, W. G., & Bryan, T. E. Ontogeny of feeding in rats IV. Taste development as measured by intake and behavioral responses to sucrose and quinine infusions. *Journal of Comparative and Physiological Psychology*, 1981, *95*, 240–251.

Hall, W. G., & Rosenblatt, J. S. Suckling behavior and intake control in the developing rat pup. *Journal of Comparative and Physiological Psychology*, 1977, *91*, 1232–1247.

Harlow, H. F., & Suomi, S. J. Nature of love—simplified. *American Psychologist*, 1970, *25*, 161–168.

Haroutunian, V., & Campbell, B. A. Development and habituation of the heart rate orienting response to auditory and visual stimuli in the rat. *Journal of Comparative and Physiological Psychology*, 1981, *95*, 166–174.

Hensel, H., & Kenshalo, D. R. Warm receptors in the nasal region of cats. *Journal of Physiology, London*, 1969, *204*, 99–112.

Hill, D. L., & Almli, C. R. Neural ontogeny of chorda tympani taste responses in the rat. *Neuroscience Abstracts*, 1979, *5*, 128.

Hinds, J. W. Autoradiographic study of histogenesis in the mouse olfactory bulb. I. Time of origin of neurons and neuroglia. *Journal of Comparative Neurology*, 1968, *134*, 287–304. (a)

Hinds, J. W. Autoradiographic study of histogenesis in the mouse olfactory bulb. II. Cell proliferation and migration. *Journal of Comparative Neurology*, 1968, *134*, 305–322. (b)

Hodos, W., & Campbell, C. B. G. *Scala naturae:* Why there is no theory in comparative psychology. *Psychological Review*, 1969, *76*, 337–350.

Hull, D. Thermoregulation in young mammals. In C. G. Whittow (Ed.), *Comparative physiology of thermoregulation* (Vol. 3). New York: Academic Press, 1973.

Jacobs, H. L., & Sharma, K. N. Taste versus calories: Sensory and metabolic signals in the control of food intake. *Annals of the New York Academy of Sciences*, 1969, *157*, 1084–1125.

Johanson, I. B., & Hall, W. G. Appetitive learning in 1-day-old rat pups. *Science*, 1979, *205*, 419–421.

Johanson, I. B., & Hall, W. G. The ontogeny of feeding in rats III. Thermal determinants of early ingestive behaviors. *Journal of Comparative and Physiological Psychology*, 1980, *94*, 977–992.

Johanson, I. B., & Teicher, M. H. Classical conditioning of an odor preference in 3-day-old rats. *Behavioral and Neural Biology*, 1980, *29*, 132–136.

Juraska, J. M., & Fifkova, E. A Golgi study of the early postnatal development of the visual cortex of the hooded rat. *Journal of Comparative Neurology*, 1979, *183*, 247–256.

Kenshalo, D. R., Hensel, H., Graziadei, P., & Fruhstorfer, H. On the anatomy and physiology and psychophysics of the cat's temperature-sensing system. In R. Dubner & Y. Kawamura (Eds.), *Oral-facial sensory and motor mechanisms*. New York: Appleton-Century Crofts, 1971.

Komisaruk, B. R. Synchrony between liblic system theta activity and rythmical behavior in rats. *Journal of Comparative and Physiological Psychology*, 1970, *70*, 482–492.

Leonard, C. M. Thermotaxis in golden hamster pups. *Journal of Comparative and Physiological Psychology*, 1974, *86*, 458–469.

Lincoln, D. W., Hill, A., & Wakerly, J. B. The milk-ejection reflex of the rat: An intermittent function not abolished by surgical levels of anesthesia. *Journal of Endrocrinology*, 1973, *57*, 459–476.

Lund, R. D., & Lund, J. S. Development of synaptic patterns in the superior colliculus of the rat. *Brain Research*, 1972, *42*, 1–20.

Lund, R. D., & Mustari, M. J. Development of the geniculocortical pathway in rats. *Journal of Comparative Neurology*, 1977, *173*, 289–306.

Martin, L. T., & Alberts, J. R. Taste aversions to mother's milk: The age-related role of nursing in acquisition and expression of a learned association. *Journal of Comparative and Physiological Psychology*, 1979, *93*, 430–445.

Martin, L. T., & Alberts, J. R. Associative learning in neonatal rats revealed by heartrate response patterns. *Journal of Comparative and Physiological Psychology*, 1982, *96*, 668–675.

Mistretta, C. M. Neurophysiological and anatomical aspects of taste development. In R. N. Aslin, J. R. Alberts, & M. R. Petersen (Eds.), *Development of perception: Psychobiological perspectives* (Vol. 1). New York: Academic Press, 1981.

Moulton, D. G. Spatio-temporal patterning of response in the olfactory system. In T. Hayashi (Ed.), *Olfaction and Taste II*, Oxford: Pergamon, 1967.

Moulton, D. G. Cell renewal in the olfactory epithelium of the mouse. In D. A. Denton & J. P. Coghlan (Eds.), *Olfaction and taste V*. New York: Academic Press, 1975.

Mozell, M. M. Spatial and temporal patterning. In L. M. Beidler (Ed.), *Handbook of sensory physiology IV, Chemical senses*, New York: Springer-Verlag, 1971.

Narayanan, C. H., Fox, M. W., & Hamburger, V. Prenatal development of spontaneous and evoked activity in the rat (*Rattus norvegicus albinus*). *Behaviour*, 1971, *29*, 100–131.

Oppenheim, R. W. Ontogenetic adaptations and retorgressive processes in the development of the nervous system and behavior: A neuroembryological perspective. In K. Connelly & H. Prechtl (Eds.), London: Spastica Society Publications, 1981.

Patrick, J. R., & Laughlin, R. M. Is the wall-seeking tendency in the white rat an instinct? *Journal of Genetic Psychology*, 1934, *44*, 378–389.

Pedersen, P. E., Greer, C. A., Stewart, W. B., & Shepherd, G. M. *2DG uptake associated with an artificial odor that elicits nipple attachment.* Paper presented at meeting of the International Society of Developmental Psychobiology, Minneapolis, Minn., October, 1982.

Pujol, R., & Hilding, D. Anatomy and physiology of the onset of auditory function. *Acta otolaryngologica*, 1973, *76*, 1–10.

Romer, A. S. *Vertebrate paleontology*, 3rd edition. Ill.: Univeristy of Chicago Press, 1966.

Rose, G. H. The development of visually evoked electrocortical responses in the rat. *Developmental Psychobiology*, 1968, *1*, 35–40.

Rosenblatt, J. S. The basis of early responses to the mother, siblings and the home and nest in altricial young of selected species of subprimate mammals. In R. A. Hinde & P. P. G. Bateson (Eds.), *Growing points in ethology*. New York: Cambridge University Press, 1976.

Rosenblatt, J. S. The sensorimotor and motivatonal bases of early behavioral development of selected altricial mammals. In N. E. Spear & B. A. Campbell (Eds.), *Ontogeny of learning and memory*. Hillsdale, N.J.: Lawrence Erlbaum Associates, 1979.

Rudy, J. W., & Cheatle, M. D. Odor-aversion learning in neonatal rats. *Science*, 1977, *198*, 845–846.

Salas, M., & Schapiro, S. Hormonal influences upon the maturation of the rat brain's responsiveness to sensory stimuli. *Physiology and Behavior*, 1970, *5*, 7–11.

Saunders, J. C., & Bock, G. R. Influences of early auditory trauma on auditory development. In G. Gottlieb (Ed.), *Studies on the development of behavior and the nervous system* (Vol. 4). New York: Academic Press, 1978.

Singh, P., & Hofer, M. A. Olfactory cues in nipple orientation and attachment in rat pups. *Neuroscience Abstracts*, 1976, *2*, 163.

Singh, S. C. The development of olfactory and hippocampal pathways in the brain of the rat. *Anatomy and embryology*, 1977, *151*, 183–199.

Small, W. Notes on the psychic development of the albino rat. *American Journal of Psychology*. 1899, *11*, 80–100.

Smith, C. G. The change in volume of the olfactory and accessory olfactory bulbs of the albino rat during postnatal life. *Journal of Comparative Neurology*, 1938, *61*, 477–508.

Smith, G. J., & Spear, N. E. Effects of the home environment on withholding behaviors and conditioning in infant and neonatal rats. *Science*, 1978, *202*, 327–329.

Smith, H. M. Biological similarities and homologies. *Systematic Zoology*, 1967, *16*, 101–102.

Smotherman, W. P. Odor aversion learning by the rat fetus. *Physiology and Behavior*, 1982, *29*, 769–771.

Taylor, A., Sluckin, W., & Hewitt, R. Changing color preferences of chicks. *Animal Behavior*, 1969, *17*, 3–8.

Tees, R. C. Perceptual development in mammals. In G. Gottlieb (Ed.), *Neural and behavioral specificity*. New York: Academic Press, 1973.

Tobach, E., Rouger, Y., & Schneirla, T. C. Development of olfactory function in the rat pup. *American Zoologist*, 1967, *7*, 792.

Vestal, B. M. Ontogeny of visual acuity in two species of deermice (*Peromyscus*). *Animal Behaviour*, 1973, *21*, 711–719.

Vestal, B. M., & King, J. A. Relationship of age at eye-opening to the first optokinetic response in deermice (*Peromyscus*). *Developmental Psychobiology*, 1968, *1*, 30–34.

Vestal, B. M., & King, J. A. Effects of repeated testing on development of visual acuity in prarie deermice. *Psychonomic Science*, 1971, *25*, 297–298.

Waite, P. M. E., & Cragg, B. G. The effect of destroying the whisker follicles in mice on the sensory nerve, the thalamocortical raditation and cortical barrel development. *Proceedings of the Royal Society of London, Series B*, 1979, *204*, 41–55.

Walk, R., & Gibson, E. J. Experiments with the visual cliff. *Psychological Monographs*, 1961, *75*, no. 519.

Weidman, T. A., & Kuwabara, T. Postnatal development of the rat retina. *Archives of Opthalmology*, 1968, *79*, 470–484.

Welker, W. I. Analysis of sniffing in the albino rat. *Behaviour*, 1964, *22*, 223–244.

Woolsey, T. A., Durham, D., Harris, R. M., Simons, D. J., & Valentino, K. L. Somatosensory development. In R. N. Aslin, J. R. Alberts, & M. R. Petersen (Eds.), *Development of perception: Psychobiological perspectives* (Vol. 1). New York: Academic Press, 1981.

5 The Ontogeny of Learning and Memory in Human Infancy

Carolyn Rovee-Collier
Rutgers University

The number and quality of the infant's accomplishments in the first year of life will probably never be equalled in any subsequent developmental period. From an experimenter's point of view, it is puzzling that these accomplishments are achieved in what could best be described as a variable and complex environment. In the laboratory, we usually attempt to maximize the opportunity for learning by eliminating multiple and presumably extraneous sources of stimulation and by removing all response opportunities other than the opportunity for the target response. The result of these efforts has been a relatively poor record of documenting the wealth and variety of the infant's early accomplishments. Paradoxically, the lack of success in laboratory demonstrations of infant learning has for almost two decades been widely accepted as evidence of the young infant's inability to learn under the more variable conditions of his natural setting: "... it is clear that newly born human infants *can learn* some responses under certain specific conditions. How much they actually *do learn* in every-day life is another matter" (Sluckin, 1970, p. 32).

In addition, the stability of learning early in infancy has been questioned. Most theories of infant development (e.g., Piaget, 1952; Watson, 1930) have assumed that the increasing number and complexity of behaviors within the first year of life in particular are products of a gradual and continuous process whereby the effects of the infant's experiences progressively accrue. Subsequent behaviors are constructed from and shaped by these experiences; they do not abruptly emerge as new competences at a given point in maturation (but see Gesell, 1928, and Kagan, 1979). Implicit in these accounts is the assumption that the infant can retain the effects of prior experiences over sufficiently long intervals that subsequent experiences could, in fact, cumulate with them. Yet the

103

extensive documentation of infantile amnesia (e.g., Allport, 1937; Freud, 1935; Schachtel, 1947; for review, see Spear, 1978) raises serious questions regarding the durability of early memories over lengthy periods of development. In addition, the very limited durations that have been projected for memories in the first 5 to 6 months of life, and in the first 2 to 3 months in particular (Werner & Perlmutter, 1979), challenge the assumption that an infant's prior experiences can influence his subsequent behavior even within a relatively limited period of development.

For a number of years our research has focused on the problem of learning in the first few postpartum months. Our work began with the relatively simple questions of "Can the infant learn?", "How early?", and "What?" (Rovee-Collier & Gekoski, 1979; Rovee-Collier & Lipsitt, 1982). These rapidly changed to "Can the young infant remember what he has learned?", "For how long?", and "Under what conditions?" (Fagen & Rovee-Collier, 1982; Rovee-Collier & Fagen, 1981). More recently, we have begun to address the problem of the ontogeny of memory. This has led us to explore infant learning and memory within and between relatively brief developmental periods and to consider the mechanism by which subsequent performance might be subject to modification by prior learning experiences. Our findings have differed in some major ways from those of other investigators who study memory in young infants. Because our procedures also differ, a brief overview of the techniques that have been applied to the study of infant memory is in order.

TECHNIQUES USED IN THE STUDY OF EARLY MEMORY

Over the past decade, most of the research on infant memory has involved what might be described as "novelty detection" procedures. These paradigms owe varying degrees of debt to Sokolov's (1963) model of the habituation of the orienting reflex and exploit the fact that infants older than 10 to 12 weeks typically spend more time looking at a novel than at a previously exposed stimulus. Presumably, when an organism encounters a stimulus, it begins to construct an internal representation (i.e., a memory engram) of it. The more complete the representation, the less the organism orients or attends to that stimulus. Thus once the engram is complete, the infant will orient to stimuli for which internal representation is not complete. Extended further, an infant will fixate stimuli on the basis of their relatively greater novelty. Retention of a prior stimulus, then, is inferred from the greater amount of looking time allocated to a previously unexposed or relatively novel stimulus than to the previously familiarized stimulus.

Three variations of the Sokolovian paradigm have been applied frequently to the study of memory in human infants. All involve measures of some aspect of the infant's visual behavior (e.g., length of first fixation, total looking time, etc.). The first, a relatively uncontaminated version of the paradigm, involves repeated presentations of a standard stimulus either for a fixed number of trials or for a fixed amount of cumulative looking time, or until a predetermined criterion of habituation has been reached. At this point, a given interval of time is allowed to elapse and then the infant is tested with the standard stimulus again. If visual fixation persists at a low level on the test trial, it is assumed that the infant has remembered the standard. Forgetting is inferred from the extent of recovery following the delay. Using such procedures, researchers typically report retention intervals ranging from 15 to 90 seconds (e.g., Pancrantz & Cohen, 1970; for review, see Werner & Perlmutter, 1979).

A highly similar procedure has been used with operants that produce access to a visual reinforcer (e.g., Hopkins, Zelazo, Jacobson, & Kagan, 1976; Siqueland, 1968, 1969). After the initial increase in operant rate indexing acquisition, response rate subsequently declines as a function of increasing exposure to the unchanging visual reinforcer. This *satiation function* is the operant analog of the habituation function for unlearned orienting responses. As in the habituation procedure, the extent to which response rate subsequently increases following a delay is assumed to reflect the extent to which the visual reinforcer was forgotten over the delay period. In a study of 4-month-olds whose high amplitude sucks produced access to a visual reinforcer, forgetting increased sharply over delay intervals of 1, 15, 30, and 75 seconds; retention was not reliable after the 15-second delay (Stinson, 1971).

A second novelty detection paradigm involves the initial brief presentation of the standard stimulus followed by a paired-comparison test between the standard and a previously unexposed stimulus. Here, the delay between the initial trial and the test trial defines the retention interval. In effect, this procedure is analogous to a delayed matching-to-sample task except that the match is implicit, inferred from greater fixation of the novel, or nonmatching, alternative. This paradigm was devised by Fantz (1963, 1967) for the study of infant visual perception and was subsequently adapted by Fagan (1970) for the study of infant memory. Fagan (1973) has reported that 5- to 6-month-olds selectively fixate novel facial photographs after a 2-week delay and novel multidimensional black-and-white stimuli, as well as some novel elements of small stimulus patterns, after a 2-day delay.

A third variant of the Sokolovian paradigm involves the serial presentation of a "list" of visual stimuli from a common stimulus class, followed by a paired-comparison test with one of the items on the list and a novel member of the same class (Cornell, 1974; Olson, 1976). Olson found strong primacy effects in 4- to 5-month-olds after delays of 8 minutes when lists consisted of relatively homogeneous items but obtained a strong recency effect when the list contained relatively heterogeneous items.

Werner and Perlmutter (1979) have speculated that age-related memory deficits reported in studies involving visual novelty detection procedures reflect "changes in infants' ability to encode stimulus information" (p. 46), either about the standard stimulus or about interpolated distractors (see also Cohen & Gelber, 1975), rather than changes in basic retention capacity.

A CONDITIONING ANALYSIS OF INFANT MEMORY

Our approach to the study of infant memory has exploited what Bolles (1976) has described as the "logical relation" between learning and memory. It is obvious that learning could not occur without memory (see Watson, this volume). In addition, however, an organism has a number of alternative behaviors in its repertoire that it can exhibit at any moment in time. If the probability of any given response in a particular context changes not only over repeated trials but also from one session to the next, then this longer term change can be attributed to the effects of its prior experiences, or to "memory." In fact, there are many examples of long-term retention of learned behaviors by animals tested days, weeks, months, and even years after their original training (cf. Skinner, 1938, 1953). Very young human infants also show strong evidence of remembering what they have previously learned from one occasion to the next, whether the learning involved simple response-reinforcer contingencies, stimulus-stimulus contingencies, or complex discriminative contingencies.

Panneton and DeCasper (1982) reinforced the nonnutritive sucking of newborn infants, 55 hours old, with a tape recording of a female singing. By the end of the first session, infants trained on a variable ratio-5 schedule were sucking at a significantly higher rate than were infants on a variable interval-1 minute schedule. At the outset of a second session that occurred an average of 6½ hours later, infants who had previously been trained on the variable interval schedule began sucking at rates even lower than their terminal response rates of Session 1. Conversely, infants who had previously been trained on the variable ratio schedule began their second session, an average of 10½ hours later, sucking at rates higher than their terminal response rates of Session 1.

Similarly, in a classical eyelid conditioning study with 10-, 20-, and 30-day-old infants, Little (1973) found that conditioning occurred within a single 20-minute session for infants at all ages. There were no age differences in speed of learning, although the oldest group attained a higher final asymptote than did the youngest group. Of greater interest from the standpoint of long-term retention, however, infants trained with a 1500-msec interval between the CS-tone and US-air puff at 20 days of age displayed a significantly higher level of anticipatory responding in their second session 10 days later than did infants trained for the first time at the older age. This response facilitation was present even in the first block of trials in Session 2 (see Fig. 5.1). Also shown in Fig. 5.1 are the data of infants trained with a 500-msec interstimulus interval. They showed no evidence of conditioning, nor did corresponding random control groups trained at 30 days.

Although the Little (1973) study might be seen as an instance of the facility with which very young infants can learn (and remember) contingencies under

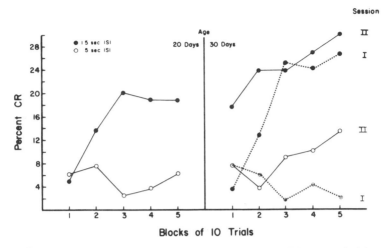

FIG. 5.1. Changes in the percentage of anticipatory eye blinks over 10-trial blocks as a function of the interstimulus interval (ISI). Infants trained when 20 days old with the 1.5-second ISI and retested 10 days later (Session II) showed no forgetting from the end of one session to the beginning of the next. The dotted lines show the performance of an age-control group trained for the first time at 30 days of age. (Little, 1973)

highly artificial laboratory conditions, instances of such learning have also been observed in naturalistic settings. For example, in a longitudinal study of inhibition of distress begun when subjects were 8 weeks old, we found that 40% of the infants, all lustily crying and tested in their own homes, already exhibited *anticipatory* quieting to the approach of a caregiver on the first trial of a multiple-trial series (Gekoski, Rovee-Collier, & Carulli-Rabinowitz, in press). This percentage increased as a function of age (see Fig. 5.2).

Finally, there is evidence that 10-week-olds remember complex stimulus-response contingencies over periods of at least 24 hours (Rovee Collier & Ca patides, 1979). Infants learned to produce movement in a distinctively colored (e.g., yellow-and-green) overhead crib mobile by means of an ankle ribbon attached to the mobile suspension hook. When the mobile was subsequently alternated for 2-minute periods with another distinctively colored mobile (e.g., blue-and-white) which could not be activated by footkicks, infants exhibited behavioral contrast, responding even more rapidly in the presence of S+ (yellow-and-green cues) than controls who continued to receive training with the same mobile without interpolated S− periods. Although the study was not designed to determine infant retention, because the procedure was carried out over 4 consecutive days, the extent of response carryover from one daily session to the next can be evaluated. As shown in Fig. 5.3, the behavioral contrast phenomenon was highly persistent, with higher response rates during S+ periods at the outset of each session. Moreover, this indicates that the infants' experience

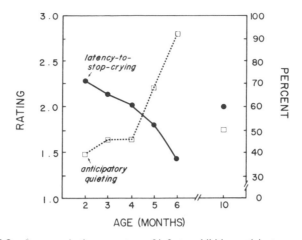

FIG. 5.2.   Increases in the percentage of infants exhibiting anticipatory quieting
over the first 6 months of age. The "CS" was the sight of the approaching
caregiver; the "UCS" was picking up the infant and administering a standardized
soothing procedure. (Gekoski et al., in press)

with the original reinforcement context of Session 1 continued to influence their
discrimination performance even 3 days later.

Thus we see that events that are predictive may be remembered for relatively
lengthy periods. In contrast, events that involve no contingency but occur randomly with respect to either the infant's own behaviors or other environmental
events are rapidly forgotten, if indeed the infant ever truly "learned" anything
about them in the first place. In fact, it would seem highly inefficient were an
infant (or an adult) to encode every visual detail that his eyes encountered, and
even more so to retain such information. This apparent *selectivity of memory
processing for contingent relations* convinced us of the value of using conditioning procedures with young infants as a means by which to approach the larger
question of the long-term impact of their early experiences.

Contextual Determinants of Retention

Over the last decade, there has been a resurgence of interest in the role of the
context in which original learning and subsequent retention testing occur
(Jenkins, 1974; Spear & Parsons, 1976; Underwood, 1969). For example, Tulving (1972) has proposed that every experience of an individual is represented in a
time-based "episodic" memory, which includes all of the contextual cues which
defined and accompanied each experience in a single representational "pack-
age." He has further proposed that access to episodic memory can be accomplished only via cues which were encoded at the time of original learning ("en-

coding specificity''). By this view, individuals seeking to retrieve memories are context-bound. Successful retention depends on the extent to which the individual can find sufficient numbers of cues in the test context that ''match'' those of the original episode. Failure to do so will result in a retrieval failure. This view emphasizes that an *available* memory (i.e., one that was originally encoded and is still in storage) will not be retrieved if the retrieval cues which mediate its access are not noticed during the retention test. Because retrieval is prerequisite to retention, most of our research has focused on this aspect of memory processing rather than on encoding or storage.

The importance of contextual cues has also captured considerable theoretical attention in the animal conditioning literature (Campbell & Spear, 1972; Estes, 1959; Johanson & Hall, this volume; Medin, 1976; Rescorla & Wagner, 1972; Spear, this volume). Our own focus on the contextual determinants of retention in human infants was strongly influenced by the procedural parallels between a conditioning analysis of infant memory and that used in animal research. For example, in both types of research the experimenter initially trains a nonverbal subject to acquire a distinctive response in a particular context and then, after an appropriate interval, asks that the subject again produce the previously acquired response in the same setting. Also, in both instances the experimenter must

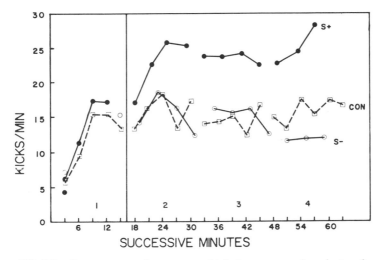

FIG. 5.3.   Response rates of two groups of infants over successive minutes of a behavioral contrast study, conducted over 4 successive days. Infants in the experimental group learned to activate a distinctively colored mobile (solid line, filled circles) and generalized that response to a second, distinctively colored mobile (open circle, Session 1). Beginning in Session 2, these infants received alternating periods of the training mobile (S+) and the second model (S−). The control group continued to receive the training model throughout the study. (Rovee-Collier & Capatides, 1979)

instruct the subject as to the nature of the task through the way in which the experimental environment is structured (cf. Campbell & Coulter, 1976).

A loose set of working assumptions, based on a contextual view of memory, has guided our research with infants. These assumptions are that (1) all retrieval is cued, and (2) retrieval can only occur when cues to which the organism selectively attended during original training are also selectively attended during the subsequent retention test. From this it follows that if novel stimuli, introduced during the retention test, elicit orienting responses, they may actually impede retrieval by drawing attention *away from* the previously noticed or familiar stimuli that must be re-noticed in order to cue retrieval. Finally, we assume that (3) the attributes that comprise a memory are independent, and can be forgotten at different rates (Spear, 1978).

Mobile Conjugate Reinforcement

For a number of years we have studied learning in 2- to 4-month-old infants using a free-operant technique, conjugate reinforcement, that was originally described by Ogden Lindsley (1956). This is a variant of a fixed ratio-one (FR 1) schedule; however, the intensity of each reinforcing consequence is proportional to the rate and/or vigor of the infant's response, varying along an intensity continuum of 0%–100%. That the infant can control two dimensions of his own reinforcing consequences, that is, frequency and intensity, may be critical in promoting the rapid acquisition that has been reported (for review, see Rovee-Collier & Gekoski, 1979). In our procedure, the movement of an overhead crib mobile is contingent upon the rate and vigor of the infant's footkicks. This is achieved by means of an ankle ribbon that is attached directly to the suspension hook of the mobile stand during reinforcement phases (see Fig. 5.4). Then, large and/or rapid kicks produce greater activation of the mobile, while small and/or slow movements produce slight jiggles of the mobile, and so forth. During nonreinforcement phases, the mobile is suspended from a second stand that bears no ribbon attachment, and kicks will not activate the mobile. It is important to emphasize that the reinforcement is the *conjugate movement* of the mobile and *not* simply the visual presence of a stationary mobile.

Infants trained in this procedure do not readily satiate to the visual reinforcer but may continue to respond to the reinforcement contingencies throughout sessions lasting 40 to 45 minutes (Rovee & Rovee, 1969) and extending over successive days, weeks, and even months (Smith, cited in Lipsitt, 1970). We speculate that the sustained efficacy of the mobile reinforcer is attributable to the relative novelty (Berlyne, 1960) that is achieved by the continuous rearrangements, in countless variations, of the familiar objects of the mobile as well as to the control per se that the infant is able to exert over its action (Skinner, 1953).

Infants who have detected the response-reinforcement contingency may smile and vocalize to the mobile, even during periods of nonreinforcement. In addi-

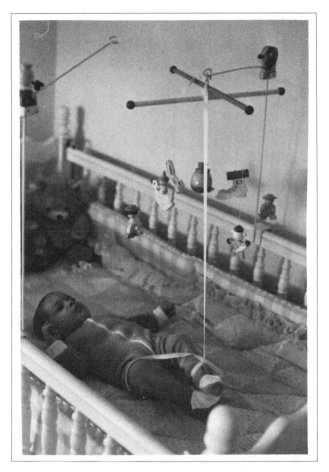

FIG. 5.4. The experimental arrangement during a reinforcement phase in the mobile conjugate reinforcement paradigm. During nonreinforcement phases the mobile is suspended from the stand shown at the left, but the ankle ribbon remains attached to the stand shown at the right. (All retention tests are administered during nonreinforcement phases.)

tion, their footkicking becomes progressively differentiated, with the movement of the leg to which the ribbon is attached achieving more vigorous and precise thrusts at a rate that exceeds that of the ineffectual leg. This highly distinctive response form is maintained during subsequent sessions. The unilateral pattern of responding can be reversed by making mobile movement contingent upon movement of the previously ineffectual leg (Rovee-Collier, Morrongiello, Aron, & Kupersmidt, 1978). This is particularly interesting for two reasons. First, there is no experimenter-imposed penalty for movement of both legs during reinforcement phases; as long as the designated leg moves, the mobile will also move. Yet the infant apparently detects the proportionality relationship and reduces the level of activity in the ineffectual limb. Second, all current tests of infant motoric development suggest that infants do not achieve unilateral responding prior to 5 or 6 months of age. However, we have seen that infants as young as 8 weeks are not only capable of selective movement of a single limb but do so readily, depending upon the "payoff." A complete sequence of unilateral responding by an 8-week-old is shown in the successive panels of Fig. 5.5.

Measurement of Infant Retention

In an early study of 24-hour retention, we found that 3-month-olds forgot little from one day to the next when tested in the mobile conjugate reinforcement paradigm (Rovee & Fagen, 1976). Babies were trained in their home cribs for 15 minutes on each of 4 days. Each session consisted of a 3-minute nonreinforcement phase preceding and following each daily 9-minute reinforcement phase. For the first 3 days, both groups (control, experimental) were trained with the same mobile. On the final day, the experimental group was tested with a novel mobile while the control group was tested with the original one. As shown in Fig. 5.6, the rate of responding at the outset of each succeeding daily session (Block R1) was simply a continuation of the rate during the final block of the immediately preceding session (E5) as long as infants were presented with the same mobile in successive sessions.

We find it useful to express an infant's response rate at the outset of a temporally distant session (the *long-term retention test*), when some degree of forgetting would be expected to have occurred, as a fraction of his response rate during the 3 minutes immediately following the acquisition phase at the end of the preceding session, when forgetting would be expected to be minimal (the *immediate retention test*). Because both measures of response rate are taken during nonreinforcement periods with no intervening reinforcement opportunities, excellent performance during the long-term test cannot be attributed to new learning. As the resulting fraction, or *retention ratio*, declines from 1.00, increased forgetting over the intersession interval is indicated (Sullivan, Rovee-Collier, & Tynes, 1979).

A second measure of retention is illustrated in the replot of the data shown in Fig. 5.6 (see Fig. 5.7). In the left panel, we see that initial (Block-1) performance improves over successive days of training. (The same improvement is seen in the right panel over the first 3 training days.) Thus irrespective of the magnitude of forgetting from the end of any given session to the beginning of the next, performance at the outset of a distant session, prior to the reintroduction of reinforcement, may still surpass the Session-1 pretraining performance level of a given infant. We express the extent to which the infant's performance during a long-term retention test continues to exceed the same infant's pretraining base-

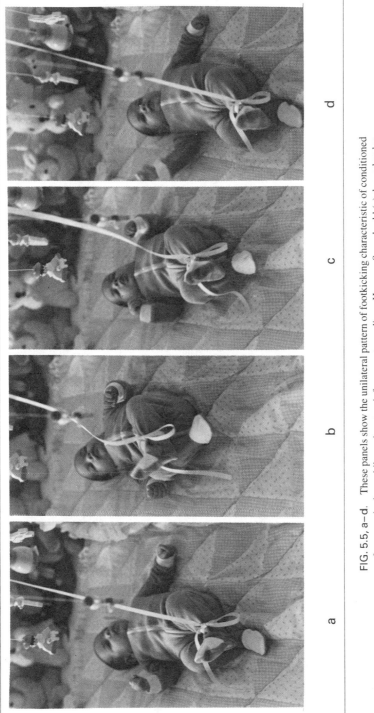

FIG. 5.5, a–d. These panels show the unilateral pattern of footkicking characteristic of conditioned performance in the mobile conjugate reinforcement paradigm. Here, an 8-week-old (a) draws her leg up and back until (b) the ribbon is slack. At this point (c) the leg starts to extend forward, and finally (d) the ribbon is taut as the infant thrusts the leg forward (toward the camera) and brings it sharply down toward the mattress.

113

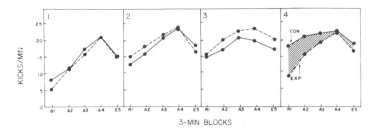

FIG. 5.6. Changes in rate of conditioned responding over successive 3-minute blocks of four daily sessions. Blocks preceded by "A" are reinforcement phases; all others are nonreinforcement phases: B1, "baseline"; E5, "immediate retention test"; R1, "long-term retention test." During the 24-hour long-term retention test in Session 4, only infants tested with their training mobile exhibited retention. (Rovee-Collier & Fagen, 1981)

line response rate in terms of a *baseline ratio,* in which a value of 1.00 indicates performance at the original pretraining level, and values greater than 1.00 presumably index some degree of retention (Davis & Rovee-Collier, 1983).

Taken together, these two measures reflect (from somewhat different perspectives) the extent to which infants' prior experiences continue to affect their behaviors (baseline ratios) and the extent to which they have forgotten the effects of their prior experiences (retention ratios). The traditional measure of the greater facility with which infants achieve relearning relative to original learning, a savings score, has not proven to be a useful index of retention in our research. We attribute this to the rapidity of original learning in the mobile paradigm. Its

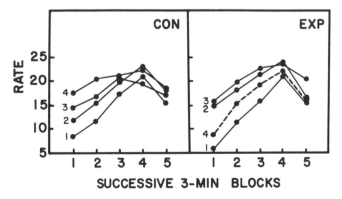

FIG. 5.7. A recharacterization of the data shown in Fig. 5.6, emphasizing the extent to which performance in the first block of each session (the long-term retention test on Days 2, 3, and 4) continues to surpass the pretraining response level recorded during the baseline block of Day 1, irrespective of the terminal response level (Block 5: the immediate retention test) on any given day.

utility is primarily in studies that involve procedures which *retard* reacquisition, yielding *negative* savings scores (Rovee-Collier & Sullivan, 1980).

Because the level of conditioned responding achieved during acquisition does not appear to be improved substantially by additional training, most of our work has involved a standard training regimen of two training sessions followed by a specified retention interval and then by a third procedurally identical session during which long-term retention is assessed. The forgetting function of independent groups of 3-month-olds tested in this paradigm is described by a progressive decline in the relative rate of conditioned responding, expressed as retention ratios, after retention intervals ranging from 24 hours to 14 days (see Fig. 5.8, solid line). Here, forgetting is complete after an interval of 2 weeks but not after 1 week (Rovee-Collier, Enright, Lucas, Fagen, & Gekoski, 1981). Extending the number of original training sessions from two to three extends the interval over which infants can successfully retrieve the contingency by 1 week (Mac-Donald, 1980). In contrast, altering the context within which retention is assessed by substituting novel components into the original training mobile dramatically disrupts retrieval after relatively short retention intervals (1–3 days) but

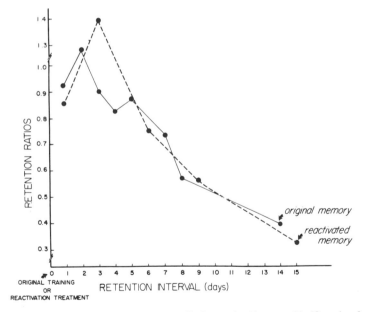

FIG. 5.8.   Retention ratios of 8 groups of infants trained between 11–13 weeks of age and tested after delays ranging from 1 to 14 days (solid line). Also shown are retention ratios of 5 groups of infants, similarly trained but who received a reactivation treatment after a retention interval of 13 days and who then subsequently received a long-term retention test either 1, 3, 6, 9, or 15 days following the reminder (dashed line). (Rovee-Collier et al., 1981)

not after lengthier ones (Rovee-Collier & Sullivan, 1980). The degree of disruption is a power function of the degree of novelty in the test mobile (Fagen, Rovee, & Kaplan, 1976). Because we assume that all retrieval is cued, we view this phenomenon as a product of the infant's robust attentional response-to-novelty: Novel cues by definition have not previously been encountered hence cannot comprise any part of the memory of a prior event; as such, they cannot cue retrieval of that event. By successfully competing with potentially effective retrieval cues (i.e., familiar stimuli) for the infant's attention, novel elements in the test context reduce the probability of retrieval by reducing the probability that familiar contextual cues will be noticed during the limited time available in the long-term retention test.

The disrupting effect of novel stimuli is illustrated in the Session-4 performance of infants in the experimental group in the Rovee and Fagen (1976) study (Figs. 5.6 and 5.7). These infants were tested in the presence of a novel mobile 24 hours following the conclusion of three daily training sessions with a highly similar mobile model. They exhibited no evidence of retention even though they had previously exhibited the characteristic day-to-day response carryover and even though the facilitative effects of 3 training days on long-term retention have been demonstrated (MacDonald, 1980). With progressively lengthier retention intervals, however, the disruptive effect on retention performance diminishes such that after a 4-day retention interval infants respond equivalently to novel and to training mobiles during the 3-minute long-term retention test (Rovee-Collier & Sullivan, 1980).

Reactivation of Infant Memories

If memories are relatively permanent, then the forgetting function shown in Fig. 5.8 may simply reflect the progressive inaccessibility of memory attributes rather than their decay or diminishing availability (cf. Tulving, 1972). From this perspective, procedures that either forestall the decreasing accessibility of memory attributes or increase the accessibility to retrieval of attributes that have become less accessible over time should yield evidence of retention after intervals longer than those predicted by the simple forgetting function. In contrast, if the forgetting function reflects either decay or loss from storage, then interventions designed to influence retrieval would not improve retention.

In a seminal study, Campbell and Jaynes (1966) reported that periodic reencounters with some aspect of the original training context could maintain conditioned responding over an interval during which it would otherwise have been forgotten (the *reinstatement* phenomenon). Critical to their finding was the observation that control groups, who either received no interpolated exposure to the training context following the completion of training or were not trained prior to the intermittent exposures to the training context, evidenced neither long-term retention nor new learning, respectively. Subsequently, Spear and Parsons

(1976) reported that a single reencounter with the reinforcer, prior to the long-term retention test but after forgetting was complete, was sufficient to restore retention to the immediate posttraining level. Their prior cuing procedure, a *reactivation treatment* (Spear, 1973), presumably primed or "stirred up" other-wise inaccessible memory attributes such that a sufficient number of them were again accessible when the organism sampled retrieval cues in the retention test context. Taken together, these two sets of research findings strengthen a retrieval-failure account of forgetting.

To assess the utility of this account for retention of memories in human infancy, we modeled a reactivation procedure after that of Spear and Parsons (1976). We presented infants trained in the standard mobile paradigm with a reminder of the reinforcer 24 hours prior to their long-term retention tests and at a point in the forgetting curve when there was no evidence that they remembered the response-reinforcement contingency. The reactivation treatment consisted of a 3-minute presentation of the original training mobile, moved by the experi-menter at the same rate that each infant had moved it for himself during the final 3 minutes of his second training session. The context within which the reminder was presented was identical to that in which the infant had originally been trained with two exceptions: (1) the ribbon was not attached to the infant's ankle, and (2) the infant was positioned under the mobile in a plastic infant seat (see Fig. 5.9). The latter was introduced to minimize limb activity. By redistributing the in-fant's weight in this way, we reduced the number of leg movements which met the definition of a footkick to 0–2 per minute (Sullivan, 1980). Even so, the topography of the response was radically different from that observed in supine infants. Two control groups, fashioned after those of Campbell and Jaynes (1966), were included to ensure that unlearned increases in activity levels, either age-related or produced by the reactivation treatment per se, did not contribute to performance during the long-term retention test.

In a dissertation, Sullivan (1980) found that a reactivation treatment admin-istered 13 days following the completion of training not only alleviated the forgetting of 3-month-olds during the long-term retention test administered on the following day but also restored their conditioned responding to a level char-acteristically seen after only a 24-hour retention interval (see also Sullivan, 1982). A reactivation treatment administered 27 days following the completion of training (Rovee-Collier, Sullivan, Enright, Lucas, & Fagen, 1980) is equally effective in alleviating forgetting. In subsequent studies, we have found that the forgetting function following a single reminder is almost identical to that follow-ing the conclusion of original training (see Fig. 5.8, dashed line; Rovee-Collier et al., 1981) and that the reactivation treatment is effective only if the original training mobile is presented as the reminder (Enright, 1981). A novel mobile is ineffective in alleviating forgetting even though infants have previously exhib-ited evidence that they do not differentiate novel from familiar mobiles after intervals longer than 3 days (Rovee-Collier & Sullivan, 1980). Also, a stimulus

FIG. 5.9.   The experimental arrangement during a reactivation treatment, administered here to an 8-week-old infant. The arrangement of the mobile stands is identical to that shown in Fig. 5.4.

that predicted reinforcement prior to serving as an S− in a behavioral contrast paradigm is not an effective reminder, but the S+ is (Fagen, Yengo, Rovee-Collier, & Enright, 1981). Apparently infants selectively forget stimuli that are nonpredictive. This is consistent with our earlier observation that infants tested in attentional paradigms, which do not involve contingencies, exhibit rapid forgetting. Finally, it appears that the reactivation process is time-locked; that is, once the reminder has been encountered, it takes ''time'' for the priming effect to occur. When independent groups of infants, trained 2 weeks earlier, were tested within 15 or 60 minutes of a reactivation treatment, they showed no evidence of retention. Some infants tested 8 hours following a reactivation treatment did

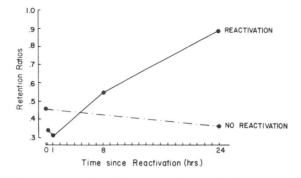

FIG. 5.10.   Retention ratios of infants receiving a reactivation treatment 13 days following the conclusion of training (solid line) or who received no reactivation treatment (broken line) but received long-term retention tests on the 13th or 14th day following the completion of training. The two groups of infants tested within 15 minutes or 1 hour of a reactivation treatment are responding at operant level. (Fagen et al., 1981)

exhibit evidence of retention, with the correlation between retention ratios and amount of time spent sleeping between the reminder and the long-term retention test being .75! However, infants tested 24 hours following a reactivation treatment exhibited retention ratios indicative of no forgetting. The postreactivation recovery function, shown in Fig. 5.10, can be viewed as the product of a recruitment process in which increasing numbers of memory attributes become accessible to retrieval over the interval following the priming or reactivation stimulus (Fagen, Hoffman, Rovee-Collier, & Thompson, 1981).

THE ONTOGENY OF MEMORY

The efficacy of a single reactivation treatment in alleviating the forgetting of 3-month-olds after periods as long as a month demonstrates clearly that memories of the very young infant are not immediately lost but can continue to influence behavior over relatively lengthy periods. This also raises the possibility that memories may remain available as potential influences after even lengthier developmental periods. However, this possibility, originally suggested by Campbell and Jaynes (1966), does not preclude the possibility that some memory attributes are lost, decay, or become permanently inaccessible over major developmental periods.

Studies of the ontogeny of memory in animals other than humans have generally yielded evidence of retention deficits in younger organisms (for a collection of these findings, see Spear & Campbell, 1979). These deficits appear in procedures which assess simple forgetting following an original training procedure as well as in procedures which assess the alleviation of forgetting following the presentation of a reminder (e.g., Spear & Parsons, 1976). A number of accounts of these ontogenetic differences have been proposed. Campbell and Spear (1972) suggested that age-related differences in the perception of the test context relative to the context in which learning originally occurred may severely limit the number of effective retrieval cues that could be sampled during the long-term retention test. Such perceptual changes might result, for example, from changes in the size of the organism relative to the size of the training-test apparatus. In addition, they proposed that major neurological reorganization may reduce the accessibility of memories (see also Campbell & Coulter, 1976), although Miller and Berk (1977, 1979) have demonstrated that this factor does not account for infantile amnesia in all species. Other accounts attribute the poorer retention by younger than by older organisms to age-related differences in either memory content (Gordon, 1979) or the efficacy of various training factors (Coulter, 1979).

With the exception of Little (1973) and Martin (1975), no researchers have systematically addressed the problem of ontogenetic changes in the memorial abilities of infants during the first several months of life. Because the period from 8 to 12 weeks is characterized by marked changes in neurological organization (Conel, 1941, 1947), sleep-waking patterns (Sterman, 1979), reflexive activity (Bergström, 1969; McGraw, 1943), and visual perception (Aslin, this volume; Bronson, 1974, 1982), the study of infant memory during this transition period might provide some insights into the adequacy of these various accounts. This possibility led us to initiate a series of studies in which 8-week-olds were trained in the mobile conjugate reinforcement paradigm and tested for retention of the contingency following various retention intervals and following a reactivation treatment. In addition, we have attempted to characterize differences in original conditioning as a function of age, amount and distribution of training, and stimulus preference.

Age Differences in Retention

In a recently completed dissertation, Vander Linde (1982) compared the retention of 8- and 13-week-old infants following single-session training in the mobile conjugate reinforcement paradigm for 6, 12, or 18 minutes. Although lengthier training periods produced higher final levels of conditioning, infants in the two age groups did not differ in terms of either the speed or asymptote of conditioning (see Fig. 5.11). When retention was assessed during the 3-minute immediate retention test at the conclusion of training, the age groups performed equivalently and showed no evidence of forgetting.

During the long-term retention test a week later, however, 13-week-olds exhibited significantly better retention as indexed by both retention and baseline ratios. Baseline ratios of 8-week-olds trained for 12 and 18 minutes and of 13-

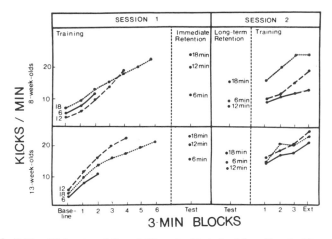

FIG. 5.11.   Kick rates of 8- and 13-week-olds trained for either 6, 12, or 18 minutes in a single session and tested 7 days later. (Vander Linde, 1982)

week-olds trained for 18 minutes continued to exceed 1.00 after one week. The baseline ratios of the 12-minute, 8-week-old group must be interpreted with caution, however, insofar as their pretraining kick rates were very low, and their 7-day retention ratios did not provide convergent evidence that they remembered the response-reinforcement contingency. (In subsequent studies, we have found that 8-week-olds trained for either 12 or 18 minutes evidence no retention after a 2-week interval, whereas 13-week-olds trained for a single 18-minute session do.) Step-wise multiple regression analyses indicated that the single best predictor of long-term retention was not age but an individual infant's performance during original conditioning. The more an infant's peak performance in any minute of acquisition exceeded that infant's pretraining response rate, the better was that infant's retention. This factor, the *peak performance* ratio, predicted 85% of the variance associated with the baseline ratio retention index a week later. While age was also a significant parameter estimate, it accounted for only a small portion (2%) of the variance in comparison.

Recently we have obtained forgetting functions of independent groups of 8-week-olds who were trained in our standard 2-session paradigm and tested after different intervals. Their retention ratios are compared with those of 13-week-olds who were similarly trained and tested in Fig. 5.12. While 13-week-olds continue to respond significantly in excess of their pretraining baseline levels for as long as 8 days following the conclusion of training, 8-week-olds show no evidence of retention after intervals longer than 3 to 5 days. Figure 5.13 shows the footkick data obtained from three of these groups of 8-week-olds during the two training sessions and the retention test session administered 1, 3, or 6 days following the completion of training. The acquisition data of the three indepen-

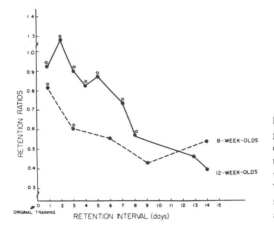

FIG. 5.12. Retention ratios of five groups of 8-week-olds, tested after delays of 1–14 days, compared with the retention ratios of 11- to 13-week-olds after comparable delays. The stars indicate those points that significantly surpass baseline levels as well.

dent groups are pooled in this figure. As can be seen, the infants show little if any response carry-over from the first to the second training session and, forgetting is orderly, with no evidence of retention after an interval of 6 days. These data are consistent with Vander Linde's (1982) report of retention deficits in the younger age group.

In spite of their deficit in retention following original training, however, 8-week-olds were highly responsive to a reactivation treatment administered 17 days after the conclusion of training (Davis & Rovee-Collier, 1983; see Fig. 5.14). When tested 24 hours later, their level of conditioned responding had recovered to the level exhibited during the immediate retention test. The apparently aberrant point in the first block of reacquisition (Block 2) during the long-term retention test session reflects a reliable cessation of activity in response to

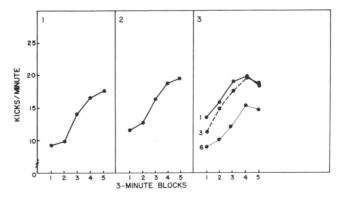

FIG. 5.13. The training and retention test session footkick data of 3 groups of 8-week-olds. Only infants tested 1 or 3 days following the completion of two training sessions exhibit retention.

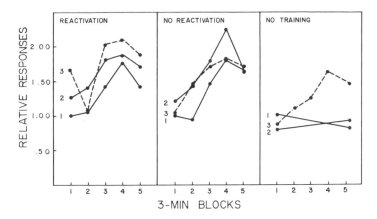

FIG. 5.14.   Mean relative response rates (response rate/minute divided by mean baseline response rate/minute) of 8-week-olds during a retention test session (Session 3, dashed line) administered 18 days following the conclusion of two successive daily training sessions (Reactivation, No Reactivation groups) or following exposure-only (no acquisition phase) to the mobile during the original two sessions (No Training group). The Reactivation and the No Training groups received a 3-minute reactivation treatment 24 hours before the long-term retention test session. Forgetting is evident in the initial block of Session 3 on the part of all but the infants in the Reactivation group. (Davis & Rovee-Collier, 1983)

the sudden, initial movements of the mobile. This reaction has been observed previously in 9-week-olds following a sudden change in some aspect of the mobile reinforcer but is not seen in 12- or 15-week-olds (Gekoski, 1977).

Age Differences in Visual Exploration

Spear and Parsons (1976) had reported that a reminder alleviated forgetting by rat pups, trained at 16 days of age, after 7 but not after 28 days. Conceivably, 8-week-olds might not respond to a reactivation treatment if the retention interval were extended. However, interpretation of the data that would result from such a manipulation would be clouded by potential differences in the stimulus features which the infants would be likely to notice during original training and later, during the long-term retention test. Because we have taken the position that retrieval occurs when the infant selectively notices cues previously noticed during original training, age-related changes in the salience of certain stimulus features would obviously impede, and possibly even preclude, retrieval (see also Gordon, 1979).

There are now considerable data (e.g., Aslin, this volume; Bronson, 1982; Milewski & Siqueland, 1975; Volkmann & Dobson, 1976) suggesting that age differences in visual exploration produce differences in the contents of memories of younger and older infants and, hence, contribute to their retention differences. Not only do the stimulus features which infants selectively fixate change with age, but so also does the nature of their visual perception (Aslin, this chapter). For example, Gekoski (1977) has reported that infants at 9 but not at 12 or 15 weeks of age exhibit more rapid acquisition when achromatic rather than chromatic mobiles serve as the visual reinforcers in the mobile conjugate reinforcement paradigm. A similar observation has been reported by Milewski and Siqueland (1975) in a study of 4-week-olds trained in the high-amplitude sucking paradigm. It is likely that the degree of contrast, rather than the presence or absence of color per se, is the critical dimension underlying the relative efficacy of these stimuli for young infants. At 4 months, however, the color of the mobile markedly influences response rate (Smith, cited by Lipsitt, 1970). Infants of this age fixate blue stimuli for lengthier periods than green stimuli (Bornstein, 1975) and respond at higher rates to activate a blue mobile than a green one (Fagen, 1980). Moreover, they respond selectively to the color of their training mobile (blue, green) after a 24-hour retention interval (Fagen, 1983).

In addition to changes in the relative salience of various stimulus features, the manner in which the infant samples his visual environment also changes with age. For example, the number of gaze shifts that an infant makes from one stimulus to the next in a visual array increases over the first 3 postnatal months (Volkmann & Dobson, 1976). Thus infants at 8 weeks of age are likely to fixate fewer of the components suspended from the overhead mobile in a fixed period of time than are infants 1 month older. (However, they may be encoding much more of the detail in only one or two components.) If the mobile component that they first encounter during a retention test is not one that they had previously inspected, then it could not cue retrieval. Moreover, fixation of that stimulus for a lengthy period reduces the opportunity to sample other components that were previously encountered.

While ontogenetic changes in target scanning and tracking undoubtedly account for a large part of the retention deficit that we have observed in younger infants, we now think that a failure to incorporate *nontarget* contextual information into the memorial representation may also contribute to their poorer retention. We have been repeatedly struck by the fact that 2-month-olds allocate little, if any, of their session time to stimuli other than the mobile per se. From the moment the mobile is suspended overhead to the moment it is removed, their eyes rarely leave it. In contrast, we have previously reported (Fagen et al., 1976; Rovee & Fagen, 1976; Sullivan et al., 1979) that 3-month-olds fixate the mobile almost continuously during reinforcement periods but intermittently shift their gaze away from it during nonreinforcement periods at the beginning and end of each session. It is during these nonreinforcement periods, in fact, when we measure retention (the long-term and immediate retention tests, respectively). We have never observed an infant "staring into space" during these nonreinforcement periods; rather, they specifically fixate the crib bumper, one or both

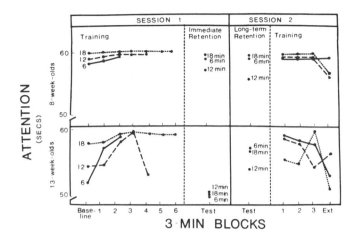

FIG. 5.15. (a)   Mean seconds per minute of looking time exhibited by 8- and 13-week-olds trained for either 6, 12, or 18 minutes in the mobile conjugate reinforcement paradigm. Looking time was recorded when an infant's head and eyes were oriented in the direction of the mobile. Session 2 occurred 7 days after Session 1 (see also Fig. 5.11). Nonreinforcement periods include baseline, the immediate retention test, the long-term retention test, and extinction blocks. (Vander Linde, 1982)

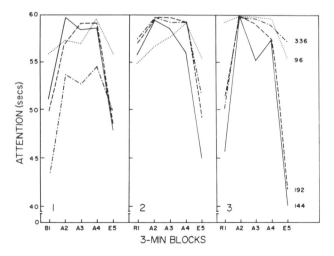

(b)   Mean seconds per minute of looking time exhibited by infants who were 12 to 13 weeks old during original training (Sessions 1, 2). The final retention test session occurred 96, 144, 192, or 336 hours (2 weeks) later. Here, the decreased visual attention during nonreinforcement periods is striking, particularly when infants were tested at 14–15 weeks of age. Nonreinforcement periods are the first and last blocks of each session (B1, E5, R1, etc.). (Sullivan et al., 1979) mobile stands, the ribbon, etc. These observations have led us to speculate that older infants obtain a richer web of memory attributes, corresponding to a greater portion of the context in which the episode occurs, than do younger infants. Although the amount of nontarget fixation may be only a matter of seconds in some instances, no one knows how long it takes to encode a bit of information. Moreover, response differences to novel and prefamiliarized stimuli in visual novelty detection paradigms are also usually on the order of only a few seconds. Thus the critical aspect of this hypothesis is not the magnitude of the difference in contextual fixations but the fact that the difference is highly reliable and that younger infants exhibit virtually no fixations of nontarget stimuli.

Differences in fixation times of 8- and 13-week-olds are illustrated in Fig. 5.15. Some of these data (Fig. 5.15a) were obtained at the same time as the footkick data previously depicted in Fig. 5.11. If younger infants encode fewer contextual cues as memory attributes, then there are fewer cues available to them to cue retrieval. Even if tested after an interval of sufficient length that their looking patterns would have changed, when more of the context would be sampled, noticing these additional contextual cues subsequently would not facilitate retrieval because they would not have been encoded with the original event.

The Effect of Training Conditions on Retention

Could retrieval be facilitated by providing infants with a greater number of contextual cues? Coulter (1979) reported that distributing the conditioning trials of 18-day-old rat pups over 1, 2, or 3 days did not influence immediate retention but did affect it after 28 days, with three sessions of 3 trials each (the most distributed condition) proving superior. The same procedure, when administered to adult rats, had no differential effect: Retention was good in all conditions. Coulter hypothesized that the additional and varied *session onset cues,* gained from multiple sessions, were responsible for improving retention in the younger animals.

In a second study of her dissertation, Vander Linde (1982) was similarly able to improve the long-term retention of 8-week-olds by distributing their minutes of training time over multiple sessions. Infants received either a single 18-minute session or three 6-minute sessions (one per day). To assess the efficacy of greater or lesser spacing between sessions, she allowed 24 hours to intervene between sessions for some infants and 48 hours for others. During retention tests administered 2 weeks later, infants whose trials had been distributed into three sessions exhibited response rates that significantly exceeded their pretraining baseline level (baseline ratios indicative of remembering), whereas infants for whom all training had occurred in a single session evidenced complete forgetting (see Fig. 5.16). It is interesting that infants with 48 hours interpolated between sessions displayed poorer retention than those with 24 hours between sessions. The facili-

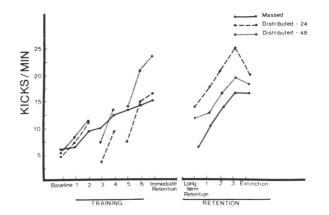

FIG. 5.16. Mean responses/minute of 8-week-olds who received 18 minutes of contingency training in either a single session (solid line) or in 3 sessions of 6 min each; in the latter instance, groups were trained with either 24-hour (dashed line) or 48-hour (dotted line) intersession intervals. The long-term retention test was administered 14 days following the completion of training. (Vander Linde, 1982)

tative influence of distributed trials may result not only from increased numbers of session onset cues, but also from the forced disruption of looking behavior in the 8-week-old. With each new presentation of the mobile, the younger infant has the possibility of encountering different mobile components than he previously had viewed. This, in essence, *forces* an increase in the number of different stimuli that he fixates during training. While this may result in relatively poor day-to-day response carryover, with additional training the carryover should improve. In fact, this effect can be seen at the outset of the second daily session in both distributed groups.

In contrast, distributing the training trials of 3-month-olds does not facilitate retention after a 2-week interval (Enright, Fagen, Rovee-Collier, & Caniglia, in press). Infants who received a single 18-minute session exhibited excellent retention during the 14-day retention test; infants who received two 9-minute sessions exhibited retention after 1 but not 2 weeks; and infants whose training was distributed into three 6-minute sessions evidenced no retention even after a week. All, however, performed equivalently during the immediate retention test. Here, disruption of visual attention does not increase the number of contextual cues that the infants are already likely to sample. If anything, the robust response-to-novelty interferes with attention to the familiar retrieval cues at the outset of succeeding sessions, thus allowing the briefer daily training group less time to locate the familiar retrieval cues. In fact, when the opportunity to inspect the mobile is provided "gratis" at the outset of a session, infants exhibit retention at a level of those trained in a single, arduous session.

Age Differences in Acquisition

In a review of infant animal learning and memory research, Campbell and Coulter (1976) disclaimed differences in original acquisition as a factor underlying differences in retention. For the most part, the training tasks used in animal research have been relatively simple and learned readily by all age groups. Vander Linde's (1982) finding that 8-week-olds did not differ in speed or level of conditioning from 13-week-olds but did show a significant retention deficit would seem to confirm Campbell and Coulter's conclusion. Similarly, Little (1973) had reported that 10- and 20-day-old infants exhibited equivalent acquisition of a conditioned eyelid response, yet only the 20-day-old group evidenced significant retention of the conditioned response 10 days later.

Longitudinal studies of human infant learning have been rare in Western culture, partly owing to the inaccessibility of a subject population for longitudinal research. Yet demonstrations of age-related changes in infant learning have resulted almost exclusively from this type of research approach (Papousek, 1967). Although the rapidity with which the mobile conjugate reinforcement task is learned over the age span of 2 to 4 months would seem to make this task inappropriate for the study of ontogenetic differences in conditioning (cf. Vander Linde, 1982), the considerable variability among infants trained at younger ages prompted Gekoski (1977) to initiate a study involving several traditional measures of visual exploration in which the same group of infants was repeatedly tested over the transitional period of 2 to 4 months. One of the tasks, simple acquisition and extinction in the mobile conjugate reinforcement paradigm, yielded clear-cut developmental differences (see Fig. 5.17).

At 9 weeks of age, only half of the infants achieved response rates that reliably exceeded their baseline level during the reinforcement phase; all but one of the infants that failed to learn the response-reinforcement contingency in the first of two sessions were trained with a chromatic mobile. During extinction, response rate continued to increase. These findings have been replicated by Davis and Rovee-Collier, (1983, Experiment 1). When retrained at 12 weeks of age, conditioning performance was asymptotic by the third 3-minute block of acquisition. While responding did not decrease during extinction, it did not continue to increase as it had 3 weeks earlier. Finally, during the 15-week test, infants increased response rate reliably by the second 3-minute block of acquisition and also decreased response rate reliably in extinction. The overall response level increased as a function of age, and the chromatic mobile was associated with higher levels of response at the older ages than was the achromatic mobile.

It could be argued that Gekoski's findings reflect the cumulative impact of the infants' prior experiences. Could not the presence of the mobile during the 3-minute baseline period at the outset of each subsequent session serve as a reminder or reactivation treatment for the response-reinforcement contingency? In view of Fagen et al.'s (1981) finding, that a reactivation treatment is ineffective

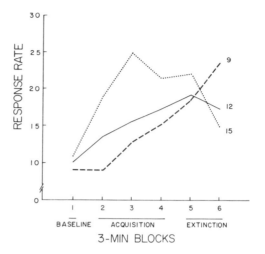

FIG. 5.17. Learning curves of infants trained for the first time at 9 weeks of age and retrained subsequently at 12 and at 15 weeks of age. (Gekoski, 1977)

in facilitating retrieval within an hour, and in many instances even within 8 hours, of its administration when presented after an even shorter retention interval (2 weeks) than that used by Gekoski, the changes in the form of conditioning that she observed can probably be attributed to age-related factors exclusive of a memorial contribution. Finally it is worth noting that premature infants, matched in terms of conceptional age (53 weeks) with full-terms, produce acquisition functions virtually identical to those described for younger infants (Davis & Rovee-Collier, 1983; Gekoski, 1977). Although preterms and full-terms do not differ during the immediate retention test, the preterms show complete forgetting of the contingency, but the full-terms still remember it a week later (Gekoski & Pearlman, 1981).

It is interesting to speculate that the age-related differences in response rate during acquisition may *not* have reflected genuine differences in learning but, rather, age differences in the preferred or effective properties of the visual reinforcer. Since younger infants have a greater lag time in tracking a moving stimulus than older ones (see Aslin, this volume), mobile objects that move rapidly as a result of higher kick rates would present difficulties for sustained fixation or tracking by the younger group. Moreover, since the mobile objects reverse direction and return in a variable path, depending upon kick rate, infants might actually completely "lose sight" of them and find, instead, that different objects have suddenly entered their visual field (only to disappear again). We have observed that low rates of kicking in many 8-week-olds are frequently accompanied by the response-bursting and patterning as well as by the unilateral thrusting (see Fig. 5.5) that is characteristic of more rapidly kicking older infants who have learned the contingency. Moreover, many 8-week-old infants begin to cry during acquisition when kicking reaches a high rate. According to their mothers, they are "frustrated." In addition, the increase in kick rate during extinction exhibited by 8- and 9-week-olds (Davis & Rovee-Collier, 1983; Gekoski, 1977) may *not* reflect a failure to detect the change in the contingency but, rather, an increase in effort associated with the change. This "elbow" effect is characteristic of operant behavior of animals early in the extinction phase and has previously been observed in 3-month-olds in the mobile conjugate reinforcement paradigm following a reduction in the number of mobile components (hence in the intensity of visual stimulation) during acquisition (Fagen & Rovee, 1976). Because conjugate reinforcement paradigms permit the subject to achieve his own preferred level of reinforcing stimulation at any moment in time, we view Gekoski's findings as support for our hypothesis of age-related differences in the contents of infant memories.

From this perspective, let us reconsider the demonstrated efficacy of a reactivation treatment administered to 8-week-olds after a retention interval of almost 3 weeks—the interval between repeated tests used by Gekoski (1977). Even though the preference for rate of visual stimulation has apparently changed over the 3-week period, administration of the previously experienced and self-produced rate of mobile movement to the now older infant is an effective reminder. It remains for future research to determine whether movement of the training mobile at a rate preferred at 3 months but not previously seen 3 weeks earlier can, in fact, serve as an effective reminder. We predict that it would not.

CONCLUSIONS

The data that we have obtained thus far strongly suggest that the most parsimonious account of age-related differences in retention by human infants in the first half-year of life is in terms of differences in the contents of their memories. Manipulations which increase the number or accessibility of the attributes that were presumably encoded as a part of an episode also increase the probability of retention days or weeks later. We have found no evidence to support the notion that there are developmental differences in the mechanisms that underlie memory processing and no evidence that retention deficits on the part of younger infants are attributable either to insufficient encoding or to loss from storage, as has been the prevailing view. Although the cues that are effective in retrieval, and the elaboration of strategies for retrieval, may change over longer developmental periods, the groundwork for the progressive accrual of information over the infancy period has clearly been laid very early in life.

The original question of how early experiences build on each other may find an answer in the reinstatement mechanism. If reactivation or reinstatement can be effective after an interval as long as a month, then it is likely to be effective after intervals even longer. We are currently pursuing this possibility. However, since a memory is likely to be modified by the current context in which it is retrieved, even if not overtly displayed, then it is also possible that memories may be "updated" or even forgotten with changing contexts over successive retrievals. Solving this problem will be a major methodological challenge for future research.

ACKNOWLEDGMENTS

The research described in this chapter was supported by Grant Nos. MH32307 and MH24711 from the National Institute of Mental Health. I am indebted to John Santa, Byron Campbell, and Norman Spear, whose research inspired this work and whose criticisms and suggestions along with those of my husband, George Collier, have sharpened its theoretical and methodological focus. In addition, a number of outstanding graduate students have made substantial contributions to the research program and to the ideas behind it: Janet Davis, Mary Enright, Jeff Fagen, Marcy Gekoski, Marge Sullivan, and Eleanor Vander Linde. Without them and without the undergraduates who contributed long hours and many miles in pursuit of infants, there would be no chapter.

REFERENCES

Allport, G. W. *Personality: A psychological interpretation.* New York: Holt, 1937.
Bergström, R. M. Electrical parameters of the brain during ontogeny. In R. J. Robinson (Ed.), *Brain and early behaviour.* London: Academic Press, 1969.
Berlyne, D. E. *Conflict, arousal and curiosity.* New York: McGraw-Hill, 1960.
Bolles, R. C. Some relationships between learning and memory. In D. L. Medin, W. A. Roberts, & R. T. Davis (Eds.), *Processes of animal memory.* Hillsdale, N.J.: Lawrence Erlbaum Associates, 1976.
Bornstein, M. H. Qualities of color vision in infancy. *Journal of Experimental Child Psychology,* 1975, *19,* 401–419.
Bronson, G. The postnatal growth of visual capacity. *Child Development,* 1974, *45,* 873–890.
Bronson, G. W. *Scanning patterns of human infancy: Implications for visual learning.* Norwood, N.J.: Ablex, 1982.
Campbell, B. A., & Coulter, X. Neural and psychological processes underlying the development of learning and memory. In T. J. Tighe & R. N. Leaton (Eds.), *Habituation: Perspectives from child development, animal behavior, and neurophysiology.* Hillsdale, N.J.: Lawrence Erlbaum Associates, 1976.
Campbell, B. A., & Jaynes, J. Reinstatement. *Psychological Review,* 1966, *73,* 478–480.
Campbell, B. A., & Spear, N. E. Ontogeny of memory. *Psychological Review,* 1972, 79, 215–236.
Cohen, L. B., & Gelber, E. R. Infant visual memory. In L. B. Cohen & P. Salapatek (Eds.), *Infant perception: From sensation to cognition* (Vol. 1). New York: Academic Press, 1975.
Cornell, E. H. Infants' discrimination of photographs of faces following redundant presentations. *Journal of Experimental Child Psychology,* 1974, *18,* 98–106.
Conel, J. L. *The postnatal development of the human cerebral cortex. II. Cortex of the one-month infant.* Cambridge, Mass.: Harvard University Press, 1941
Conel, J. L. *The postnatal development of the human cerebral cortex. III. Cortex of the three-month infant.* Cambridge, Mass.: Harvard University Press, 1947.
Coulter, X. The determinants of infantile amnesia. In N. E. Spear & B. A. Campbell (Eds.), *Ontogeny of learning and memory.* Hillsdale, N.J.: Lawrence Erlbaum Associates, 1979.

Davis, J. *Alleviated forgetting in 8-week-old infants.* Paper presented at the meeting of the Eastern Psychological Association, Hartford, Conn., April 1980.

Enright, M. K. *Comparison of newly acquired and reactivated memories in three-month-old infants.* Unpublished doctoral dissertation, Rutgers University, 1981.

Enright, M. K., Rovee-Collier, C. K., Fagen, J. W., & Caniglia, K. The effects of distributed training on retention of operant conditioning in human infants. *Journal of Experimental Child Psychology,* in press.

Estes, W. K. The statistical approach to learning theory. In S. Koch (Ed.), *Psychology: A study of a sicence* (Vol. 2). New York: McGraw-Hill, 1959.

Fagan, J. F. Memory in the infant. *Journal of Experimental Child Psychology,* 1970, *9,* 217–226.

Fagan, J. F. Infants' delayed recognition memory and forgetting. *Journal of Experimental Child Psychology,* 1973, *16,* 424–450.

Fagen, J. W. Stimulus preference, reinforcer effectiveness, and relational responding in infants. *Child Development,* 1980, *51,* 372–378.

Fagen, J. W. *Long-term memory for stimulus color in young infants.* Paper presented at the meeting of the Society for Research in Child Development, Detroit, Mich., 1983.

Fagen, J. W., Hoffman, M., Rovee-Collier, C. K., & Thompson, S. *Reminiscence following reactivation of infant memory: What a difference a day makes.* Paper presented at the meeting of the Society for Research in Child Development, Boston, Mass., April 1981.

Fagen, J. W., & Rovee, C. K. Effects of quantitative shifts in a visual reinforcer on the instrumental response of infants. *Journal of Experimental Child Psychology,* 1976, *21,* 349–360.

Fagen, J. W., & Rovee-Collier, C. K. A conditioning analysis of infant memory: How do we know that they know what we know they knew? In R. L. Isaacson & N. E. Spear (Eds.), *The expression of knowledge,* New York: Plenum, 1982.

Fagen, J. W., Rovee, C. K., & Kaplan, M. G. Psychophysical scaling of stimulus similarity in 3-month-old infants and adults. *Journal of Experimental Child Psychology,* 1976, *22,* 272–281.

Fagen, J. W., Yengo, L. A., Rovee-Collier, C. K., & Enright, M. K. Reactivation of a visual discrimination in early infancy. *Developmental Psychology,* 1981, *17,* 266–274.

Fantz, R. L. Pattern vision in newborn infants. *Science,* 1963, *140,* 296–297.

Fantz, R. L. Visual perception and experience in early infancy: A look at the hidden side of behavior development. In H. W. Stevenson, E. H. Hess, & H. L. Rheingold (Eds.), *Early behavior: Comparative and developmental approaches.* New York: Wiley, 1967.

Freud, S. *A general introduction to psychoanalysis.* New York: Clarion Books, 1935.

Gekoski, M. J. Visual attention and operant conditioning in infancy: A second look (Doctoral dissertation, Rutgers University, 1977.) *Dissertation Abstracts International,* 1977, *38,* 875B. (University Microfilms No. 77–17, 533)

Gekoski, M. J., & Pearlman, M. A. *Early learning and memory in the preterm infant.* Paper presented at the meeting of the International Society for the Study of Behavioural Development, Toronto, Canada, August 1981.

Gekoski, M. J., Rovee-Collier, C. K., & Carulli-Rabinowitz, V. A longitudinal analysis of inhibition of infant distress: The origins of social expectations. *Infant Behavior and Development,* in press.

Gesell, A. *Infancy and human growth.* New York: Macmillan, 1928.

Gordon, W. C. Age: Is it a constraint on memory content? In N. E. Spear & B. A. Campbell (Eds.), *The ontogeny of learning and memory.* Hillsdale, N.J.: Lawrence Erlbaum Associates, 1979.

Hopkins, J. R., Zelazo, P. R., Jacobson, S. W., & Kagan, J. Infant sensitivity to stimulus schema discrepancy. *Genetic Psychology Monographs,* 1976, *93,* 27–62.

Jenkins, J. J. Remember that old theory of memory? Well, forget it! *American Psychologist,* 1974, *29,* 785–795.

Kagan, J. Growing by leaps: The form of early cognitive development. *The Sciences,* 1979, *19,* 8–12, 32.

Lindsley, O. R. Operant conditioning methods applied to research in chronic schizophrenia. *Psychiatric Research Reports*, 1956, *5*, 118–139.

Lipsitt, L. P. Developmental psychology. In A. Gilgen (Ed.), *Contemporary scientific psychology*. New York: Academic Press, 1970.

Little, A. H. A comparative study of trace and delay conditioning in the human infant (Doctoral dissertation, Brown University, 1973). *Dissertation Abstracts International*, 1974, *34*, 5224B. (University Microfilms No. 74-0346)

MacDonald, S. *Effect of amount of training on long-term retention of three-month-old infants*. Unpublished honor's thesis, Douglass College, Rutgers University, 1980.

Martin, R. M. Effects of familiar and complex stimuli on infant attention. *Developmental Psychology*, 1975, *11*, 178–185.

McGraw, M. B. *Neuromuscular maturation of the human infant*. New York: Columbia University Press, 1943.

Medin, D. L. Animal models and memory models. In D. L. Medin, W. A. Roberts, & R. Davis (Eds.), *Processes in animal memory*. Hillsdale, N.J.: Lawrence Erlbaum Associates, 1976.

Milewski, A. E., & Siqueland, E. R. Discrimination of color and pattern novelty in one-month old infants. *Journal of Experimental Child Psychology*, 1975, *19*, 122–136.

Miller, R. R., & Berk, A. M. Retention over metamorphosis in the African claw-toed frog. *Journal of Experimental Psychology: Animal Behavior Processes*, 1977, *3*, 343–356.

Miller, R. R., & Berk, A. M. Sources of infantile amnesia. In N. E. Spear & B. A. Campbell (Eds.), *Ontogeny of learning and memory*. Hillsdale, N.J.: Lawrence Erlbaum Associates, 1979.

Olson, G. M. An information-processing analysis of visual memory and habituation in infants. In T. J. Tighe & R. N. Leaton (Eds.), *Habituation: Perspectives from child development, animal behavior, and neurophysiology*. Hillsdale, N.J.: Lawrence Erlbaum Associates, 1976.

Pancrantz, P. J., & Cohen, L. B. Recovery of habituation in infants. *Journal of Experimental Child Psychology*, 1970, *9*, 208–216.

Papousek, H. Experimental studies of appetitional behavior in human newborns and infants. In H. W. Stevenson, E. H. Hess, & H. L. Rheingold (Eds.), *Early behavior: Comparative and developmental approaches*. New York: Wiley, 1967.

Panneton, R. , & DeCasper,A., *Newborns are sensitive to temporal and behavioral contingencies*. Paper presented at the meeting of the International Conference on Infant Studies, Austin, Texas, March 1982.

Piaget, J. *Origins of intelligence in children*. New York: International Universities Press, 1952.

Rescorla, R. A., & Wagner, A. R. A theory of Pavlovian conditioning: Variations in the effectiveness of reinforcement and nonreinforcement. In A. H. Black & W. F. Prokasy (Eds.), *Classical conditioning II: Current research and theory*. New York: Appleton-Century-Crofts, 1972.

Rovee, C. K., & Fagen, J. W. Extended conditioning and 24-hour retention in infants. *Journal of Experimental Child Psychology*, 1976, *21*, 1–11.

Rovee, C. K., & Rovee, D. T. Conjugate reinforcement of infant exploratory behavior. *Journal of Experimental Child Psychology*, 1969, *8*, 33–39.

Rovee-Collier, C. K., & Capatides, J. B. Positive behavioral contrast in 3-month-old infants on multiple conjugate reinforcement schedules. *Journal of the Experimental Analysis of Behavior*, 1979, *32*, 15–27.

Rovee-Collier, C. K., Enright, M. K., Lucas, D., Fagen, J. W., & Gekoski, M. J. The forgetting of newly acquired and reactivated memories of 3-month-old infants. *Infant Behavior and Development*, 1981, *4*, 317–331.

Rovee-Collier, C. K., & Fagen, J. W. The retrieval of memory in early infancy. In L. P. Lipsitt (Ed.), *Advances in infancy research* (Vol. 1). Norwood, N.J.: Ablex Pub. Corp., 1981.

Rovee-Collier, C. K., & Gekoski, M. J. The economics of infancy: A review of conjugate reinforcement. In H. W. Reese & L. P. Lipsitt (Eds.), *Advances in child development and behavior* (Vol. 13). New York: Academic Press, 1979.

Rovee-Collier, C. K., & Lipsitt, L. P. Learning, adaptation, and memory. In P. Stratton (Ed.), *Psychobiology of the newborn*. London: Wiley, 1982.

Rovee-Collier, C. K., Morrongiello, B. A., Aron, M., & Kupersmidt, J. Topographical response differentiation and reversal in 3-month-old infants. *Infant Behavior and Development*, 1978, *1*, 323–333.

Rovee-Collier, C. K., & Sullivan, M. W. Organization of infant memory. *Journal of Experimental Psychology: Human Learning and Memory*, 1980, *6*, 798–807.

Rovee-Collier, C. K., Sullivan, M. W., Enright, M. K., Lucas, D., & Fagen, J. W. Reactivation of infant memory. *Science*, 1980, *208*, 1159–1161.

Schachtel, E. G. On memory and childhood amnesia. *Psychiatry*, 1947, *10*, 1–26.

Siqueland, E. R. *Visual reinforcement and exploratory behavior in infants*. Paper presented at the meeting of the Society for Research in Child Development, Worcester, Mass., 1968.

Siqueland, E. R. *The development of instrumental exploratory behavior during the first year of human life*. Paper presented at the meeting of the Society for Research in Child Development, Santa Monica, Calif., March 1969.

Skinner, B. F. *The behavior of organisms: An experimental analysis*. New York: Appleton-Century-Crofts, 1938.

Skinner, B. F. *Science and human behavior*. New York: Macmillan, 1953.

Sluckin, W. *Early learning in man and animal*. London: George Allen & Unwin, 1970.

Sokolov, E. N. *Perception and the conditioned reflex*. New York: Macmillan, 1963.

Spear, N. E. Retrieval of memory in animals. *Psychological Review*, 1973, *80*, 163–194.

Spear, N. E. *The processing of memories: Forgetting and retention*. Hillsdale, N.J.: Lawrence Erlbaum Associates, 1978.

Spear, N. E., & Campbell, B. A. *Ontogeny of learning and memory*. Hillsdale, N.J.: Lawrence Erlbaum Associates, 1979.

Spear, N. E., & Parsons, P. J. Analysis of a reactivation treatment: Ontogenetic determinants of alleviated forgetting. In D. L. Medin, W. A. Roberts, & R. T. Davis (Eds.), *Processes of animal memory*. Hillsdale, N.J.: Lawrence Erlbaum Associates, 1976.

Sterman, M. B. Ontogeny of sleep: Implications for function In R. Drucker-Colin, M. Shkurovich, & M. B. Sterman (Eds.), *The functions of sleep*. New York: Academic Press, 1979.

Stinson, F. S. Visual short-term memory in four-month infants. (Doctoral dissertation, Brown University, 1971). *Dissertation Abstracts International*, 1973, *33*, 3998–3999B. (University Microfilms No. 73–2340).

Sullivan, M. W. Infant learning in a memory paradigm: Long-term retention and alleviated forgetting (Doctoral dissertation, Rutgers University, 1980). *Dissertation Abstracts International*, 1980, *40*, 5259B. (University Microfilms No. 80–8923).

Sullivan, M. W. Reactivation: Priming forgotten memories in human infants. *Child Development*, 1982, *53*, 516–523.

Sullivan, M. W., Rovee-Collier, C. K., Tynes, D. M. A conditioning analysis of infant long-term memory. *Child Development*, 1979, *50*, 555–556.

Tulving, E. Episodic and semantic memory. In E. Tulving & W. Donaldson (Eds.), *Organization of memory*. New York: Academic Press, 1972.

Underwood, B. J. Attributes of memory. *Psychological Review*, 1969, *76*, 559–573.

Vander Linde, E. *The effects of training factors on acquisition and retention in early infancy*. Unpublished doctoral dissertation, Rutgers University, 1982.

Volkmann, F. C., & Dobson, M. V. Infant responses of ocular fixation to moving visual stimuli. *Journal of Experimental Child Psychology*, 1976, *22*, 86–99.

Watson, J. B. *Behaviorism* (1st ed.). Chicago: University of Chicago Press, 1930.

Werner, J. S., & Perlmutter, M. Development of visual memory in infants. In H. W. Reese & L. P. Lipsitt (Eds.), *Advances in child development and behavior* (Vol. 14). New York: Academic Press, 1979.

6

Ontogeny of Appetitive Learning: Independent Ingestion as a Model Motivational System

Ingrid B. Johanson
Florida Atlantic University

W. G. Hall
Duke University

INTRODUCTION

The psychobiological study of how learning and memory develop has been plagued by a paradox. On the one hand, there is an enormous amount of evidence that early experiences can exert lasting effects on later behavior (see Hunt, 1979 for review). On the other hand, there are numerous studies that indicate poor memory in infants (Campbell & Coulter, 1976; Spear, this volume). These seemingly contradictory observations are slowly being reconciled, now, largely because of a change in how we view infants and infant behavior.

Drawing from both developmental biology and psychology, the emerging approach, rather than emphasizing infants' deficiencies and their immaturity, views infants at any one stage of development as being particularly well adapted to their environment (Oppenheim, 1981). By acknowledging the infant's unique behavioral competence at each age, as well as incorporating age-specific motoric capabilities into their experimental strategy, researchers have been able to demonstrate that newborns of many mammalian species are capable of quite complex learning (e.g., beagle puppies, Bacon & Stanley, 1970; kittens, Bloch & Martinoy, 1981; human infants, Rovee-Collier, Sullivan, Enright, Lucas, & Fagen, 1980 and present volume). Studies such as these, and our own to be discussed below, demonstrate that in the context of an age-appropriate paradigm a broad group of altricial and precocial infants possess fundamental learning capabilities, and thus the neural mechanisms to subserve them. The question is no longer "Do young infants learn?", but becomes a more complicated and demanding query into the ontogenetic course of learning processes (prophesied by Campbell & Coulter, 1976). How does learning change during development? How do we identify these changes in process within the totality and confounds of the developing organism? And finally, how do each of these interacting changes affect memories for early events?

To date, our own orientation to these questions has been to provide a description of the early sensory and motor competence of one species, rat, and with respect to one behavioral system, ingestion. We have tried to comprehend the manner in which the ingestive system is at each age adapted to the organism's status, as well as the manner in which factors influencing the system change. This provides a context in which to explore learning in terms of how infants incorporate particular types of experiences related to ingestion at particular stages of development. In the following sections, we first describe a simple ingestive system of infant rats, showing how sensory determinants of this behavior change developmentally and how the response system matures. We then demonstrate how this "motivational" system can subserve or mediate a number of types of learning and show how the learning, and memory for it, are dependent on the sensory and motor constraints characteristic of a specific age. These data will, we hope, provide some perspectives on the kinds of issues that need to be addressed in studying the ontogeny of learning.

A Few Comments on Infant Rats

Many psychobiological studies of learning development have utilized rodent neonates, especially infant rats. The rat pup is not simply a subject of convenience; it is uniquely suited for such analysis by virtue of its initial primitive state and subsequent rapid development. In the few weeks after birth, rat pups undergo a remarkable transition, from helpless, underdeveloped, altricial neonates—blind, deaf, naked, and inactive—to fully-furred, active, and adultlike weanlings. As a result, in rat pups there is an evolving array of physiological and behavioral states compressed into a short period of time. Each of these represents a timely adaptation of the developing organism, providing us with the opportunity to evaluate behavioral mechanisms through a series of adaptive stages.

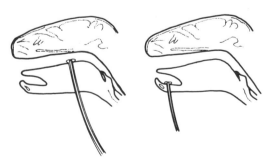

FIG. 6.1. Diagrams of sagittal sections through the heads of infant rats indicating the location of posterior (left) and anterior (right) oral cannulae. Milk delivered at the back of the tongue is reflexively swallowed and intake is independent of deprivational state; milk infused into the front of the pup's mouth is either moved to the back of the mouth and swallowed, or is actively rejected, depending on deprivational state.

Moreover, it provides the opportunity to relate neural development, which is also impressive in the postnatal period, to changing behavioral processes and learning and memory capabilities. This same neural and behavioral immaturity does pose special challenges to those interested in studying early behavior, but many innovative methodologies have been developed in the last 10 years.

INGESTIVE BEHAVIOR: A PROTOTYPIC MOTIVATIONAL SYSTEM

General Characteristics

Our studies have as their basis an ingestive system in infant rats that can be studied apart from suckling and the normal mother-infant interactive situation. This system offers many experimental advantages over suckling as a study system. More importantly, it is a system that has continuity into adult behavior, and, as will be seen, possesses many affective or motivational characteristics from early ages. Suckling, while a fascinating form of ingestion in its own right, seems to have little representation in adult behavior (Hall & Williams, in press) and thus does not offer as good an opportunity for longitudinal analysis.

The essential features of the early ingestive system are as follows: From birth, infant rats actively ingest milk infused into their mouths through intraoral cannulas (Fig. 6.1, Hall, 1979a,b). These cannulas have been used for most of the work we describe because they allow a high degree of control over stimulus presentation, but similar active ingestion can also be demonstrated when milk or other diets are spread on the floor underneath pups (Hall & Bryan, 1980). The amount of diet pups consume depends on their deprivational state. Nondeprived pups consume very little, but as length of food deprivation increases, so does milk intake. Thus, intake in young rats is already under physiological control.

Significantly, intake in deprived pups less than 9 days of age is accompanied by a dramatic behavioral activation (Fig. 6.2), characterized by mouthing, probing, rolling, and excited locomotion. As pups grow older, these global activational responses disappear and when pups are fed they engage more exclusively in ingestive responding.

Sensory Determinants of Ingestion

Two types of sensory factors contribute to the control of early ingestion, general contextual sensory cues and the specific sensory stimuli of food and feeding. The meaning and significance of both types of sensory control changes developmentally.

General Contextual Cues. We were able to demonstrate ingestion in neonates (where others had not) simply because we fed pups in *warm* test incubators

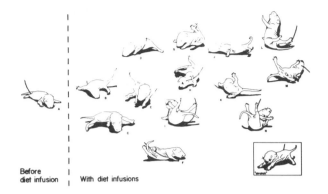

Before
diet infusion   With diet infusions

FIG. 6.2.   Diagram of some of the behaviors shown by 3-day-old pups in response to milk infusions. The individual drawings do not portray an actual sequence, but do give examples of pups' initial response to infusion with mouthing
and probing of the floor (B, C) that becomes more vigorous and is extended to
twisting and locomotion (D, E, F, G). Pups then often roll and curl (H, I) and
exhibit forms of locomotion, probing, reaching, and posturing (J–N). Some of
these responses appear to be fragments of adult behavior patterns (e.g., grooming), while others may be search patterns used in suckling. Some of the positions
are also suggestive of righting attempts, but more often than not, these movements
are initiated from an upright position.

(32°–34°C). Vigorous ingestive behavior, including intake and behavioral activation, was shown only by pups fed in a warm environment (Johanson & Hall,
1980). If oral diet infusions were made at room temperature (22°–24°C), pups
did not ingest, but rather rejected the diets (Fig. 6.3). Further studies revealed
that it was pups' perception of ambient temperature, rather than their general
body temperature, that played the primary role in determining ingestion and
activity. Pups that had their body temperatures cooled to 29°C (36°C is normal
nest temperature) before being fed immediately ingested diet and became active
when placed in a warm environment. In contrast, warm pups immediately offered food in a cool environment refused to ingest. Thus, even at very young
ages, pups' perception of their environment made a significant permissive contribution to how they responded to specific feeding stimuli and in particular
whether food was actively and excitedly responded to.

While we found temperature to be an important permissive cue for young
pups, control of ingestion by contextual cues became more complex in older
pups. At 6 days of age, the additional presence of home odors enhanced the vigor
of ingestive behaviors, and by 12 days, the presence of a sibling significantly
increased food intake (Johanson & Hall, 1981). Thus, the functioning of the
early ingestive system seems to be dependent on an increasingly complex contextual sensory control. Pups seem to interpret the significance of new types of
stimuli (such as food infused into their mouths) on the basis of environmental

conditions, and the conditions to which they attend change dramatically in just 2 weeks. We do not know yet whether these later types of environmental constraints are elaborated on the initial temperature-dependence system, or whether they represent additional neural control systems superimposed on the more primitive system.

Specific Stimuli.   Responsiveness to specific ingestive stimuli (given a permissive context) also changes developmentally (Hall & Bryan, 1981). When intake and behavior were studied in a series of experiments in which various concentrations of either quinine or sucrose were infused, it was found that young pups did not differentiate these solutions from water (Fig. 6.4). By 6 days of age, though, pups increased their intake and behavioral activity to sucrose infusions, while failing to detect quinine. Only at 9 days of age did pups begin to respond to the bitter characteristics of quinine by rejecting it. Developmental changes are also known to occur in olfactory and oral-tactile systems.

These changes in the effects of both general environmental cues and specific ingestive stimuli illustrate one of the difficult problems for developmental studies of more complex behavioral processes such as learning (also see Rudy et al., this volume). It is very difficult to equate stimuli, or the interpretation of stimuli, from one age to another. If the taste of sucrose is different at 6 days and 25 days, what stimulus does an investigator give a 25-day-old to test its memory for a 6-day taste experience? Descriptive studies like ours, while not answering such questions, certainly call attention to their troublesomeness.

Response Characteristics

As we mentioned earlier, the behavioral activation seen in response to diet infusions diminishes with age. Pups older than 9 days of age tend to just lower their snouts and lap when a milk infusion is made, much as if they thought the milk was on the floor in front of them. In other studies (Hall & Bryan, 1980), we have also shown that as pups grow older they get better at directing their re-

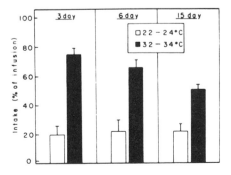

FIG. 6.3.   Mean intake of 3-, 6-, and 15-day-old pups fed in either a cool (22°–24°C) or warm (32°–34°C) environment. Milk intake is severely depressed in cool environments.

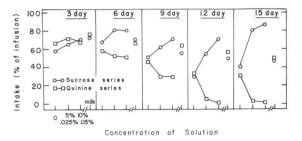

FIG. 6.4.   Mean intake data for 24-hour-deprived pups of various ages, in either sucrose- or quinine-infusion series. Intake data are expressed as a percentage of the infusion that was consumed; total infusion volume was equal to 2.5% of the average weight of pups of each age.

sponses towards food. Neonates are unable to consume milk efficiently if it is restricted to a small area of the test container, whereas pups over 9 days of age can direct their ingestive responses to the milk and consume it effectively.

This shift from generalized activation to more directed activity could represent a general shift in neural functioning. When young pups are aroused or excited, a number of behavior patterns are recruited—perhaps virtually all the behavioral fragments that the pups have available. Activation in older pups, though, seems to excite more specific and appropriate output systems. Recent electrical stimulation studies (Moran, Lew, & Blass, 1981) depicts this process nicely. Medial forebrain bundle (reward and arousal pathways) stimulation in young pups elicits an array of behaviors (very similar to those in Fig. 6.2). In older pups stimulation tends to elicit only a single behavior pattern, though the pattern varies among animals.

As with developmentally changing sensory function, developmentally changing response patterns complicate the ontogenetic study of behavioral processes. For example, if a response or group of responses come to be associated with a particular stimulus in the infant, with what should that stimulus be associated in an older animal where the early response system has perhaps differentiated into several separately elicitable response systems? Such questions are, perhaps, not as troubling as they are instructive, for data bearing on them may provide considerable information on organizational processes operating within the brain of maturing animals.

INCORPORATING EXPERIENCE INTO THE INGESTIVE SYSTEM

We have now set the stage for a demonstration of learning processes that relate directly to early ingestion and a consideration of this learning in relation to developmental changes occurring within the ingestive system. We should point out early learning in rats has been convincingly demonstrated, but primarily within the context of aversive and noningestion related learning. An early study by Caldwell and Werboff (1962) reported simple escape learning in newborn rats: neonates presented with a vibrotactile CS prior to footshock showed conditioned limb withdrawal to the CS. More complex escape and avoidance learning was reported in pups from 1 to 2 weeks of age (Misanin, Nagy, Keiser, & Bowen, 1971; Schulenburg, Riccio, & Stikes, 1971; Smith & Spear, 1978).

Aversion learning has also been well documented within the area of ingestive responding. For example, Rudy and Cheatle (1977) found that 2-day-old pups learn and retain for at least 6 days an aversion to an odor associated with illness, and taste aversions have also been conditioned in rat neonates (Martin & Alberts, 1979). This paradigm has been successfully used to demonstrate conditioning at the youngest age yet reported: rat fetuses exposed, on Day 20 of gestation, to a taste/odor stimulus paired with LiCl-induced illness show a marked aversion to that stimulus 16 days after birth (Stickrod, Kimble, & Smotherman, 1982).

The ingestive motivational system is, however, primarily an appetitive system. Until very recently, relatively little work had been done on the appetitive learning capabilities of infant rats, although we must assume that normally there are many opportunities for infants of most species to be influenced by positively reinforcing events, such as food, warmth, and maternal care. An early study by Thoman, Wetzel, and Levine (1968) reported that pups as young as 3 days learned to recognize a tube used to feed them. This recognition was not seen in pups intubated but not fed through the tube. Unfortunately, the findings were confounded by the fact that control pups were returned to the dam and were hence in a different deprivational state than the tube-fed, incubator-reared pups. Most of the differences in recognition (activity and mouthing) may have, in fact, reflected these differences in deprivational state.

Our involvement in the ontogeny of appetitive learning began with the speculation that the behavioral activation shown by young pups to milk infusions was an external manifestation of positive affect, and the occurrence of primitive reinforcement or reward (given the similar behavioral profile elicited by medial forebrain bundle stimulation, this becomes less speculative [Moran et al., 1981]). Would learning occur with respect to (1) the ingestive responses themselves, (2) orientation to stimuli in the environment associated with food, and (3) integrated operant response patterns that would produce milk reward?

Response Conditioning

To determine whether pups' ingestive responses (see Fig. 6.2) could come to be elicited by cues associated with feeding, we developed a classical conditioning procedure in which a novel odor was paired with milk infusions. The odor was presented by pumping a light stream of cedar odor into a pup's test container. The onset of the odor cue preceded milk infusion by 5 seconds, and odor continued during a 5-second milk infusion. We gave pups 15 to 20 trials, spaced

4 minutes apart. This allowed the behavioral reaction to the milk infusion to subside somewhat before the next trial. Pups' behavior was scored during this 5-second interval, as well as 1 minute before and 1 minute after milk infusion.

From 3 to 12 days of age, pups that were exposed to cedar odor before each milk infusion showed conditioned responding (anticipatory mouthing, probing, and activity) to the odor after 4 to 5 training trials. Controls that were exposed to milk only, cedar only, or milk for 15 trials and then cedar/milk pairings for 5 trials (as a control for sensitization) all showed no change in responding over training (Fig. 6.5 for mouthing responses at all ages).

Ten minutes after the last training trial, pups were given five trials with cedar alone, spaced 2 minutes apart. During these trials, trained 3- and 6-day-old pups were much more active than their controls in the minute following cedar onset, and at all ages trained pups mouthed and probed more than controls (Fig. 6.6, for mouthing at all ages). Such conditioned responding developed only if odor preceded milk infusions during training, in that pups that received "backward conditioning" treatment (milk before cedar exposure) did not differ from controls in level of activity, mouthing, or probing during these trials. While 1-day-old pups did not show any evidence of learning on the same day they were trained, they did mouth and probe more than controls 24 hours after training, and we discuss this later. The conditioned responding appeared to be elicited with some degree of specificity. Three-, 6- and 9-day-old pups trained with a cedar airstream as the conditioned stimulus showed conditioned mouthing and probing to the odor of cedar after training, but were unresponsive to either clove or unscented airstreams (Fig. 6.7). However, this is not to say that ingestive re-

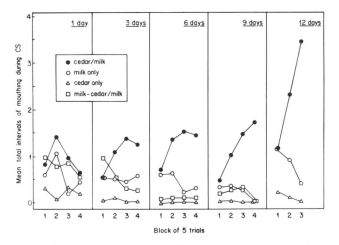

FIG. 6.5.   Mean mouthing scores in the CS interval during training of 1-, 3-, 6-, 9-, and 12-day-old pups. Trials are presented in blocks of five trials. The maximum mouthing score is 5.

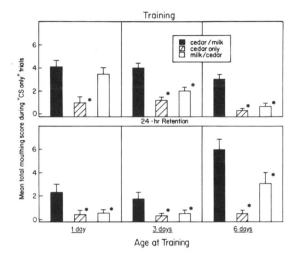

FIG. 6.6.   Mean mouthing scores of 1-, 3-, and 6-day-old pups during five trials of CS exposure alone at the end of the training session. The scores were obtained by totaling ratings in the CS interval and the four subsequent 15-second intervals (5 intervals scored per trial for five trials). The maximum mouthing score is 25.

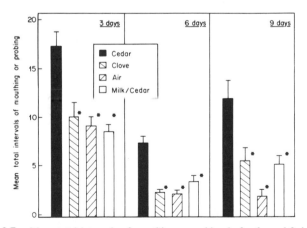

FIG. 6.7.   Mean total intervals of mouthing or probing in 3-, 6-, and 9-day-old pups tested for generalization of conditioned responding. Pups were trained using cedar odor as the CS, and were then tested either with cedar, clove, or an unscented airstream during "CS only" trials. Pups responded only to the cedar airstream with mouthing or probing.

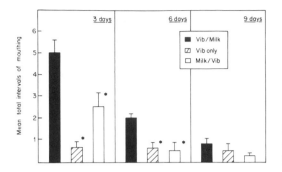

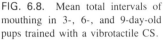

FIG. 6.8. Mean total intervals of mouthing in 3-, 6-, and 9-day-old pups trained with a vibrotactile CS.

sponses cannot be conditioned to other types of conditioned stimuli. Three- and 6-day-olds, trained with a vibrotactile CS, showed conditioned mouthing to the vibration alone after training (though the levels of responding were lower than seen with the odor CS; Fig. 6.8). Similarly, Rudy and Hyson (1981) have observed conditioning of mouthing to an auditory CS starting at about 14 days of age. However, it appears that for younger pups and our particular procedures, at least, the olfactory cue produced much more robust conditioning.

Conditioning of ingestive responses depended on pups' internal state. Three-day-old pups that were dehydrated with hypertonic saline probed a bit more to the odor CS following odor/milk pairings, but showed no conditioned activity or mouthing, despite having actively mouthed to milk infusions during training.

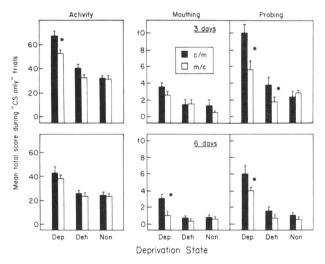

FIG. 6.9. Mean activity, mouthing, and probing scores for dehydrated and non-deprived 3- and 6-day-old pups, compared with 24-hr-deprived pups.

Nondeprived 3-day-olds and both dehydrated and nondeprived 6-day-olds showed no evidence of conditioning at all (Fig. 6.9). Thus, conditioning of components of ingestive responding depends on pups' deprivational state.

Conditioning of an Orientation to an Odor

Inspired by the odor aversion paradigm developed by Rudy and Cheatle (1977), we assessed pups' relative preference for odors that were associated with oral milk infusions. For this analysis, we chose an odor—cedar—that is usually aversive to pups reared in pine bedding, to determine whether we could change the pups' normal withdrawal response to the odor to one of approach. The cedar airstream was presented for 15 seconds before a brief milk infusion. Controls were exposed to cedar only, infused with milk only, infused with milk and then later exposed to cedar, or were untreated. After 10 training trials, pups were given a two-choice test similar to the one used by Cornwell (1975) and Rudy and Cheatle (1977). Pups were placed on a screen suspended over a container that had pine-scented shavings on one side and cedar-scented shavings on the other side. We measured time spent over pine or cedar in five 1-minute trials.

Deprived 3-day-old pups that were exposed to cedar odor prior to milk infusions spent more time over cedar than any of the controls, and they also spent much more time over cedar than pine (Fig. 6.10). In fact, 8 of 10 trained pups spent twice as much time over cedar as pine. Of 40 pups in the four control groups, only 2 showed such a preference for cedar odor (Johanson & Teicher, 1980; Johanson & Hall, 1982). Conditioning occurred at 6 days as well, but was less robust than at 3 days. Six-day-old pups did not spend more time over cedar than pine, but they no longer showed the marked aversion to cedar seen in their

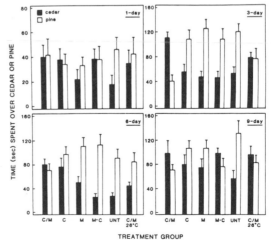

FIG. 6.10. Mean time spent over cedar or pine for 3-day-old pups. Experimental pups (C/M) were given 10 cedar/milk pairings. Controls received cedar exposure alone (C); milk infusions alone (M); milk infusions followed by cedar exposure (M/C); no treatment (UNT); or cedar/milk C/M pairings at 26°C.

controls. The altered response to cedar was retained by both 3- and 6-day-olds for at least 24 hours, indicating good retention after just a few training trials. At 1 and 9 days of age, there was surprisingly no evidence that pairing cedar odor with milk altered pups' relative preference for cedar. This is not to say that these pups did not associate cedar with milk, since we have found that both 1- and 9-day-olds showed conditioning of components of their ingestive responding to cedar odor.

As was the case with response conditioning, deprivational state is an important determinant of whether pups' responses to an odor are altered as a result of pairing with milk. Both nondeprived and dehydrated 3- and 6-day-old pups that received the training treatment did not spend more time over cedar than pine and behaved similarly to littermate controls. A possible explanation for why deprivation is necessary for conditioning is that it creates a state of activation or "arousal" in pups. In fact, there is now growing evidence that activation, along with milk infusions, may play a major role in early olfactory learning. Pederson and Williams (1980) report that stimulating pups (by amphetamine injection or by stroking with a soft brush) in the presence of an odor results in pups' preferentially attaching to nipples scented with that odor. More recently, Brake (1981) found that any of several methods for producing activation (e.g., tail pinch, exposure to salivary gland odor, or stroking) could be paired with a novel odor to produce a relative preference for that odor. This suggests that activation per se is reinforcing to infant rats. In our own work, simple exposure to cedar odor following amphetamine treatment was not sufficient to produce altered orientation to cedar odor; only pups given cedar/milk pairings showed conditioning. This does not rule out the importance of activation in our paradigm, but it does suggest that specific forms of activation may be required for conditioning to occur.

Because warmth appears to be such an important contextual determinant of pups' response to milk, it was not surprising that warmth enhances the reinforcing aspects of milk. Fewer 3-day-olds oriented toward cedar if the cedar/milk pairings occurred at room temperature, rather than in a warm incubator, and by 6 days, warmth was necessary for conditioning to occur. This finding provided our first evidence that the same contextual cues that influence pups' ingestive behavior would also modulate the rewarding aspects of milk infusions. What we feel may be the case, but do not have data for yet, is that like ingestive motivation, the necessary conditions for learning will become increasingly complex as pups grow older and that other factors in pups' environments will come to serve as perceptual constraints on the occurrence of learning. We believe that we have a model in this process of how major changes can occur in the kinds of experiences that infants integrate into their response patterns, and in particular how the same experiences can have markedly different effects at different ages. Indeed, this process calls attention to developmental differences in attention and perception.

Operant Conditioning in Neonates

Recently, progress has been made in assessing appetitive instrumental learning by using simple locomotor tasks and rewards appropriate to neonates. For example, Bulut and Altman (1974) found that 6- to 10-day-old pups could acquire and reverse a spatial discrimination when the reward was exposure to the nest. Similarly, pups about 1 week of age will learn to choose one arm of a Y-maze (Kenny & Blass, 1977) or increase their runway running speed (Amsel, Burdette, & Letz, 1976) for the opportunity to suckle their anesthetized dam. Since our interest was in learning in newborns, these various runway or maze tasks were inappropriate. The task that we developed took advantage of an upward probing response that we had occasionally observed when pups were fed with milk. One- and 3-day-old pups were placed in a styrofoam cup and were required to probe up into a terrycloth covered paddle over their heads (Fig. 6.11). If a pup probed with sufficient force, an infusion pump was turned on and a small amount of milk was delivered into the pup's mouth via an intraoral cannula.

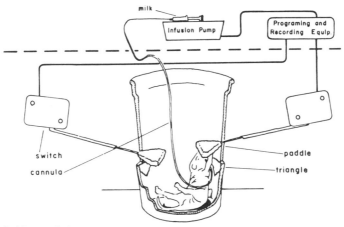

FIG. 6.11. Diagram of the apparatus used for the operant learning experiments. The test container was a styrofoam cup. Terrycloth covered paddles extended into the container and were mounted 3–4 cm from the floor. An upward force of 3 to 3.5 g was required to activate an infusion. In the simple learning paradigm, pups were provided with one paddle. In the discrimination situation (shown here), two different odors were placed on terrycloth triangles below the paddles. An upward probe into one paddle produced a small milk infusion into the pup's mouth; a probe into the other paddle only triggered a counter. The test container was placed inside an incubator maintained at 34°C. An infusion pump and recording equipment were located outside the incubator.

We found that pups as young as 1 day were capable of appetitive learning for milk reward (Johanson & Hall, 1979). Pups learned to probe into the paddle for milk reward and did so several hundred times over the 12 to 16 hours of testing (Fig. 6.12a). In contrast, yoked controls (pups that received milk whenever the experimental pup responded, but their own paddle was ineffective) and deprived controls (pups that had a paddle but did not receive milk) probed at much lower rates. As would be expected, rates of responding for experimental pups and controls were initially quite similar, but after a few hours of training, experimental pups probed at much higher rates. The experimental pups frequently showed bursts of responding, followed by long periods without responding. During extinction, experimental pups initially responded at higher rates than controls. There was considerable variability in the extent to which their responding declined over the 6-hour extinction period. Typically, however, pups showed decreased responding, with occasional bursts of responding at high rates.

Three-day-old pups were tested for retention of the learned response 24 hours after the initial training. They were returned to test containers and allowed to respond for 6 hours, with no milk reward. Of 6 pups tested in this way, 5 responded at higher rates than their controls, though the absolute number of responses was quite variable. Thus, some pups trained at 3 days can retain the learned response for at least 24 hours.

To determine whether deprived neonates were capable of more complex discrimination learning, we placed two paddles in pups' test containers, each la-

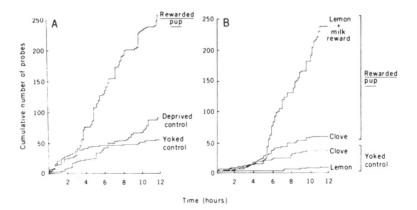

FIG. 6.12.   (A) Cumulative number of probes (in 10-minute intervals) into the paddle made by a representative 1-day-old pup that was rewarded with a small oral milk infusion for each probe. The littermate "yoked control" and "deprived control" pups made considerably fewer probes over the 12 hours of testing. (B) Cumulative number of upward probes (in 10-minute intervals) made by a representative pup in the discrimination situation. The pup appeared to have learned to discriminate the paddle that rewarded it from the one that did not. This pup's littermate yoked control did little probing and did not show a discrimination.

beled with a different odor and only one of which provided milk. One- and 3-day-old experimental pups learned to discriminate between the two paddles and restricted their probing response to the paddle that produced milk (Fig. 6.12b). For example, at 3 days, experimental pups responded an average of 288 times (16-hour total) on the rewarding paddle compared to an average of 111 times on the nonrewarding paddle. Yoked controls responded at a lower overall rate and failed to discriminate between the two paddles (mean 16 hour totals, 94 vs. 92). If the paddles were reversed (so that the previously rewarding paddle was now ineffective and probes into the previously ineffective paddle were now rewarded) pups continued at first to respond at a high rate to the paddle that previously produced reward, but eventually shifted their responding to the new rewarding paddle.

Time-lapse videotape recording of pups' behavior during training has provided additional information about changes in response topography that occur over training. We found that 3-day-old pups generally became more "efficient" in their probing responses. Initially, there were many incomplete probes (that is, pups made contact with the paddles, but with insufficient force to activate an infusion). As training progressed, there was a marked decline in the number of incomplete probes in four of five trained pups. Further, the approach used by the pups varied during training, from an upward reach into the paddle to a more direct, "head-on" push into the paddle (Fig. 6.13).

Because the response we chose to reinforce is also occasionally elicited by the reinforcer, we were concerned that perhaps the milk was activating the experimental pups when they were near the rewarding paddle, thus inflating the number of responses and our estimate of learning. However, when we counted initiations of bouts of responding (an initiation being a response not preceded by another response for at least 30 seconds), we found that 1-day-old experimental pups initiated responding more than controls, and they also initiated responding on the rewarding paddle more than the nonrewarding paddle. Further, from videotape analysis, it is clear that many of the bouts were initiated from a distance and were not elicited by random contact with the paddle.

To obtain learning in young pups, we have chosen response, reinforcer, and stimulus conditions that are all highly related. While the various controls rule out potential artifacts (such as sensitization), it is probably the case that young pups are well "prepared," in Seligman's (1970) sense, to acquire the upward probing response. In fact, there are probably severe constraints on the kinds of behavioral plasticity that can be shown by young pups. Specifically the probing response that is rewarded is also occasionally elicited by the milk, a situation reminiscent of the phenomenon of "autoshaping." In fact, there are probably several types of associative process involved in this "operant" paddle-probing paradigm, including classically conditioned associations between stimuli. Separate analysis of these conditioned associations (see above) may reveal some of the ways in which classical conditioning and instrumental learning interact to produce adap-

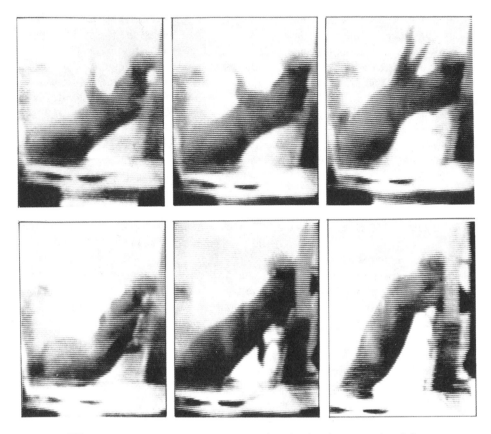

FIG. 6.13.   Photographs from a video monitor showing the topography of the probing responses used by 3-day-old pups in the operant learning situation. The top three photos show a sequence in which a pup probes upward while on its back; the bottom three show a sequence in which a pup pushes its head into the paddle while standing on its hindlimbs. Variations of these probing responses are seen during the operant conditioning.

tive behavior. One virtue of the ingestive system as a model motivational system is that these different types of associative learning can be studied using the same reward or reinforcer.

ONTOGENY OF MEMORY

A recurring theme in current studies of the ontogeny of learning and memory is the recognition that some of the problem in detecting effects of earlier training may result from the manner in which the infant is asked to remember. Frequently, infants' retention is assessed without any additional exposure to training stimuli and as a result is quite poor. However, it now appears that some of the memory deficit observed in infants can be alleviated, or reinstated, by providing "reminder" cues: brief exposures to some aspects of the original training experience, such as the conditioned stimulus or the reinforcer (e.g., in rats, Campbell & Randall, 1976; Haroutunian & Riccio, 1979; Riccio & Haroutunian, 1979; Spear & Smith, 1978; and in humans, Rovee-Collier et al., 1980 and this volume). It may also be that some of the memory deficit results from age-related differences in stimulus selection. That is, the stimuli that an infant attends to in an early learning situation may not be attended to in the same fashion or degree as it grows older (Gordon, 1979). Also, along these lines, it seems reasonable that an acquired response may undergo considerable modification as pups mature, so that the same stimulus that elicited a conditioned response at one age elicits a different response at a later age (e.g., Smith, 1980). To the extent that this is true, a comparison of what is learned at one age with what is remembered at a later age might reveal how response systems are organized and how they change over development.

With these considerations in mind, we became interested in an assessment of long-term memory in pups. We have demonstrated 24-hour retention of both the operant "upward-probing" response and the classically conditioned orientation preference, but the procedure for the classical conditioning of pups' ingestive responses has provided us with the most useful tool with which to assess the ontogeny of long-term memory. We found that pups trained at 1 day of age and then tested 1 day later mouthed and probed to the odor, although they showed little evidence of conditioning on the day they were trained (Fig. 6.14). This finding raises the intriguing possibility that pups show evidence of learning many hours later as a result of having a period of consolidation, or because of the maturation of some components (though not the associative ones) of the learned response system. In addition, 1-day-old pups that were tested for retention 1 day after training and again 3 days after training showed retention of conditioned activity and mouthing at 3 days, whereas pups retested for the first time at 3 days did not. This suggests that the intervening experience with the CS 1 day after training served to "reactivate" the memory.

Conditioned responding to the odor CS was retained for 6 days in 3-day-old pups, and for at least 9 days in 6-day-olds, indicating substantial long-term retention of the odor/milk association (Fig. 6.14). What is of particular interest is the observation that the response profile for activity, mouthing, and probing was more typical of the age at retesting, rather than the age at training. For example, pups trained at 6 days no longer became active to cedar odor at 9 days, though they did mouth and probe (note on Fig. 6.14 that pups trained for the first time at 9 days did not become active to the CS). Possibly, the conditioned response profile changes as the pups mature because, rather than learning a specific

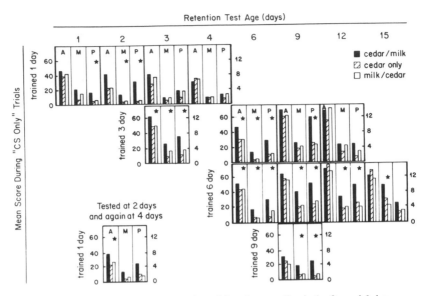

FIG. 6.14.   Long-term retention of conditioned responding in 1-, 3-, and 6-day-old rat pups. The figure shows mean activity, mouthing, and probing scores for pups trained at 1 day of age, and retested 1, 2, or 3 days later, and for pups trained at 3 or 6 days of age and tested 3, 6, or 9 days later.

stimulus-response relationship, pups learned a more general association between the CS and a developing ingestive behavior system. That is, the response profile changed because the same CS that elicited one response pattern at a younger age somehow gained access to the now more mature response system at a later age. It may simply be that certain ingestive behaviors were not as strongly conditioned, or were learned less readily or extinguished more easily, and for these reasons they disappeared more rapidly. However, a convincing case could be made if in retention the CS elicited a more mature response not observed in original training.

AGE-RELATED CONSTRAINTS ON LEARNING AND MEMORY

While there is now overwhelming evidence that infants can learn and remember, we still know very little about the basic mechanism and processes involved in neonatal learning. That is, what do infants learn in a given situation, and why do they learn what they learn?

The current conceptual approach to the ontogeny of learning encourages not only study of conditioning mechanisms as they become more and more complex but also suggests an assessment of how these mechanisms fulfill adaptive needs at each stage in development. Moreover, the current approach calls attention to the special constraints on learning processes that apply to each of these stages. Indeed, the hallmark of studies in early learning and memory is the focus on the nature of the process and the conditions required for early learning to occur.

Contextual Constraints on Learning

The infant's awareness or perception of its environment has become a central theme in recent studies of learning. For example, the context in which infants are trained appears to play an important role in how well they learn and remember. Infant rats trained in the presence of home environment cues acquired shock-escape (Smith & Spear, 1981) and passive-avoidance (Smith & Spear, 1978) responses more quickly. Similarly, the presence of siblings facilitates odor aversion learning in 2-day-old pups (Smith & Spear, 1980). On the other hand, acquisition of taste aversions is hampered by training in the home environment in 18-day-old pups, but not 21-day-old pups or adults (Infurna, Steinert, & Spear, 1979). The suckling context also interferes with acquisition of taste aversions. Ten-day-old pups that received intraoral infusions of milk followed by illness developed strong taste aversions, but only if they were not suckling when they tasted the milk (Martin & Alberts, 1979). The blocking effect of the suckling context appears to be task specific, however, in that 11-day-old pups that received pairings of odor and milk while suckling learned a relative preference for the odor (Brake, 1981). This suggests that the suckling context may prevent pups from learning about aversive events, whereas learning about positive events is unaffected.

All of these studies have in common the idea that infant learning is particularly vulnerable to contextual cues, especially cues from the nest, mother, and siblings. In our own work, the finding that warmth is a necessary condition for both feeding behavior and the development of orientation preference suggests that perhaps temperature is a major constraint on pups' affective responses to milk. The finding that as pups grow older, other types of cues affect their ingestion, and that these cues become increasingly complex with age, suggests that these same cues may similarly modulate learning as pups grow older. In fact, the absence of these cues (e.g., particularly social stimuli) may explain in part the poor conditioning of orientation preference observed in older pups. On the other hand, these cues may function quite differently in the conditioning of consummatory responses, for example, the components of ingestive responding. We would predict, in fact, that pups trained at room temperature would show conditioned responding, but conditioning of their *aversion* responses, rather than their ingestive responses, inasmuch as pups reject milk presented to them unless they are in a warm environment.

Such a changing dependence on contextual cues may also have important implications for infant memory. Gordon (1979) suggests that there are age-related differences in the types of stimuli that infants attend to in a given learning context. The implication is that at different ages, different stimulus features are judged relevant and are incorporated into long-term memory storage. Thus, memory deficits result because the now older animal selectively attends to other sensory cues, which do not match the cues attended to during the original training. Some support for this idea has come from a study by Solheim, Hensler, and Spear (1980). They found that the retention performance of preweanling rats was quite poor if the sensory context during retention testing was markedly different from that during training, suggesting that infants may attend to different (and often "irrelevant") features of the environment than adults. Furthermore, it may not be sufficient to simply duplicate the environment in which an infant was trained in order to obtain good retention of learning. Rather, it may be necessary to take into account the (now older) pups' changing dependence on other types of sensory cues, as well, in order to fully tap the infants' memory capabilities.

Age-Related Changes in Response Systems

In addition to ontogenetic changes in the types of sensory cues that infants attend to and learn about, there are also changes in their response systems. This issue has been addressed by Smith (1980), who suggests that learning and memory can be greatly facilitated by considering pups' "age-specific behavior patterns." Along this line, we feel that it is essential, when assessing retention, to consider and evaluate changes in the response system as pups mature. As pups grow older, specific responses may not be retained and elicited by a conditioned stimulus, though the stimulus may elicit other behaviors more appropriate to the pups' present age. In fact, our initial exploration of long-term retention of conditioned ingestive responses suggests that this may be the case. It is becoming increasingly clear that it is only by careful analysis of the ontogenetic changes occurring in both stimulus selectivity and response systems that a meaningful assessment of infant learning and memory can begin.

CONCLUSIONS

We have now described three different types of learning paradigm—all suited to even newborn pups and all having as their basis the developing ingestive behavior system of infant rats. One virtue of working within this framework is that we have a common motivational system—independent feeding—within which to assess several different types of conditioning process. Further, the ingestive behavior system is itself a developing system, and subject to increasingly complex controls. As such, it provides a rich source of both empirical data and theoretical considerations to the study of appetitive learning.

Each of the paradigms described above assesses a change in a different component of the response chain for "food-getting" behavior. First, cues associated with feeding can come to elicit conditioned consummatory reponses (Johanson, Hall, & Polefrone, submitted). Second, pups will learn to orient to an odor cue associated with milk, perhaps ensuring that pups remain in areas where feeding occurs (e.g., Johanson & Hall, 1982; Johanson & Teicher, 1980). Finally, pups learn to emit certain behaviors that are reliably followed by milk reward, and this responding can come under discriminative control (Johanson & Hall, 1979). Thus, in certain contexts, behaviors are performed that produce food. So, both appetitive and consummatory phases of pups' ingestive behavior can come to be modified by cues associated with feeding.

What is especially evident—both from our own work and from other recent work in early learning—is the remarkable learning capabilities of infant rats. Indeed, far from being incapable of associative learning, even newborns appear capable of learning a variety of tasks, from quite simple habituation to rather more complex discriminative operants. It is clear that if any ontogenetic changes occur in learning processes, it is probably in higher order processes. For example, infant rats show age-related differences in both latent inhibition (Johanson, unpublished observations; Rudy & Cheatle, 1979) and a second-order conditioning of odor aversions (Cheatle & Rudy, 1979), though there are no marked age differences in performance on the primary task. We have thus progressed from asking "Do young infants learn?" to much more complex questions regarding the changing contextual constraints on learning, the organization of response systems, and the ontogenesis of higher order learning processes.

REFERENCES

Amsel, A., Burdette, D. R., & Letz, R. Appetitive learning, patterned alternation, and extinction in 10-d-old rats with non-lactating suckling as reward. *Nature,* 1976, *262,* 816–818.

Bacon, W. E., & Stanley, W. C. Reversal learning in neonatal dogs. *Journal of Comparative and Physiological Psychology,* 1970, *3,* 344–350.

Bloch, S. A., & Martinoya, C. Reactivity to light and development of classical cardiac conditioning in the kitten. *Developmental Psychobiology,* 1981, *14,* 83–92.

Brake, S. C. Suckling infant rats learn a preference for a novel olfactory stimulus paired with milk delivery. *Science,* 1981, *211,* 506–508.

Bulut, F. G., & Altman, J. Spatial and tactile discimination learning in infant rats motivated by homing. *Developmental Psychobiology,* 1974, *7,* 465–473.

Caldwell, D. F., & Werboff, J. Classical conditioning in newborn rats. *Science,* 1962, *136,* 1118–1119.

Campbell, B. A., & Coulter, X. The ontogenesis of learning and memory. In M. R. Rosenzweig & E. L. Bennett (Eds.), *Neural mechanisms of learning and memory.* Cambridge: MIT Press, 1976.

Campbell, B. A., & Randall, P. K. The effect of reinstatement stimulus conditions on the maintenance of long-term memory. *Developmental Psychobiology,* 1976, *9,* 325–334.

Cheatle, M. D., & Rudy, J. W. Ontogeny of second-order odor-aversion conditioning in neonatal rats. *Journal of Experimental Psychology: Animal Behavior Processes,* 1979, *5,* 142–151.

Cornwell, C. A. Golden hamster pups adapt to complex rearing odors. *Behavioral Biology,* 1975, *14,* 175–188.

Gordon, W. C. Age: Is it a constraint on memory content? In N. E. Spear & B. A. Campbell (Eds.), *Ontogeny of learning and memory.* Hillsdale, N.J.: Lawrence Erlbaum Associates, 1979.

Hall, W. G. Feeding and behavioral activation in infant rats. *Science,* 1979, *205,* 206–209. (a)

Hall, W. G. The ontogeny of feeding in rats: I. Ingestion and behavioral responses to oral infusions. *Journal of Comparative and Physiological Psychology,* 1979, *93,* 977–1000. (b)

Hall, W. G., & Bryan, T. E. The ontogeny of feeding in rats: II. Independent ingestive behavior. *Journal of Comparative and Physiological Psychology,* 1980, *94,* 746–756.

Hall, W. G., & Bryan, T. E. The ontogeny of feeding in rats: IV. Taste development as measured by intake and behavioral responses to oral infusions of sucrose and quinine. *Journal of Comparative and Physiological Psychology,* 1981, *95,* 240–251.

Hall, W. G., & Williams, C. L. Suckling isn't feeding, or is it? A search for developmental continuities. In J. S. Rosenblatt, R. A. Hinde, C. Beer, & M. C. Busnel (Eds.), *Advances in the study of animal behavior* (Vol. 13), in press, 1983.

Haroutunian, V., & Riccio, D. C. Drug-induced ''arousal'' and the effectiveness of CS exposure in the reinstatement of memory. *Behavioral and Neural Biology,* 1979, *26,* 115–120.

Hunt, J. M. Psychological development: Early experience. *Annual Review of Psychology,* 1979, *30,* 102–144.

Infurna, R. N., Steinert, P. A., & Spear, N. E. Ontogenetic changes in the modulation of taste aversion learning by home environmental cues in rats. *Journal of Comparative and Physiological Psychology,* 1979, *93,* 1097–1108.

Johanson, I. B., & Hall, W. G. Appetitive learning in 1-day-old rat pups. *Science,* 1979, *205,* 419–421.

Johanson, I. B., & Hall, W. G. The ontogeny of feeding in rats: III. Thermal determinants of early ingestive responding. *Journal of Comparative and Physiological Psychology,* 1980, *94,* 977–992.

Johanson, I. B., & Hall, W. G. The ontogeny of feeding in rats: V. The influence of texture, home odor, and sibling presence on ingestive responding. *Journal of Comparative and Physiological Psychology,* 1981, *95,* 837–847.

Johanson, I. B., & Hall, W. G. Appetitive conditioning in neonatal rats: Conditioned orientation to a novel odor. *Developmental Psychobiology,* 1982, *15,* 379–397.

Johanson, I. B., Hall, W. G., & Polefrone, J. M. Appetitive conditioning in neonatal rats: Conditioned ingestive responding to stimuli paired with oral infusions of milk. Manuscript submitted.

Johanson, I. B., & Teicher, M. H. Classical conditioning of an odor preference in 3-day-old rats. *Behavioral and Neural Biology,* 1980, *29,* 132–136.

Kenny, J. T., & Blass, E. M. Suckling as incentive to instrumental learning in preweanling rats. *Science,* 1977, *196,* 898–899.

Martin, L. T., & Alberts, J. R. Taste aversions to mother's milk: The age-related role of nursing in acquisition and expression of a learned association. *Journal of Comparative and Physiological Psychology,* 1979, *93,* 430–445.

Misanin, J. R., Nagy, Z. M., Keiser, E. F., & Bowen, W. Emergence of long-term memory in the neonatal rat. *Journal of Comparative and Physiologial Psychology,* 1971, *77,* 188–199.

Moran, T. H., Lew, M. F., & Blass, E. M. Intracranial self-stimulation in 3-day-old rat pups. *Science,* 1981, *214,* 1366–1368.

Oppenheim, R. W. Ontogenetic adaptations and retrogressive processes in the development of the nervous system and behavior: A neuroembryological perspective. In K. J. Connolly & H. F. R. Prechtl (Eds.), *Maturation and development: Biological and psychological perspectives.* Philadelphia: Lippincott, 1981.

Pedersen, P. E., & Williams, C. L. *Nipple attachment elicited by a novel odor: A demonstration of early olfactory learning in young pups.* Paper presented at the annual meeting of the International Society for Developmental Psychobiology, Cincinnati, 1980.

Riccio, D. C., & Haroutunian, V. Some approaches to the alleviation of ontogenetic memory deficits. In N. E. Spear & B. A. Campbell (Eds.), *Ontogeny of learning and memory.* Hillsdale, N.J.: Lawrence Erlbaum Associates, 1979.

Rovee-Collier, C. K., Sullivan, M. W., Enright, M., Lucas, D., & Fagen, J. W. Reactivation of infant memory. *Science,* 1980, *208,* 1159–1161.
Rudy, J. W., & Cheatle, M. D. Odor-aversion learning in neonatal rats. *Science,* 1977, *198,* 845–846.
Rudy, J. W., & Cheatle, M. D. Ontogeny of associative learning: Acquisition of odor aversions by neonatal rats. In N. E. Spear & B. A. Campbell (Eds.), *Ontogeny of learning and memory.* Hillsdale, N.J.: Lawrence Erlbaum Associates, 1979.
Rudy, J. W., & Hyson, R. L. *Ontogenetic differences in simple and differential Pavlovian conditioning in infant rats.* Paper presented at the annual meeting of the International Society for Developmental Psychobiology, New Orleans, 1981.
Schulenburg, C. J., Riccio, D. C., & Stikes, E. R. Acquisition and retention of passive-avoidance response as a function of age in rats. *Journal of Comparative and Physiological Psychology,* 1971, *74,* 75–83.
Seligman, M. E. P. On the generality of the laws of learning. *Psychological Reviews,* 1970, *77,* 406–418.
Smith, G. J. *Age-specific defense behaviors: Constraints on ontogeny of learning and memory.* Unpublished doctoral dissertation, State University of New York at Binghamton, 1980.
Smith, G. J., & Spear, N. E. Effects of the home environment on withholding behaviors and conditioning in infant and neonatal rats. *Science,* 1978, *202,* 327–329.
Smith, G. J., & Spear, N. E. Facilitation of conditioning in two-day-old rats by training in the presence of conspecifics. *Behavioral and Neural Biology,* 1980, *28,* 491–495.
Smith, G. J., & Spear, N. E. Home environmental stimuli facilitate learning of shock escape discrimination in rats 7–11 days of age. *Behavioral and Neural Biology,* 1981, *31,* 360–365.
Solheim, G. S., Hensler, J. G., & Spear, N. E. Age-dependent contextual effects on short-term active avoidance retention in rats. *Behavioral and Neural Biology,* 1980, *30,* 250–259.
Spear, N. E., & Smith, G. J. Alleviation of forgetting in preweanling rats. *Developmental Psychobiology,* 1978, *11,* 513–529.
Stickrod, G., Kimble, D. P., & Smotherman, W. P. In utero taste/odor aversion conditioning in the rat. *Physiology and Behavior,* 1982, *82,* 5–7.
Thoman, E. B., Wetzel, A., & Levine, S. Learning in the neonatal rat. *Animal Behaviour,* 1968, *16,* 54–57.

7 Memory in Learning: Analysis of Three Momentary Reactions of Infants

John S. Watson
University of California, Berkeley

In the mid-seventies, I reviewed the state of infant memory research for an edition of the *Encyclopédie de la Pléiade* on Psychology (Piaget, Bronkart, & Mounound[1]). Although my personal interest in memory processes was with regard to their relevance to the acquisition phase of response-reward learning, the more general review was an educating experience. In the effort to organize the diverse array of relevant research I found it useful to distinguish between what I called reactive, regenerative, and associative memory.

Reactive memory was proposed as a basis for sensing that an experience is one that has occurred on some occasion previously as opposed to being a novel experience. An example would be when an infant smiles at an object because it is familiar.

Regenerative memory was proposed as a basis of altering present experience so that is shares features—either stimulus structure or behavioral content—with some past experience. An example would be when an infant produces sounds he has heard or made in the past.

Associative memory was proposed as the joining of two or more memories of different experiences, particularly as these occur at different points in time. For example, if an infant is to learn that thrusts of his feet will shake a mobile attached to his crib, then memory of the mobile must in some way be linked with memory of his feet thrusts. And if he is to learn that the sound of his nursery door opening is usually soon followed by the appearance of his mother's face, then

---

[1] My chapter "Memory in infancy." was to appear in J. Piaget, J. P. Bronkart & P. Mounoud (Eds.), *Encyclopédie de la Pléiade: La Psychologie,* Paris: Gallimard. At the time of this writing, it is not clear whether Gallimard will complete the project which was initiated prior to Piaget's death.

memory of her face must be linked to memory of the sounds of the nursery door. Thus, associative memory is a conjunction of memories of two or more prior experiences displayed by the fact that later exposure to one of the experiences (Ey) leads to behavior (B) which implies a composite memory (My, Mx) of the past association of experiences (Ey-Ex), the assumption being that experience (Ey) activates memory (My) which associatively activates additional memory (Mx) which is also reflected in the resulting behavior B. Table 7.1 presents a comparison of the three types of infant memory in these diagrammatic terms. Reference to this comparison should make it clear that associative memory is similar to regenerative memory in that they both involve behavior which implies memory of an absent object or event (Mx), but in the case of associative memory, the behavior need not recreate the absent experience. Table 7.1 also points up that while associative memory is similar to reactive memory in that they both occur at the instigation of the recurrence of an experience (E), in the case of associative memory the behavior (B) not only implies memory (My) of the existent experience (Ey), it also implies the active memory (Mx) of the absent but associated experience (Ex).

Each of these three categories benefits from a further division by the classical distinction between short-term (a few seconds) and long-term (more than a few minutes) memory function. The resulting division of the existing research on infant memory led me to draw two basic conclusions: (1) there is substantial evidence that human infants display memory capacity in each of the categories, and (2) the developmental picture varied in somewhat surprising manner from one category to another.

During the 7 years since the writing of that review, considerable advancement in research has occurred in some of these categorical domains (Cohen & Gelber, 1975; Fagen & Rovee-Collier, 1982; Fagan & Singer, in press; Rovee-Collier & Sullivan, 1980). Given the diversity of contributors to this volume, there is no need for me to extend my previous overview of the general topic of infant memory capacities. Instead I will take the opportunity to describe some recent work I have been doing on the formation of an associative memory of response-reward contingency in young infants—specifically on the role of constituent memory processes participating in formation of a response-reward association.

TABLE 7.1
Comparison of Three Types of Infant Memory

	Activation	Implied Memory	Behavioral Consequence
Reactive	Ex ⟶	Mx ⟶	B
Regenerative	? ⟶	Mx ⟶	B ⟶ Ex
Associative	Ey ⟶	My + Mx ⟶	B

Because the scope of this volume extends beyond concern for memory in human infancy, I will conclude my discussion with some thoughts on a few topics of research in the broader field of animal memory processes. Before I begin reporting my specific work, however, let me set the stage by introducing a conceptual distinction between "memory *of* learning" and "memory *in* learning" as this pertains to instrumental or operant learning (a similar distinction could be made for classical conditioning).

MEMORY OF LEARNING VERSUS MEMORY IN LEARNING

What I am calling "memory *of* learning" encompasses evidence that the subject has formed an associative memory based on prior learning experience. The classical studies of proactive and retroactive interference are focused on the formation and retention of this kind of memory. Tests of recognition or probes for recall are employed to assess the status of the memory for the focal association. Retroactive interference effects or facilitative reinstatement effects are manipulated by interposing some experience between the time the original learning occurred and the time memory *of* that learning is assessed. Within the past few years great advancement has occurred in our accumulation of information about the human infant's memory *of* learning and his/her sensitivity to subsequent interfering and facilitating experience. Rovee-Collier and her colleagues are responsible for most of that exciting work and she reviews the present state of that research in her chapter of this volume.

One can contrast the concern for memory *of* learning with what I am calling memory *in* learning. The latter is introduced to make reference to memory processes that participate in the formation of a learned association. A classical example of concern for memory *in* learning is provided by studies of the effects of delayed reinforcement. Another is provided by studies of the effects of intertrial interval. The concern here is with how formation of a learned association may be affected by the temporal separation of the constituent units of the basic association. There is an explicit assumption (somewhat tautologically conceived) that if the temporal delay of reward exceeds the subject's memory span then no association will form. On the basis of a fair amount of research to date, it would seem that the human infant, within the first 6 months at least, possesses a memory span for reward delay that is less than 3 seconds (Millar, 1972; Millar & Watson, 1979; Ramey & Ourth, 1971).

Another example of memory *in* learning comes from some earlier work of mine (Watson, 1966) wherein I was attempting to assess a theoretical model of how the infant performs what I termed "contingency analysis"—meaning loosely, how he forms the notion that a particular stimulus is contingent on a particular behavior. I was proposing that the infant began contingency analysis at the time the interesting or rewarding stimulus occurred and the analytic process involved searching memory for a record of the prior (and presumed) effective behavior. The analysis was hypothesized to carry a commitment to repeating the selected behavior under the implicit assumption that this emission of the response would provide a test of the correctness of selection. A concern for memory arose in this theoretical model. It was assumed that the infant's selected response would be subject to the biological constraint of "memory trace fading" and thus the usefulness of the selected response (even if correct) as a test would be lost if the response were not emitted before the end of what I termed the "contingency memory span." Using data from studies of operant conditioning of selective fixation, I was able to obtain evidence that the correctness of the young infant's fixation of one of two spatial positions (3-inch white circles separated by 8 inches on the horizontal axis of a black background) was significantly related to time since he had made the preceding correct and immediately rewarded fixation. Infants' responses following each of the first three rewarded fixations were analyzed. Although I will not take the space here to repeat the statistical basis of the data analysis, the summary plot of results in Fig. 7.1 will suffice to illustrate the basis for concluding that the infants appeared to possess a contingency memory that formed about 2 seconds following reward of the preceding fixation and then lasted until about 5 to 7 seconds following that response-reward experience.

It should be clear that this "contingency memory" function is conceptually and operationally distinct from the memory function assessed be reward delay. They are both examples of memory *in* learning as opposed to memory *of* learning, but they are distinct measurement functions—reward-delay memory being a measurement of response probability as a function of time separating behavior and its subsequent reward, while contingency memory is a measurement of

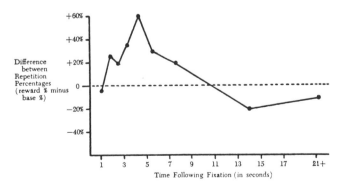

FIG. 7.1. Observed relation between change in rate of fixation repetition and the time following rewarded fixation. From Watson (1966).

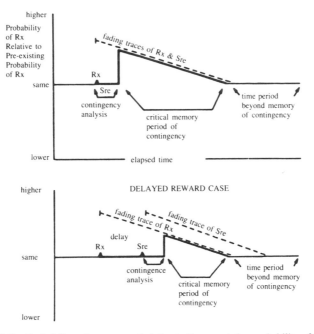

FIG. 7.2.   Probability of a response (relative to the preexisting probability of that response) as a function of time, for immediate reward (upper panel) and delayed reward (lower panel). From Watson (1974).

response probability as a function of time separating reward and the subject's subsequent response.

It is possible, of course, that the two measurement procedures are in fact assessing the same underlying psychological process—their difference in estimate of memory span (3 vs. 5 to 7 seconds) being a consequence of the measurement procedure. I previously offered one conception of the manner in which contingency memory span and reward delay span might simply be two conditions of measuring response memory trace (Watson, 1974). Consider the effect of reward delay on the contingency memory function as shown in Fig. 7.2. Under the assumption that contingency analysis begins in reaction to reward occurrence, the inner boundary of contingency memory span will be displaced in time to the extent that reward is delayed. If one now assumes that the outer boundary of contingency memory is set by the time of prior response occurrence, then it seems clear that the effective time of contingency memory will be severely diminished by delay of reward. Put simply, because contingency memory is memory of the selected response trace, then it would seem reasonable to suspect that the later it is selected the shorter will be the span of time it will be available to guide subsequent response emission. As I point out later, I now believe that this conception may be too simple, but it should help illustrate the general features of the task of examining the potential role of memory processes in the formation of response-reward association.

Let me now turn to some recent methodological and empirical developments from my research on infant response-reward learning that I believe bear directly on the topic of memory *in* learning.

THE ANALYSIS OF "MOMENTARY REACTIONS"

I will present data on what I am tentatively calling three forms of "momentary reaction," each of which appears to play a role in the young infant's adaptation to a contingency between his behavior and a subsequent stimulus event. The reactions I am considering are (1) reaction to the stimulus, (2) reaction to the response—or perhaps it would be clearer to say reaction to having responded, and (3) reaction to a response-stimulus pairing. It is possibly surprising only to me that these three forms of momentary reaction turn out to have a close family resemblance to the three forms of memory process I found within the infant memory literature—namely the stimulus reaction, response reaction, and R-S pair reaction appear to reflect short-term forms of reactive, regenerative, and associative memory respectively.

I have turned to these momentary reactions (which I define below) because the method that I used with fixation responses to assess my "contingency aware-ness" model clearly left something to be desired. First of all, that method was focused on a situation in which two mutually exclusive responses compete for occurrence. That is, the fixation data were obtained in a response-choice situa-tion in which the infant could look to the right circle or to the left circle but not to both at the same time. The momentary probabilities of responding were therefore *relative* probabilities of making one response versus the other. This is not a bad thing per se; it is just somewhat limited in its potential for assessing the model. Although the relative probability did show the predicted positive bulge in the temporal distribution of momentary probability, one cannot tell whether that bulge was due to a positive bulge in the absolute momentary probability of the rewarded response or to a negative bulge in the absolute momentary probability of the nonrewarded response. Moreover, while the situation involving mutually exclusive responses is not a rare situation in life, the more general case of instrumental or operant learning involves single or nonexclusive responses. It was desirable, therefore, that a method be worked out for the testing of the model in the context of nonexclusive responses. I will now describe a method of conditional probability analysis of the temporal contingency between nonexclu-sive events and the results of applying that analysis to response records of 16-week-old infants who were presented the opportunity to control the movement of a TV image by kicks of the right leg. The method involves analysis of event times as these are recorded over a period of many repetitions of the events of interest.

THE METHOD OF CONDITIONAL PROBABILITY ANALYSIS

In general, conditional probability analysis involves estimating the probability of a particular class of event (X) as conditional upon the occurrence of a particular class of event (Y). This probability is usually written P(X/Y) and is read "the probability of X given Y." As I have discussed elsewhere (Watson, 1979), statement of a conditional probability requires reference to a specific span (sometimes called a "bin" or "window") of time (t) in relation to the base event (Y). In the present analyses, the analytic bin is a span (t = 3 seconds) following the occurrence of Y (referred to as Yt). Imagine that in a period of 10 minutes, one observed 20 X's and 30 Y's. For each occurrence of Y, one would ask whether or not an X occurred in the specified span of 3 seconds following Y. Assume the answer were yes for 15 of the 30 Y's. In that case, the conditional probability P(X/Yt) would be 15/30 or .50.

Assuming our 3-second span was a time bin beginning with the occurrence of each Y and ending 3 seconds later, then we might conclude that the conditional probability of X within 3 seconds following Y is .50. To check whether this value is beyond chance expectancy, one would want to compare the observed value with the probability of observing an X within a 3-second time bin chosen at random. This chance value will depend directly upon the temporal rate or density of X (i.e., the number of X's to have occurred during the overall 10-minute observation period). The random-based or unconditional probability of X is given by the formula P(X/Random t) = $1 - e^{-\lambda t}$ where e is the natural log, λ is the observed rate of X over the observation period (e.g. 20 X's/600 seconds), and t is the 3-second bin. This unconditional probability of X for a 3-second span can be compared to the observed conditional probability of X following Y.

As depicted in the examples of Fig. 7.3, if the observed conditional probability of X is greater than the unconditional, one might call this elicitation of X by Y. If the observed conditional probability of X is less than the unconditional, one might call this suppression of X by Y. If the conditional and unconditional values were the same then one would have no basis for assuming any reaction of X to the occurrence of Y.

Figure 7.3 illustrates an additional feature of conditional probability analysis that distinguishes it from the analysis of inter-event times (e.g., inter-response times) which has had a long history of use in animal memory and learning studies (e.g., McGill, 1963). The conditional probability analysis allows a displacement or lag to exist between the setting event (Y) and the temporal bin (e.g., the 3-

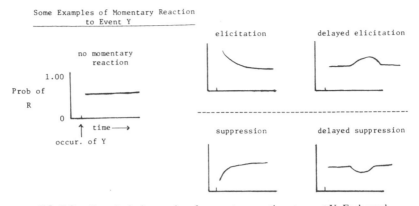

FIG. 7.3.   Hypothetical examples of momentary reactions to event Y. Each graph depicts the conditional probability of a response as a function of the time since event Y.

second span) in which one looks for any occurrence of the focal event (X). Thus one might ask what is the conditional probability of X occurring in a 3-second span which starts 6 seconds after the occurrence of Y. In this analysis it is not relevant whether or not the focal event X occurs in the time between Y and the start of the relevant temporal bin (the span from 6 to 9 seconds following Y), and this allows the method to be far more sensitive to delayed effects than is possible in an analysis of the distribution of inter-event times.[2] Figure 7.3 illustrates instances of both delayed elicitation and delayed suppression.

Let me now share some results of applying the conditional probability analysis to the response records of a sample of 16-week-old infants. The infants were exposed to an instrumental contingency affording either perfect control of a social reward or virtually no control of that stimulus. As illustrated in Fig. 7.4, subjects were seated in front of a color television monitor. For a 1-minute Base Period, the infants saw the "frozen" image of a woman's life-size face. For the next 4 minutes, right foot-movement could cause the image to become enlivened (silent smiling and mouth movement) for a fixed reward length of 2 seconds. Pressure sensitive pillows under the infants' feet were monitored by computer that, in turn, controlled the TV image by advancing and stopping a video tape recording of the woman's expressive facial movement. For infants given perfect

---

[2]To highlight the contrast between conditional probability analysis and inter-event time analysis, one need only note that conditional probability analysis might well uncover a strong delayed elicitation (e.g., in a 3-second bin which is lagged 10 seconds) in a set of data wherein all inter-event times within the observed distribution of intervals were shorter than the specified delay (e.g., less than 10 seconds). In other words, delayed elicitation need not be accompanied by long intervals since the analysis disregards events that occur during the lag time.

control, the social reward was presented immediately following each right foot-movement that caused sufficient pressure on the pillow. For infants with virtually no control, the computer delivered reward for only 10% of the right foot-movements and randomly delivered an average of eight rewards per minute noncontingently so that these infants received virtually the same number of rewards (mean per minute = 6.6) as those having perfect control (mean per minute = 5.8) but for these infants 90% of the rewards were occurring independent of behavior. For simplicity I shall refer to the two groups as representing the contingent and the noncontingent stimulus conditions respectively. These subjects actually were drawn as samples for an experimental examination of a contextual variable that turned out to have no significant effect on learning either directly or interactively with the contingency manipulation.

At the end of 4 minutes of contingent or noncontingent stimulation, infants were removed from the seat for a pause of 3 to 4 minutes prior to an attempt to return them for a second 4-minute session. My laboratory employs a stringent criterion of acceptable state in the effort to avoid artifactual rises in kicking rate due to fussiness. A session is terminated if the infant displays any fussiness (i.e., grimacing and/or crying) for more than 15 seconds consecutively or more than two or three times of shorter duration. Thus, of a starting sample of 146, 97 completed the first session, but only 33 went on to complete both sessions and the intervening pause in an alert and unperturbed disposition.

As shown in panel A of Fig. 7.5, general behavior rate of the two groups during the first session distinguished between the contingency conditions. As expected on the basis of prior research (Watson, 1972; Watson, 1979), the contingent stimulus group tended to increase rate of foot movement from Base to

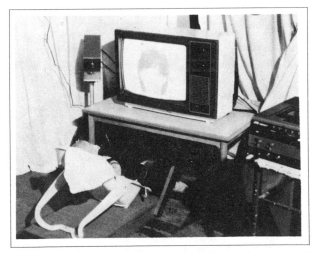

FIG. 7.4.   Apparatus used to obtain response records from 16-week-old infants.

4th minute of contingency ($t = 3.06$, 55df $p < .01$), while the noncontingent stimulus group showed no significant rise in rate over Base rate ($t < 1$, 40 df, NS). If anything, the noncontingent stimulation tends to suppress rate as implied by the behavior of the subsample that completed two sessions, which is presented in panel B of Fig. 7.5.

The preceding analyses are reported here to establish the fact that the standard evaluation of response rate change as a *general reaction* to stimulus contingency did support the conclusion that these 16-week-old infants were sensitive to the manipulation of contingency (100% vs. 10%) in this laboratory arrangement of instrumental control. The data records of these subjects therefore provide an essentially ideal opportunity to evaluate the set of three *momentary reactions* that we assume participate in the formation of the learning which is eventually reflected in any general change in response rate.

The three momentary reactions of interest are (1) *Reaction to the response itself:* (R/Rt), the conditional probability of the focal response given time following a prior occurrence of that response, (2) *Reaction to the stimulus:* (R/S*t), the conditional probability of the focal response given time following a prior occurrence of the stimulus, and (3) *Reaction to R-S* contingency:* (R/R-S*t), the conditional probability of the focal response given time following a prior contingent occurrence of the stimulus.

Analysis of the Reaction to the Response Itself (R/Rt)

The momentary reaction of the infant to having responded is of interest under two conditions. First it is important to discover what this momentary reaction is during the base period. In the absence of the stimulus, does the infant emit foot movements randomly in time or is some temporal dependency evident such that

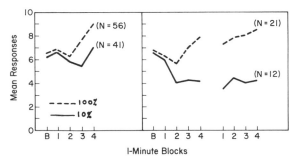

FIG. 7.5.   For 16-week-olds controlling TV face, average number of criterial responses (i.e., kicks) per minute for 1-minute trial blocks as a function of contingency (100% versus 10%). The data in panel A are for 97 infants who completed one 4-minute session successfully; the data in panel B are for the subset of 33 infants who successfully completed two 4-minute sessions.

REACTION TO RESPONSE
BASE PERIOD

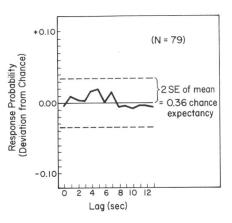

FIG. 7.6. Momentary reaction to the response itself during the 1-minute baseline period. The abscissa is the lag (in sec) between the occurrence of a response and the onset of a 3-second time bin. The ordinate is the mean deviation of the observed conditional probability of the response from the level of chance expectancy.

the response is potentiated or suppressed following its occurrence? And if some dependency exists, is it immediate or delayed? Any notable dependency would carry an implication of short-term regenerative memory as defined above—that is, the experience of responding can be said to have been retained (memory) for as long as regeneration is influenced.

Figure 7.6 presents the results of analyzing the conditional probability (R/Rt) for the right foot-responses occurring during the 1-minute base period of all subjects who completed at least the first session and made at least five responses during the minute (N = 79).[3] This and all subsequent graphs involve plotting the deviation of the observed conditional probability of the response from the level of chance expectancy (i.e., the unconditional probability of the response). For ease of comparison all analyses are based on an analytic time bin of 3 seconds. This span was chosen as a compromise between descriptive detail favored by smaller bin size and statistical stability favored by larger bin size. The graph is the plotting of the average difference between observed and chance expectancy at each of 14 lagged placements of the 3-second bin—that is, from 0 through 13 seconds following the setting event (in this case, occurrence of a response). The analysis for each of the 14 lags involved calculating the observed and expected values for each infant (because chance expectancy is a direct function of an infant's particular response rate) and then deriving the mean and standard error of the mean of observed minus chance expectancy. Each graph includes a set of

---

[3]In each of the following analyses of conditional probability, an arbitrary criterion of at least 5 target (x) events and 5 base (y) events per sampling period (e.g., T = 2 minutes) were required for entry into the analysis in order to obtain a minimal stability of sampling per subject. This explains slight variation in sample sizes for the two portions of a given four minute session.

lines representing the average of 2 standard errors above and below the axis of no-difference. Points exceeding these margins are taken to indicate reliable deviations from a null hypothesis specifying no difference between the conditional and the unconditional probability.

Figure 7.6 shows all lagged bins to exhibit values well within the margins of statistical unreliability. In short, it would seem that during the Base Period, right foot-movement occurs as if the infant were a random generator. Once emitted, a right foot-movement appears to exercise no modulating influence on the probability of a subsequent right-foot movement. There is no evidence of short-term regenerative memory occurring in this situation.

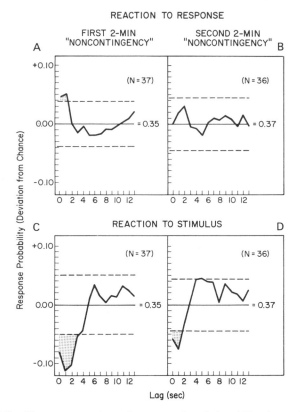

FIG. 7.7. Momentary reaction to the response (panels A and B) and to a stimulus (C and D) for noncontingent presentation of the reward stimulus. In all panels the ordinate is the mean deviation of the observed conditional probability of the response from the chance expectancy. For panels A and B the abscissa is the lag between the occurrence of a response and the onset of a 3-second bin during the first 2 minutes (panel A) and second 2 minutes (panel B) of noncontingent stimulation. For panels C and D, the lag refers to the time between presentation of the social stimulus and the onset of a 3-second bin.

Consider now what happens when the reward stimulus begins occurring non-contingently as displayed in Fig. 7.7A. During the first 2 minutes of exposure to noncontingent reward, the infant's momentary reaction to having responded is strikingly different from that observed in the Base Period. Now there would appear to be a significant elicitation effect wherein having made a response tends to immediately elicit another. For a span of perhaps 3 or 4 seconds, there is evidence of regenerative memory—the tendency to respond is influenced by the experience of having responded seconds earlier. As shown in Fig. 7.7B, this reaction appears to fade rapidly so that it is no longer present in the second 2 minutes of exposure to noncontingent stimulation.

Analysis of the Reaction to the Stimulus (R/S*t)

Let us turn now to the infant's momentary reaction to the noncontingent stimulus. Knowing something about the character of this momentary reaction will help us interpret the potential reaction to contingent occurrences of the stimulus, but it is of interest on its own as well. Does the social stimulus have any direct effect on foot movement? If so, is it an eliciting or suppressing effect? We have already seen an indirect or contextual effect wherein the regenerative tendency of foot movement was apparently influenced for a brief period by the occurrence of noncontingent stimulation. But that effect does not describe the momentary reaction of the response to a specific occurrence of the stimulus. To obtain that description, the conditional probability of the response must be calculated directly on the base of stimulus occurrence times.

Figures 7.7C and 7.7D present the results of the analysis of (R/S*t) for the two 2-minute blocks of the first session. It would seem that a rather strong momentary reaction occurred to the stimulus which is maximal in the 3-second span beginning 1 second following the stimulus. There is some indication that the magnitude and duration of this momentary suppression effect habituates a bit with repeated exposure to the stimulus.

Analysis of the Reaction to R-S* Contingency (R/R-S*t)

The infants' reaction to a contingency experience can now be examined with reasonable sophistication. We have some understanding of infants' reactions to each of the components of an R-S* contingency. If the contingency is of no special importance, then one should expect the observed momentary reaction to be a simple combination of effects already observed for the separable occurrences of R and S*. As we have seen, the separate effects are quite the opposite of one another—at least so during the initial 2 minutes of exposure to the recurrent stimulus. During this time, the response has an immediate elicitation effect upon itself while the stimulus has an immediate suppression effect upon the response. Given the apparent greater strength of the suppression effect, a simple combination of effects would predict an R-S* conjunction to produce a suppression effect of lesser magnitude than that produced by the stimulus alone. In the second 2-minute block, the fact that the response regenerative effect appears to habituate more rapidly than the stimulus suppression effect would lead one to predict an aggregate increase in suppression from an R-S* conjunction.

Examination of Figs. 7.8A and 7.8B shows a pattern of effects that includes each of the above predictions. The initial reaction to R-S* conjunction is less suppression than observed for S* alone, and the continuation of recurrent exposure is accompanied by an increase in the suppression effect to virtually the same level observed for S* alone in the second 2-minute block.

So it would seem that the immediate momentary reaction to an R-S* conjunction is explicable as some simple summation of the momentary reactions to the individual components of that conjunction. However, further examination of Figs. 7.8A and 7.8B indicates the presence of a delayed momentary reaction to R-S* conjunction that is not accountable as a summation of the component effects. Between 5 and 10 seconds following an R-S* conjunction, the infants' probability of foot movement becomes reliably greater than chance expectancy. The strength of this delayed elicitation effect appears to increase from the first to the second half of the 4-minute contingency experiences. It also appears to continue increasing with additional experience of the contingency as indicated by the contrast in momentary reaction exhibited in the second 4-minute session versus the first session for the 21 infants who completed two sessions (see Figs. 7.9A and 7.9B).

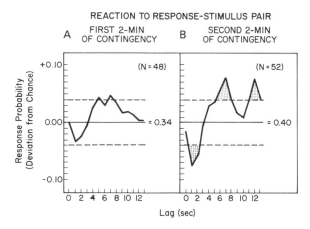

FIG. 7.8.   Momentary reaction to R-S* contingency. The ordinate is the mean deviation of the observed conditional probability of the response from the chance expectancy. The abscissa is the lag between R-S* conjunction and the onset of a 3-second bin for the first (panel A) and second (panel B) two minutes of contingent stimulation.

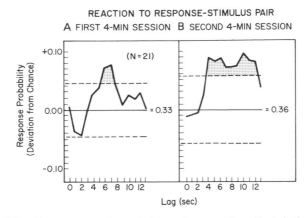

FIG. 7.9.   Momentary reaction to R-S* contingency. The ordinate is the mean
deviation of the observed conditional probability of the response from the chance
expectancy. The abscissa is the lag between R-S* conjunction and the onset of a 3-
second bin for the first 4 minutes of contingent stimulation (panel A) and the
second 4 minutes (panel B).

CONCLUSIONS AND IMPLICATIONS

Let me now propose what I think these momentary reaction data suggest for our
understanding of learning and memory in human infants. I will follow that by
noting the potential relevance of the data and my associated inferences for some
general issues in animal memory and learning.

First consider the momentary reaction to S*. Although investigators of infant
perception have long been taking advantage of response suppression to novel
stimuli—most notable in the so-called habituation-recovery method of measuring
perceptual sensitivity—they have commonly concluded that repeated exposure to
a stimulus can be expected to lead to progressive reduction of its salience or
arousal value as evidenced in the habituation of initial responsiveness (Cohen &
Gelber, 1975; Kagan & Lewis, 1965). Our analysis of momentary reaction to the
TV stimulus presented *non*contingently did uncover this classic pattern. However, when the same stimulus was presented contingently, infants evidenced the
formation and growth of an elicitation reaction. On the surface, at least, this
contrast suggests that the R-S* conjunction may increase the memory or significance of the stimulus. To rule out the possibility that this apparent increase in
salience is not due solely to an underlying change in regenerative response
memory will require additional research, but for the moment the idea that R-S*
contingency experience can increase stimulus significance and/or stimulus memory has an appealing fit with some earlier findings of the arousing effects of R-S*
contingency on social responsiveness (Watson 1972, 1979).

The results of our analysis of momentary reaction to the subjects' *response* are also notable. Recall that we found no evidence of short-term regenerative memory during the base period; but as the noncontingent stimulus began to occur, the infants' response pattern shifted in time from random to a regenerative pattern. My tentative interpretation of this finding is that when the infant experiences a situation of potential contingency (i.e., prior to determining the recurring stimulus is *not* contingent), special investment is made in logging behavioral emission (in effect the infant becomes analogous to what we would describe as *deliberate* or *reflective*). I am assuming that this facilitation of emission by the trace of a prior emission is not necessarily an attempt to control the stimulus but simply the byproduct of the active memory trace. As others before me, I am assuming that the relatively undifferentiated state of the infants' psychological functions allows that memory will "spill over" into action more frequently than we would expect of older subjects (at least those both sane and conscious). The only novel aspect of my assumption is that I am proposing that the infant increases a commitment to response memory as an effect of the exposure to stimuli that hold the potential of being contingent on some response.

The results of the momentary reaction to an R-S* pairing are admittedly my favorite. They provide nice support for the contingency memory model I have been working on for some years now. They also suggest a significant modification of that model. In the original formulation, the outerbound of contingency memory was specified by the trace decay of the response. On the basis of the momentary reaction data, it would seem that contingency memory would be best conceived as having a life span of its own. It would appear capable of lasting far longer than either the independent trace effects of the stimulus as measured by reactive memory for the stimulus occurring noncontingently, or the independent trace effects of the response as measured by regenerative memory during noncontingent stimulation episodes. Moreover, the boundary of contingency memory appears readily extended by continued exposure to a contingency. I did not suspect such flexibility would be the case. I am excited by the potential opportunity this flexibility offers for studies of the specific role of contingency memory in transfer of learning.

Developmental Implications

The positive effects of contingency experience on the length of contingency memory naturally leads to a question of whether the short-term forms of reactive, regenerative, and associative memory are affected in any general ways by experience and/or maturation during infancy. Although the data reported here were limited to a sampling of 16-week-olds, the method of analysis is potentially applicable to a broad age range. Future studies with samples of younger and older infants will be necessary for any definitive conclusion on the question of development, but some speculation on the matter is possible at this time.

If one assumes that longer retention is the sign of a more capable memory system and adds to that an assumption that most capacities improve with development, then one might well expect to observe a progressive lengthening of each form of memory. It is my guess, however, that while the preceding conclusion is probably generally true of long-term memory systems, it is probably not true for two of the three short-term forms discussed in this chapter. Rather, I believe the short-term regenerative memory of response and reactive memory of stimulus will be found to become shorter in duration if they change at all with age. I base this surmise primarily on some data relevant to short-term regenerative memory of response.

Piaget's (1952) description of the primary circular reaction stage of sensory-motor intelligence is relevant here. This notable tendency of infants to repeat behaviors as if stimulated by the fact of having just made the response generally disappears by the fourth month. One potential interpretation of this is that the repetition is the effect of (as well as an index of) the active short-term memory trace of prior responding. The longer the trace lasts, the greater the probability of repetition. If so, then it is equally conceivable that the waning of the "repetition compulsion" of the stage of primary circular reactions is itself a reflection of a foreshortening of the short-term memory trace for responses.

It is easy to imagine functional advantages deriving from a rapid movement of experiential records through short-term and on to long-term storage—at least so for pure stimulus or pure response memory. Reciprocally, one can imagine even disruptive effects of a vivid and lingering short-term memory of responses and/or stimuli (analogous to visual disruption by strong afterimages). Yet the same would not seem so for the case of short-term contingency memory. If contingency memory is to guide response selection and confirmation in the infant's adaptation to an existing response-stimulus contingency, then some reasonably protracted short-term memory of the contingency experience would be advantageous. As we have seen in the analysis above, the momentary reaction to the R-S* pairing is not only distinct from the individual (or conceivable combination) momentary reactions to the stimulus and response alone, it is also a much longer lasting reaction. It is my guess that future research will chart a progressive extension of contingency memory, which, in turn, will be associated with the infant's development of increasing capacity to perceive and cope with contingencies in the surrounding world.

Implications for Animal Research

The implications I would draw from my work for the larger domain of animal memory and learning can be stated as two general points. The first is comparatively simple. It is this. The analysis of memory functions has been dominated by an investment in assessing memory for stimuli. This seems so for studies of both short-term and long-term memory and for studies of associative and nonassociative memory. Some notable exceptions come to mind in the classic work on learning response alternation patterns (e.g., RR-LL-RR; Hunter, 1928) and in certain studies of delayed reaction—although the latter really began as an investigation of stimulus memory only to be altered by discovery that many animals were apparently guiding subsequent behavior by referencing response storage (Hunter, 1913).

There would seem no intrinsic reason for greater interest or potential value in the study of stimulus memory, so I suspect the history of our investment has been directed by the greater ease of experimental manipulation of stimuli than responses. That is no small attraction, but I would now conclude that memory-for-response deserves some renewed attention—at least within the topical area of memory *in* learning. Recent conceptual advances in our general appreciation for the ''biological constraints'' that may distinguish the adaptive functions of different species argue for the likelihood that we will discover different patterns of *reactive, regenerative*, and *associative* memory from one species to another—if not also from one adaptive context to another for a particular species (e.g., will social stimuli engage longer reactive memory than nonsocial? will a cry be sensitive to longer reinforcement delay than a smile?).

My second point is a little more elaborate. Basically, it is that research on animal memory and learning will possibly benefit from examining the potential interaction of memory *in* learning with memory *of* learning. To illustrate the point I will consider two provocative areas of animal learning research: work on the interference or ''helplessness'' effect of exposure to noncontingent reinforcement or punishment; and work on what some researchers call ''response marking'' effects that appear to allow an animal to form associative memory for a response-stimulus pairing that involves surprisingly long delay of reinforcement.

Consider first a peculiar aspect of the interference effect uncovered by Seligman and Maier (1967; Maier & Seligman, 1976). Recall that the essential finding is that noncontingent exposure to a particular stimulus will lead to subsequent difficulty for a subject learning to control that stimulus when it is later made contingent on an available response. Why is it that a particular response can have a long history of not being followed by reinforcement without any apparent interference effect? Seligman has occasionally treated the experience of an ineffective response as much the same as the experience of a noncontingent stimulus (Seligman, 1975). Clearly they both imply a lack of contingency—that is, they both violate the concept of an R-S* association. Yet they have distinctly different effects, and their effects appear to trade forms following experience in which the stimulus is controlled by the response. Prior to experience of control, experience of the response as not followed by the stimulus has no detrimental consequence on the potential for later learning of the association, but there is great interference caused by experience of the stimulus occurring independent of the response. By contrast, following a contingency experience in which the stimulus *is* controlled, failure of the contingency by occurrence of an ineffective response will cause emotional and behavioral depression as in classical extinction reactions. Yet if the contingency (at least in cases of positive reinforcement) fails by the occurrence of response-independent stimuli, the subject maintains some level of control of the stimulus in what is termed the "counter freeloading" effect (Singh, 1970).

I view these contrasting effects of R and S* to imply that associative memory is initiated as a process by stimulus experience but not by response experience. Once initiated, I suspect response experience plays an important role in a verification process that involves some sort of memory-guided expectancy and some mechanisms for confirmation/disconfirmation of the specific R-S* association tentatively formed.

Some of us who have proposed contingency as opposed to contiguity as the "glue" in R-S* learning have implicitly assumed that the subject has access to a reasonably accurate historic record of the serial temporal distribution of past responses and stimuli. Complete evaluation of contingency requires taking into account responses emitted that have not been rewarded and stimuli that have not been preceded by a response, as well as the instances of temporally conjoined (with or without delay) response-stimulus pairing. Those of us who have been concerned with the subject's evaluation of "pairing by chance" have also assumed the subject modifies the estimate of contingency by some evaluation of stimulus and/or response density. This requires some evaluation of the *total time* involved in the *historic sample* of the serial events being accessed (see discussion of Gibbon's versus Wagner-Rescorla's models by Jenkins, Barnes & Barrera, 1981). This is surely assuming a lot. To the extent we take this assumption seriously, it follows that we must view the problem of memory to be not only one for individual events but for a span or time frame of events (in my contingency model I have referred to this as T, Watson, 1979). This "historic sample memory" is a concept quite distinct from contingency memory, response memory, or stimulus memory. With introduction of this historic sample concept one must wonder how far it extends—what determines its boundaries? I have assumed that contingency analysis begins with experience of the significant stimulus. I have also just proposed that response memory is activated or accentuated in the context of contingency experience. Yet one must wonder what sample boundary exists at the time of the first reward experience. In the absence of prior reward stimuli, response memory will presumably be weak—at least, that is what should be expected in the absence of any other form of accentuation of response memory. This line of thought leads me to consider the recent animal studies on delayed reinforcement as potentially very relevant to the question of sample memory boundary.

Garcia's (Garcia, Ervin, & Koelling, 1966) discovery of taste aversion conditioning while using prolonged delay of reinforcement was a resounding shock to proponents of the contiguity model of learning. How could a rat or coyote associate the aversive stimuli of illness to the response of eating novel food hours previously? While taste cues appear to play an essential role in these species, Wilcoxon, Dragoin, and Kral (1971) were able to show virtually the same effect mediated by visual cues in quail. It is not altogether clear whether these dramatic demonstrations of associative memory formation are what should be viewed as R-S versus S-S associations, but recent investigations of *non*aversive conditioning under prolonged delay of reinforcement lead me to suspect that R-S learning can be assisted by direct manipulation of response memory with a procedure called "response marking."

Lett (1974) found that food reward for T maze learning was effective with reward delays up to 1–8 minutes as a function of "marking" the correct response by handling the rat immediately following alley choice. Liebermann, McIntosh, and Thomas (1979) found that auditory and visual stimuli, as well as handling, will provide the marking effect for food delays that, on their own, will not support learning a correct alley choice. Roberts (1982, personal communication) has since extended this line of investigation to a *non*spatial discrimination procedure using lights and sounds as marking stimuli for delays of food reward up to 16 seconds with rats given a simple lever press task. More work needs to be done to assure that these marking effects are not due to some form of direct or secondary reinforcement effects of the marking stimuli. However, the findings to date are encouraging for the view that investigation of processes of memory *in* learning, particularly response memory, is a potentially fertile territory for future research in both memory and learning of animals and human infants.

ACKNOWLEDGMENTS

Research reported here was supported by grants *HD-14393* and *HD-11436* to the author from the National Institute of Child Health and Human Development. Thanks are extended to Dr. Louise Hayes, Richard Ewy, Curt Samuels, Zeynep Biringen, Clare Friedman, and Deborah Bremer for their assistance in the collection and analysis of data.

REFERENCES

Cohen, L. B., & Gelber, E. R. Infant visual memory. In L. Cohen & P. Salapatek (Eds.), *Infant perception: From sensation to cognition* (Vol. 1). New York: Academic Press, 1975.
Fagan, J. F., & Singer, L. T. Infant recognition memory as a measure of intelligence. In L. P. Lipsitt (Ed.), *Advances in infancy research* (Vol. 2). Norwood, N.J.: Ablex, in press.
Fagen, J. W., & Rovee-Collier, C. K. A conditioning analysis of infant memory: How do we know that they know what we know they knew? In R. L. Isaacson & N. E. Spear (Eds.), *The expression of knowledge*. New York: Plenum, 1982.
Garcia, J., Ervin, F. R., & Koelling, R. A. Learning with prolonged delay of reinforcement. *Psychonomic Science*, 1966, 5, 121–122.
Hunter, W. S. The delayed reaction in animals and children. *Behavior Monographs*, 1913, 2, 52–62.

Hunter, W. S. The behavior of raccoons in a double alternation temporal maze. *Journal of Genetic Psychology*, 1928, *35*, 374–388.

Jenkins, H. M., Barnes, R. A., & Barrera, F. J. Why autoshaping depends on trial spacing. In C. M. Locurto, H. S. Terrace, & J. Gibbon (Eds.), *Autoshaping and conditioning theory*. New York: Academic Press, 1981.

Kagan, J., & Lewis, M. Studies of attention in the human infant. *Merrill-Palmer Quarterly*, 1965, *11*, 95–128.

Lett, B. T. Visual discrimination learning with a 1-minute delay of reward. *Learning and Motivation*, 1974, *5*, 174–181.

Lieberman, D. A., McIntosh, D. C., & Thomas, G. V. Learning when reward is delayed: A marking hypothesis. *Journal of Experimental Psychology: Animal Behavior Processes*, 1979, *5*, 224–242.

Maier, S. F., & Seligman, M. E. P. Learned helplessness: Theory and evidence. *Journal of Experimental Psychology: General*, 1976, *105*, 3–46.

McGill, W. J. Stochastic latency mechanisms. In R. D. Luce, R. R. Bush, & E. Galanter (Eds.), *Handbook of Mathematical Psychology* (Vol. 1). New York: John Wiley, 1963.

Millar, W. S. A study of operant conditioning under delayed reinforcement in early infancy. *Monographs of the Society for Research in Child Development*, 1972, No. 147.

Millar, W. S., & Watson, J. S. The effect of delayed feedback on infant learning reexamined. *Child Development*, 1979, *50*, 747–751.

Piaget, J. *The origins of intelligence in children*. New York: International Universities Press, 1952.

Ramey, C. T., & Ourth, L. L. Delayed reinforcement and vocalization rates of infants. *Child Development*, 1971, *42*, 291–297.

Roberts, S. Personal communication, March 1982, Berkeley, California.

Rovee-Collier, C. K., & Sullivan, M. W. Organization of infant memory. *Journal of Experimental Psychology: Human Learning and Memory*, 1980, *6*, 798–807.

Seligman, M. E. P., & Maier, S. F. Failure to escape traumatic shock. *Journal of Experimental Psychology*, 1967, *74*, 1–9.

Seligman, M. E. P. *Helplessness: On depression, development and death*. San Francisco: Freeman, 1975.

Singh, D. Preference for bar pressing to obtain reward over freeloading in rats and children. *Journal of Comparative and Physiological Psychology*, 1970, *73*, 320–327.

Watson, J. S. The development and generalization of "contingency awareness" in early infancy: Some hypotheses. *Merrill-Palmer Quarterly*, 1966, *12*, 123–135.

Watson, J. S. Memory and "contingency analysis" in infant learning. *Merrill-Palmer Quarterly*, 1967, *13*, 55–76.

Watson, J. S. Smiling, cooing, and "the game." *Merrill-Palmer Quarterly*, 1972, *18*, 323–339.

Watson, J. S. *Early infant learning: some roles and measures of memory, thinking and trying*. Invited address to British Psychological Association, Bangor, Wales, 1974.

Watson, J. S. Perception of contingency as a determinant of social responsiveness. In E. Thoman (Ed.), *The origins of social responsiveness*. New York: Lawrence Erlbaum Associates, 1979.

Wilcoxon, H. C., Dragoin, W. B., & Kral, P. A. Illness-induced aversions in rat and quail: relative saliences of visual and gustatory cues. *Science*, 1971, *171*, 826–828.

8

A Developmental Analysis of the Rat's Learned Reactions to Gustatory and Auditory Stimulation

Jerry W. Rudy
Mark B. Vogt
Richard L. Hyson
University of Colorado

INTRODUCTION

Learning processes often play a major role in behavioral adaptation. A learned outcome of an organism-environment interaction depends, of course, upon adequate functioning of the sensory processes that allow the organism to experience the critical events of its world and the memory processes that store representations of experienced events and their relation to one another. The newborn of many species, including humans, are altricial, however. They are born with immature central nervous systems (CNS) and limited sensory and motor processes, relative to their adult counterparts. Consequently, there are serious constraints on the learning potential of such organisms. Indeed one of the remarkable features of altricial animals is the change in their learning capacity that occurs as their sensory systems and central nervous systems develop. As witnessed by the contributions to this volume and preceding ones (Kail & Hagen, 1977; Spear & Campbell, 1979), there has been and continues to be considerable interest in the ontogenesis of learning and memory processes by researchers studying both humans and nonhumans.

In our chapter, we focus on the ontogenesis of learning in nonhumans. First, we briefly discuss some of the important methodological advances in the study of infant animals. Second, we point to some of the limitations of our knowledge about the ontogenesis of animal learning processes. Third, we discuss some conceptual issues that surround this problem area and suggest what we think is a viable research strategy for advancing our understanding of the ontogenesis of learning. Finally, we review some of the recent empirical work from our laboratory to illustrate some advantages of this approach.

RECENT ADVANCES IN THE STUDY OF NEONATAL
LEARNING

In their review of the literature on the ontogenesis of animal learning and memory, Campbell and Coulter (1976) concluded their section on neonatal learning by noting that "given that task demands are appropriate to the neonatal state, learning apparently occurs without difficulty" (p. 211). However, a major limiting factor in our knowledge of the neonate's learning capacities and how they change during ontogeny is the difficulty one faces in assessing these capacities in organisms that have immature sensory and motor processes. The neonate's incomplete sensory development restricts the kinds of stimulus events it can learn about, and its underdeveloped motoric processes make it difficult to obtain behavioral measures that can index any learning that might occur.

Perhaps the most notable advance in the study of the ontogenesis of animal learning and memory since Campbell and Coulter's (1976) review has been the development of a variety of behavioral procedures for assessing the neonate's learning capacity, especially those of the rat. These advances in the study of learning are due, in part, to researchers becoming educated about the "Umwelt" (von Uxeküll, 1957) of the infant rat and developing methodologies predicated on some knowledge of the neonate's relation to its environment.

Like other altricial newborns, the early behavior of the rat is organized around its mother, its siblings, and the nest site. Because its auditory and visual systems do not become functional until well into the second week after birth, the pup's early behavioral reactions are controlled by thermotactile, olfactory, and gustatory stimulation (Rosenblatt, 1979). In addition, because the newborn pup is totally dependent on its mother for nutritive needs, much of its early behavior is devoted to attaching and suckling at the dam's nipple.

Armed with some knowledge of the salient events in the neonatal rat's environment, investigators since the Campbell and Coulter (1976) review have begun to make some inroads into the newborn rat's potential to learn.

Two features of contemporary research are prominent. First, most researchers have employed Pavlovian-like conditioning procedures to probe the learning potential of the neonatal rat. Second, these procedures have most often been used to produce learned changes in the neonate's response to olfactory stimulation. The first point reflects that Pavlovian procedures permit the experimenter great control over the to-be-learned-about events and that the learning experience can be given to the pup independent of its limited behavioral repertoire. The second point reflects that the olfactory system is to some extent functional at birth and that olfactory stimulation plays a major role in organizing and controlling the suckling behavior of the neonate (cf. Teicher & Blass, 1976, 1977).

We now know that learned changes in the neonate's response to olfactory stimuli can be brought about by a variety of experiences. The pup's preference for an odor can be reduced if it experiences that odor paired with either drug-induced illness (Haroutunian & Campbell, 1979; Rudy & Cheatle, 1977, 1979;

Smith & Spear, 1978) or electrical shock (Bryan, reported by Spear, 1979). Its preference for an odor can be enhanced if it experiences that odor paired with either milk infusion (Johanson & Teicher, 1980; Johanson & Hall, 1982), the smell of its mother's saliva, the stroking of its genitalia, the pinching of its tail (Sullivan & Brake, 1981) or the act of suckling (Brake, 1981).

In addition, an odor paired with an inter-oral milk infusion can acquire the power to evoke the mouthing response, elicited unconditionally by the milk infusion itself (Johanson & Hall, 1982, this volume; Johanson, Polefrone, & Hall, 1981).

Although the majority of contemporary investigations into the learning potential of the neonate have centered on Pavlovian paradigms, several researchers have employed instrumental conditioning procedures to produce learned behavior changes. For example, Kenny and Blass (1977) have demonstrated that 7-day-old pups can learn a spatial discrimination when the correct choice is reinforced by the opportunity to suckle a dry nipple. Amsel, Burdette, and Letz (1976) have found that the opportunity to suckle will reinforce increased running speed in a straight alley (see Amsel, 1979, for a summary of this and related work).

SOME LIMITATIONS

It is evident from the above discussion that a number of behavioral procedures are now available to the researcher interested in exploring the learning potential of the neonatal rat and how it changes during ontogenesis. Moreover, several systematic empirical reports centered on one or more of these methodologies have now appeared (cf. Amsel, 1979; Bryan, reported by Spear, 1979; Johanson & Hall, 1982, this volume; Rudy & Cheatle, 1979).

Nevertheless, we have been more impressed with the promise these methodological advances hold for increasing our understanding of the changes in learning potential that occur during ontogenesis than we are with any actual accomplishments toward this goal.

In our view, this is because, to date, there has been very little progress toward the development of a conceptual framework in which to place many of the existing findings and to serve as a guide to future research. In the next sections of this chapter, we sketch such a framework and outline the research strategy it suggests. We then illustrate the usefulness of this approach by describing two lines of research that we have been pursuing.

TOWARD A DEVELOPMENTAL ANALYSIS OF LEARNING

Before discussing issues that surround the ontogenesis of learning, it is useful to consider briefly the concept of learning. Learning, of course, is a theoretical abstraction, an inference one makes on the basis of observing a change in an organism's behavioral reaction to some component of its environment that can be attributed to its prior experience with that environmental event. We call those unobserved, inferred processes, presumed to mediate the experienced-induced behavioral change, learning processes.

As Rescorla and Holland (1976) have noted, investigators of animal learning have focused primarily on analysis of three kinds of experience: (a) presentation of a stimulus event independently of other events (noncontingent stimulus exposure paradigms), (b) presentation of a stimulus contingent upon the occurrence of another stimulus (Pavlovian conditioning paradigms), and (c) presentation of a stimulus event contingent upon some response of the animal (instrumental conditioning paradigms).

The organism's learning processes can then be viewed as extracting and recording from its experience memory representations of (a) the events it experiences, (b) the temporal, spatial, and sequential relation of the experienced events to each other, and (c) the relationship between its own actions to stimulus events that precede and follow the act. Thus, as a consequence of a particular environmental interaction, an organism *potentially* might acquire knowledge that an event exists, knowledge of that event's relation to other events, and knowledge of that event's relation to its own behavior (cf. Rescorla & Holland, 1976).

Ontogenesis and Constraints on Learning

The word potentially is emphasized in the preceding paragraph because an organism-environment interaction need not give rise to a learned change in behavior of any sort. What, if anything, is learned is determined and constrained by biological characteristics of the organism. Therefore, it may be helpful to discuss some of the organismic variables that can constrain the learning.

The first requirement for learning of any sort, of course, is sensory systems appropriate for detecting the environmental stimulation with which the organism is nominally interacting. Obviously, an event not detected cannot be learned about. It does not follow, however, that an organism equipped with sensory systems appropriate for detecting particular stimulus events will necessarily learn and remember anything about the events per se or their relation to each other. Even though the sensory processes necessary for event detection may be present, we can imagine that the learning processes that generate a memory representation for the events may well be absent. Moreover, even though an animal may possess the processes necessary for sensing events and generating memory representations of them, it may lack the *integrative* (associative) processes for learning anything about their relation to each other.

The results of the well-known "cue to consequences" experiment reported by Garcia and Koelling (1966) illustrate this last point. They reported that the drinking response of adult rats was suppressed by an auditory-visual stimulus compound previously paired with electric shock, but this same compound paired with illness failed to suppress drinking. They also reported that a taste cue suppressed drinking when paired with illness but not when paired with shock.

From this pattern of results one can infer that the rat has the sensory processes necessary to detect the four stimulus events and in some sense has a memory for these events. The important implication often drawn from these data, however, is that there may be constraints on the rat's ability to integrate these events. It evidently can easily associate the taste-illness experience (interoceptive events) and the auditory-visual compound with shock (exteroceptive events), but it may not have the same potential for integrating the taste and shock experience or the auditory-visual compound with illness.

It is apparent why it may be appropriate to place the question of the ontogenesis of learning into the more general context of biological constraints on learning. The concept of biological constraints emphasizes that it is the *organism* that is the ultimate determiner of just what aspects of the environment will be learned about, and that different species are predisposed to learn or not learn about different events and about different inter-event relations. The point is that just as species differ in the biological machinery that interfaces them with the environment, so may members of the same species differ during ontogenesis. That is to say, the same organismic variables that determine and constrain what different species learn are also likely to be major sources of variation in learning during ontogenesis.

Placing the question of the ontogenesis of learning into the general context of biological constraints on learning also helps us to appreciate that the learned outcome of an organism-environment interaction is not the product of a single process. It is the orchestrated result of many processes which, during ontogenesis, can be at different levels of functional maturation.

This analysis suggests that the developmental analysis of learning can be conceptualized as a research program designed to determine the comparative functioning, during ontogenesis, of the various component processes that contribute to learned behavioral changes (cf. Gollin, 1965).

The Research Strategy

To determine the set of processes involved in producing any learned behavior change in any organism is challenge enough. To then attempt to make comparative statements about how these processes differ as a function of an organismic variable such as age is a problem of almost overwhelming magnitude.

Our thinking about how to proceed on this problem has been heavily influenced by Gollin (1965, 1970). The essence of Gollin's (1965) idea is that the contribution of any organismic variable (age, genes, brain lesion, species, etc.) to differences in learning potential can only be determined by research designs that vary *both* the organismic variable and the experimental assessment task. Experiments simply comparing the performance of different-aged subjects on a *single* behavioral task can yield age-related differences. They leave untouched, however, the question of process differences that are responsible for the effect. To determine the comparative functioning of the processes involved requires both the subject's age and the assessment procedures to be varied in the same research context. Gollin (1965) has called this a *levels × levels* design, where one level is the organismic variable and the other level is the task variable.

Such research designs can then yield a matrix of data that will provide information about *both* performance *differences,* which are correlated with the organismic variables (e.g., age), and *similarities* that exist despite organism variation. Tentative conclusions or hypotheses about the comparative functioning of the subjects representing different levels of the organismic variable are arrived at by consideration of this matrix of results. These can then be evaluated through additional experimental probes tailored to comment more precisely on the hypotheses.

It should be emphasized that the success of such a program depends critically on the battery of tasks employed to compare subjects representing different levels of some organismic variable. Ideally they should be logically structured to vary along some dimensions that will permit the results to comment on theoretical suppositions that guide the research.

Our experimental work is guided by the view that learning depends upon the sensory processes that mediate the organism's detection and discrimination of environmental events and interface with learning processes that generate (a) memory representations of the experienced stimulus events (event memory processes), and (b) representations of the temporal, spatial, and sequential relations among the experienced events (integrative memory processes). A major goal of our experimental efforts then is to provide information about the comparative function of these processes during ontogenesis. Thus, we attempt to assess different-aged subjects with tasks that index the comparative state of these elementary processes.

Summary

The main points of this discussion may be summarized as follows. The learned outcome of an organism-environment interaction is the orchestrated product of many processes. These include the organism's sensory, event-memory, and integrative-memory processes. What an organism can learn can be constrained by ontogenetic differences in the functional maturity of any of these processes. A primary goal in the developmental analysis of learning is to determine the comparative functioning of these processes in subjects representing different points in the ontogenetic continuum. Reaching this goal can be facilitated by a research strategy centered on what Gollin (1965) has termed a *levels × levels* design in which both the organismic variable (age) and task variable are systematically manipulated so as to provide the researcher with information about both the similarities and differences that exist among different-aged subjects.

SOME ILLUSTRATIONS OF THIS APPROACH

To illustrate the application of this approach, we will describe some of our recent empirical work concerned with a developmental analysis of learning processes mediating the rat's behavioral reaction to two classes of events, gustatory and auditory stimulation. The rat's gustatory system is functional shortly after birth (cf. Mistretta, 1981). Its auditory system, however, is relatively late in developing (Clopton, 1981; Rubel, 1978).

Learning About Gustatory Stimulation

Behavioral reactions to gustatory stimulation can be a matter of life or death because the gustatory receptors are the final point of evaluating (to ingest or reject) a potential food source. Learning and memory processes contribute to the rat's behavioral response to gustatory stimulation in at least two ways (cf. Barker, Best, & Domjan, 1977). First, they reduce the rat's neophobic tendencies (Barnett, 1958). The rat typically ingests very little of a novel food source. Its intake of a particular food source, however, increases as a consequence of repeated experience with that source (cf. Domjan, 1977). Second, the rat acquires aversion to foods that, if ingested, are followed by illness. The adult rat's integrative learning processes in this domain are legendary. It can learn to avoid a specific food source even when illness does not occur until several hours after the ingestional act (Revusky & Garcia, 1970). Presumably, both of these effects, reduced neophobia and food aversion learning, in part, involve learned changes in the rat's response to the gustatory components of the food source.

One of us, Vogt, has begun a developmental analysis of the processes contributing to the rat's learned reaction to gustatory stimulation. This research was designed to determine the relationship, during ontogenesis, of the sensory processes mediating detection of the taste stimulus and those involved in producing learned changes in the pup's behavioral reaction to that taste stimulus. Across several experiments, Vogt has assessed different-aged pups (Sprague-Dawley derived Holtzman rats bred in our laboratory) with behavioral tests that reveal the comparative functioning of (a) the *sensory* processes mediating detection of the taste stimulus, (b) the *integrative* process involved in the production of learned taste aversion, and (c) the *recognition* or event memory processes that mediate reduced neophobic reactions to a taste stimulus.

Sensory Processes

Hall and Bryan (1981) have recently introduced a set of behavioral procedures that can be used to assess the ontogenesis of the processes mediating detection of a gustatory stimulus. Briefly, the gustatory stimulus is infused directly into the pup's mouth through a tongue cannula (cf. Hall & Rosenblatt, 1977). The pup is weighed just prior to and immediately after the infusion. The difference in the pup's pre- and post-infusion weight indexes the amount of fluid the pup consumed. By comparing the amount of the test fluid pups consume with the amount of a standard (e.g., distilled water) consumed by other pups, one can infer whether or not the pups are detecting the difference between the test and standard solution.

Hall and Bryan (1981) have used this procedure to study the development of the rat pup's sensitivity to a 10% sucrose solution. Essentially, they have reported differences in the 6-day-old pup's intake of sucrose versus distilled water and that this difference increases substantially with age (until the pup is about 15 days old).

Vogt's initial experiment was modeled after Hall and Bryan's (1980). Nondeprived pups, 6, 9, 12, or 15 days old, were infused via a cheek cannula (see Rudy and Hyson, 1982) with a fixed amount (3% of their body weight infused over a 3-minute time period) of either a 10% sucrose solution or distilled water.

The results of this experiment are presented in Fig. 8.1 as the mean percentage weight gained, obtained by dividing the amount of weight gained as a result of the infusion by the pup's pre-infusion body weight. This figure shows that pups at each test age ingested more of the sucrose solution than of the distilled water and that in general this difference increased with age. Thus, these findings replicate the earlier work of Hall and Bryan.

Integrative Learning Processes

Given that pups at all ages differentiated between sucrose and water, implying that at each age the sensory processes for detecting sucrose were functional, Vogt

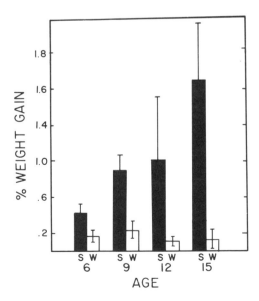

FIG. 8.1. Mean percent weight gain as a function of age. Key: S = sucrose infusion; W = distilled water infusion. Bars indicate standard errors.

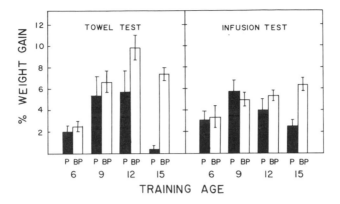

FIG. 8.2.   Mean percent weight gain as a function of training age. Key: P =
Paired presentation of sucrose and LiCl; BP = Backward pairing of sucrose and
LiCl. Bars indicate standard errors.

assessed what pups at these training ages learn from a taste experience. The first
of these results that we report comes from an experiment designed to study
integrative learning involving the sucrose solution as one event and a LiCl-
induced illness as the other. Immediately following their infusion with the
sucrose solution, the pups in the sensory detection experiment each received an
injection of a .15M LiCl solution (2% body weight). To determine if pups given
this paired presentation of sucrose and LiCl (Group P) acquired an aversion to
sucrose, another set of pups at each age received a backward pairing (Group BP)
of these events. Two hours prior to the sucrose infusion those pups received an
injection of LiCl.

Forty-eight hours after training, when deprived of the mother for 24 hours, the
pups were tested for an acquired aversion to sucrose. Half of the animals in each
training condition were tested with the infusion procedure. They received 5% of
their body weight of the sucrose solution, infused over an 8-minute test period.
The other half were tested using another procedure used by Hall and Bryan
(1980) to measure the infant rat's ingestion behavior, the so-called "towel test."
Pups in the "towel test" procedure were placed for 20 minutes on a terry-cloth
towel soaked in the sucrose solution. Percentage weight gain was the dependent
variable used in both tests.

As one can see in Fig. 8.2, the same general pattern of results was produced
by both test procedures. Note that the pup's training age was a major source of
variance among the training conditions. There were no differences between
Groups P and BP when pups were trained at 6 and 9 days of age. There were
reliable differences between these two groups, on both measures, when the pups
were trained when 15 days old. Only the towel test, however, produced a reliable
difference between these two training conditions for pups that were conditioned

when 12 days old. The failure to obtain a reliable difference among 12-day-olds with the infusion test proved to be due to a "ceiling effect" imposed by the infusion procedure. All pups in this experiment were given an infusion of 5% of their body weight during the 8-minute test period. When the test infusion was increased to 10% of their body weight in a follow-up experiment, a reliable difference between 12-day-olds in Groups P versus BP was observed. Thus, the two test (towel versus infusion) procedures yield the same results: No evidence of a learned taste aversion (integrative learning) until the pups were at least 12 days old at the time of training.

These results become especially interesting when they are considered in relation to the results of the sensory detection test (see Fig. 8.1). Recall pups at every age behaved differentially to the sucrose and distilled water. The behavior of the 9- and 12-day-olds in fact was almost identical on the detection task. That pups 9 days old or less failed to display evidence of learning an aversion to the sucrose whereas pups 12 or 15 days old do display such evidence suggests a *dissociation* during ontogenesis between the sensory processes that detect a gustatory stimulus and the integrative processes that mediate acquisition of aversion to that stimulus.

There are, however, many alternatives to the view that the 9-day-old pup does not have the integrative processes necessary for learning the taste aversion. One argument against this position is that even though the 9-day-old can clearly detect a sucrose experience, it fails to learn an aversion to it because the mechanisms whereby LiCl induces such aversions are not yet developed. This hypothesis, however, seems quite unlikely given the large number of published experiments indicating that LiCl can induce learned odor aversions in rats only 2 to 6 days old (cf. Haroutunian & Campbell, 1979; Rudy & Cheatle, 1977, 1979; Smith & Spear, 1978).

Another possibility is that, even though the 9-day-old pup can detect the 10% sucrose solution, this stimulus is not sufficiently salient to be associated with illness. Perhaps a more concentrated sucrose solution (20%) could be associated with illness. Vogt, however, has attempted to condition 9-day-old pups to a 20% sucrose solution. He found no evidence of conditioning, whether or not these animals were later tested for aversion to a 20% or 10% solution.

The data presented in Fig. 8.3 are from an experiment designed to comment on two other interpretations. Both of these possibilities center on the notion that pups 9 days old do indeed acquire an aversion to sucrose paired with illness but that no evidence of this learning is observed for some other reason. One possibility is that there is forgetting over the 48-hour retention interval separating training and testing. The other is that learning is not detected because the response system that is involved in rejecting a taste with acquired aversive properties has not yet developed.

To comment on these two hypotheses, Vogt gave one set of 9-day-old pups a sucrose (10%)-LiCl pairing (Group P) and another set a backward pairing of

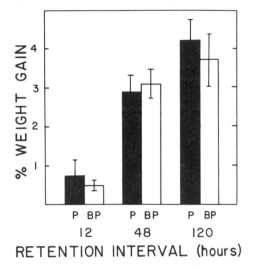

FIG. 8.3. Mean percent weight gain as a function of the retention interval separating training and testing. The pups were 9 days old on training day. Key: P = Paired presentation of sucrose and LiCl; BP = Backward pairing of sucrose and LiCl. Bars indicate standard errors.

these events; LiCl was administered 120 minutes prior to the sucrose solution (Group BP). Animals from each of these two treatment conditions were then tested (infusion test) either 12, 48, or 120 hours later.

As one can see in Fig. 8.3, there were no differences between the two training groups at any retention interval. Unfortunately, the intake of both groups at the 12-hour retention interval was relatively small and this "floor effect" might have prevented one from detecting an effect of the pairing operation. Nevertheless, the failure to find a difference when the retention interval was reduced from 48 to 12 hours offers no support for the notion that there was appreciable forgetting over the 48-hour retention interval. The failure to find evidence of learning when the retention interval was increased to 120 hours provides no support for the view that learning was not detected because the response system mediating the effects of this learning was not yet developed. Recall that pups trained when 12 days old and tested when 14 days old displayed evidence of aversion to sucrose, indicating that the response system involved was functional when pups are 14 days old. Pups conditioned when 9 days old and tested 120 hours later were 14 days old at the time of testing and should have displayed evidence of learning the taste aversion, if this learning was simply awaiting the development of the response system.

To summarize the results to this point: Pups 6 to 15 days old behave differentially when infused with a 10% sucrose solution compared to distilled water. This suggests that sensory processes mediating detection of the sucrose solution are functional in animals at each of these ages. Pups 12 and 15 days old apparently learn an aversion to sucrose when it is paired with LiCl but pups 9 days old or less do not. We have suggested that there may be an ontogenetic dissociation of the sensory processes mediating detection of sucrose and the integrative processes mediating learned taste aversions. Experiments designed to test alternative conceptions of these data have not provided any data that challenge this conception.

The strongest support for the notion that there are ontogenetic constraints imposed on the rat pup's acquisition of a taste aversion by underdeveloped integrative processes, however, is provided by the next experiment. Recall that both 12- and 15-day-old pups acquired aversions to sucrose followed by LiCl-induced illness. Recall also that adult rats can learn aversions to tastes that are separated several hours from illness.

It seems reasonable to suppose that the acquisition of aversion to a taste stimulus separated from illness by an appreciable delay requires more fully developed integrative processes than when there is no appreciable delay. If there is ontogenetic constraint on the integrative processes mediating taste aversion learning, we might then expect to see that even though 12- and 15-day-old pups behave similarly when a minimal delay separates the sucrose-LiCl injection, they might differ when a longer delay is imposed.

The results of Vogt's experiment to test this reasoning are presented in Fig. 8.4. It shows that 15-day-old pups acquire an aversion to sucrose even when a 60-minute delay separated the sucrose and LiCl episodes. The 12-day-old pups, however, did not learn the aversion under these training conditions.

It is of interest to note that this ontogenetic effect is quite general. It has been reported by both Rudy and Cheatle (1979), who employed an odor aversion task, and Gregg, Kittrell, Domjan, and Amsel (1978), who used a saccharin solution in a taste aversion task.

These results provide considerable support for the view of an ontogenetic dissociation between the development of the sensory processes that detect

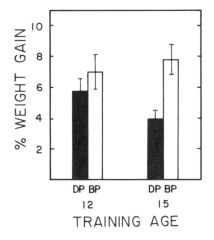

FIG. 8.4. Mean percent weight gain as a function of training age. Key: DP = Delayed pairing; pups in this group received a sucrose infusion 60 minutes prior to the LiCl injection; BP = Backward pairing; pups in this group received the LiCl injection 120 minutes prior to the sucrose infusion. Bars indicate standard errors.

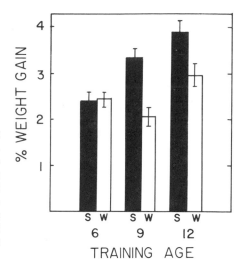

FIG. 8.5. Mean percent weight gain as a function of training age. Key: S = Sucrose: pups in this group were infused with a sucrose solution on the training day; W = Distilled water; pups in this group were infused with distilled water on the training day. All pups were infused with sucrose on the test day. Bars indicate standard errors.

sucrose and the integrative processes that allow the pup to learn aversion to that taste. The 12-day-old pup clearly discriminates sucrose and water and it can learn an aversion to sucrose when LiCl is injected immediately after the sucrose infusion. That it then fails to learn the aversion when a delay between the sucrose and LiCl events is added does not seem to be easily attributable to the processes mediating response to the stimulus events per se. Instead, it appears that the ontogenetic constraint is due to underdeveloped integrative processes.

Recognition Processes

We have suggested that there is an ontogenetic dissociation of the sensory processes mediating the pup's detection of sucrose and the integrative processes mediating learning of an aversion to sucrose. The final experiment by Vogt that we describe was intended to determine the developmental relationship of the learning processes mediating the rat's recognition of, or event memory for, a previously experienced taste to those processes involved in detection and integrative learning.

Recall that the rat is neophobic (Barnett, 1958). It ingests more of a flavor when it has been previously experienced (familiar) than when it is novel. Vogt exploited this phenomenon to get an index of the learning processes that give rise to the rat's memory for a taste event. The experiment was quite simple: Non-deprived pups, 6, 9, or 12 days old, were infused with either a 10% sucrose solution or distilled water. Forty-eight hours later, all pups were tested while 24 hours deprived by being infused with the 10% sucrose solution.

The results of this experiment are presented in Fig. 8.5. Note that there are age-related differences between the two training conditions. Pups preexposed to sucrose when 6 days old did not differ from pups that were given distilled water. Pups preexposed to sucrose when 9 and 12 days old, however, consumed more sucrose on the test day than did the non-preexposed pups. Thus, the evidence suggests that only the 9- and 12-day-old pups recognized the sucrose as familiar.

Summary of Gustatory Experiments

This completes the survey of some of our experiments on the rat's gustatory system. By assessing the performance of different-aged pups with several different tasks (levels x levels design; Gollin, 1965), we have gained some insight into the comparative functioning, during ontogenesis, of processes involved in (a) *detection* of a gustatory event, (b) *recognition* of a gustatory event as previously experienced, and (c) the *integration* of a gustatory experience with an illness episode.

The 6-day-old rat evidently can discriminate to some degree between sucrose and water but appears not to remember a sucrose experience nor to integrate a sucrose and illness experience. The 9-day-old pup can discriminate sucrose from water and can remember a sucrose experience. It evidently cannot, however, integrate a sucrose-illness experience. The 12-day-old pup can discriminate sucrose from water, it can remember an experience with sucrose, and it can integrate a sucrose-illness experience, provided that the sucrose and LiCl are presented in relatively close temporal proximity to each other. Long delays, however, seriously diminish the 12-day-old pup's ability to integrate these events. The 15-day-old pup, in addition to being able to discriminate sucrose from water and to integrate the sucrose-illness events under minimal delay conditions, can also do so even when a 60-minute delay separates these events.

Thus, generally sepaking, the processes subserving relatively simple functions of taste detection and recognition appear to emerge prior to those involved in the more complex integrative functions that mediate taste aversion learning.

Learning About Auditory Stimulation

We now consider some of our research that has been directed at a developmental analysis of processes involved in the rat's learned reactions to change in its acoustic environment. It was noted earlier that the rat's auditory system is relatively late in developing. Both behavioral and electrophysiological research (Brunjes & Alberts, 1981; Clopton, 1981; Crowley & Hepp-Raymond, 1966; Wada, 1923) suggest that the rat begins to respond to sound when about 10 days old. The opening of the auditory meatus, an event of major importance to the rat's response to sound, however, does not occur until the rat is about 12 days old.

Our developmental analysis of learning in the auditory system starts with pups in the 10 to 12-day-old range and makes use of Pavlovian conditioning procedures as a means of inducing learned behavioral reactions to acoustic stimulation. First, we briefly describe the procedure we (Rudy & Hyson, 1982) have developed for this purpose. Then we describe how we have begun to exploit it to developmentally analyze instances of relatively simple and more complex kinds of integrative learning involving auditory stimulation.

The Conditioning Procedure

To study ontogenetic changes in the processes mediating learning about the acoustic environment we (Rudy & Hyson, 1982) have developed a Pavlovian conditioning task that can be easily employed with pups 10 to 25 days old. The unconditioned stimulus (US) in this procedure is a 10% sucrose solution (.10 ml), infused directly into the pup's mouth through a cannula implanted in its cheek. This stimulus evokes, unconditionally, vigorous mouthing activity, the opening and closing of the pup's jaw. This behavior comes to be evoked as a conditioned response to an auditory stimulus paired with sucrose infusion. The dependent variable that serves as our index of learning is the time, during the CS, that the pup is engaged in mouthing. We obtain this measure from video recordings of the conditioning sessions. In all of these experiments, the pups were deprived for 12–14 hours of food and water by separating the litters from the mother.

That this procedure is an effective one for studying integrative learning involving an auditory stimulus is illustrated by the experiment Rudy and Hyson (1982) reported. In this experiment, a 2000 Hz, 92 dB tone served as the CS. The tone was presented for 15 seconds and the US infusion was initiated 10 seconds after CS onset. There were 10 trials per session, separated by about 6 minutes. The pups were 12 days old at the start of the training.

The results of this experiment are displayed in Fig. 8.6. This figure presents not only data for pups that received CS-US pairings, but also data for pups that received a number of conventional control treatments (cf. Rescorla, 1967). It is apparent that the CS-US pairing treatment generated substantial mouthing behavior to the CS, whereas neither of the control treatments did so. Thus, we can be assured that the mouthing behavior displayed by pups in the pairing condition reflects integrative or associative learning.

Simple Integration

The first step toward an ontogenetic analysis of the learning processes involved in this task was taken by Hyson. Using the same training parameters as those Rudy and Hyson employed, he compared pups that were 10, 12, 14, or 16 days old at the start of training. The results of this experiment are presented in Fig. 8.7. To understand these data, it is useful to conceptualize the experiment as one designed to yield positive transfer. In this case, if one assumed that the sensory

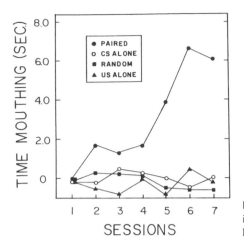

FIG. 8.6.   Mean time mouthing during the 10-second CS period. (From Rudy & Hyson, 1982.)

and integrative processes mediating acquisition of conditioned responding were similarly functional in pups of all ages, then one would expect that the conditioned response should emerge at an earlier age, the younger the pups were at the start of training.

The results, however, do not completely conform to this expectation. For example, one would expect that the conditioned response of pups that were 10 and 12 days old at the start of training would emerge before that of pups that were 14 days old. As can be seen in Fig. 8.7, this was clearly not the case. Pups that started when 14 days old did exhibit more responding when 16 days old than did pups that started at 16 days of age.

Thus, there is no evidence that the training trials administered to pups less than 14 days old contributed toward acquisition of conditioned responding to the

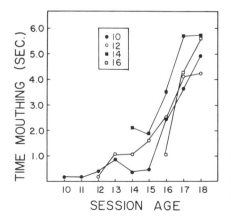

FIG. 8.7.   Mean time mouthing during the 10-second CS period by pups either 10, 12, 14, or 16 days old at the start of training. The CS was a 2000 Hz (92dB) tone.

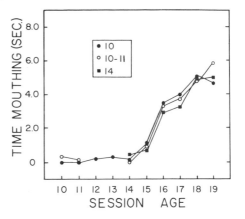

FIG. 8.8.   Mean time mouthing during the 10-second CS period by pups 10 or 14 days old at the start of training. The CS was a 2000 Hz (92dB) tone.

tone. Evidently the processes mediating this learning are not equally functional in pups 10 to 16 days old.

Data presented in Fig. 8.8 are consistent with this conclusion. Pups in this experiment were either 10 or 14 days old at the start of training. One set of 10-day-olds, Group 10, received daily training sessions throughout the experiment. The other set, Group 10–11, received training when 10 and 11 days old and on Days 14–19 after birth. It is clear that the additional training given pups in these two groups gave them no advantage over the pups that were 14 days old at the start.

It is of some interest to identify more clearly just why pups less than 14 days old failed to condition to the 2000 Hz tone, whereas older pups did. The most obvious possibilities center on the functional capabilities of the processes mediating the pup's commerce with the CS and US events per se. On the one hand, pups less than 14 days old might fail to condition because the processes mediating the action of the sucrose US are too immature to promote conditioning. On the other hand, the sensory processes mediating response to the auditory system may be too immature to permit conditioning to the auditory CS (2000 Hz tone).

Hyson conducted an experiment that comments on both of these alternatives. Pups 10, 12, or 14 days old at the start of the experiment were given daily conditioning sessions in which a new auditory CS, a train of clicks (22 cps, 90 dB) served as the CS. All other parameters were the same as those in the previous experiments. Given these parameters, any evidence of conditioning by pups less than 14 days old would argue against the notion that processes mediating the effects of the sucrose US are not sufficiently developed to produce conditioning. Such evidence would also suggest that the previously observed failure of 10 to 13-day-old pups to condition to the 2000 Hz tone was likely due to an immature auditory system.

The results of this experiment are presented in Fig. 8.9. It is evident that pups that began training when 12 days old benefited from the extra training they

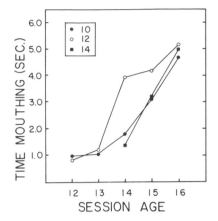

FIG. 8.9. Mean time mouthing during the 10-second CS period by pups 10, 12, or 14 days old at the start of training. The CS was a train of clicks (22cps, 90dB).

received, relative to pups that started when 14 days old. Note that the 12-day-old pups displayed substantially more conditioned responding on Day 14 than did the pups that started training when 14 days old.

Pups that started training when 10 days old, however, did not benefit from the training they received on Days 10 and 11. In fact, they not only failed to differ on Day 12 from pups started when 12 days old, they also did not differ on Day 14 from pups not started until they were 14 days old. This latter finding suggests that the training pups received on Days 10 and 11 had a detrimental effect on their ability to benefit from the training they received on Days 12 and 13. The general implications of this experiment, however, are best seen if we compare its results with those of the previous experiments. When the CS was a 2000 Hz tone, there was no evidence that training influenced the acquisition of conditioned responding until the pups were at least 14 days old. When a train of clicks (22 cps) was the CS, no evidence was obtained that pups 10 to 11 days old benefited from training, but there was substantial evidence that pups 12 to 13 days old benefited from training.

This last fact implies that the processes mediating the action of the sucrose US are sufficiently mature to promote conditioning in pups 12 to 13 days old. The failure of 12 to 13-day-old pups to condition when the 2000 Hz tone was the CS would then appear to be due to constraints imposed by some aspects of the auditory system. Evidently, this system is sufficiently developed to allow conditioning to the train of clicks but will not accommodate the 2000 Hz tone. It will be of considerable interest in the future to provide a better characterization of the critical differences between these two auditory events that permit conditioning to one but not the other by 12 to 13-day-olds.

That 10 to 11-day-old pups failed to condition regardless of the CS could reflect constraints imposed by either an immature auditory system or the system mediating the effects of the sucrose US. It is probable, however, that a primary constraint is in the immature auditory system, probably in the periphery. Recall that the auditory meatus does not open until the pup is about 12 days old, and its presence drastically attenuates the sound intensity (cf. Crowley & Hepp-Raymond, 1966).

Complex Integration

The simple Pavlovian task we employed in the above studies requires that a pup be able to detect change in its acoustic environment, detect the occurrence of the sucrose US, and be capable of integrating the relation between these events. The meaning of acoustic stimulation, however, also can vary with its frequency. Given two tones of different frequency (e.g., 2000 Hz and 900 Hz), presentation of one (T_1+) might be paired with the sucrose US, but the occurrence of the other (T_2-) might be nonreinforced.

This paradigm is called differential Pavlovian conditioning. When an animal is exposed to the two training episodes, T_1+ and T_2-, in principle, it can learn that one event, T_1, signals US occurrence and the other, T_2, does not. Evidence of such learning is provided when the subject behaves differentially to T_1 and T_2. For the organism to learn these relations, however, requires that it be able to discriminate between the two tones and integrate their occurrence appropriately with US occurrence and absence. Differential Pavlovian conditioning thus would appear to place greater demands on the organism's learning capacity than would simple Pavlovian conditioning.

The final experiments we describe were designed to provide information about the ontogeny of the processes that are involved in the differential conditioning paradigm. The procedures were similar to those in the previous studies. Two auditory events, usually a 2000 Hz and 900 Hz tone (92 dB), served as CSs and the US was an infusion of a 10% sucrose solution. Typically the 2000 Hz tone was paired with the US (T_1+) and the 900 Hz tone was nonreinforced (T_2-). During a daily session, pups received eight trials of each type, according to an irregular sequence. These trials were separated on the average by 4 minutes.

Our first experiment with this procedure compared pups that were either 12, 14, or 16 days old at the start of training. The results of this experiment are presented in Fig. 8.10. It is evident that rat pups can learn to respond differentially to the two auditory CSs. The more interesting outcome revealed by this figure, however, is that regardless of the age (12, 14, or 16 days old) at which pups started training, differential mouthing to the two CSs did not emerge until they were about 19 days old. It appears as if the conditioning trials given to pups less than 16 days old contributed little if anything to the subsequent emergence of differential responding. This implies, of course, that there are important differences between 12- to 14- and 16-day-olds in the processes that contribute to this learned behavior change.

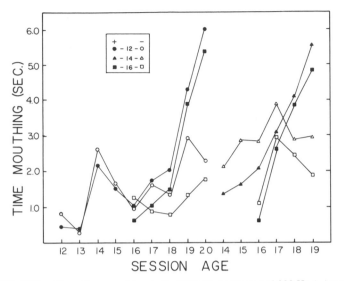

FIG. 8.10.   Mean time mouthing to the 2000 Hz (+) tone and 900 Hz (−) tone by pups that were either 12, 14, or 16 days old at the start of training. The data in the left of this figure are from 12- and 16-day-old pups from the same litters. Those in the right are from 14- and 16-day-old pups from another set of litters.

The two additional experiments confirm this conclusion and specify more precisely just when the processes that mediate this learning are functional. These experiments employed a *negative transfer* design. They each consisted of two training phases. Control pups received the same training in both phases, the 2000 Hz tone was paired with the US and the 900 Hz tone was nonreinforced. This was not the case for the pups in the experimental condition. During Phase 1 they experienced the 900 Hz tone paired with the US and the 2000 Hz tone was nonreinforced. In Phase 2, this relationship was *reversed*. The 2000 Hz tone was now paired with the US and the 900 Hz tone was nonreinforced. Thus, during Phase 2, the pups in the control and experimental conditions were trained on the same problem. They differed with respect to the training they received during Phase 1.

Our reasoning was that until the processes mediating differential conditioning are functional, the emergence of differential responding in Phase 2 would be *independent* of which of the two cues was reinforced or nonreinforced in Phase 1. Once these processes are functional, however, the treatment given the experimental animals in Phase 1 should produce negative transfer. It should interfere with the emergence of appropriate differential responding on Phase 2. Thus if the Phase 1 training, administered to experimental pups of a given age produces negative transfer, one can reasonably infer that the processes mediating differential conditioning are functional at that age.

Figure 8.11 presents the results of an experiment that exploited this strategy. In this experiment, the pups received Phase 1 training on either Days 14–16 or 16–18 after birth. For half of the subjects the training received in Phase 1 and Phase 2 was identical. The 2000 Hz tone was reinforced and the 900 Hz tone was nonreinforced.

The remaining subjects received the training designed to produce negative transfer. In Phase 1, the 900 Hz tone was reinforced and the 2000 Hz tone was nonreinforced. In Phase 2 this relationship was reversed.

It is evident that reversal training on Days 16–18 markedly interfered with the acquisition of appropriate differential responding to the stimuli in Phase 2 (i.e., produced negative transfer). In contrast, the pups that received reversal training on Days 14–16 displayed no evidence of negative transfer. Differential respond-ing appropriate to the contingencies operating in Phase 2 emerge on the same day (Day 19) for both the reversed and nonreversed control pups started at this age.

Figure 8.12 presents the results of a second experiment that exploited the negative transfer logic. In this case, pups received Phase 1 reversal training on Days 15–16 or 16–17 after birth. As one can see from Fig. 8.12, reversal training interfered with the acquisition of differential responding appropriate to Phase 2 by the pups that were 16 to 17 days old but had no effect on the Phase 2 behavior of the pups that were 15 to 16 days old.

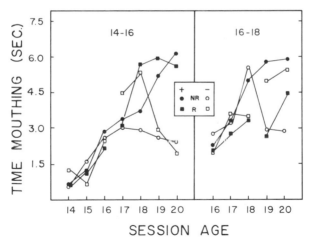

FIG. 8.11.   Mean time mouthing during differential conditioning. The 2000 Hz tone was reinforced (+) and the 900 Hz tone was nonreinforced (−) throughout both phases of training for pups in the nonreversal (NR) control group. This relationship was reversed (R) during Phase 1 training for pups in the experimental group. All pups received the same training during Phase 2. The data for pups that receive Phase 1 training on Days 14–16 are presented in the left panel; those for pups that received Phase 1 training on Days 16–18 are presented in the right panel.

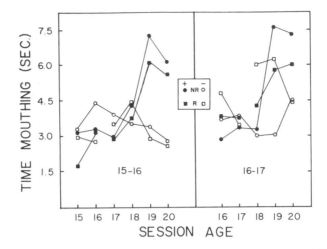

FIG. 8.12.   Mean time mouthing during differential conditioning. The 2000 Hz
tone was reinforced (+) and the 900 Hz tone was nonreinforced (−) throughout
the experiment for pups in the nonreversal (NR) control group. This relationship
was reversed (R) during Phase 1 training for pups in the experimental group. All
pups received the same training in Phase 2. The data for pups that received Phase 1
training on Days 15 and 16 are presented in the left panel; that for pups that
received Phase 1 training on Days 16 and 17 are presented in the right panel.

To summarize the results of these two experiments, the emergence of appropriate differential responding during Phase 2 training was *independent* of the
nature of Phase 1 training if the pups were less than 17 days old during Phase 1.
When they were at least 17 days old, however, reversal training in Phase 1
strongly interfered with the emergence of differential responding in Phase 2.

If one accepts the logic of the negative transfer design, these data imply that it
is not until the pup is about 17 days old that the processes mediating the acquisition of differential responding to the 2000 Hz versus 900 Hz tone are functional.
Or, put more cautiously, one cannot detect any evidence that the training given
pups prior to this age contributes to the emergence of appropriate differential
responding.

These experiments have revealed that there are ontogenetic differences in the
processes mediating the acquisition of differential conditioned responding to
auditory stimulation. They do not, however, tell us anything about the nature of
the difference. The final experiment we describe was intended to provide some
insight into the nature of the ontogenetic constraint imposed on the 12- to 16-day-
old pups' learning of this task.

There is considerable evidence that early in the development of the auditory
system its response to auditory frequencies is not as well "tuned" as it will later
be. The work of Rubel and Rosenthal (1975) has made this point for the chicken.

More recently, Campbell and Haroutunian (in press) have provided evidence that this is also true for the rat. Using a habituation of heart rate response to acoustic stimulation paradigm, they found that the frequency generalization gradient for habituation is much broader in rats 16 to 17 days old than for 19- to 20-day-old pups. This suggests that during its early development, the auditory system does not detect differences in frequency as well as it will when it is fully developed.

This conclusion has a strong implication for why our rats less than 17 days old are not benefiting from differential conditioning trials. It suggests that, at some level, the 2000 Hz and 900 Hz tones are functionally equivalent. This would certainly explain why reversal training had no influence on their later learning to respond appropriately.

If this is true, then perhaps pups less than 17 days old can learn to behave differentially to auditory CSs if the physical similarity of these stimuli is decreased. We evaluated this idea by exposing rat pups to either the standard 2000 Hz versus 900 Hz problem used in the previous studies, or by giving them a presumably *easier* problem, 2500 Hz versus 500 Hz. In each case the pups were 13 days old at the start of Phase 1 training, and half of the pups assigned to each problem were given reversal training over Days 13–15 (Phase 1) before being transferred, when 16 days old, to the target problem in Phase 2. Control animals received training on the target problem in both phases of training.

The Phase 2 results of this experiment are presented in Fig. 8.13. The left panel displays the behavior of pups asked to learn the standard 2000 Hz versus 900 Hz problem. It replicates our previous findings. Reversal training in Phase 1 does not interfere with the 13- to 15-day-old pups' learning the final discrimination. In contrast, as one can see in the right panel, reversal training drastically interfered with the pups' learning the 2500 versus 500 Hz discrimination.

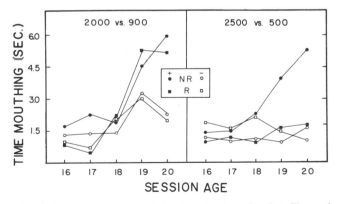

FIG. 8.13.   Mean time mouthing during differential conditioning. The results of the 2000 Hz versus 900 Hz problem are presented in the left panel; those of the 2500 Hz versus 500 Hz problem are presented in the right panel. All pups received Phase 1 training over Days 13–15.

This pattern of results certainly supports the view that an important constraint of the infant rat's ability to learn to respond differentially to two auditory stimuli is imposed by the processes that enable it to detect the differences between them. The 13- to 15-day-old pups can learn to respond differentially to 2500 Hz versus 500 Hz tones but evidently cannot learn to respond differentially to 2000 Hz versus 900 Hz tones.

Summary of Auditory Studies

This ends the description of our experimental studies on the rat's ability to learn about acoustic stimulation during a period of time when the auditory system is changing dramatically (cf. Clopton, 1981; Rubel, 1978). Our experiments have focused on pups that differ in age by no more than a week (10- to 16-day-old pups). Nevertheless, when pups in these age ranges are assessed by a variety of conditioning tasks, we see some important differences and similarities among them.

First, the studies of simple Pavlovian conditioning revealed no evidence that 10- to 11-day-old pups can associate sound with sucrose, even though pups this age might be able to detect sound (e.g., Brunjes & Alberts, 1980; Crowley & Hepp-Raymond, 1966; Wada, 1923). This was true whether a 2000 Hz tone or train of clicks was the CS. We also failed to find evidence that 12- to 13-day-old pups will condition to the 2000 Hz tone. Pups this age, however, were able to condition to the train of clicks. By the time pups are 14 to 15 days old we found evidence that they condition to both the 2000 Hz tone and train of clicks.

Second, even though our studies of simple Pavlovian conditioning suggest that pups 14 days old are capable of conditioning to a 2000 Hz tone, our studies of the more complex, differential Pavlovian conditioning task provided no evidence that pups less than 17 days old can condition differentially to a 2000 Hz versus 900 Hz tone. Pups only 13 to 15 days old, however, learned to respond differentially when the physical difference between the two auditory CSs was increased (i.e., 2500 Hz versus 500 Hz).

When these results are considered together with those of Wada (1923) and Brunjes and Alberts (1981) one can begin to gain some insight into the functional development of the rat's auditory system. The auditory system is sufficiently developed at 10 days after birth to mediate primitive unlearned behavioral reactions to sound (Brunjes & Alberts, 1981; Wada, 1923). The processes participating in the acquisition of conditioned or learned responses to sound, however, do not appear capable of supporting the integrative learning necessary for such behavior until the pup is 12 to 13 days old. Even at that age not all auditory stimuli that can be conditioned to by older pups (e.g., 2000 Hz tone) will be effective at this age. Although the 12- to 13-day-old pup is capable of detecting a change in its acoustic environment and integrating it with the occurrence of some other event (e.g., sucrose infusion), the systems that allow the rat pup to learn to respond differentially to sounds of different frequency continue to develop until the rat is at least 17 days old.

SUMMARY AND CONCLUSIONS

Our major concern in this chapter was to address what we see as a fundamental stumbling block to a developmental analysis of learning, the absence of a systematic framework to guide experimenters to the kinds of questions that, when addressed, will provide some insight into the ontogenesis of learning in altricial animals.

In our view, the learned changes in behavior that result from an organism-environment interaction are usefully viewed as representing the orchestrated product of many processes. These include the sensory processes that place the organism in contact with the environment and that interface with the more central processes that generate memory representations of experienced stimulus events (event memory processes) and representations of the various spatial, temporal, and sequential relationships among them (integrative memory processes).

From a developmental perspective, we might expect that during ontogenesis these processes will be at different levels of functional maturity. Consequently, the same nominal experience applied to organisms at different points during ontogenesis may have quite different effects on their subsequent behavior. Said otherwise, what an organism extracts or learns from its interaction with the environment may vary substantially, depending upon what components of the system, that combine to generate learning, are functional.

We assume then that there are ontogenetically determined sources of constraint that place limits on just what an organism can extract from its interactions with the environment. The goal of a developmental analysis of learning from this perspective is to uncover those sources of constraint and how they change during ontogenesis.

In pursuit of this goal, we have followed the research strategy recommended by Gollin (1965), termed a *levels × levels* approach. He argued that to arrive at some understanding of the relative learning capacities or constraints thereon of different-aged organisms requires that they be assessed with a battery of behavioral tasks selected so as to provide information about both their similarities and differences.

To illustrate the application of this approach we described some of our work directed at a developmental analysis of the processes that contribute to the rat's learned behavioral reaction to gustatory and auditory stimulation. In both cases, an array of behavioral tasks was used to determine the comparative functioning of the processes that contribute to the rat's learned reaction to these classes of stimuli. In both cases the evidence suggests a dissociation, during ontogenesis, of the onset of function in the relevant sensory system and the onset of function in the learning processes engaged by these events. It also appears that the learning processes that mediate the effects of relatively simple tasks emerge before those required by relatively more complex or demanding tasks. These generalizations, of course, must be viewed with caution. Our task here, however, is not to convince the reader that we can offer, at this time, powerful generalizations about the ontogenesis of learning but to suggest that continued application of this strategy will put us in a more favorable position to do so.

ACKNOWLEDGMENTS

This research project was supported in part by BRSG Grant RR07013–1980, awarded by the Biomedical Research Support Grant Program, Division of Research Resources, National Institute of Health and by Grant BNS-8207654, awarded by the National Science Foundation. We thank Drs. Thomas Minor and Fernando Oberdieck for critically reading the earlier versions of this manuscript.

REFERENCES

Amsel, A. The ontogeny of appetitive learning and persistence in the rat. In N. E. Spear & B. A. Campbell (Eds.), *Ontogeny of learning and memory*. Hillsdale, N.J.: Lawrence Erlbaum Associates, 1979.

Amsel, A., Burdette, D. R., & Letz, R. Appetitive learning, patterned alternation, and extinction in 10-day-old rats with non-lactating suckling as reward. *Nature*, 1976, *262*, 816–818.

Barker, L. M., Best, M. R., & Domjan, M. *Learning mechanisms in food selection*. Waco, Texas: Baylor University Press, 1977.

Barnett, S. A. Experiments on "neophobia" in wild and laboratory rats. *British Journal of Psychology*, 1958, *49*, 195–201.

Brake, S. Suckling infant rats learn a preference for a novel olfactory stimulus paired with milk delivery. *Science*, 1981, *211*, 506–508.

Brunjes, P. E., & Alberts, J. R., Development of early visual and auditory function in normal and hypothyroid rats. *Behavioral and Neural Biology*, 1981, *31*, 393–412.

Campbell, B. A., & Coulter, X. The ontogenesis of learning and memory. In M. R. Rosenzweig & E. L. Bennett (Eds.), *Neural mechanisms of learning and memory*. Cambridge: MIT Press, 1976.

Campbell, B. A., & Haroutunian, V. Perceptual sharpening in the developing rat. *Journal of Comparative Psychology*, in press.

Clopton, B. M. Neurophysiological and anatomical aspects of auditory development. In R. N. Aslin, J. R. Alberts, & M. R. Peterson (Eds.), *Development of perception* (Vol. 1). New York: Academic Press, 1981.

Crowley, D. E., & Hepp-Raymond, M. C. Development of cochlear function in the ear of the infant rat. *Journal of Comparative and Physiological Psychology*, 1966, *93*, 977–1000.

Domjan, M. Attenuation and enhancement of neophobia for edible substances. In L. M. Barker, M. R. Best, & M. Domjan (Eds.), *Learning mechanisms in food selection*. Waco, Texas: Baylor University Press, 1977.

Garcia, J., & Koelling, R. A. Relation of cue to consequence in avoidance learning. *Psychonomic Science*, 1966, *4*, 123–124.

Gollin, E. S. A developmental approach to learning and cognition. In L. P. Lipsitt, & C. C. Spiker (Eds.), *Advances in child development and behavior* (Vol. 2). New York: Academic Press, 1965.

Gollin, E. S. A developmental analysis of learning. In J. Hellmuth (Ed.), *Cognitive studies* (Vol. 1). New York: Brunner/Mazel, 1970.

Gregg, B., Kittrell, E. M. W., Domjan, M., & Amsel, A. Ingestional aversion learning in preweanling rats. *Journal of Comparative and Physiological Psychology,* 1978, *92,* 785–795.

Hall, W. G., & Bryan, T. E. The ontogeny of feeding in rats: II. Independent ingestive behavior. *Journal of Comparative and Physiological Psychology,* 1980, *94,* 746–756.

Hall, W. G., & Bryan, T. E. The ontogeny of feeding in rats: IV. Taste development as measured by intake and behavioral responses to oral infusions of sucrose and quinine. *Journal of Comparative and Physiological Psychology,* 1981, *95,* 240–251.

Hall, W. G., & Rosenblatt, J. S. Suckling behavior and intake control in the developing rat pup. *Journal of Comparative and Physiological Psychology,* 1977, *91,* 1232–1247.

Haroutunian, V., & Campbell, B. A. The emergence of interoceptive and exteroceptive control of behavior in rats. *Science,* 1979, *205,* 927–929.

Johanson, I. B., & Hall, W. G. Appetitive learning in 1 day old rat pups. *Science,* 1979, *205,* 419–421.

Johanson, I., & Hall, W. G. Appetitive conditioning in neonatal rats: Conditioned orientation to a novel odor. *Developmental Psychobiology,* 1982, *15,* 379–397.

Johanson, I. B., & Teicher, M. H. Classical conditioning of an odor preference in 3 day old rats. *Behavioral and Neural Biology,* 1980, *29,* 132–136.

Johanson, I. B., Polefrone, J. M., & Hall, W. G. *Classical conditioned activation in neonatal rats.* Meetings of the International Society for Developmental Psychobiology, New Orleans, November 12–15, 1981.

Kail, R. V., & Hagen, J. W. (Eds.). *Perspective on the development of memory and cognition.* Hillsdale, N.J.: Lawrence Erlbaum Associates, 1977.

Kenny, J. T., & Blass, E. M. Suckling as incentive to instrumental learning in preweanling rats. *Science,* 1977, *196,* 898–899.

Mistretta, C. Neurophysiological and anatomical aspects of taste development. In R. N. Aslin, J. R. Alberts, & M. R. Peterson (Eds.), *Development of perception* (Vol. 1). New York: Academic Press, 1981.

Rescorla, R. A. Pavlovian conditioning and its proper control procedures. *Psychological Review,* 1967, *74,* 71–80.

Rescorla, R. A., & Holland, P. C. Some behavioral approaches to the study of learning. In E. Bennett & M. R. Rosensweig (Eds.), *Neural mechanisms of learning and memory.* Cambridge, Mass.: MIT Press, 1976.

Revusky, S. H., & Garcia, J. Learned associations over long delays. In G. H. Bower & J. T. Spence (Eds.), *The psychology of learning and motivation: Advances in research and theory* (Vol. 4). New York: Academic Press, 1970.

Rosenblatt, J. S. The sensorimotor and motivational basis of early behavioral development of selected altricial mammals. In N. E. Spear & B. A. Campbell (Eds.), *Ontogeny of learning and memory.* Hillsdale, N.J.: Lawrence Erlbaum Associates, 1979.

Rubel, E. W. Ontogeny of structure and function in the vertebrate auditory system. In M. Jacobson (Ed.), *Handbook of sensory physiology.* Berlin: Springer-Verlag, 1978.

Rubel, E. W., & Rosenthal, M. The ontogeny of auditory frequency generalization in the chicken. *Journal of Experimental Psychology: Animal Behavior Process,* 1975, *1,* 287–297.

Rudy, J. W. & Cheatle, M. D. Odor aversion learning by neonatal rats. *Science,* 1977, *198,* 845–846.

Rudy, J. W., & Cheatle, M. D. Ontogeny of associative learning: Acquisition of odor aversions by neonatal rats. In N. E. Spear & B. A. Campbell (Eds.), *Ontogeny of learning and memory.* Hillsdale, N.J.: Lawrence Erlbaum Associates, 1979.

Rudy, J. W., & Hyson, R. L. Consummatory response conditioning to an auditory stimulus in neonatal rats. *Behavioral and Neural Biology*, 1982, *34*, 209–214.

Smith, G. J., & Spear, N. E. Effects of the home environment on withholding behavior and conditioning in infant and neonatal rats. *Science*, 1978, *202*, 327–329.

Spear, N. E. Memory storage factors leading to infantile amnesia. In G. H. Bower (Ed.), *The psychology of learning and memory* (Vol. 13). New York: Academic Press, 1979.

Spear, N. E., & Campbell, B. A. (Eds.). *Ontogeny of learning and memory*. Hillsdale, N.J.: Lawrence Erlbaum Associates, 1979.

Sullivan, R. M., & Brake, S. C. *Reinforcement and activation in infant rats*. Meetings of the International Society for Developmental Psychobiology. New Orleans, November 12–15, 1980.

Teicher, M. H., & Blass, E. M. Suckling in newborn rats: Eliminated by nipple lavage, reinstated by pup saliva. *Science*, 1976, *193*, 422–425.

Teicher, M. H., & Blass, E. M. First suckling response of the newborn albino rat: The roles of olfaction and amniotic fluid. *Science*, 1977, *198*, 635–636.

von Uexküll, J. A stroll through the worlds of animals and men. In C. H. Schiller (Ed.), *Instinctive behavior*. New York: International Universities Press, Inc., 1957.

Wada, T. W. Anatomical and physiological studies of the albino rat. *American Anatomical Memoirs*, 1923, *10*, 1–174.

9 Individual Differences in Infant Memory: Forgotten but not Gone

Theodore D. Wachs
Purdue University

Individual differences have been an annoyance rather than a challenge to the experimenter. His goal is to control behavior, and variation within treatments is proof that he has not succeeded. Individual variation is cast into that outer darkness known as "error variance." For reasons both statistical and philosophical, error variance is to be reduced by any possible device. You turn to animals of a cheap and short-lived species, so that you can use subjects with controlled heredity and controlled experience. You select human subjects from a narrow subculture. You decorticate your subject by cutting neurons or by giving him an environment so meaningless that his unique responses disappear. You increase the number of cases to obtain stable averages, or you reduce N to 1 as Skinner does. But whatever your device, your goal in the experimental tradition is to get those embarrassing differential variables out of sight. (Cronbach, 1957, p. 674.)

Although noted over 25 years ago, the exorcism of individual differences described by Cronbach, continues today.[1] While one might assume that developmental psychology could be that area of psychology most tolerant of the notion

---

[1]Following Kraemer and Korner (1976), I am defining individual differences as variability among individuals that cannot be attributed to differential experimental treatment, unreliability of measurements, or random, unstable, subject variability (see Kraemer and Kroner for statistical approaches to quantifying these dimensions). Individual differences may be studied between groups when groups are differentiated on the basis of specific individual parameters, or they may be studied within groups of individuals. I consider both approaches in this paper.

of individual differences, this assumption would be incorrect (Horowitz, 1969). Given the predominance of the experimental model in developmental psychology (McCall, 1977), individual differences are all too often dismissed as trival, unstable variations that can have little impact upon later development (Kopp, 1978). Within developmental psychology, individual differences have been neglected in favor of an emphasis on "universal" processes of development (Jeffrey & Cohen, 1971; Kopp, 1978; Wachs, 1977). The possible impact of individual differences upon development has rarely been seen as a legitimate field of study, but rather as a nuisance that must be directly suppressed. This suppression is typically carried out through rigorous experimental controls which minimize any chance of individual differences appearing (Horowitz, 1969), through dropping of subjects who do not conform exactly to the experimenter's needs (Horowitz, 1969), or through use of statistical designs that do not allow the emergence of individual differences in any form beyond that of error variance (Wachs & Gruen, 1982).

Yet, despite decades of not so benign neglect, individual differences are not disappearing. Particularly in infancy, individual differences continue to appear. Recent evidence over the past decade has increasingly emphasized the relevance of individual differences to our understanding of infant development across a wide range of areas. These include *infant learning* (Fitzgerald & Brackbill, 1977; Horowitz, 1969; Watson, Hayes, Dorman, & Vietze, 1980), *attentional process* (Field, 1981; Friedman & Jacobs, 1981; McCall & McGhee, 1977; Molfese & Molfese, 1979; Williams & Golinski, 1979), *self regulatory processes* (Kopp, 1982), *language development* (Hardy-Brown, Plomin, & DeFries, 1981; Nelson, 1977), *cognitive development* (Black, Steinschneider, & Sheehe, 1979; Johnson & Brody, 1977; Lamb, Garn, & Keating, 1981), *emotional development* (Gunnar-Vongnechten, 1978), *exploratory behavior* (Sigman, 1976), *bio-behavioral organization* (Brackbill, 1979; Dixon, Tronick, Keefe, & Brazelton, 1982), *reactivity to environmental stimulation* (Wachs, 1977, 1979, in press; Wachs & Gandour, in press), and *social interaction patterns* (Field, 1981; Harmon, Morgan, & Klein, 1977; Hittelman & Dickes, 1979; Waters, Vaughn, & Egeland, 1980). Even more critically, we are also beginning to see the integration of individual difference parameters into theoretical models of the processes involved. This integration is found across such diverse areas as *developmental mental retardation* (Ramey, MacPhee, & Yates, in press), *early social development* (Harmon et al, 1977; Field, 1981), *early cognitive development* (McCall, 1981), *the impact of early environment upon development* (Thomas & Chess, 1976; Wachs & Gruen, 1982), *classical conditioning* (Fitzgerald & Brackbill, 1976), and *language development* (Nelson, 1981). This integration of individual difference parameters into theoretical models is quite unusual, given the traditional reluctance of developmental theorists to consider individual differences as relevant for theory (Horowitz, 1969; Kopp, 1978).

In the area of infant memory, while there is evidence for individual differences (as will be shown below), there appears to be considerable reluctance to consider individual differences as salient for memory development. In spite of problems in applying adult memory models to infancy (Werner & Perlmutter, 1979), the bulk of infant memory theory has been derived from adult information processing models (Olson, 1976; Ratner, 1980). These models are firmly rooted within the classic experimental tradition. The implications of this tradition for the study of individual differences have been noted earlier. As a result, beyond the study of age changes in memory, there has been little emphasis or interest in individual differences in either memory performance or memory processes in infancy. Authors of major reviews in the area of infant memory either assume individual differences are of little importance (Rovee-Collier & Fagen, 1981), or note the existence of individual differences but make no attempt to integrate individual differences into theoretical models emerging from these reviews (Cohen, 1976; Cohen & Gelber, 1975; Olson, 1976; Werner & Perlmutter, 1979).

It is the thesis of the present chapter that replicable individual differences in infant memory performance and processes do exist. As will be documented, these individual differences can be attributed to specific biological characteristics of the organism, or to specific environmental circumstances encountered by the individual. The existence of individual differences in infant memory means that research designs or theoretical models that do not allow consideration of these differences are not likely to promote an understanding of early memory development, as it normally occurs.

THE EXISTENCE OF INDIVIDUAL DIFFERENCES IN INFANT MEMORY PERFORMANCE

The bulk of evidence for individual differences in infant memory has dealt with the question of differences in level of memory performance. Performance is typically measured either by recognition memory paridigms (habituation rate, preference for novel stimuli after exposure to a series of familiar stimuli) or through use of object permanence tasks (which are more likely to tap aspects of recall memory).

One obvious individual difference parameter is age differences in memory, and changes in memory strategies associated with age. There do appear to be reliable age changes in memory performance and processes in infancy and these changes have already been reviewed in detail by Cohen and Gelber (1975). Given the existence of this review, I will not consider this particular aspect of individual differences in great detail. Besides age differences, there appear to be two other classes of individual difference parameters related to differences in memory performance. This first class includes biological, neurological, and biomedical factors; the second class includes the organism's previous experience.

Biological Factors

The largest body of available evidence relates difference in biomedical diagnosis to performance differences on recognition memory tasks. Much of the available evidence has compared risk (i.e., preterm) infants with nonrisk infants. In general, risk infants show significantly poorer performance than nonrisk infants on both novelty recognition (Fagan & Singer, in press; Rose, 1980; Sigman & Parmelee, 1974) and habituation tasks (Eisenberg, Coursin, & Rupp, 1966). These differences occur even when risk and nonrisk groups are matched on conceptual age (Fagan & Singer, in press). Most explanations of these differences utilize a developmental lag model, wherein memory performance of older risk infants resembles that of younger nonrisk infants (Rose, 1980). Differences between risk and nonrisk infants are particularly noticeable on more complex tasks such as crossmodal recognition memory, wherein the novel stimuli are in a different modality than the familiarization stimuli (Rose, Gottfried, & Bridger, 1978). For this type of task, 12-month-old risk infants evidence memory performance comparable to that of 6-month-old nonrisk infants (Rose, Gottfried, & Bridger, 1979). Similar developmental lags in memory have also been shown in habituation tasks (Cohen, 1981) and in novelty recognition tasks when Down's syndrome infants are compared to normal infants (Fagan & Singer, in press; Miranda & Fantz, 1974).

Using another type of risk population, Schexnider, Bell, Shebilske, and Quinn (1981) have recently reported significantly greater recovery to novel stimuli in a dishabituation paradigm for 12-month-old infants having few (3 or less) minor physical anomalies, as compared to infants having a high number (5 or more) of minor physical anomalies. These results are complicated by an interaction between anomaly level and whether dishabituation testing occurred before or after a pediatric exam. Based on these order effects in their results, Schexnider et al. (1981) hypothesize that infants with many minor anomalies have a short-term memory deficit that is accentuated by fatigue. The nature of these order effects suggests an alternative explanation however; namely, that infants with minor physical anomalies are more distracted by new situations, and this distractibility interferes with the development of schemata. This alternative explanation would be congruent with other data showing a differential impact of novelty of test setting upon attentional process in males and females (Weizmann, Cohen, & Pratt, 1971). This distractibility hypothesis may also account for the slower habituation and dishabituation shown by infants with a history of illnesses associated with fever (Haskins, Collier, Ramey, & Hirschbiel, 1978).

The above studies are primarily between-group comparisons, wherein the impact of individual differences is ascertained by comparing groups of infants with and without a specific biomedical problem. Within-group biomedical risk studies are also available. In these studies individual differences in memory performance are related to within-group differences on specific biomedical parameters. Again, much of the available evidence is based on premature infants.

Using a high amplitude sucking paradigm, wherein infant sucking produced visual stimuli that were either familiar or novel, Werner and Siqueland (1978) reported that the degree of recovery of sucking for novel stimuli was positively related to birth weight and gestational age and negatively related to postnatal complications in a group of *1-week-old* premature infants. By 3 to 5 months (corrected age), birth weight and gestational age were no longer related to recovery, although frequency of postnatal complications was still significantly and negatively related (Siqueland, 1981). Using 7-month-old (corrected age) preterms, Rose (1980) reported no relationship of birth weight, gestational age, or biomedical complications to degree of recovery in a visual recognition task.

The pattern across these three studies suggests a recovery in memory performance from the effects of biomedical risk, as preterm infants get older. What mediates this recovery? At least two possibilities exist. One possibility is that the initial memory performance of young preterms was inhibited by biomedical factors correlated with (prematurity), which lose their salience over time (Sameroff & Chandler, 1975). One example of such a correlated biomedical parameter is maternal anesthesia. In general, preterm infants are more likely to be exposed to higher relative levels of anesthetic drugs than full-term infants (White & Brackbill, 1981). Moreau and Birch (1974) report that while maternal anesthesia does not depress the responsivity of the newborn infant, it does lengthen habituation of the neonate to both auditory and touch stimuli. The continued impact of maternal anesthesia upon 4 months' recognition memory has also been demonstrated (Sigman cited in Brackbill, 1979). With an eventual fading or compensation for the impact of early biomedical problem correlates, such as anesthesia, we would predict the pattern observed; namely, major within-group differences early in life (Werner & Siqueland, 1978) which became attenuated over time (Siqueland, 1981) and ultimately disappeared (Rose, 1980).

Although a potential explanation for the change in within-group correlations, this hypothesized recovery process could be seen as difficult to reconcile with the between-group data we have noted earlier, indicating depressed memory performance in preterm infants beyond 7 months of age (Fagan & Singer, in press). However, a recovery from specific perinatal influences does not mean that the infant is immune from other conditions *associated with risk status,* which may continue to depress memory performance. The most obvious example of a parameter associated both with infant risk status and with deficits in memory performance is social class (Lewis & Goldberg, 1969; Rose et al., 1978). Preterms tend to come from lower SES backgrounds and low SES is associated with memory deficits in infancy.

Overall, the evidence suggests that in terms of understanding the influence of biomedical parameters upon differences in infant memory performance, it may be incorrect to view this process as a series of specific point-to-point relationships. Rather, following the model of Sameroff and Chandler (1975), it may be more correct to consider the relevance of a variety of biomedical and environmental factors, *which are associated with risk status,* and *which may lead to variability in infants' memory performance at different age levels.* Put another way, we may be dealing with a system of influences, rather than one or two specific and isolated factors. Within-group longitudinal studies, looking at changes in parameters influencing memory performance as the infant develops, would be extremely useful in helping us understand the nature of this system.

In addition to risk status and retardation, data reported by Fagan and Singer (in press) also suggest the possibility that the nutritional status of the infant may be another biological factor associated with variation in infant memory performance. Specifically, these authors reported significantly poorer recognition memory, through 6 months (corrected age), for infants suffering from intrauterine growth retardation and failure-to-thrive syndrome, as compared to nonrisk infants or to premature infants whose weight was appropriate for their gestational age. Similarly, Klein, Forbes, and Nader (1975) report that school-age children diagnosed as having congenital pyloric stenosis in *early infancy* (a medical condition producing malnutrition—it is correctable by surgery) had impaired visual and auditory short-term memory when compared to siblings and matched controls who did not have pyloric stenosis in infancy. These authors further report that the degree of short-term memory impairment was significantly correlated with the degree of malnutrition resulting from the pyloric stenosis in infancy. In contrast to this data, the potential relationship between nutritional status and memory has not been verified by other studies. Studies directly comparing malnourished and nourished infants on such diverse tasks as habituation (Lester, Klein, & Martinez, 1975), novelty recognition (Lasky & Klein, 1980), and object permanence (Dasen, Lavalle, Retshitzki, & Reinhardt, 1977), all report differences between malnourished and nourished infants on attention, efficiency of information processing, and persistence, but not on memory performance. Given that intrauterine growth retardation is often associated with maternal biomedical problems (Kopp & Parmelee, 1979), while pyloric stenosis is a biomedical problem associated with infant malnutrition, it may well be that malnutrition influences memory only when it covaries with specific biomedical problems.

One remaining area where individual biological parameters may relate to differences in early memory performance involves the organism's genetic composition. Studies with adults clearly suggest a modest, but significant, genetic component for short-term memory (Cole et al., 1979). While little research has been done on this topic with infants, what research is available is supportive of the hypothesis that individual, genotypic differences may relate to differences in memory performance. Specifically, using indirect measures of object permanence taken from the Bayley, data from the Louisville Twin study (Matheney, 1975) indicate significantly greater concordance for monozygotic twins then dizygotic twins. Similarly, data from the Colorado adoption project (DeFries, Plomin, Vandenberg, & Kuse, 1981), using direct measures of object permanence, yielded significant correlations between measures of adult memory and infants' object permanence scores for biological parents and offspring, but not for adopted parents and offspring. In terms of future research, given that early recognition memory has been hypothesized to be an index of general intelligence (Fagan & Singer, in press), studies on the extent and nature of genetic influences upon this aspect of early memory would seem an obvious direction to go.

Individual Differences in Infant Memory Performance as a Function of the Environment

As with infrahuman research, there appears to be a direct tie between the reinstatement model of early memory and early experience. Reinstatement is traditionally defined as a periodic repetition or reminder of an earlier experience. Theorists in infant memory have pointed to the importance of reinstatements for stabilizing the impact of the infant's early experience over time. (Rovee-Collier & Fagen, 1981). This conclusion is based on studies which train infants on a conditioning task and then assess the degree to which exposing the infant to stimulus elements used in the conditioning task aids in long-term retention of conditioning (Rovee-Collier, Sullivan, Enright, Lucas, & Fagen, 1980). However, infant memory theorists do not appear to have considered the converse side of their argument; namely, that *individual differences in reinstatement history* are a form of early experience that may lead to individual differences in infant memory performance. By individual differences in reinstatement history I am referring to differences in the degree to which infants *continue* to encounter, *in their natural environment,* previously encountered stimuli or contiguous relationships. Specific stimuli could be faces or forms; contiguous relations could include pairings between cup and milk or between a box and an object contained in that box. Although infrahuman studies have successfully used reinstatement situations analogous to those described above (Wachs, 1973), there have been virtually no data collected on the extent to which *reinstatement experiences occur in the infant's natural environment or how these naturally occurring reinstatement experiences are translated into individual differences* in infants' recognition or recall memory. Rather, what we find is a collection of atheoretical studies relating variation in early experience parameters to variation in performance on various types of early memory tasks. However, even within this diverse group of studies certain consistencies emerge.[2]

The most consistent relationship that emerges from literature relating early experience to early memory performance involves physical contact (i.e., tactual-kinesthetic stimulation of the infant). Specifically, a positive relationship is consistently found between variations in early memory performance and amount of physical contact stimulation encountered by or provided to the infant in the first year. This relationship occurs whether early memory is measured by habituation (Lewis & Goldberg, 1969), recognition of novelty (Rose, 1980), or object permanence (Wachs & Gruen, 1982).

In terms of other environmental parameters, variation in the amount and variety of inanimate and social stimulation, encountered by or provided to the infant, has been found to be positively related to variation in infant memory during the first year. The pattern of results suggests that variability of stimulation is more critical than the presence of specific environmental factors like verbal stimulation or encouraging infant attention (Ruddy & Bornstein, 1982). The relationship of environmental variability to infant memory is found both for habituation (Riksen-Walraven, 1978) and object permanence (Wachs & Gruen, 1982). A direct test for the relevance of amount and variety to infant recognition of novelty has not yet been reported in the literature. However, McCall and Kennedy (1980) do report that infants who were exposed to greater amounts of stimulus variability did show greater attention to more complex novel stimuli than infants who were exposed to stimuli with little variability. Although this study was designed as a test of McCall and McGhee's (1977) discrepancy hypothesis, the relevance of this finding to recognition memory seems clear.

Naturally occurring variability in object responsivity or adult responsivity to the infant's social signals has also been consistently and positively related to variation in early object permanence performance (Wachs & Gruen, 1982). The relationship of these types of contingencies to habituation is less clear. Lewis and Goldberg (1969) have reported a positive relationship between rate of response decrement on an habituation task and degree of adult responsivity to infants' vocalization and distress signals. In contrast, Riksen-Walraven (1978) reports that training parents to be more responsive to the infant's signals, while related to level of infant's exploratory behavior, was unrelated to infants' habituation performance. Given the fact that infants in these two studies were 12 months of age

---

[2]My emphasis here will be on the relationship between variation in specific environmental parameters and variation in indices of infant memory performance. Relationships between more global environmental indices (social class, orphanage rearing, or provision of global enrichment to the infant) and infant memory performance have also been demonstrated (Decarie, 1965; Lewis & Goldberg, 1969; Paraskevopoulos & Hunt, 1971; Rose, et al., 1978). However, the undifferentiated nature of the environmental indices in these studies makes interpretation difficult. I also restrict my review to infant memory, as measured in the first year of life. Evidence for environmental parameters which influence variation in early memory after this time is scarce but does exist (Ratner, 1980).

when tested on habituation, age differences cannot explain the discrepant pattern of results for contingencies.

Overall, the pattern of available evidence indicates that variations in infant memory performance are associated with variations in specific environmental parameters encountered by or provided to infants. Given the atheoretical nature of the studies done up to this point (only the Riksen-Walraven paper was based on theory, in terms of environmental parameters selected), the general consistency of results, while pleasing, does not offer firm directions for future research. The most obvious direction would be to use theoretical models of infant memory as a guide for predicting which specific environmental parameters would be most relevant for early memory development. As I noted earlier, the most obvious memory theory would undoubtedly be the reinstatement model. Based upon this model, it would be predicted that variation in level of infants' recognition or recall memory for specific stimuli or concepts would be related to *variation in the frequency and context with which infants encountered naturally occurring environmental events encompassing these stimuli and concepts.* Specifically, it would be predicted that *memory for specific stimuli* would be related to the frequency of repetition of infant contact with events encompassing these stimuli *within a specific context.* Thus, the strength of an infant's recognition of a specific form would be related to the amount of time a mobile containing that form remained in place over the infant's crib. In contrast it would be predicted that *memory for concepts* would be related to the frequency of infant contact with contiguous events encompassing these concepts *across* different contexts. Thus, the strength of an infant's recall memory (eg., object permanence) would be related to the frequency of infant contact with different boxes containing different objects. Development of studies to test these predictions would require a close collaboration between researchers involved in the experimental study of memory and those interested in the naturalistic measurement of infant environment. Such a collaboration, while perhaps difficult to achieve, offers the potential for expanding both theoretical models of infant memory and theoretical models of early environmental action.

INDIVIDUAL DIFFERENCES IN EARLY MEMORY PROCESSES

Up to the present time I have been discussing individual differences in infant memory performance. Such individual differences in performance could be used to argue that global models of memory that do not take account of individual difference parameters may be inadequate. However, to paraphrase an argument made in the area of learning, it could also be argued that more or less efficient memory performance does not necessarily mean different memory processes (Logue, 1979). A global memory theorist could assume that while individual differences may predict (trival) differences in memory efficiency, the *basic processes* of memory are the same across all individuals at a given age. Unfortunately, there has been relatively little research (beyond age differences) on the question of individual differences in memory processes. What theory and evidence are available do suggest the potential validity of the counter-hypothesis; namely, that individual differences may affect early memory processes as well as early memory performance. Two areas of investigation seem to be salient here, one dealing with style, the other with sex.[3]

One distinction that has been in the early memory literature for some time is the distinction between "fast" and "slow" habituators (McCall & Kagan, 1970). Research in this area (Miller, Sinnott, Short & Haines, 1976) could be used to suggest the possibility that differences in habituation rate may reflect differences in the nature of information processing between these groups. However, most explanations of these differences center around variation in information-processing rate and not on the nature of information processing itself. Thus, Cohen and Gelber (1975) have suggested that the differences between fast and slow habituators may be due to slow habituators taking more trials to begin processing than fast habituators. Werner and Perlmutter (1979) hypothesize that differences are due to the slow habituators needing more time to encode information than fast habituators. A similar "quantitative" explanation (maturational differences) may also serve to explain the relationship between individual differences in consistency of looking responses and the attention-releasing aspects of performance in habituation tasks, as reported by Cohen (1976). (Though sex differences in other response measures besides looking [smiling or vocalization, McCall, 1972] cannot easily be explained by purely quantitative mechanisms such as maturation).

Such quantitative explanations would not easily fit recent data reported by McCall (1979). Specifically, McCall (1979) has identified three clusters of children who show distinctively different types of habituation *patterns*. Given these individual response patterns, McCall suggests that the standard practice of grouping data, as done in most traditional experimental studies of memory, may be highly misleading. The fact that McCall reports *differences in patterns of*

---

[3]A third potential individual difference factor, rarely mentioned in the literature, involves those infants who are unable to complete the experimental proceedure. Subject loss rates may run as high as 75% with certain proceedures (Richardson & McCluskey, 1981). It has generally been assumed that subject losses are primarily due to state related factors (Lewis & Johnson, 1971), and are thus random. An alternative hypothesis is that these losses are not due to random states, but rather are associated with unique, individual traits. What little evidence is available on this question does not support the assumption of random subject loss. Subject loss appears to be associated with both subject characteristics such as sex (Richardson & McCluskey, 1981), and with infant processing characteristics such as attentional patterns (Lewis & Johnson, 1971; Richardson & McCluskey, 1981). Whether these individual differences would effect performance or processing is unclear. In either case non-random subject loss would certainly restrict the generalizability of theories of infant memory, if not the nature of these theories as well.

habituation and not simply in rate of habituation supports the hypothesis that individual infants may be using different styles of information processing, which are reflected in pattern differences in habituation and dishabituation.

A second area where potential processing differences are possible lies in the study of sex differences in early memory. While evidence for sex differences in memory performance have been inconsistent (Cohen & Gelber, 1975), available data do suggest that there may be differential sensitivity of the sexes to kinds of information most easily stored. Specifically, evidence suggests that females store motor information (Cohen & Gelber, 1975), environmental contingencies (Cohen, 1973), and auditory and social cues (McGuinness & Pribram, 1979) more easily than males. Males store information more easily about the physical aspects of the environment (Cohen, 1973), and nonsocial visual cues (McGuinness & Pribram, 1979). This differential sensitivity to different stimulus classes is not a phenomenon restricted only to early memory; differential sensitivity of males and females to informational content has also been reported in studies of early learning (Watson, 1969; Watson et al., 1980). In addition to differential sensitivity to information stored, some evidence suggests that during the attention-getting stage in memory testing, females may compare a currently perceived stimulus with the previously stored stimulus; this aspect of processing may not be utilized by males (Cohen, 1973).

Attempts have been made to explain these types of sex differences as a quantitative phenomenon, by suggesting that males and females may be at different developmental stages (McCall & McGee, 1976). However, in a recent paper, McGuinness and Pribram (1979) summarize evidence from a wide variety of studies and come to the conclusion that sex differences in preferred modalities or information may reflect the use of *different neural systems* for processing and storing information by males and females. McGuinness and Pribram (1979) specifically hypothesize that sex differences in sensitivity to stimuli in different modalities may be mediated by sex differences in central nervous system arousal and activation processes. In terms of other systems, McGuiness and Pribram see little evidence that differences in hemispheric specialization relate to differential stimulus sensitivity. However, recent data by Lewkowicz and Turkewitz (1982), indicating a complex relationship between age and sex of infant and hemispheric utilization in processing different types of auditory input, suggest that McGuinness and Pribram may have been premature in denying the relevance of early hemispheric specialization to differential sensitivity.

One major implication of the McGuinness and Pribram (1979) hypothesis is that sex differences in infant memory for stimuli in different modalities cannot be attributed to simple quantitative phenomena like maturation. Rather, their position would suggest that different neurologically based memory processes may have to be evoked to explain male-female differences in information storage.

If McGuinness and Pribram are correct, there are two areas of future investigation that emerge. First, if central nervous system differences underlie sex differences, it is quite plausible to hypothesize that the differences in memory efficiency between risk and normal infants reviewed earlier may also be due to the operation of different processing systems. Infants with biologically based central nervous system deficits may process and store information in distinctively different ways than do infants with intact central nervous systems.

Second, as part of their model, McGuinness and Pribram (1979) hypothesize that the *initial impact* of central nervous system differences in sensitivity to stimuli in different modalities may be *maintained and expanded* by differential experience with stimuli in the preferred modality. This suggests the possibility that differential exposure to different types of experience (for example physical versus vocal stimuli) may also lead to the operation of differential memory processes for storing information in preferred and nonpreferred modalities. By combining these two possibilities, a complex process can be envisioned wherein individual differences in memory efficiency and processing are seen as initially due to biologically based individual differences in modality preference. These initial differences are expanded by encountered environments which either match or do not match the biologically based modality preferences. Obviously, this is an extremely speculative position. However, this position has some empirical basis and cannot be dismissed simply because the possibility of individual differences in memory processing violates our treasured notions of parsimony, or our desire to have a single model that explains all aspects of memory. The possibility of multiple determinants of individual differences in memory performance and pattern is not inconsistent with the complexity of early memory, as we know it (McCall, 1979).

CONCLUSIONS

What I hope has been demonstrated by this review is that, in terms of individual differences, the area of infant memory development is no different from other developmental areas. In spite of our best efforts to ignore, control, or otherwise suppress the existence of individual differences, they continue to emerge. Certainly, there can be little doubt that individual differences in memory performance exist, as a function of specific individual, biomedical, or environmental parameters. There is also more than a remote possibility that there may also be individual differences in memory processes, which are associated with different biological or environmental parameters.

While my review has dealt primarily with memory at the human level, the same points could also be made in regard to infrahuman studies of early memory development. In general, infrahuman research and theory have shown little interest in individual difference parameters (Donegan, Whitlow, & Wagner, 1976). However, individual differences in memory performance have been demonstrated at the infrahuman level, not only as a function of such obvious parameters as integrity of the central nervous system (Thompson & Spencer, 1966) and strain of organism studied (Mathieu, Bouchard, Granger, & Herscovitch, 1976), but also as a function of such individual characteristics as responsiveness to stimulation (Donegan, et al., 1976) and innate biological rhythms (Holloway & Wansley, 1973). Further, individual differences in experiential history have formed the basis for one of the major models of infrahuman memory development—the reinstatement model (Spear & Parsons, 1976), though this model is not typically discussed in terms of individual differences. Even more critically, arguments have been made, within an evolutionary framework, that *processes* of infrahuman memory may vary as a function of the evolutionary history of the organism. Within this viewpoint, there is no obvious rationale for assuming a general process of memory development over and above that based on common organization of the central nervous system or common evolutionary history (D'Amato & Cox, 1976; Rozin & Kalat, 1971). Particularly in terms of species differences in memory processes (Roberts & Grant, 1976), evidence is available which supports this viewpoint (though care must be taken to distinguish process-based species differences from differences due to simple physical or behavioral factors [D'Amato, Safarjan, & Salmon, 1981]). Given the possibilities of individual differences, what are the implications for future research and theorizing in the area of infant memory?

In terms of research, the most obvious conclusion must be that now is perhaps the time to begin the systematic study rather than the systematic suppression of individual differences in infant memory. A first step would be to identify specific parameters that are reliably associated with differences in infant memory performance. One approach would be to measure memory performance in different modalities across a wide variety of tasks, using infants stratified on specific biomedical or environmental parameters. An alternative approach would be the use of clustering techniques, as exemplified in the work of McCall (1979), to identify groups of infants who showed specific patterns of recall that are reliably different from the patterns shown by other clusters of infants.

Identification of individual parameters or individual characteristics represents only a first step, however. As Medin (1976) has pointed out, at some point we must ask what specific *processes* underlie identified individual differences. Identification of processes underlying individual differences in memory performance would contribute greatly to our knowledge of how memory develops. Perhaps even more importantly, the question of what processes underlie individual differences in early memory may form a common meeting ground for those interested in the human and infrahuman study of memory. As has been noted, all too often there is little interaction between human and infrahuman researchers (Medin, 1976). In part, this lack of interaction is a function of different organisms and paradigms used in the infrahuman and human literature. However, the infrahuman organism offers an excellent means of testing questions generated at the human level, in terms of identifying specific neurobiological or environmental factors that may underlie individual differences in memory. One potential interface is seen in the suggestion by Leaton and Tighe (1976) that infrahuman neurophysiological research may be useful in clarifying the meaning of state-habituation relationships that have been detailed with human infants.

In terms of theory, as noted earlier, most existing human memory theories have no place for individual differences. To the extent that individual differences exist, such theories are obviously incomplete. Reliance on incomplete theories may give great comfort to the theoretician but do little to advance our understanding of the phenomena under study. Given that individual differences exist in memory performance and processing, theories must take account of these differences. Given the complexity of individual differences, it may be necessary, for a time, to rely on mini-theories of memory, encompassing memory only within a specific population or within a specific set of conditions. The ultimate aim would be an integration of these mini-theories into a larger scale theory that would account for population and individual differences in both memory performance and processing, across a wide variety of tasks. We are obviously a long way from such an integrated theory. However, denying the obvious fact that individual differences exist will not bring us much closer. It is perhaps time to bring individual differences back from the outer darkness into the main stream of psychology. The area of infant memory seems as good a place to start as any.

ACKNOWLEDGMENTS

Special thanks go to Bob McCall for his detailed review of a preliminary draft of this paper, as well as for providing some very critical references. Thanks are also due to Rob Kail for his very incisive editing.

REFERENCES

Black, L., Steinschneider, A., & Sheehe, P. Neonatal respiratory instability and infant development. *Child Development,* 1979, *50,* 561–564.

Brackbill, Y. Obstetrical medication and infant behavior. In J. Osofsky (Ed.), *Handbook of infant development.* New York: Wiley, 1979.

Cohen, L. A two process model of visual attention. *Merrill-Palmer Quarterly,* 1973, *19,* 157–180.

Cohen, L. Habituation of infant visual attention. In T. Tighe & R. Leaton (Eds.), *Habituation: Perspectives from child development, animal behavior, and neurophysiology.* Hillsdale, N.J.: Lawrence Erlbaum Associates, 1976.

Cohen, L. Examination of habituation as a measure of aberrant infant development. In S. Friedman, & M. Sigman (Eds.), *Pre-term birth and psychological development.* New York: Academic Press, 1981.

Cohen, L., & Gelber, E. Infant visual memory. In L. Cohen & P. Salapatek (Eds.), *Infant perception: From sensation to cognition* (Vol. 1). New York: Academic Press, 1975.

Cole, R., Johnson, R. Ahern, F., Kuse, A., McClearn, G., Vandenberg, S., & Wilson, J. A family study of memory processes and their relation to cognitive test scores. *Intelligence,* 1979, *3,* 127–138.

Cronbach, L. The two disciplines of scientific psychology. *American Psychologist,* 1957, *12,* 671–684.

D'Amato, M., & Cox, J. Delay of consequences and short term memory in monkeys. In D. Medin, W. Roberts, & R. Davis (Eds.), *Process of animal memory.* Hillsdale, N.J.: Lawrence Erlbaum Associates, 1976.

D'Amato, M., Safarjan, W., & Salmon, M. Long delay conditioning and instrumental learning: Some new findings. In N. Spear & R. Miller (Eds.), *Information processing in animals.* Hillsdale, N.J.: Lawrence Erlbaum Associates, 1981.

Dasen, T., Lavallee, N., Retschitzki, J. & Reinhardt, M. Early moderate malnutrition and the development of sensorimotor intelligence. *Journal of Tropical Pediatrics and Environmental Child Health,* 1977, *23,* 146–157.

Decarie, T. *Intelligence and affectivity in early childhood.* New York: International University Press, 1965.

DeFries, J., Plomin, R., Vandenberg, S., & Kuse, A. Parent offspring resemblance for cognitive abilities in the Colorado adoption project. *Intelligence,* 1981, *5,* 245–277.

Dixon, S., Tronick, E., Keefe, C., & Brazelton, T. Perinatal circumstances and new born outcome among the Gusii of Kenya. *Infant Behavior and Development,* 1982, *5,* 11–32.

Donegan, W., Whitlow, J., & Wagner, A. *Post trial reinstatement of the CS in Pavlovian conditioning.* Unpublished manuscript. Cited in J. Whitlow, The dynamics of episodic processing in Pavlovian conditioning, In D. Medin, W. Roberts, & R. Davis (Eds.), *Processing animal memory.* Hillsdale, N.J.: Lawrence Erlbaum Associates, 1976.

Eisenberg, R., Coursin, D., & Rupp, N. Habituation to an acoustic pattern as an index of differences among human neonates. *Journal of Acoustic Research,* 1966, *6,* 239–248.

Fagan, J., & Singer, L. Infant recognition memory as a measure of intelligence. In L. Lipsitt (Ed.), *Advances in infancy research* (Vol. 2). Norwood, N.J.: Ablex Publishing, in press.

Field, T. Infant arousal, attention and affect during early interaction. In L. Lipsitt (Ed.), *Advances in infancy research* (Vol. 1). Norwood, N.J.: Ablex Publishing, 1981.

Fitzgerald, H., & Brackbill, Y. Classical conditioning in infancy: developmental constraints. *Psychological Bulletin,* 1976, *83,* 353–376.

Friedman, S., & Jacobs, B. Sex differents in neonate behavioral responsiveness to repeated auditory stimulation. *Infant Behavior and Development,* 1981, *4,* 175–183.

Gunnar-Vongnechten, M. Changing a frightening toy into a pleasant toy by allowing the infant to control its actions. *Development Psychology,* 1978, *14,* 157–162.

Hardy-Brown, K., Plomin, R., & DeFries, J. Genetic and environmental influences on the rate of communicative development in the first year of life. *Development Psychology,* 1981, *17,* 704–717.

Harmon, R., Morgan, G., & Klein, R. Determinants of normal variation in infants negative reactions to unfamiliar adults. *Journal of the American Academy of Child Psychiatry,* 1977, *16,* 670–683.

Haskins, R., Collier, A., Ramey, C., & Hirschbiel, P. The effect of mild illness on habituation in the first year of life. *Journal of Pediatric Psychology,* 1978, *3,* 150–155.

Hittelman, J., & Dickes, R. Sex differences in neonatal eye contact time. *Merrill-Palmer Quarterly,* 1979, *21,* 171–184.

Holloway, F., & Wansley, F. Multiphasic retention deficits at periodic intervals after passsive avoidance learning. *Science,* 1973, *180,* 268–270.

Horowitz, F. Learning, development, research and individual differences. In L. Lipsitt & H. Reese (Eds.). *Advances in child development and behavior* (Vol. 4). New York: Academic Press, 1969.

Jeffrey, W., & Cohen, L. Habituation in the human infant. In H. Reese (Ed.), *Advances in child development and behavior* (Vol. 6). New York: Academic Press, 1971.

Johnson, D., & Brody, N. Visual habituation, sensorimotor development and tempo of play in one year old infants. *Child Development,* 1977, *48,* 315–319.

Klein, P., Forbes, G., & Nader, P. Effects of starvation in infancy (Pyloric stenosis) on subsequent learning abilities. *Journal of Pediatrics,* 1975, *83,* 8–15.

Kopp, C. Individual differences and intervention for infants and young children. *Journal of Pediatric Psychology,* 1978, *3,* 145–149.

Kopp, C. Antecedents of self-regulation: A developmental perspective. *Developmental Psychology,* 1982, *18,* 199–214.

Kopp, C., & Parmelee, A. Prenatal and perinatal influences on infant behavior. In J. Osofsky *Handbook of infant development.* New York: Wiley, 1979.

Kraemer, H., & Korner, A. Statistical alternatives in assessing reliability, consistency and individual differences for quantitative measures. *Psychological Bulletin,* 1976, *83,* 914–921.

Lamb, M., Garn, S., & Keating, M. Correlation between sociability and cognitive performance among 8 months olds. *Child Development,* 1981, *52,* 711–713.

Lasky, R., & Klein, R. Fixation of the standard and novelty preference in six month old well and malnourished infants. *Merrill-Palmer Quarterly,* 1980, *26,* 171–178.

Leaton, R., & Tighe, T. Comparison between habituation research at the developmental and animal neurophysiological levels. In T. Tighe & R. Leaton (Eds.), *Habituation: Perspectives from child development, animal behavior, and neurophysiology.* Hillsdale, N.J.: Lawrence Erlbaum Associates.

Lester, B., Klein, R., & Martinez, S. The use of habituation in the study of the effects of infantile malnutrition. *Developmental Psychobiology,* 1975, *8,* 451–456.

Lewis, M., & Goldberg, S. Perceptual cognitive development in infancy: A generalized expectancy model as a function of the mother infant interaction. *Merrill-Palmer Quarterly,* 1969, *15,* 81–100.

Lewis, M., & Johnson, N. What's thrown out with bathwater: A baby? *Child Development,* 1971, *42,* 1053–1055.

Lewkowicz, D., & Turkewitz, G. Influences of hemispheric specialization in sensory processing on reaching in infants: Age and gender related effects. *Developmental Psychology,* 1982, *18,* 301–318.

Logue, A. Taste aversion and the generality of the laws of learning. *Psychological Bulletin,* 1979, *86,* 276–296.

Matheney, A. Twins: Concordance for Piagetian-equivalent items derived from the Bayley mental test. *Developmental Psychology,* 1975, *11,* 224–227.

Mathieu, M., Bouchard, M., Granger, L. & Herscovitch, J. Piagetan object permanence in Cebus, Capucinus, Lagothrica Flavicauda & Pan Troglodytes, *Animal Behavior,* 1976, *24,* 585–588.

McCall, R. Smiling and vocalization in infants as indices of perceptual-cognitive processing. *Merrill-Palmer Quarterly,* 1972, *18,* 341–347.

McCall, R. Challenges to a science of developmental psychology. *Child Development,* 1977, *48,* 333–344.

McCall, R. Individual differences in the pattern of habituation at five and 10 months of age. *Developmental Psychology,* 1979, *15,* 559–569.

McCall, R. Nature-nurture and the two realms of development: a proposed integration with respect to mental development. *Child Development,* 1981, *52,* 1–12.

McCall, R., & Kagan, J. Individual differences in the infants distribution of attention to stimulus discrepancy. *Developmental Psychology,* 1970, *2,* 90–98.

McCall, R., & Kennedy, C. Subjective uncertainty, variability of experience and the infants response to discrepancy. *Child Development,* 1980, *51,* 285–287.

McCall, R., & McGhee, P. The discrepancy hypothesis of attention and affect in infants. In I. Uzgiris & F. Weizmann (Eds.), *Structuring of experience.* New York: Plenum, 1977.

McGuinness, D., & Pribram, K. The origins of sensory bias in the development of gender differences in perception and cognition. In M. Bortner (Ed.), *Cognitive growth and development.* New York: Bruner-Mazel, 1979.

Medin, D. Animal models and memory models. In D. Medin, W. Roberts, & R. Davis (Eds.), *Processes of animal memory.* Hillsdale, N.J.: Lawrence Erlbaum Associates, 1976.

Miller, D., Sinnott, J., Short, E., & Haines, A. Individual differences in habituation rates and object concept performance. *Child Development,* 1976, *47,* 528–531.

Miranda, S., & Fantz, R. Recognition memory in Down Syndrome and normal infants. *Child Development,* 1974, *45,* 651–660.

Molfese, D., & Molfese, V. Hemisphere and stimulus differences as reflected in the cortical responses of newborn infants to speech stimuli. *Developmental Pyschology,* 1979, *15,* 505–511.

Moreau, T., & Birch, H. Relationship between obstetrical general anesthesia and rate of neonatal habituation to repeated stimulation. *Developmental Medicine and Child Neurology,* 1974, *16,* 612–619.

Nelson, K. First steps in language acquisition. *Journal of the American Academy of Child Psychiatry,* 1977, *16,* 563–583.

Nelson, K. Individual differences in language development: Implications for development and language. *Developmental Psychology,* 1981, *17,* 170–187.

Olson, G. An information processing analysis of visual memory and habituation in infants. In T. Tighe & R. Leaton (Eds.), *Habituation: Perspectives from child development, animal behavior, and neurophysiology.* Hillsdale, N.J.: Lawrence Erlbaum Associates, 1976.

Paraskcvopoulos, J., & Hunt, J. McV. Object construction and imitation under differing conditions of rearing. *Journal of Genetic Psychology,* 1971, *119,* 301–321.

Ramey, C., Macphee, D., & Yates, K. Preventing developmental retardation: a general systems model. In L. Bond & J. Joffe (Eds.), *Facilitating infant and early childhood development.* Hanover, N.H.: University Press of New England, in press.

Ratner, H. The role of social context in memory development. In M. Perlmutter (Ed.), *New directions for child development: Children's memory.* San Francisco: Jossey-Bass, 1980.

Richardson, G., & McCluskey, K. *Subject loss in infancy research: How biasing is it?* Paper presented to the International Society for the Study of Behavioral Development, Toronto, August 1981.

Riksen-Walraven, J. Effects of caregiver behavior on habituation rate and self efficacy in infants. *International Journal of Behavioral Development,* 1978, *1,* 105–130.

Roberts, W., & Grant, T. Studies of short time memory in the pigeon using the delayed matching to sample procedure. In D. Medin, W. Roberts, & R. Davis, (Eds.), *Processes of animal memory.* Hillsdale, N.J.: Lawrence Erlbaum Associates, 1976.

Rose, S. Enhancing visual recognition memory in preterm infants. *Developmental Psychology,* 1980, *16,* 85–92.

Rose, S., Gottfried, A., & Bridger, W. Cross-modal transfer in infants: relationship to prematurity and socioeconomic background. *Developmental Psychology,* 1978, *14,* 643–652.

Rose, S., Gottfried, A. & Bridger, W. Effect of haptic cues on visual recognition memory in full-term and pre-term infants. *Infant Behavior and Development,* 1979, *2,* 55–67.

Rovee-Collier, C., & Fagen, J. The retrieval of memory in early infancy. In L. Lipsitt (Ed.), *Advances in infancy research* (Vol. 1). Norwood, N.J.: Ablex, 1981.

Rovee-Collier, C., Sullivan, M., Enright, M., Lucas, D., & Fagen, J. Reactivation of infant memory, *Science,* 1980, *208,* 1159–1161.

Rozin, P., & Kalat, J. Specific hungers and poison avoidance as adaptive specializations of learning. *Psychological Review,* 1971, *78,* 459–486.

Ruddy, M., & Bornstein, M. Cognitive correlates of infant attention and maternal stimulation over the first year of life. *Child Development,* 1982, *53,* 183–188.

Sameroff, A., & Chandler, M. Reproductive risk and the continuum of care taking causality. In F. Horowitz (Ed.), *Review of child development research* (Vol. 4). Chicago: University of Chicago Press, 1975.

Schexnider, V., Bell, R., Shebilske, W., & Quinn, P. Habituation of visual attention in infants with minor physical anomalies. *Child Development,* 1981, *52,* 812–818.

Sigman, M. Early development of preterm and full term infants. *Child Development,* 1976, *47,* 606–612.

Sigman, M., & Parmelee, A. Visual preferences of 4 month old premature and fullterm infants. *Child Development,* 1974, *45,* 959–965.

Siqueland, E. Studies of visual recognition memory in pre-term infants: Differences in development as a function of perinatal morbidity factors. In S. Friedman & M. Sigman (Eds.), *Preterm birth and psychological development.* New York: Academic Press, 1981.

Spear, N., & Parsons, P. Analysis of a reactivation treatment: Ontogenetic determinants of alleviated forgetting. In G. Medin, W. Roberts, & R. Davis (Eds.), *Processes of animal memory.* Hillsdale, N.J.: Lawrence Erlbaum Associates, 1976.

Thomas, A., & Chess, S. Behavioral individuality in childhood. In L. Aronson, E. Tobach, G. Lehrman, & J. Rosenblatt (Eds.), *Development and the evolution of behavior.* San Francisco: Jossey-Bass, 1976.

Thompson, R., & Spencer, W. Habituation: A model phenomenon for the study of neuronal substrates of behavior. *Psychological Review,* 1966, *76,* 16–43.

Wachs, T. D. Reinstatement of early experiences and later learning: An animal analog for human development. *Developmental Psychobiology,* 1973, *6,* 437–444.

Wachs, T. D. The optimal stimulation hypothesis and early development. In I. Uzgiris & F. Weizmann (Eds.). *The structuring of experience.* New York: Plenum, 1977.

Wachs, T. D. Proximal experience and early cognitive-intellectual development: The physical environment. *Merrill-Palmer Quarterly,* 1979, *25,* 3–41.

Wachs, T. D. Proximal experience and early cognitive-intellectual development: The social environment. In A. Gottfried (Ed.), *Home environment and early mental development.* New York: Academic Press, in press.

Wachs, T. D., & Gandour, M. J. Temperament, environment and six month cognitive-intellectual development: A test of the organismic specificity hypothesis. *International Journal of Behavioral Development,* in press.

Wachs, T. D., & Gruen, G. *Early experience and human development.* New York: Plenum, 1982.

Waters, E., Vaughn, B., & Egeland, B. Individual-differences in infant mother attachment relationships at age one. *Child Development,* 1980, *51,* 208–216.

Watson, J. Operant conditioning of visual fixation in infants under visual and auditory reinforcement. *Developmental Psychology,* 1969, *1,* 508–516.

Watson, J., Hayes, L., Dorman, L., & Vietze, P. Infant sex differences in operant fixation with visual and auditory reinforcement. *Infant Behavior and Development,* 1980, *3,* 107–114.

Weizmann, F., Cohen, L., & Pratt, J. Novelty, familiarity and the development of infant attention. *Developmental Psychology,* 1971, *4,* 149–154.

Werner, J., & Perlmutter, M. Development of visual memory in infants. In H. Reese & L. Lipsitt (Eds.), *Advances in child behavior and development* (Vol. 14). New York: Academic Press, 1979.

Werner, J., & Siqueland, E. Visual recognition memory in the preterm infant. *Infant Behavior and Development,* 1978, *1,* 79–94.

White, K., & Brackbill, Y. Visual development in pre and full term infants. In S. Friedman & M. Sigman (Eds.), *Pre-term birth and psychological development.* New York: Academic Press, 1981.

Williams, L., & Golinski, J. Infant behavioral states and speech sound discrimination. *Child Development,* 1979, *50,* 1243–1246.

10 Ontogenetic Differences in Stimulus Selection During Conditioning

Norman E. Spear
David Kucharski
State University of New York

This chapter is concerned with ontogenetic differences in what, among the multitude of elements comprising an episode, is "selected" to form one's representation of that episode in memory. The basic topic of stimulus selection, sometimes discussed under the heading "selective learning" or "selective attention," is so broadly pervasive an issue that one hardly knows where to begin in discussing it. Adding the complication of ontogenetic differences in this process multiplies the difficulty further. As one vehicle for focus within this topic, we shall describe why our laboratory began studying this topic a few years ago.

Our study of the ontogeny of stimulus selection arose from interest in infantile amnesia. "Infantile amnesia" is the term used by Freud to refer to the adult human's ineffectiveness in remembering episodes that took place prior to the age of about 3 years. Within the past 10–15 years an animal model of this phenomenon has been developed and applied toward its understanding, as witnessed by a number of reviews (Campbell & Coulter, 1976; Campbell & Spear, 1972; Spear, 1978, 1979a,b; Spear & Campbell, 1979).

Experimental analyses of infantile amnesia through this animal model have been infrequent and fairly unsuccessful. Better progress toward understanding this phenomenon has been limited by a number of factors: the experiments themselves are difficult, time consuming, and prone to a variety of methodological mistakes (the basic caveats in this work were laid out in a general sense by Campbell, 1967, and repeated in some of the reviews cited above); the learning process itself is not well understood ontogenetically; and perhaps in part because the learning is not well understood, theories of ontogenetic differences in forgetting have been developed less tightly than one might prefer. There is by no means a shortage of theories of infantile amnesia (for reviews see those just cited and in addition, Tomkins, 1970, and White & Pillemer, 1979). It is only that the theories have not been sufficiently constrained by data to permit a narrowing of focus and decisive experiments.

Given these circumstances, our laboratory set out a few years ago to focus on two matters of substance that promised steady progress. One was rather technical—the development of tests of learning and memory especially adapted for rats from infancy to adulthood. The other was the general issue of what is learned and what remembered by the developing animal—the issue of "stimulus selection."

ECOLOGICALLY DRIVEN ADVANCES IN BEHAVIORAL TECHNOLOGY

The first task for our laboratory was to devise tests of learning for preweanling rats that were more sensitive ecologically than those "borrowed" from studies originally designed for adults, and yet sufficiently flexible to assess special characteristics of stimulus selection for rats of any age. It was fortunate that the same notion had occurred to a variety of other scientists across the United States, and fortunate also that they were a good deal more inventive than we were in solving this problem. A good sample of these technical innovations can be found in the report of the symposium held at Binghamton in the late 1970s (Spear & Campbell, 1979) and in chapters in the present volume (Campbell; Johanson & Hall; and Rudy, Vogt, & Hyson). These new tests indicated that when the "question" of whether learning had occurred was phrased properly to the developing rat, mouse, or cat, and when the form of the animal's "answer" was suited to its response capabilities, the associative capacities of the infants of these species were found to be a very great deal more effective than had previously been suspected. We return shortly to some illustrations.

The technical development of more suitable tests of the ontogeny of learning and memory provided in addition some information spinoff of theoretical importance. It became evident that in a plainly practical sense, we in this business might best adhere to a view something like that of Anohkin (1964) in acknowledging a certain age-specificity in what will be learned. At one level this is no more than a truism. Sensory capacity is in some stages of infancy simply inadequate for learning certain events merely because of inadequate detection, and likewise, the motor system can be inadequate for expression of learning merely because of insufficient capability in movement or coordination of movement. This sort of constraint is trivial for the understanding of learning and memory; it is assumed that such differences are taken into account methodologically or conclusions about learning and memory simply are not made.

But there is more to it than that. An ontogenetic gap may exist between the time a sensory-motor system becomes functional for some purposes and the point at which it is modifiable by experience. In other words, even when the constituents for information input and behavioral expression are otherwise functional, they may not be ready to take part in the processes of learning and memory. This possibility, which is not yet certain, has gained credibility by careful ecological considerations such as those illustrated in the work of Anohkin (1964). Spear (this volume) has suggested that such considerations were responsible for technological advances leading to evidence for capability in learning and memory at ages much younger than previously supposed. That chapter also indicated the selectivity, apparently age-specific, in what is learned and remembered at these ages. This point is implied also in the chapters by Campbell, by Alberts, and by Johanson and Hall, and is an explicit component of the chapter by Rudy et al. (this volume). The major purpose of the present chapter is to describe our recent empirical investigations of such age-related differences in stimulus selection for learning and memory.

FOCUS ON STIMULUS SELECTION

Elsewhere in this volume it is illustrated that in contrast to what had appeared to be severe limitations in the associative capacity of infant animals, recent tests show that from birth onward the infant and neonatal rat are capable of learning a great deal. From a general perspective this alone is neither surprising nor very interesting. As also mentioned elsewhere, the central nervous system of the newborn rat is a much more impressive structure than that of many simpler animals that have shown good associative capacity, and the infant rat's brain is in some sense more complete than that of decorticate animals (and persons) that have little difficulty in simple conditioning and learning (Spear, this volume). What seems of more interest is the nature of the solution to the problem, the steps taken to permit observation of the associative processes in these very young organisms.

The solution was based on close observation of the infant animal, consequential appreciation of its fundamental biological problem of growth, and some insight into the systems it regularly applies for the procurement, consumption, and conservation of the calories needed for this growth. The special techniques applied for adaptation by the infant differ ontogenetically, and are fairly specific. A basic implication is that at each ontogenetic stage from birth onward, the developing animal has a special mission, a particular focus in its behavior that leads to its selecting for learning only a fraction of those things that could be learned in any particular episode. We may expect, therefore, that this selective learning (stimulus selection) will differ ontogenetically in regular fashion. This topic is addressed with data in the present chapter.

There are at least three other reasons to be concerned with ontogenetic changes in stimulus selection. First, this topic addresses the contemporary question of how general the laws of learning and memory can be. If an infant shows learning to Episode A but not Episode B, is it because these episodes are controlled by such different systems that principles regulating their learning simply make no contact with one another? To say that more specifically and simply, a 15-day-old rat that finds food equally predicted by both an odor and a location will more likely learn about the odor, whereas an adult rat will more likely learn about the location; is this because these rats differ in what they could possibly learn, what they would more probably learn, or in what they "prefer" to express about what they have learned? The second reason for studying stimulus selection ontogenetically in the rat is because this topic has begun to be studied increasingly with human infants as well as older children. There is an opportunity not only for fruitful interaction between these types of studies but also for the application of animal models toward determining the physiological basis of these common behaviors.

The third reason, the one that provided most of the impetus for our present work, is that ontogenetic change in stimulus selection is potentially a viable explanation of infantile amnesia. Potential relationships between ontogenetic differences in stimulus selection and ontogenetic differences in forgetting (i.e., infantile amnesia; Spear, 1979a, b) have been discussed elsewhere. There is no need to review the details of this argument, and the relationships can be stated simply. Suppose preweanlings learn different things than adults about an episode—acquire a different set of attributes to represent the episode in memory (for the majority of the data reported in this chapter the youngest rats were 18 days old at conditioning, perhaps too old for designation as infants; these animals are referred to henceforth as "preweanlings"). If so they might be expected to forget more than adults if they had acquired either too few attributes to promote effective memory retrieval later or if they had acquired the "wrong" ones, those that happened to be most susceptible to prevalent sources of forgetting, such as interference.

We will see that this preliminary approach now seems, perhaps not surprisingly, to be at least half wrong and probably incomplete. Some of our data suggest that the infant does not acquire fewer memory attributes that an adult to represent an episode and may in fact acquire more. Other evidence indicates, however, that the quality of the attributes, the way the preweanling represents an episode, may be significantly different from that of the adult.

It is probably necessary at this point to resolve the apparent discrepancy between ontogenetic differences in *what* is learned—differences proposed here as determinants of corresponding differences in forgetting—and ontogenetic differences in *degree* of learning—which must be held constant to justify ontogenetic conclusions about age differences in forgetting. The issue is one of experimental design. The fact is that we can control degree of learning, defined operationally, by holding constant across ages the probability with which an acquired memory is manifested in the absence of the source of forgetting introduced for experimental purposes. Experimental control of this factor, using whatever are the best techniques available, is necessary to permit conclusions about interactions between age and the source of forgetting.

It is fundamental, however, that *what is learned may exceed that which is necessary and sufficient for full behavioral manifestation of that learning as designated by the experimenter*. This allows for a great deal of undetected variation in how an episode is in fact represented in memory. It is such qualitative differences in what is learned, hypothetically linked to ontogenetic status, that may provide explanatory factors in respect to infantile amnesia. When such differences are identified and shown capable of being placed under experimental control, they will in the future become sources of experimental confounding rather than sources of explanation for infantile amnesia. But at present, the identification of age-related differences in what is learned is interesting and important itself for a variety of issues pertaining to the ontogeny of perception, learning and forgetting.

TESTS OF ONTOGENETIC CHANGES IN WHAT IS LEARNED IN CONDITIONING WITH A MULTI-ELEMENT CS

We began with some general hypotheses about ontogenetic differences in the selection of what will be learned from multiple-event episodes. Focus was on two kinds of episodes. For one class of episode the events predicting the reinforcer occur simultaneously and so provide redundant information with respect to its prediction. The alternative is the class of episode in which events that precede and predict the reinforcer occur sequentially.

We initially hypothesized a simple ontogenetic increase in the effectiveness with which animals process multiple events. In other words, we expected that the older the animal between neotony and adulthood, the more likely would it learn about the predictive value of redundant events. We based this on the perhaps naive assumptions that the learning of such redundancy would have adaptive value for later retention, and that between neotony and adulthood a general increase in the capacity for processing large amounts of information would accommodate the apparently increasing need to process these amounts. In spite of the lack of solid evidence for an ontogenetic increase in processing capacity (see Spear, this volume) we were influenced by some gross neurophysiological evidence (e.g., that during the second half of the rat's first month of life, the number of synapses in the cortex increases more than tenfold).

A second hypothesis was concerned with the integration of temporally separate events. We felt that relative to adults, younger animals would have more difficulty integrating sequentially presented events such as the elements of a conditioned stimulus in classical conditioning. The evidence with infant rats, limited though it was, indicated severe deficits in conditioning with long intervals between the CS and US (trace conditioning), a possibly special deficit in second order conditioning when a neutral stimulus was paired successively rather than simultaneously with an established CS, and a special sensitivity in infant rats to retroactive and proactive interferences that seemed likely to leave them vulnerable to such effects when learning sequentially presented events (Steinert, Infurna, Jardula, & Spear, 1979; Cheatle, 1980; and Smith & Spear, 1981, respectively). We therefore expected that in processing multiple-event episodes, younger animals would be at a particular disadvantage with sequential compared to simultaneous presentation of events.

We tested ontogenetic differences in what is learned about redundant contextual events in both classical conditioning and instrumental learning. We found, somewhat to our surprise, that changes in ambient odors between conditioning of either type and testing were more disruptive for rats during their third week of life than in adulthood (e.g., Newman, Caza, & Spear, 1982; Solheim, Hensler, & Spear, 1980). We did not expect this. From the limited-capacity notion, it had seemed that the younger animals would be less likely than adults to process redundant contextual information. But these data suggested the opposite relationship. This paradigm, however, did not permit firm inferences about ontogenetic differences in what was learned about the redundant context. For instance, perhaps the adults noticed and learned as much about the change in context as the preweanlings, but their performance established by the contingencies of the more immediate task was less subject to disruption. Although our experiments had included a number of implicit tests that would seem to eliminate this possibility, it could not be eliminated entirely with this sort of design. What was needed was a more direct assessment of what is learned. We felt that the best way to do this would be to assess the conditioning of multiple elements in a conditioned stimulus.

Age-Related Differences in Learning of Elements in a Compound Stimulus

Our ontogenetic study of this kind began with a Ph.D. dissertation by Pamela Steinert (Steinert, 1981). Steinert presented 18-day-old or adult rats with two successive flavors (tastes) that were either explicitly paired with illness induced by LiCl injection (with a 1-hour delay between the taste [CS] and LiCL [US]) or explicitly unpaired with the US (24-hour CS-US delay). Each rat experienced its taste through solution drunk from the (needle absent) end of a syringe. With this procedure, used in all our studies of this kind, we could carefully control the quantities of the two solutions given each rat and the temporal relationships either between the two tastes or between a taste and the LiCl injection. A variety of different kinds of tastes were administered and the effects of amount of taste were investigated in other portions of the thesis. We emphasize here only those conditions in which sucrose solution and (decaffeinated) coffee solution provided the stimulus compound. The concentrations of these different tastes were selected from pilot experiments so as to yield, following their individual pairing with illness, equivalent strengths of aversion conditioning. These solutions were presented in succession, one immediately following the other, and in this study order of presentation seemed to have no effect on conditioning (due apparently to the 1-hour delay between CS and US). To simplify presentation of this and subsequent studies, we will refer only to the conditioning of aversion to the sucrose solution, which was always tested with a two-bottle procedure in which the animal had a choice between sucrose solution or water (testing of coffee required a single-bottle test the results of which are less clearly interpretable for our purposes).

In the experiments of primary interest here (Experiments 2b, 3, and 4, Steinert, 1981), Steinert varied othogonally the amount and flavor of solution in each of the two elements of the successive compound while holding constant the total amount of solution given the animal in each condition. Infants given the same amount of coffee as sucrose received .3 ml on two successive occasions, one of coffee and the other of sucrose; those given less coffee than sucrose received .1 ml coffee and .5 ml sucrose; and those given more coffee than sucrose received .5 ml coffee and .1 ml sucrose solution. For adults the ratios were identical, but the amounts of each solution were multiplied by a factor of 10.

The results of primary interest here are more easily described than was the method. They deal with "overshadowing," decreased conditioning to one stimulus element due to the presence of a more salient element. A clear test of ontogenetic difference in overshadowing was not possible in Steinert's study because single-solution, single-amount control conditions were not included in these experiments and the 1-hour CS-US delay nearly maximized the adult superiority in conditioning, leaving little room to detect a further difference. Two of Steinert's results nevertheless suggested more overshadowing by infants than adults. First, the correlations between the degrees of conditioning to the sucrose and coffee components were positive for adults, indicating conditioning strength was allocated about equally or proportionally to the two CS elements so that the more conditioning to one element, the greater the conditioning to the other; these correlations were negative for preweanlings, suggesting that the younger animals tended to condition to one element only at the expense of the other, so that the stronger the conditioning to one element, the weaker the conditioning to the other.

The second result of special interest arose initially by accident when, for reasons that need not be explained here, extraneous novel odors were present during conditioning in one experiment. This seemed to impair conditioning particularly in the preweanlings. Steinert tested this directly (Experiment 4) by exposing half the infants to their conditioning treatment in the presence of an extraneous novel odor and half in the absence of this odor. The effect of this extraneous odor was to drastically reduce conditioning to the sucrose solution, for all amounts of sucrose-relative-to-coffee in the stimulus compounds. Although Steinert did not directly test the influence of the extraneous odor on adult conditioning, data published at about the time of this experiment had suggested that for adults, such an extraneous odor might facilitate ("potentiate") rather than impair conditioning of a taste aversion in adults (Clarke, Westbrook, & Irwin, 1979; Rusiniak, Hankins, Garcia, & Brett, 1979; although these studies reported the opposite order of potentiation—odor by flavor—there was little hard evidence that potentiation must be unidirectional).

It began to look as if the preweanling's capacity for learning and memory had been overloaded in Steinert's experiment. Greater overshadowing in the preweanlings than in the adults, especially when the distracting odor was present, seemed to be indicated by the correlations between the aversions to the coffee and sucrose elements. For adults, the correlation was $+.47$; for preweanlings without the distracting odor, the correlation was $-.41$; and for preweanlings with the distracting odor, the correlation was $-.55$. When Steinert devised an index based on control conditions that would indicate, according to an arbitrary criterion, when a taste was and was not "avoided," the percentages of subjects avoiding both the coffee and sucrose tastes were 67%, 25%, and 6% for adults, preweanlings, and preweanlings with distracting odors, respectively.

Steinert's Results Present a Paradox.   The correlations in Steinert's thesis seemed to indicate that the preweanlings tended to learn about only one of the two elements in the CS while the adults learned about both. This would be consistent with the general notion of a limited memory capacity among preweanlings. But it seemed inconsistent with other evidence.

For instance, Steinert's correlations would seem to indicate greater overshadowing among the preweanlings than the adults, or more generally, more selective learning among the preweanlings than the adults. Yet the general trend of the evidence with humans indicates less selectivity in learning among younger subjects (Kail & Hagen, 1977, 1982). What little evidence was available seemed to indicate the same for animals also, as implied by our data suggesting greater learning about redundant contextual events, and hence less selective learning, among younger subjects. Yet it seemed premature to consider this evidence as inconsistent with that of Steinert (1981). The experiments under comparison were only remotely related to one another so far as the ontogeny of stimulus selection is concerned. Furthermore, the general significance of Steinert's correlations was uncertain because the age-related differences seemed due primarily to those groups in which the CS elements differed in both amount and quality of flavor. We therefore began a series of experiments to assess and extend the results of Steinert, testing age-related differences in the processing of stimulus compounds that consisted of distinctly different tastes. At the same time we conducted a variety of experiments to assess the generality of the ontogeny of stimulus selection with different kinds of conditioned stimuli. One such series is mentioned briefly because it helps to provide perspective on the central problem.

We (with Patricia Caza) presented rats a single-taste CS or a CS compound of two different tastes, accompanied or not accompanied by an extraneous odor. For some subjects, these conditions predicted illness and for others they did not (explicitly unpaired control conditions). When a single taste (sucrose solution) was presented in the context of an ambient odor (methyl salicylate), we were surprised to find that the preweanlings showed more *potentiation* than the adults. In other words, conditioning of an aversion to sucrose solution was more effective when presented in the context of the odor than when presented alone—that is, potentiation occurred—and the effect was greater for preweanlings than for adults.

We also found that with a two-flavor CS in which sucrose solution was consumed first followed immediately by ingestion of methyl salicylate in solution (or vice versa), conditioning to the sucrose solution tended to be less than when it was presented alone—that is, overshadowing occurred—whether or not it was accompanied by an ambient (methyl salicylate) odor. This overshadowing effect tended to be greater for adults than for preweanlings.

Each of these results suggested that the preweanlings were less selective than adults in what they had noticed or learned about the redundant aspects of the CS or odor context. It also seemed that the temporal relationships between stimulus elements might be especially important, not only for the form taken by stimulus selection generally but also for ontogenetic differences in this effect. When the occurrence of the sucrose taste and the methyl salicylate odor was simultaneous, potentiation was found; but when the sucrose and methyl salicylate tastes occurred successively—temporally separate—overshadowing was found. At about the same time we were conducting the above experiments, Rescorla and his colleagues also were finding that conditioning of pigeons or rats to a CS compound was quite different when the elements of the compound were presented simultaneously than when presented successively, with potentiation more likely in the former case (Rescorla & Durlach, 1981). And of particular importance ontogenetically, Cheatle (1980) had completed his Ph.D. thesis, which indicated that especially for very young rats (4 days old), second-order conditioning occurred with a simultaneous compound of two distinct odors but not with successive presentation of these odors, although older subjects (8 days old) showed second-order conditioning in both cases (Cheatle, 1980; also see Rudy and Cheatle, 1979). This suggested that we should compare the influence of these two kinds of conditioned stimuli, successive and simultaneous compounds, under circumstances in which better temporal control could be exerted than was possible with our ambient odor.

Conditioned Aversions to Multiple Versus Single Flavors.   The first experiment manipulated several variables during the taste-illness conditioning episodes, using procedures like those of Steinert (1981). The major variable of interest was the temporal proximity of the taste presentations. One group of animals received a coffee presentation (a fixed quantity delivered into the mouth via a syringe) followed 1 hour later by a sucrose presentation (or vice versa; this constituted the basic "single"-element CS condition while maintaining equated experience with each taste); a second group of animals received a coffee presentation followed 30 seconds later by a sucrose presentation (or vice versa); for the final group of animals, the sucrose and coffee tastes were mixed in the same solution. A second variable was the delay between the last CS element(s) and the US (injection of LiCl to induce internal malaise): 2 minutes, 1 hour, or 24 hours. The final analytic variable was order of testing. The first test was given 4 days after conditioning, and the second was given 24 hours after the first. Half of the animals received a sucrose preference test (sucrose intake / sucrose + water intake) first and a coffee intake test second, and for the remaining subjects order of test was reversed.

We must limit our main focus to a few of the more interesting comparisons with respect to sucrose aversions. Animals given successive presentations of tastes were compared to those given the sucrose presentation 1 hour following the coffee presentation, as were the animals given the simultaneous presentation of the two tastes. The successive presentations resulted in overshadowinglike results replicating the previous findings of Revusky (1971). In other words, sucrose aversion was attenuated when a second taste was presented in a sequential manner during conditioning. However, animals given a simultaneous presentation of the same two tastes demonstrated potentiation (cf. Rescorla, 1981). Put another way, these subjects developed a stronger sucrose aversion if coffee was mixed with the sucrose solution as the CS. The most striking finding was that while preweanlings demonstrated about equal or more overshadowing than adults when the tastes were presented sequentially, they demonstrated much more potentiation when the tastes were presented simultaneously. Lett (1982) has suggested that prior exposure to a compound taste may be necessary for potentiation, yet the present potentiation effect (see Fig. 10.1) was obtained without any previous exposure to the taste-compound solution. In other words, animals given a simultaneous presentation of sucrose and coffee as their CS demonstrated stronger sucrose aversion than animals given only sucrose during conditioning, and this effect was greater for preweanlings than adults.

Preweanling animals demonstrated poorer long-delay learning than adults. While the single-element CS aversions were about equal for the preweanlings and adults if the CS-US delay was 2 minutes, the preweanlings demonstrated weaker aversions than adults if the CS-US delay was 1 hour. This was to be expected from previous evidence. What was not expected was the elimination of this effect among animals given the simultaneous presentation of the two tastes as their CS. The benefits due to potentiation were so strong for the preweanlings

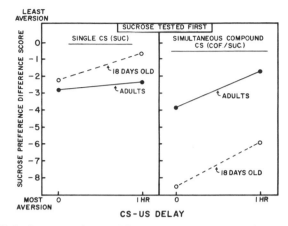

FIG. 10.1   Sucrose preference differences scores ([sucrose preference score for each individual experimental subject−X̄ sucrose preference score for respective control group]÷standard deviation of respective control group) for preweanling and adult animals conditioned with either sucrose or the coffee/sucrose compound, as a function of delay between taste presentation and LiCl injection.

that the deficits due to long-delay learning were overridden. This result is seen in Fig. 10.1.

The final major result of this experiment was that the potentiated sucrose aversion was strongly attenuated if the animals received a coffee intake test prior to the sucrose preference test. The magnitude of this effect was stronger for the preweanling animals than for the adults and is illustrated in Fig. 10.2. Because the coffee intake test did not include any administration of LiCl, it may be considered an extinction trial. The implications of this result will be discussed below. However, it should be noted that Lett (1982) had suggested that preexposure to the compound taste should have been necessary for this result also.

Another experiment was, essentially, one of several replications of the above. Preweanling and adult rats were given as their CS either saccharin, salt, or a simultaneous compound presentation of saccharin and salt. In the present experiment, preweanling animals that were conditioned on the compound taste demonstrated better saccharin aversions (potentiation) than those animals conditioned on saccharin alone. This was not the case for the adult animals. Again, these results were obtained without prior exposure to the compound. Similar results pertaining to long-delay learning and extinction replicated the findings of the first experiment. These results are illustrated in Fig. 10.3.

Another example of this series of experiments employed several different taste and odor stimuli. Animals of both age groups received conditioning presentations of either sucrose, sucrose presented simultaneously with a lemon-flavored

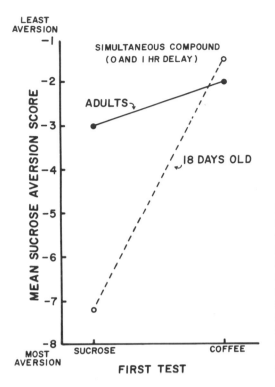

FIG. 10.2. Sucrose aversion (preference difference) scores for preweanlings and adults conditioned on the coffee/sucrose compound as a function of test order. Each test also served as an extinction experience so, for example, the sucrose aversion score for rats tested first on coffee estimates sucrose aversion after some extinction of the coffee aversion. The effect of delay between taste presentation and LiCl injection (0 and 1-hour delay) was collapsed.

solution, sucrose presented simultaneously with ambient methyl salicylate, or sucrose presented simultaneously with a lemon solution and ambient methyl salicylate. If the CS was lemon solution presented sequentially with the sucrose solution, animals of both age groups demonstrated attenuated sucrose aversions relative to animals for which the CS was sucrose alone. However, for all instances in which the CS consisted of a simultaneous compound of two or more elements, preweanlings animals had greater potentiation or less overshadowing than adults.

A Comment on Theory. According to the multiple association theory, potentiation is due to the addition of within-compound associations (between CS elements) to those between each of the CS elements and the US (Rescorla & Durlach, 1981; Spear & Kucharski, 1983). In the above experiments one element could be associated with the second, which is itself aversive due to conditioning, so the net aversion to the first becomes inflated beyond its direct association with the US. Preweanlings could be more likely than adults to form multiple associations. However, this theory is hard pressed to account for the overshadowing that

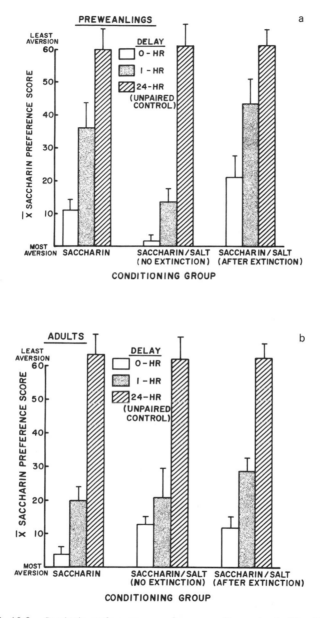

FIG. 10.3.   Saccharin preference scores for preweanlings animals (Fig. 10.3a) and adult animals (Fig. 10.3b) as a function of taste-illness delay (0, 1, or 24 hours) and conditioning group. Animals were conditioned with just saccharin or a saccharin/salt compound. Animals trained in the compound either did or did not experience a salt intake test prior to the saccharin preference test.

occurs when the same stimuli are presented in rapid succession. A further difficulty with this interpretation arose from our next experiment.

The multiple association theory of potentiation expects that nonreinforced presentations of either the compound itself or both elements separately should result in equal extinction of the aversion to the compound. If rats are given a pairing of a sucrose/coffee simultaneous compound CS with LiCl, followed by exposure to sucrose alone and to coffee alone, the sucrose-illness and coffee-illness association should undergo equal extinction; because the aversion to the compound is mediated through these two aversions, the aversion to the compound should undergo the same degree of extinction. According to the "Gestalt" or configuration theory (Rescorla, 1981), the compound is treated by the animal as a different entity from its separate elements. Relative to a single-element CS the greater net intensity of the configured "blob" of two elements leads to its stronger conditioning, but generalization decrement reduces this advantage when a single element, rather than the compound is tested. The net result can be potentiation. This view expects that nonreinforced presentations of the element should be less effective than nonreinforced presentations of the compound for extinction of the aversion to the compound.

We found that when preweanling animals were conditioned to the simultaneous compound of sucrose and coffee and then given nonreinforced presentations of one or both elements, the aversion to the *compound* was only mildly attenuated, less so than for adults. This result was replicated when degree of extinction of each element was equated carefully for adults and preweanlings and in circumstances in which the effect of extinction of the compound itself was about equal for the two age groups. These facts seem consistent with the notion that preweanlings do not form representations of the individual taste elements in a simultaneous compound during conditioning. Only when the elements are presented in isolation, as in the testing or extinction sessions, do these animals form such representations. The adult animals seemed to view the simultaneous compound CS differently, as made up of a "sweet" and "bitter" component for instance, and to form appropriate representations of each element in addition to a configured representation of the compound (Spear & Kucharski, 1983).

Although these results indicate that preweanling animals are more likely than adults to form a configured representation of the compound stimulus, these results by themselves do not account for their greater potentiation. Booth and Hammond (1971) found that when "configural conditioning" occurred to the compound, the components became ineffective as CSs when presented alone. Indeed, some authors have proposed that any responding to the components is mediated solely through stimulus generalization. This could predict greater overshadowing rather than greater potentiation by the younger rats. Two further studies from our laboratory indicate, however, that greater CS intensity (which presumably accompanies an increased number of elements in a CS) facilitates conditioning more for preweanlings than for adults. Furthermore, the generalization decrement from testing with a stimulus less intense than the CS is less for the younger animals (Spear & Kucharski, 1983). Taken together, these facts tend to support the view that the greater potentiation seen in younger animals is a net consequence of (1) their greater boost in conditioning strength due to the higher CS intensity of a compound than a single-element CS, and (2) their lesser generalization decrement when a single-element test follows conditioning with the stimulus compound.

Summary. These tests of stimulus selection in the conditioning of a flavor aversion gave us several kinds of information. First, age-related differences in the conditioned aversion to a single flavor were magnified when conditioning involved a multiple-flavor CS, relative to a single-flavor CS. Second, the form of this effect was markedly dependent on whether the elements of the CS occurred simultaneously or successively. Relative to when a particular element had been presented alone during conditioning, conditioning to that element was either more enhanced or less impaired for preweanlings than adults when that element appeared in simultaneous combination with another during conditioning. But when that element appeared with another in succession during conditioning, its conditioning was somewhat *more* impaired for preweanlings than adults. This effect was reflected in still another way: conditioning to a particular element was stronger for preweanlings than for adults when that element had appeared with another in a simultaneous CS compound but was weaker for preweanlings than adults when that element had appeared in a successive compound as the CS. These relationships held whether the CS-US delay in conditioning was 2 minutes or 1 hour. Third, in comparison to adults, preweanlings had a greater increase in conditioning strength with higher intensities of the CS (with intensity of the test stimulus held constant). This was so whether the "intensity increase" was produced by a simple increase in the concentration of the single flavor constituting the CS or by increase in the concentration of an element paired with that flavor to form a compound CS (Spear & Kucharski, 1983). Also, the conditioning manifested by preweanlings was less impaired than that of the adult when the test stimulus differed somewhat from the conditioning stimulus. Finally, each of these results was replicated with each of several combinations of flavors.

Further Tests of These Ontogenetic Differences in Stimulus Selection

Our subsequent experiments on this topic focused on the ontogenetic differences in conditioning to a simultaneous compound CS. This decision arose in part because the ontogenetic differences were simply larger with a simultaneous than a successive compound. But also, phenomena associated with simultaneous compounds were closer to other issues we were testing at the time, and solutions to these issues seemed likely to provide important steps toward understanding a process of vital ontogenetic importance—perceptual learning.

Our next series of experiments was conducted to assess the ontogeny of stimulus selection with simultaneous CS compounds in circumstances other than flavor aversion. We did not want our conclusions tied only to circumstances in which a flavor aversion is induced by injections of LiCl. There are uncertain central effects of the latter, and certain cases of stimulus selection with this paradigm are viewed by some as a quite special case (Lett, 1982). Within a completely different set of procedures, therefore, we assessed the aversion conditioned to an odor arising from pairing a footshock with a simultaneous compound consisting of that odor and another.

Potentiation with an Odor-Odor CS in Simultaneous Compound.   This study tested animals of the same ages as in our flavor-conditioning series, either 18 days old or 60 to 80 days old ("preweanlings" and "adults," respectively). In addition, 8-day-old rats ("infants") also were tested. For each age group, the general question was how conditioning of an aversion to odor A would differ when (1) odor A was paired with footshock in comparison to when (2) a simultaneous compound of odor A and odor B was paired with that footshock.

The conditioning procedure involved pairing a CS+ (either odor A, odor B, or A+B) with footshock and a CS− (odor C) with the absence of footshock. In this experiment, odors A and B were lemon and orange (or vice versa) and the CS− odor was methyl salicylate. On each conditioning trial the rat was exposed to the CS− for 20 seconds, then to the CS+ for 20 seconds, during which two-second footshocks of 1 mA each were delivered, one beginning the 8th second, the other beginning the 18th.

Each animal was given four such conditioning trials followed by two odor preference tests, given in counterbalanced order. One test compared the animal's relative preference for the vicinity of the lemon odor (one element of the CS+) that emanated from a convex piece of fur in the wall of one end of an alley, relative to that of a novel odor, amyl acetate, that came from a similarly placed piece of fur in the opposite end of the alley. For the other test, the comparison was between orange (the other element of the CS+) and amyl acetate. The question was what percentage of the 5-minute test would be spent in the half of the alley nearest lemon or orange. To the extent that this was less for the experimental (conditioned) rats than for control animals given the same experience but without the pairing of an odor and footshock, an aversion to lemon or orange was verified.

To summarize so far, the basis of the experimental design was a 3 × 3 factorial in which rats 8, 18, or 60 days postnatal had footshock paired with either lemon odor, orange odor, or lemon and orange odors presented simultaneously. The complete experimental design involved two other orthogonal variables. One was the contingency between these odors and footshock; in addition there were for each of the nine basic experimental conditions, explicitly unpaired control groups given four footshocks 1 hour prior to receiving the same "conditioning" treatment as the experimental animals but without footshock. The other variable was the order of testing; half the animals were tested for their lemon preference first and half for their orange preference first. The reason for testing the orange preferences of animals conditioned with lemon and the lemon preferences for animals conditioned with orange was to test for generalization between these two odors. This provided an important control condition to which we shall return.

The basic results of this experiment are shown in Fig. 10.4, which indicates conditioned aversions to lemon, and Fig. 10.5, which indicates conditioned aversions to orange. The same basic phenomena were found in both cases, with only a slight divergence in terms of statistical significance. The 8-day-old animals had significant aversive conditioning when either a single odor or the compound odor served as the CS+, but the degree of conditioning did not differ. In other words, the youngest rats showed neither overshadowing nor potentiation. But the results were quite different for the older animals.

Both the 18-day-old and 60-day-old animals conditioned differently to the compound than to a single odor, but in opposite directions. In terms of the

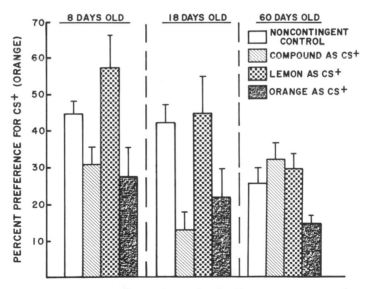

FIG. 10.4   Percentage preference for orange odor (time spent on orange ÷ time spent on orange and banana) among 8-, 18-, or 60-day-old animals as a function of conditioning group. Animals had been given paired presentations of either lemon, orange, or lemon/orange odor compound with footshock. Additional animals had received unpaired presentations of orange odor and footshock.

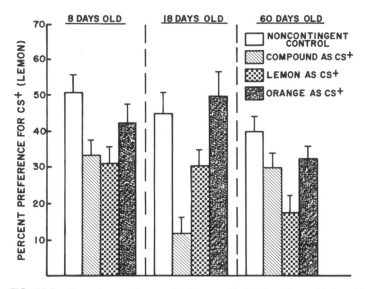

FIG. 10.5. Percentage preference for lemon odor by 8-, 18-, or 60-day-old
animals as a function of conditioning group. Animals received paired presentations of either lemon, orange, or lemon/orange odor compound with footshock.
Additional animals received unpaired presentations of lemon odor and footshock.

conditioned aversion to lemon, 18-day-old rats expressed potentiation—greater
lemon aversion if the CS+ was the compound than if the lemon odor alone. The
60-day-old animals, however, expressed overshadowing—weaker aversion to
lemon following conditioning with the compound than following conditioning
with lemon alone as the CS+. It can be seen that the same effects, potentiation
for the 18-day-olds but overshadowing for the 60-day-olds, were seen in terms of
the conditioned aversion to orange. For both the cases of lemon and orange, the
interaction between age and treatment condition was statistically significant.
Finally, at no age was there significant generalization between orange and lemon; animals conditioned with lemon as their CS+ showed no aversion to orange,
and those conditioned with orange as the CS+ showed no aversion to lemon.

To summarize the basic results, there appeared a distinct ontogenetic difference in conditioning to a single odor when that odor was presented alone as
the CS+ in comparison to when it had been presented in simultaneous compound
with another odor. For 8-day-olds, conditioning to the odor seemed neither
weaker nor stronger in the latter case. For 18-day-olds, however, conditioning of
an odor was stronger when it was presented in compound with another than when
it was presented alone. And for 60-day-olds, conditioning to an odor was weaker
when presented with another odor in compound than when presented alone. To
say this another way, 18-day-olds displayed potentiation, 60-day-olds, overshadowing, and 8-day-olds, neither.

For present purposes the most significant aspect of these data is the faithfulness with which they replicate the basic phenomena observed in terms of conditioning of a flavor aversion. We were somewhat surprised that the 8-day-olds showed neither potentiation nor overshadowing. This result suggests caution in concluding that the different phenomena observed in the 18- and 60-day-old animals reflect a single process that merely increases ontogenetically in monotonic fashion.

Our next step was to investigate in another manner, perhaps more directly, the differential integration of the elements of the stimulus compound among preweanling (18 days old) and adult animals. We use the term "integration" to remain neutral with respect to whether the preweanlings and adults differ primarily in their perceptual/cognitive treatment of the compound or in their associative/cognitive treatment. We remain open as to whether it is the case that the younger animals are more likely than adults to treat a taste-taste or odor-odor compound in integral rather than separable fashion (see Spear, this volume), or whether they are instead more likely than adults to form multiple associations in these circumstances, although our own evidence is more supportive of the former view. Either interpretation would, however, lead to the prediction that preweanlings should show greater "sensory preconditioning" than adults. If an odor-odor simultaneous compound were presented without pairing it with any particular reinforcer, we should expect the consequential integration among the two odors (i.e., the sensory preconditioning) to be greater for the younger animals. But if something other than age-related perceptual or associative dispositions were responsible for the above results, the preweanlings might not show more odor-odor integration than adults in this paradigm. This was the subject of our next experiment.

Sensory Preconditioning with an Odor-Odor Combination.   The question of sensory preconditioning is, will a relationship between two stimulus elements be acquired by virtue of mere exposure to these two elements presented together, in this case simultaneously. The strategy for deciding this is really quite simple. Following exposure to the two elements the value of one is changed, either decreased or increased. To the extent that the two elements had been integrated when the animal experienced them concurrently, the value of the other element is expected to increase or decrease correspondingly.

In the present experiment two odors were presented together. The value of one odor was then decreased by pairing it with a footshock. The question was, how aversive did the previously paired odor become as a consequence?

In actual practice our experiment design and procedure were a good bit more complicated than in the abstract case, but the reader will be spared the full details. Two factors must be mentioned, however, one procedural and one of design. (1) For conditioning an aversion to an odor by pairing it with a footshock, it has seemed necessary to present the animal a different odor in the same context, but explicitly unpaired with footshock. The conditioning is expressed as a greater preference for the latter (CS−) than the former (CS+), but one cannot determine a priori whether the CS− or the CS+ accrued the more associative strength. For the experimental conditions, therefore, each animal was exposed to two pairs of odors, a lemon/orange combination and a banana/methyl combination. This was followed by two conditioning trials in which the banana odor was paired with footshock and the lemon odor with the absence of footshock. The test then assessed preference for orange relative to methyl. (2) There were two basic control conditions, one given the pre-exposure to the odors and the test but without intervening conditioning and another given the conditioning and the test but without the pre-exposure.

A series of experiments with this paradigm was conducted by Joan Brandt in our laboratory, but the full series need not be described here. Comparisons of special relevance involve the sensory preconditioning observed among animals of either of three ages, 10, 15, or 50 to 60 days postnatal.

The results of the odor preference test may be seen in Fig. 10.6. This figure shows percentage preference for methyl. Methyl originally had been paired with banana and a conditioned aversion later was formed to banana. Therefore, the lower the percentage time in Fig. 10.6, the more the sensory preconditioning. It is quite clear that substantial preconditioning occurred for the 15-day-old animals, with some sign of the effect in 10-day-old animals but none in the adults. For statistical analysis the two control conditions at each age level, which did not differ, were collapsed for comparison with the experimental groups. It was determined by analysis of variance that significant sensory preconditioning occurred for both the 15- and 10-day-old animals but not for the adults.

At this stage in this series we are cautious about the meaning of these age-related differences. The greater sensory preconditioning in the 15-day-olds could be due to their greater integration of the two paired odors, but other explanations have not been thoroughly eliminated. For instance, the present effect could be derived either from the 15-day-olds' greater responsiveness to the initial (pre-exposure) pairing of the odors or from their greater conditioning of an aversion to the single odor in Stage 2. Previous data in our laboratory, however, suggest that neither effect is likely. First, a series of experiments by Caza and Spear (in preparation) indicated that the consequence of a 3-minute exposure to a novel odor was about the same for 15-day-old rats and adults (in both cases preference for this odor increases). This suggests that in the present series as well, these two groups did not differ in their responsiveness to the paired odors during pre-exposure. Second, an experiment by Kessler and Spear (reported by Spear, 1979) indicated that the strength of the aversion conditioned by pairing an odor with a footshock was about equal for 18-day-old and adult rats, and we have seen no indication that 15-day-olds and 18-day-olds differ in this respect. We therefore conclude, tentatively, that odor-odor integration in these circumstances is greater for preweanlings (15-day-olds) than for adults.

It is significant that this tendency for preweanlings to show more integration

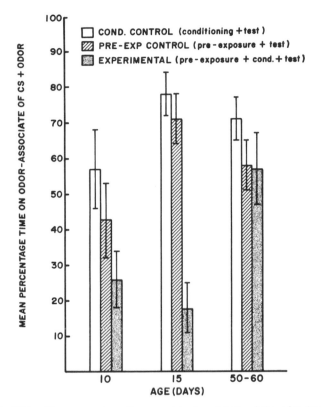

FIG. 10.6.   Mean percentage time spent in the vicinity of the odor (methyl salicylate) previously paired with the CS+ odor (banana) in the experimental condition and each of two control conditions, for 10-, 15-, and 60-day-old rats. Lines above and below the bars indicate standard error of the mean.

among stimulus elements than adults occurred in circumstances quite similar to those in which preweanlings of almost the same age (18 days) had greater potentiation in conditioning of a flavor aversion than did adults. Potentiation has also seemed to depend on such integration, as we described earlier. What begins to emerge is the generalization that preweanlings are more likely than adults to perceptually or associatively integrate the elements of a simultaneous compound stimulus. This disposition may in some cases be reflected as less "stimulus selection" by the younger animals.

SUMMARY

Our previous experiments had indicated that during their third postnatal week, the conditioned responding of preweanling animals is more disrupted by a contextual change than is the case for adults. It was as if the younger animals were less selective than adults in learning about redundant or irrelevant context in the presence of the more urgent contingencies of the conditioning task at hand. The Ph.D. thesis of Steinert (1981) indicated that with successive presentation of two stimulus elements, there was a greater tendency for the younger animals to learn about one CS element only at the expense of learning the other. A third set of experiments, a Ph.D. thesis by Caza (1982), tended to support the former conclusion. Caza's study was intended primarily to investigate the role of central catecholamines in mediating ontogenetic differences in stimulus selection, but two aspects of the behavior of her animals not given drugs are of interest here. First, the younger (15 days old) animals exhibited less blocking than the adults. Specifically, for preweanlings relative to adults, prior conditioning to a distinctive location yielded less impairment in subsequent conditioning of an aversion to an odor presented in compound with that same location. The preweanlings also tended to show less overshadowing of the odor by the location than did the adults. But this study, too, had used simultaneous stimulus compounds, that is, a compound of an odor presented simultaneously with a distinctive location that predicted footshock.

Collectively, these studies indicated that ontogenetic differences in stimulus selection might depend on whether the alternative stimulus elements occur simultaneously or successively. We then conducted a series of experiments to assess stimulus selection in terms of the conditioning of an aversion to a single flavor. That flavor alone was either paired with an induced illness, or the flavor was presented with another distinctive flavor, simultaneously or successively, and that combination paired with an induced illness. Preweanlings and adults differed markedly in their conditioning in these circumstances. With simultaneous presentation of paired flavors, conditioning to a flavor was greater than if only that flavor had been presented singly as the CS (potentiation), and this effect was far greater for preweanlings than adults. But when the two flavors were presented in close succession, there was a tendency toward overshadowing, and this effect tended to be greater for adults than for preweanlings.

Our empirical analysis focused on the case of the simultaneous compound. In a variety of experiments using several different combinations of flavors we consistently found that (1) the preweanlings showed greater potentiation than the adults, and (2) in the rare case in which potentiation was not significant, the preweanlings showed less overshadowing than adults. A further set of experiments with this paradigm tended to support the notion that the preweanlings were more likely than adults to form a configuration of the compound, to treat it as an integral rather than a separable compound—to differ, in other words, in their perceptual/cognitive processing of the simultaneous compound. Our results tended to favor the interpretation that for preweanling rats, stimulus selection in the strict sense may not be an issue in their treatment of stimuli in a simultaneous compound. At this age, the animal may simply not perceive discrete and separate elements of such a compound and so may have no occasion to ''select'' one or the other. But although our analysis tended to confirm such a perceptual or "Gestalt" interpretation, it would appear premature to dismiss the possibility that the preweanling rats are more likely than adults to form a variety of discrete associations among the elements in an episode. And if so, we could expect that these would be relatively fragile associations, eliminated readily by virtue of the younger animals' greater susceptibility to extinction (cf. Spear, this volume; Spear & Kucharski, 1983). What comes to mind with this latter interpretation is an analogy with the process of neural development in the brain, in essence a process of overproduction and selective pruning.

Our final two sets of experiments employed a quite different conditioning paradigm, one involving odors and footshocks rather than flavors and illnesses. This series confirmed that in these circumstances too, preweanlings in their third postnatal week show greater potentiation than adults. The adults tended toward overshadowing in this study. We also determined with this paradigm that even in the absence of any special event of biological significance such as a footshock or illness, preweanlings were more likely than adults to integrate two simultaneously occurring odors. Whether this greater integration by the younger animals is a perceptual/cognitive matter or an associative/cognitive matter is yet to be decided.

The purpose of this chapter has been to report a series of experiments that assessed age-related changes in what is learned about multiple-event episodes. Beyond answers to specific questions from theory, two working generalizations emerged to guide our subsequent work. First, the circumstances we have studied do not seem to require considerations of capacity limitations among immature animals; it does not seem that, relative to adults, younger animals merely learn fewer of the many elements possible within an episode. Yet, the circumstances of our experiments probably are not the sort that would be expected to fully challenge the animal's capacity for information processing, at least not in the sense of "divided attention" or a "necessarily selective allocation of associative strength." As Riley and his colleagues have noted in a series of important analytical papers (e.g., Riley, 1983; Riley & Leith, 1976; Riley & Roitblatt, 1978) there probably is little real challenge of this kind to information processing in a large proportion of contemporary experiments that have tested what is learned about multiple-event episodes, particularly those with rats as subjects. Perhaps with more severe limitations on processing time, ontogenetic differences in such capacity may be seen. But in our circumstances none appeared.

Second, the effects of age on learning seem markedly different with reference to episodes in which the events appear simultaneously, in comparison with those in which events occur successively. There would appear to be at least three long-range implications of this. One is that what may be manifested here is a general ontogenetic increase in the capacity to integrate information across time, an effect exhibited also in the younger organism's special difficulties with retention over short or long intervals and in conditioning with long intervals between CS and US. Another implication addresses ontogenetic differences in response to contextual stimuli. What has seemed an age-related disposition to process redundant contextual features during conditioning may be understood through appreciation that at least in the case of contemporary context (Spear, 1976), contextual features may join with discriminative or conditioned stimuli to form a simultaneous compound. Finally, what seems to be demanded by the age-related differences in response to simultaneously presented events is further understanding of developmental changes in perception, quite beyond those in sensory detection. For this purpose there is no better source in my opinion than the general arena of perceptual learning mapped out so well by Gibson (1969). With further emphasis on this topic we may have to rely more heavily than ever on the notion that a great deal of the ontogeny of learning and memory must focus on changes that are not easily characterized as associative, at least not in the traditional sense.

ACKNOWLEDGMENT

Preparation of this chapter was supported by a grant from the National Institute of Mental Health (1 RO1 MH35219). I am grateful for the excellent secretarial assistance of Teri Tanenhaus and the technical assistance of Norman G. Richter with regard to data reported in this chapter.

REFERENCES

Anohkin, P. K. Systemogenesis as a general regulator of brain development. In W. A. Himwich & H. E. Himwich (Eds.), *The developing brain: Progress in brain research*. Amsterdam: Elsevier, 1964.

Booth, J. J., & Hammond, L. J. Configural conditioning: Greater fear in rats to compound than component through overtraining of the compound. *Journal of Experimental Psychology*, 1971, 87, 255–262.

Campbell, B. A. Developmental studies of learning and motivation in infraprimate mammals. In H. W. Stevenson, E. H. Hess, & H. L. Rheingold (Eds.), *Early behavior: Comparative and developmental approaches*. New York: John Wiley & Sons, 1967.

Campbell, B. A., & Coulter, X. Ontogeny of learning and memory. In M. R. Rosenzweig (Ed.), *Neural mechanisms of learning and memory*. Cambridge: MIT Press, 1976.

Campbell, B. A., & Spear, N. E. Ontogeny of memory. *Psychological Review*, 1972, 79, 215–236.

Caza, P. *Noradrenergic influences on selective attention: Interactions with development*. Unpublished Ph.D. Thesis, State University of New York at Binghamton, 1982.

Cheatle, M. D. *Ontogenetic differences in mechanisms of second-order conditioning*. Unpublished Ph.D. Thesis, Princeton University, Princeton, N.J., 1980.

Clarke, J. C., Westbrook, R. F., & Irwin, J. Potentiation instead of overshadowing in the pigeon. *Behavioral and Neural Biology*, 1979, 25, 18–29.

Gibson, E. J. *Principles of perceptual learning and development*. New York: Appleton-Century-Crofts, 1969.

Kail, R. V., & Hagen, J. W. (Eds.). *Perspectives on the development of memory and cognition.* Hillsdale, N.J.: Lawrence Erlbaum Associates, 1977.

Kail, R. V., & Hagen, J. W. Memory in Childhood. In B. B. Wolman (Ed.), *Handbook of developmental psychology.* Englewood Cliffs, N.J.: Prentice Hall, 1982.

Lett, B. T. Taste potentiation in poison-avoidance learning. In R. Herrnstein (Ed.), *Harvard Symposium on Quantitative Analysis of Behavior* (Vol. 4). Hillsdale, N.J.: Lawrence Erlbaum Associates, 1982.

Newman, S., Caza, P. A., & Spear, N. E. *Ontogenetic differences in response to contextual stimuli.* Paper presented at meetings of Eastern Psychological Association, Baltimore, April 1982.

Rescorla, R. A. Simultaneous associations. In P. Harzum & M. D. Zeiler (Eds.), *Predictability, correlation and contingency.* New York: John Wiley & Sons, 1981.

Rescorla, R. A., & Durlach, P. J. Within-event learning and Pavlovian conditioning. In N. E. Spear & R. R. Miller (Eds.), *Information processing in animals: Memory mechanisms.* Hillsdale, N.J.: Lawrence Erlbaum Associates, 1981.

Revusky, S. The role of interference in association over a delay. In W. K. Honig & P. H. R. James (Eds.), *Animal memory.* New York: Academic Press, 1971.

Riley, D. A. Do pigeons decompose stimulus compounds? In H. Roitblatt, T. Bever, & H. Terrace (Eds.), *Animal cognition.* Hillsdale, N.J.: Lawrence Erlbaum Associates, 1983, in press.

Riley, D. A., & Leith, C. R. Multidimensional psychophysics and selective attention in animals. *Psychological Bulletin,* 1976, *83,* 138–160.

Riley, D. A., & Roitblatt, H. L. Selective attention and related cognitive processes in pigeons. In S. H. Hulse, H. Fowler, & W. K. Honig (Eds.), *Cognitive processes in animal behavior.* Hillsdale, N.J.: Lawrence Erlbaum Associates, 1978.

Rudy, J. W., & Cheatle, M. D. Ontogeny of associative learning: Acquisition of odor-aversions by neonatal rats. In N. E. Spear & B. A. Campbell (Eds.), *Ontogeny of learning and memory.* Hillsdale, N.J.: Lawrence Erlbaum Associates, 1979.

Rusiniak, K. W., Hankins, W. G., Garcia, J. & Brett, L. P. Flavor-illness aversions: Potentiation of odor by taste in rats. *Behavioral and Neural Biology,* 1979, *25,* 1–17.

Smith, G. J., & Spear, N. E. Role of proactive interference in infantile forgetting. *Animal Learning & Behavior,* 1981, *9,* 371–380.

Solheim, G. S., Hensler, J. G., & Spear, N. E. Age-dependent contextual effects on short-term active avoidance retention in rats. *Behavioral and Neural Biology,* 1980, *30,* 250–259.

Spear, N. E. Retrieval of memories. In W. K. Estes (Ed.), *Handbook of learning and cognitive processes* (Vol. 4), *Attention and memory.* Hillsdale, N.J.: Lawrence Erlbaum Associates, 1976.

Spear, N. E. *The processing of memories: Forgetting and retention.* Hillsdale, N.J.: Lawrence Erlbaum Associates, 1978.

Spear, N. E. Memory storage factors in infantile amnesia. In G. Bower (Ed.), *The Psychology of learning and motivation* (Vol. 13). New York: Academic Press, 1979. (a)

Spear, N. E. Experimental analysis of infantile amnesia. In J. F. Kihlstrom & F. J. Evans (Eds.), *Functional disorders of memory.* Hillsdale, N.J.: Lawrence Erlbaum Associates, 1979. (b)

Spear, N. E., & Campbell, B. A. *Ontogeny of learning and memory.* Hillsdale, N.J.: Lawrence Erlbaum Associates, 1979.

Spear, N. E., & Kucharski, D. Ontogenetic differences in the processing of multi-element stimuli: Potentiation and overshadowing. In H. Roitblatt, T. Bever, & H. Terrace (Eds.), *Animal cognition.* Hillsdale, N.J.: Lawrence Erlbaum Associates, 1983, in press.

Steinert, P. A. *Stimulus selection among preweanling and adult rats as a function of CS amount and quality using a taste-aversion paradigm.* Unpublished Ph.D. dissertation, State University of New York at Binghamton, 1981.

Steinert, P. A., Infurna, R. N., Jardula, M. F., & Spear, N. E. Effects of CS concentration on long-delay taste aversion in preweanling and adult rats. *Behavioral and Neural Biology,* 1979, *27,* 487–502.

Tompkins, S. S. A theory of memory. In J. S. Antrobus (Ed.), *Cognition and affect*. Boston: Little, Brown, 1970.

White, S. H., & Pillemer, D. P. Childhood amnesia and the development of a socially accessible memory system. In J. F. Kihlstrom & F. J. Evans (Eds.), *Functional disorders of memory*. Hillsdale, N.J.: Lawrence Erlbaum Associates, 1979.

11 Continuities and Discontinuities in Early Human Memory Paradigms, Processes, and Performance

Marion Perlmutter
University of Minnesota

Understanding about memory is, in many ways, constrained by the situations and tasks in which it has been investigated. While a variety of experimental paradigms have been used to study memory, these hardly are representative of the numerous situations in which memory actually is used in everyday life (see Neisser, 1982; Perlmutter, 1980b). For example, while most experimental memory tasks test for deliberate, short-term retention of discrete stimuli (e.g., word lists), most everyday use of memory involves nondeliberate, long-term retention of complex events. Yet, because each memory task requires different cognitive processing, it has been difficult to integrate research findings from even the limited range of paradigms that have been used to study memory. Moreover, because different paradigms have been used with different species and different age groups, it has been difficult to synthesize a comparative or developmental perspective on memory.

In this chapter, an approach for considering continuities and discontinuities in memory is suggested. A general model is presented in order to specify (1) the task characteristics of paradigms used to investigate memory, and (2) the cognitive processes required for demonstrating memory in these paradigms. By using this model, continuities and discontinuities in the *paradigms* and *processes* should become apparent. A selective review of the literature on memory *performance* from the initiation of life to the initiation of formal schooling is then provided, with special emphasis given to the author's own research on memory in 2- to 5-year-olds. In this program of research age-related continuities and discontinuities in performance across a variety of paradigms have been investigated in order to gain an understanding of developmental continuities and discontinuities in memory processes.

PARADIGMS

The model, shown in Fig. 11.1, provides a very general representation of situations that involve memory. Experimental memory paradigms, as well as everyday tasks involving memory, may be conceptualized into presentation and test phases. During the presentation phase, a stimulus or event that is to be remembered is experienced, and during the test phase, a response that is indicative of memory is exhibited. Thus, referring to Fig. 11.1, inferences about the remembrance of an experience (labeled presentation stimulus) that occurred at some point in time (labeled presentation phase) are derived from responses (labeled dependent measure) that are made at a later point in time (labeled test phase).

This model is extremely general, and applies to most situations involving memory. However, important differences between paradigms can be specified within this framework. For example, the type of information provided during presentation, and the amount of information available during testing, differ across paradigms, as do the dependent measures used to draw inferences about memory. Table 11.1 shows the most typical presentation stimuli, test stimuli,

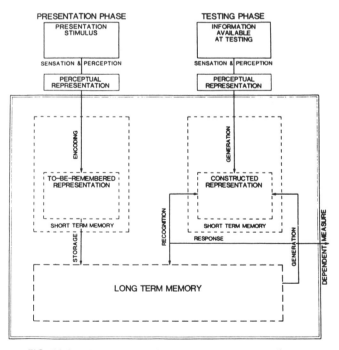

FIG. 11.1.   General model for analyzing memory paradigms.

TABLE 11.1
Typical Task Characteristics of Various Memory Paradigms

| Paradigm | Task Characteristics | | |
	Presentation Stimulus	Test Stimulus	Dependent Measure
Habituation	Visual	Presentation stimulus	Visual attention
Violation of expectations	Visual or auditory	Context	Surprise
Conditioning	Visual and motoric	Visual part of presentation stimulus	Motoric
Object permanence/delayed response	Visual	Part of presentation stimulus	Search
Language comprehension	Visual & verbal	Verbal part of presentation stimulus	Nonspecific
Language production	Visual & verbal	Visual part of presentation stimulus	Verbal
Recognition	Visual	Presentation stimulus	Nonspecific
Reconstruction	Visual	Unorganized presentation stimuli	Nonspecific
Cued recall	Visual & verbal	Visual part of presentation stimulus	Verbal
Cued recall	Verbal	Related verbal stimulus	Verbal
Imitation	Visual	Context	Motoric
Free recall	Verbal	Query	Verbal

and dependent measures used in paradigms employed to study young human memory.

The *habituation* paradigm typically has involved visual stimuli. The stimulus is presented for an extended interval, during which time visual attention, or some other relatively noncontrolled dependent measure, is monitored. A decrement in the dependent response is assumed to indicate retention, although this assumption is checked by the introduction of a novel stimulus during a dishabituation (post-test) phase.

In the *violation of expectation* paradigm a visual or auditory stimulus is presented repeatedly. Then, the experience is repeated, but without the stimulus. A surprise response is taken to indicate that the child expected the stimulus. Such an expectation depends upon retention of the prior occurrence of the stimulus in the situation.

In *conditioning* paradigms, a co-occurring visual (or auditory) stimulus and behavioral response is reinforced. If the child later repeats the response in the presence of the stimulus, memory of the stimulus response association is assumed.

In *object permanence and delayed response* paradigms a visual stimulus is hidden in an array of locations. During testing, the visual array is available, but the child must rely upon his or her memory to locate the object correctly.

Although *language comprehension* might not strictly be considered a paradigm for investigating memory, it surely indicates a child's retention of previous, perhaps numerous, pairings of a verbal label with a visual stimulus. If, when a word is uttered, a child remembers what it stands for, he or she may respond in a way (e.g., point to the appropriate object) that indicates retention and understanding of the linguistic code.

Language production also may be taken as evidence of a child's memory of prior verbal-visual pairings of stimuli. In this situation the child responds verbally to some (usually visual) stimulus.

The *recognition* paradigm is quite similar to habituation in that a visual stimulus is presented during the presentation phase and also is available during the test phase. In the recognition paradigm, however, the child is queried specifically about his or her retention. The experimenter thus relies upon the child to respond in a way that indicates memory.

In the *reconstruction* paradigm visual stimuli are presented in an organized manner during presentation, and re-presented without their original organization during testing. The child must then reinstate the original arrangement of stimulus components.

In *cued recall* paradigms stimuli are presented during the presentation phase, and during the test phase, parts of the stimuli, or information related to the stimuli, are provided. The child must then respond with verbal labels that indicate remembrance of the presentation stimuli.

In *imitation* a child repeats a motoric (or auditory) response that was presented previously. Only the general context of the test situation is provided as a cue to memory.

In the *free recall* paradigm verbal stimuli are presented during presentation. During testing, with only the prompting of a query, verbal responses are elicited to verify retention.

This brief description of memory paradigms includes only a few of the many potentially important details that define memory tasks. For example, amount of stimulus familiarization, or time interval between presentation and testing, certainly influence performance in important ways. However, these variables tend not to be confounded with paradigm. Thus, for example, relatively limited familiarization times, and brief retention intervals, generally have been used regardless of paradigm. By focusing only on paradigmatic discontinuities in (1) presentation information, (2) test information, and (3) dependent measure, important discontinuities in processing requirements should become evident.

PROCESSES

In order to respond in a fashion that indicates memory, a number of cognitive processes are assumed to operate. Very generally, during the presentation phase, the stimulus must be sensed, perceived, and encoded, and a mental representation of it must be stored. Between presentation and test, the mental representation of the stimulus must be retained. Finally, during the test phase, the stimulus must be reexperienced in some way, and a response that is indicative of this reexperience must be produced.

While there are some processing continuities across paradigms in that these general stages of processing must be carried out in all situations involving memory, there are many processing discontinuities in the specific cognitive processes required for performance in particular situations. For example, depending on the nature of the presentation stimulus, motoric, visual, or verbal encoding processes will be required during the presentation phase. In addition, depending on the information available during the test phase, the generation processes required for reexperiencing the stimulus will vary. Finally, while in some situations memory is inferred from the pattern of an automatic response, and therefore involves minimal response skills, in most cases memory is inferred from performance on tasks that involve nonmemorial response requirements, such as actions, decisions, and/or language.

In general, the paradigm characteristics discussed previously, that is, (1) the nature of information to be remembered, (2) the amount of information available in the test environment, and (3) the dependent measure indicative of memory, determine the (1) encoding, (2) generative, and (3) response processing necessary for evidencing memory. *Encoding processes* are determined by the nature of the information to be remembered. *Generation processes* are determined by the amount of information available in the test situation and the response required for performance. *Response processes* are determined by the dependent measure used to infer memory.

Conceptually, it is possible to analyze memory paradigms parametrically by independently varying each paradigm characteristic (and thus each processing requirement). In reality, however, a complete design of such paradigms does not exist. Table 11.2 summarizes the presumed encoding, generation, and response processes required for performance in the paradigms that have been used most frequently in research on memory in infants and preschool children. Progress toward understanding processing continuities and discontinuities in early memory development requires an analysis of the processing continuities and discon-

TABLE 11.2
Presumed Processing Requirements of Various Memory Paradigms

	Processing Requirements		
Paradigm	Encoding	Generation	Response
Habituation	Visual	Minimal	Minimal
Violation of expectation	Visual or auditory	Visual or auditory	Minimal
Conditioning	Visual & motoric	Motoric	Minimal
Object permanence/delayed response	Visual	Visual	Decision
Language comprehension	Visual & verbal	Visual	Decision
Language production	Visual & verbal	Verbal	Verbal
Recognition	Visual	Minimal	Decision
Reconstruction	Visual	Visual organization	Minimal
Cued Recall	Visual & verbal	Verbal	Verbal
Cued Recall	Verbal	Verbal	Verbal
Imitation	Visual	Visual	Motoric
Free recall	Verbal	Verbal	Verbal

tinuities in various paradigms used to study memory. Only after such an analysis has been carried out can the age-related continuities and discontinuities in children's performance be interpreted usefully.

In several paradigms (habituation, conditioning, and violation of expectation) inferences about memory are based on a child's nondeliberate responding (see Cohen & Gelber, 1975; Werner & Perlmutter, 1979). These paradigms involve minimal nonmemorial response processing. In contrast, in most memory paradigms (object permanence, delayed response, language comprehension, language production, recognition, reconstruction, cued recall, imitation, and free recall), the child is required to respond in a deliberate manner (see Brown, 1975; Flavell, 1977). These paradigms demand substantial nonmemorial response processing. Because the young infant is not thought to deliberately control much of his or her behavior, it is likely that the earliest evidence of memory will come from situations that do not require such deliberate responding. Indeed, there is earlier evidence of habituation, conditioning, and response to violation of expectation than there is of recall. This pattern suggests that immature response systems may limit the young infant's ability to demonstrate memory in many situations; however, information apparently is encoded and retained, even very early in life.

Moreover, there are important discontinuities in the processing requirements for habituation, conditioning, and response to violation of expectation that may be informative for understanding the earliest development of memory skills. For example, because the original presentation stimulus is present during the test phase of the habituation paradigm, minimal generative processing is required to re-experience the presentation stimulus in a habituation task. However, because the presentation stimulus is not available in its original form during the test phase of conditioning and violation of expectation situations, some cognitive generation is required for a memorial experience in these tasks. Evidence of habituation earlier than of conditioning or response to violation of expectation thus would suggest developmental limitations in infants' generative processing skills. In addition, by manipulating the information available during testing, and thus varying the generative processing requirments of the paradigm, further information about the development of generative processing can be obtained. For example, it may be possible to determine whether the ability to generate action schemes or representations precedes the ability to generate imaginal schemes or representations.

Similar analysis of more demanding memory paradigms also should be informative. For example, it might be hypothesized that verbal responding is developmentally demanding. Thus, evidence of memory from paradigms requiring verbal responses (language production, cued recall, and free recall) would be expected considerably later than from paradigms involving nonverbal responses. After controlling for response demands, however, a developmental progression that parallels the generative requirements of the memory paradigm might be hypothesized.

While this analysis suggests that age-related improvements in memory performance observed during infancy and the preschool years may be attributable to the early development of encoding, generative, and response skills, other memorial skills also are known to develop (see Kail & Hagen, 1977; Ornstein, 1978). Figures 11.2I through 11.2IV depict four proposed phases in the development of the human memory system. During the first phase, shown in Fig. 11.2I, the child possesses the *basic processes* (encoding, generation, response) already discussed. However, these processes are only in rudimentary form at birth, and during infancy and the preschool years there is much development of encoding, generation, and response skills. For example, the infant and young child becomes faster at encoding information, more facile at cognitively generating representations, and better organized in responding.

In the second phase, shown in Fig. 11.2II, *semantic influences* are added. As the child interacts with the world, a history of this experience is recorded in his or her long-term-memory. Very rapidly this accumulated knowledge is found to have an important influence on the way in which new information is encoded during presentation, as well as the way in which retained information is generated during testing. The extent of such semantic influences has been found to increase during the preschool years, and to continue to increase during later childhood (see Brown, 1975; Myers & Perlmutter, 1978).

Another addition to the memory system, shown in Fig. 11.2III, also emerges during the preschool years. At sometime around the second year of life, the child demonstrates some *awareness* of his or her memory. Thus, for example, while inferences about memory at an earlier age are derived from ongoing activities of

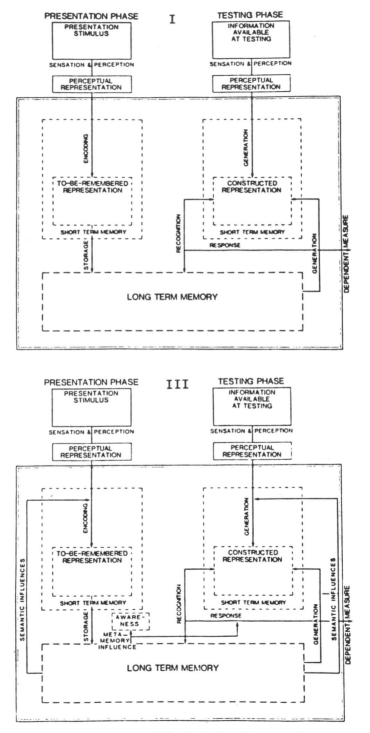

FIG. 11.2. Embellishment of processes added to

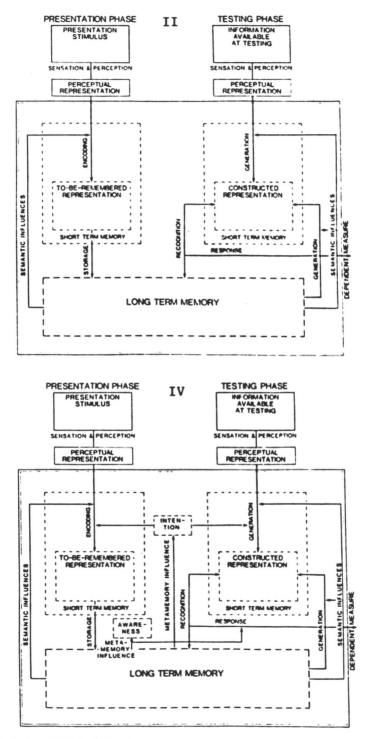

memory system over development.

the infant, after about age two, a child is able to respond to a query about his or her memory. This knowledge of memory, or cognizance of the re-experiencing of an event, is an early form of what has been termed metamemory (see Cavanaugh & Perlmutter, 1982; Flavell & Wellman, 1977).

A further addition to the memory system, shown in Fig. 11.2IV, is observed only in limited form prior to the elementary school years. With this addition, the child shows an ability to be *intentional* about the way in which he or she encodes information during presentation and generates it during testing. The assumed basis of this effective control or intentionality over memorial processing is the accumulation of remembrances about the functioning of the memory system. Thus, strategic ability is thought to derive from one's knowledge about the memory system. As such, strategy development has been viewed as a further ramification of metamemory (see Cavanaugh & Perlmutter, 1982; Flavell & Wellman, 1977).

PERFORMANCE

In reviewing the findings from research on infants and preschool children, it becomes clear that the earliest observations of memory have been in paradigms requiring limited response processing. In addition, there appears to be a developmental increase in memory performance that parallels the generative processing demands of the paradigm used to test memory, Moreover, although the data are less clear concerning a possible developmental progression in the type of information that may be retained effectively, there is some indication that effective processing of motoric information precedes effective processing of imaginal information, which is followed by effective processing of verbal information. Finally, the pattern of performance points to the influence of semantic knowledge on memory early in life, as well as to the emergence, prior to elementary school, of some awareness of memory by children, and perhaps to the beginning limited intentional control over it.

In the following portion of this section a more detailed presentation of some of the author's own research on memory in children between 2 and 5 (see also Perlmutter, 1980a; 1981; 1982) is provided. Data from a number of paradigms is summarized, with the findings organized around encoding, generative, and response processing factors that may limit preschool children's memory performance. In addition, the presentation highlights the increasing influence of semantic knowledge on memory functioning over this time span and discusses briefly the emergence of metamemorial influences.

Very generally, the procedure used in most of this research has involved the testing of younger (2- or 3-year-olds) and older (4- or 5-year-olds) preschool children in short (approximately one-half hour) memory tasks of various sorts. Children were brought to the laboratory, where, in the pretense of a game, they were shown stimuli that they were told to try to remember. Almost immediately after this presentation phase, the children were tested for their retention of the stimuli. In various experiments, the nature of the stimuli (e.g., pictures, objects, words), information in the test environment (e.g., original stimulus, visual cues, verbal cues, no cues), and response requirements (e.g., pointing, yes/no choice, verbal) were manipulated.

Encoding Factors.   Much nondevelopmental research has demonstrated that some stimuli are remembered more easily than others (see Anderson, 1980; Crowder, 1976; Lachman, Lachman, & Butterfield, 1979; Spear, 1978). For example, pictures tend to be more memorable than words. This picture superiority effect might be expected to be especially evident in young children, who are still mastering language. Indeed, to the degree that the preschool years are a time when there are increases in the facility with which language is processed, observed age-related improvements in memory performance should be especially pronounced for verbal material. This hypothesis, that increased skill in verbal processing contributes to memory improvement during the preschool years, was examined in several situations.

Perlmutter and Myers (1976) investigated 3- and 4½-year-olds' recognition of common objects that were presented verbally only (words), imaginally only (pictures), or imaginally and verbally (pictures with words). Not surprisingly, the older children performed better than the younger children, and the poorest recognition performance was observed for stimuli presented only verbally (see Fig. 11.3). Of greater interest, however, was the lack of an age x item type interaction. Apparently, the age-related improvement in recognition performance

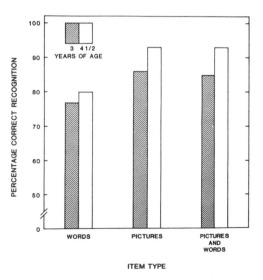

FIG. 11.3. Mean percentage correct recognition by younger and older preschool children for word, picture, and picture plus word stimuli.

over the preschool years is not attributable to increased facility specifically in the language domain.

In a delayed response paradigm, Blair, Perlmutter, and Myers (1978) investigated the possible contribution of age-related differences in the ability to process spatial, visual, or verbal information on memory performance from 2 to 4 years. In the delayed response task, there were again age-related improvements in performance, and performance was most accurate when visual and verbal cues were provided, and least accurate with only spatial cues (see Fig. 11.4). However, again, there was no age x condition interaction. It was expected that both age groups might perform comparably when only spatial cues were available, but that older children would make better use of additional cues, and therefore perform better than younger children in the other cue conditions. This hypothesis was not supported.

Response Factors.   The lack of support for the view that development of encoding skills contributes to improvements in memory performance over the preschool years points to another factor that may limit young children's memory performance, and also obscure researchers' ability to detect memory improvement. Specifically, there may be age differences in the nonmemorial response skills required to perform many of the memory tasks used with young children. Therefore, possible age differences in a number of response factors that contribute to memory performance have been investigated.

Perlmutter, Hazen, Mitchell, Grady, Cavanaugh, and Flook (1981) hypothesized that incomplete search may limit young preschool children's performance in delayed response tasks. Therefore, they compared 2- and 3-year-olds' delayed

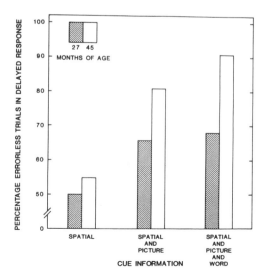

FIG. 11.4.   Mean percentage errorless trials in a delayed response task by younger and older preschool children with spatial, spatial plus picture, and spatial plus picture plus word cues.

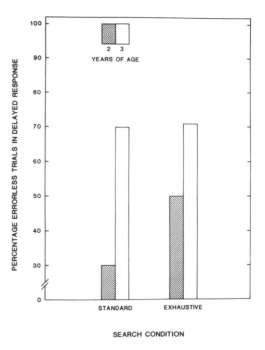

FIG. 11.5. Mean percentage errorless trials in a delayed response task
by younger and older preschool children with standard and exhaustive
search conditions.

response performance in two search conditions. In a standard search condition, children were simply told to find a hidden toy in one of nine boxes that had different pictures on each. In an exhaustive search condition, prior to finding the hidden toy, the children were asked to indicate whether the toy was in each of the nine boxes. Here, the expected age x search condition interaction was observed. While the exhaustive search procedure facilitated the younger children's performance, it had no effect on the older children (see Fig. 11.5). Thus, the age difference in delayed response performance was attenuated by the exhaustive search procedure. Apparently, unsystematic search limits younger, but not older, preschool children's delayed response performance, and this age difference contributes to the age-related improvement that is observed.

The possibility that limitations in young children's search skills also contributes to observed age differences in recognition performance has been investigated as well. Metzger and Perlmutter (1980) compared preschool and college students' performance in matching and recognition tasks involving complex pictorial scenes that either were identical to the presentation stimuli, changed only in background, changed only in detail, or changed both in background and detail. For the matching task, subjects were required to make same-different judgments to two perceptually available stimuli. Age differences in the pattern of performance in this task, therefore, should be ascribed to developmental changes in nonmemorial skills. In contrast, for the recognition task, subjects were required to indicate whether a test stimulus was the same or different than a previously shown presentation stimulus. Age differences in the pattern of performance on the recognition task therefore should reflect developmental changes that contribute to age differences in matching performance, as well as possible developmental differences in memory skills. Reaction times to perform the matching and recognition tasks are shown in Fig. 11.6, and the number of correct responses in these tasks are shown in Fig. 11.7. The reaction time data suggest that rather different scanning strategies were used by the preschool children and college students. Adults were fastest when aspects in both the background and detail differentiated the presentation and test stimuli and slowest when the presentation and test stimuli were identical. Apparently, they responded "different" as soon as a difference was detected but continued to search when there were no differences. In contrast, young children's search time was not systematically affected by the differential discriminability of presentation and test items. Moreover, as is indicated in the number correct data, children performed poorest in the most subtle change condition (same background-different details). This performance pattern can be attributed to the fact that they did not spend additional time searching for differences in detail.

Another response factor that may contribute to age differences in recognition performance relates to the decision process that is required in most recognition tasks. For example, younger children may be more or less conservative or biased than older children in indicating recognition. That is, when young children are not certain if they have seen a particular stimulus previously, they may be more (or less) likely than older children to judge it as "old." Perlmutter and Myers (1974, 1976) carried out signal detection analyses on their recognition data in order to assess independently whether there were age differences in the reten-

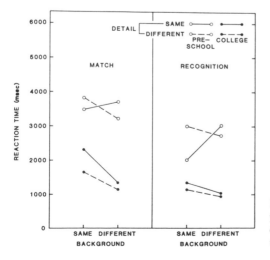

FIG. 11.6. Mean reaction times by preschool children and college students in matching and recognition tasks.

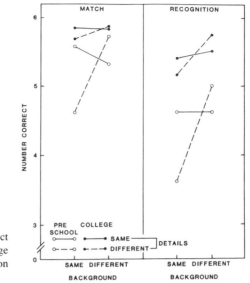

FIG. 11.7. Mean number correct by preschool children and college student in matching and recognition tasks.

tional and decision components of recognition performance. While statistically different d' measures (reflecting retentional differences) were obtained, significant age differences in C (reflecting response bias) were not.

Generative Factors. Perhaps the most obvious characteristic of preschool children's memory, at least in laboratory tasks, is the contrast between their proficient recognition and their poor recall. This point is illustrated by Fig. 11.8, which summarizes the results of several recognition studies and Fig. 11.9, which summarizes the results of several recall studies. As may be seen, recognition accuracy was over 80%, even for 3-year-olds, but recall was barely 40%, even

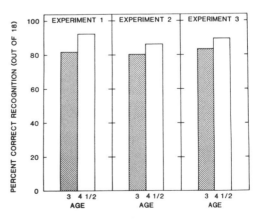

FIG. 11.8. Mean percentage correct recognition by younger and older preschool children.

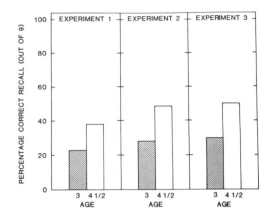

FIG. 11.9. Mean percentage correct recall by younger and older preschool children.

for 4½-year-olds. Moreover, it should be noted that the 80% recognition levels were achieved on 18-item lists, and thus represent recognition of nearly 15 items. In contrast, the 40% recall levels were achieved on 9-item lists, and thus represent recall of under 4 items. This procedural difference in list lengths was incorporated in order to maximize assessments of both recall and recognition. While a considerable difference in performance on these two tasks was observed, the young children might well have been able to recognize even more items; however, we were unable to engage them for longer periods of time.

Better performance on recognition than on recall tasks typically has been obtained with adults as well (see Anderson & Bower, 1973; Crowder, 1976; Kintsch, 1970; Perlmutter & Perlmutter, 1979). This difference usually is attributed to the greater generative processing demands of recall tasks, as compared to recognition tasks. A similar argument, of course, is applicable to the children's performance. However, it appears that young children's recognition performance approximates that of adults, but that, relative to adults, their recall is quite deficient (see Brown, 1975; Hasher & Zachs, 1979; Perlmutter & Lange, 1978). While methodological difficulties (e.g., ceiling level performance) limit definitive assessments of the relative age differences in recall and recognition, empirical evidence is consistent with theoretical analyses of the processing demands of these two tasks. Recall involves more generative processing than does recognition, and although there is some age-related improvement in recognition, there seems to be much greater age-related improvement in recall. The development of generative processing skills thus is implicated as an important factor in the early improvements observed in memory performance.

Recognition and free recall may be viewed as extremes of a continuum of memory tasks that vary in terms of the stimulus support available at time of testing. Therefore, recognition and free recall represent extremes in the generative processing required for demonstrating memory. For recognition, the original presentation stimulus typically is available; hence limited cognitive processing is required for the generation of a representation of the retained stimulus. For free recall, only the global contextual characteristics of the test environment replicate the presentation situation; thus, extensive cognitive processing is required for the generation of a representation of the retained stimulus.

A variety of other memory tasks fall between these extremes, with some, but not total, stimulus support provided during testing, and thus, with an intermediary level of cognitive processing required for the generation of a representation of the retained stimulus. For example, in some cued recall tasks, a part of the stimulus that was provided by the experimenter during presentation (e.g., context) is available during testing. These cues presumably reduce the cognitive generative demands. In other cued recall tasks, information that the subject was assumed to have encoded during presentation (e.g., category label), but that was not presented by the experimenter, is provided as a cue during testing. This information is also presumed to reduce the cognitive generative demands. The research summarized below focused on the effectiveness of various kinds of stimulus support in facilitating memory of preschool children.

Duncan, Todd, Perlmutter, and Masters (1982) hypothesized that affective information may be helpful in supporting preschool children's memory. In order to examine how affect might facilitate memory, they designed free recall, cued recall, and recognition tasks that incorporated an affect induction procedure. Just prior to the presentation of picture stimuli, as well as just prior to testing (which followed presentation after approximately 15 minutes), children were instructed to generate happy, neutral, or sad thoughts. It was expected that if the affect induced by these thoughts was the same at presentation and testing, memory would be better than if the induced affect differed during presentation and testing. That is, memory was expected to be facilitated by the reinstatement, prior to testing, of the affective state that was induced prior to presentation and inhibited by presentation of a different affective state. Systematic effects of affective state at presentation, or at test, were not found on any of the measures that were examined. Moreover, as may be seen in Table 11.3, a match between affect at presentation and test did not lead to better memory performance on any of the tasks. It appears that affective state, at least at the level that could be induced with the procedures used in this laboratory situation, is not an effective support for preschool children's memory of discrete stimuli.

Perlmutter and Myers (1979) hypothesized that spatial information might provide especially strong stimulus support for young children. Therefore, they designed a cued recall task in which each of nine presentation items was hidden in different locations of a 3 × 3 grid of boxes. It was expected that during testing the spatial information associated with the boxes would cue recall of the items hidden in them. The results of two such experiments are shown in Fig. 11.10. Experiment 1 included four conditions. In one condition the spatial memory aid was never used (control condition), in another it was available only at testing, in a third the aid was available only at presentation, and in the final condition it was

TABLE 11.3
Mean Level of Performance for Same and Different
Presentation-Test Conditions

| | Presentation-Test Condition | |
Dependent Measure	Same	Different
Free recall	3.7	4.0
Cued recall	5.0	4.9
Recognition	11.9	11.9

used both at presentation and testing. As may be seen, the spatial memory aid had virtually no effect on recall of either 3- or 4½-year-olds. Because this result was surprising, the procedure was replicated in Experiment 2, using just two conditions, the control condition, in which the spatial memory aid was never present, and the condition that was presumed to be strongest, that is, the one in which the aid was always present. Again, the spatial information available from the memory aid was not helpful to preschool children.

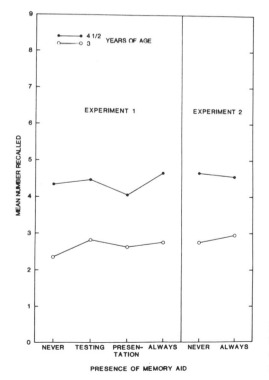

FIG. 11.10.   Mean number recalled by younger and older preschool children with or without spatial memory aid.

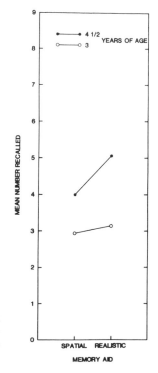

FIG. 11.11. Mean number recalled by younger and older preschool children with spatial and realistic memory aid.

In another study, Cohen, Perlmutter, and Myers (1976) considered the possibility that semantically richer spatial locations might better cue preschool children's recall. They compared preschool children's cued recall when they were provided cither with the nine-compartment spatial memory aid just described, or with a doll house that provided nine more-meaningful locations. For the younger children, cued recall was comparable in the two memory aid conditions; however, for the older children, cued recall was better when a meaningful memory aid was provided (see Fig. 11.11). Thus, the age difference was greater with a realistic memory aid. This greater facilitating effect of stimulus support for the older children is counter to the view that generative processing skill is an especially limiting factor in younger children's memory. If generative processing improves over the preschool years, then providing support for generative processing would be expected to attenuate the age difference. However, it may be important that in this case the effective support for generative processing was semantic in nature. The results thus illustrate semantic influences on the memory system of older preschool children and point to an important development that is observed over this time span, that is, the addition of a meaning driven quality to the memory system.

In another study, Perlmutter and Ricks (1979) found that stimulus support that did not depend on meaning facilitated recall, and in this case, the effect was strongest for the youngest children. They presented children nine common objects that varied in color, and tested for recall of the item names, as well as the colors of the items. The color recall measure served as an index of recall given considerable stimulus support. Because the name of the item was provided for color recall, only one of its attributes, color, had to be cognitively generated. In fact, color recall was substantially higher than was item recall (see Fig. 11.12). Moreover, given the stimulus support of the item name, the age difference in recall was attenuated.

In another series of studies, Perlmutter, Sophian, Mitchell, and Cavanaugh (1981) examined the effects of reinstating perceptual information on preschool children's recall. During presentation of some lists, target pictures were each paired with related context pictures, and during testing, the context pictures were provided as cues. It was expected that the picture cues would greatly improve recall, because they would provide considerable stimulus support during testing. Moreover, it was hypothesized that the age difference in preschool children's recall might be attenuated with the picture cues, because the stimulus support provided by these cues should reduce the generative demands of the recall task, and these generative demands were assumed to be especially problematic for the youngest children. In two experiments, the picture cues improved recall a bit, but not as dramatically as had been expected (see Fig. 11.13). Moreover, there was an age x condition interaction in the direction opposite to that predicted. The older children profited from the picture cues more than the younger children.

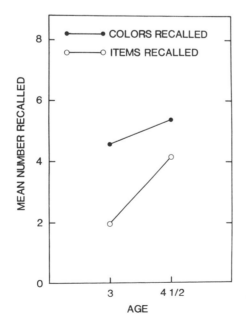

FIG. 11.12.   Mean number of items and colors recalled by younger and older preschool children.

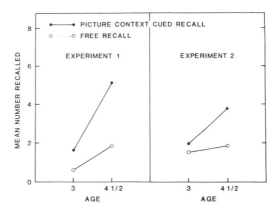

FIG. 11.13.   Mean number recalled by younger and older preschool children with no cues and with picture cues.

Another aspect of this research sheds light on the nature of these cuing effects. Pictures that were used as context during presentation and as cues during testing for some children, also were used as cues during testing for other children who had not seen them during presentation. Thus, it was possible to assess whether the pictures were effective cues, even if they were not provided during presentation, and therefore, could not perceptually contribute to a reinstatement of the presentation situation. Table 11.4 shows cued recall performance with picture cues that were provided at both presentation and test or only at test. As may be seen, the picture cues in these two conditions were just as effective; they improved recall regardless of whether they were provided at presentation. A perceptual reinstatement explanation of the picture cuing effect appears untenable. Rather, it seems likely that the children encoded the category membership of the pictures, and, since the context pictures were conceptually related to the target pictures, they appeared to use these labels as cues. The greater effectiveness of the picture cues for the older children also is consistent with the view that the pictures were translated into category cues. Category cuing would be expected to

TABLE 11.4
Mean Number Cued Recall with Pictures Provided at
Presentation and Test or Only at Test by Younger
and Older Preschool Children

	Cue Condition	
Age Group	Presentation and Test	Only Test
3	2.0	2.9
4½	3.9	3.7
Combined over age	3.0	3.9

be more effective for older children, if semantic influences become more potent with age.

Experiment 2 also permitted a more direct means to examine the nature of the picture-cuing effect. Both related and unrelated context cues were used, thereby allowing separate assessment of the perceptual reinstatement and category cuing functions of the picture cues. The effects of unrelated and related context cues are shown in Fig. 11.14. Unrelated context cuing had little effect on recall, although related context cues were beneficial, especially for older children. Apparently, the perceptual stimulus support provided by picture cues was not useful to preschool children. The limited value of the perceptual stimulus support available in unrelated contextual picture cues was surprising. It had been expected that such concrete stimulus information would be especially facilitating to young children, since it would be helpful in reinstating the enoding situation. It is possible, however, that the context pictures and target items were never encoded as integrated units. This possibility is especially plausible and would account for the limited facilitating effect of the unrelated picture cues, if, as has been suggested, preschool children do not spontaneously integrate stimulus information into compound units but rather tend to encode components individually (e.g., Elkind, 1969).

In a final experiment in this series, in order to determine whether a lack of integration of the perceptual information in the target and context items limited the effectiveness of the unrelated picture cues, a procedure for unitizing presentation of target and context stimuli was developed. The results are shown in Fig. 11.15. As may be seen, when unrelated context pictures had been unitized with target stimuli during presentation, they served as effective retrieval cues during testing. Indeed, the integrated unrelated picture cues were more beneficial than the unintegrated related picture cues, and they attenuated, rather than accentuated, age differences in recall.

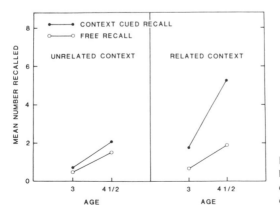

FIG. 11.14.   Mean number recalled by younger and older preschool children with no cues, related context cues, and unrelated context cues.

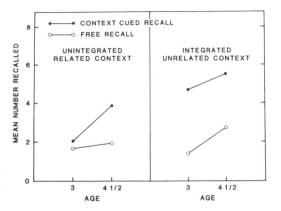

FIG. 11.15. Mean number recalled by younger and older preschool children with no cues, unintegrated related context cues, and integrated unrelated context cues.

Whereas the research just discussed examined the effectiveness of concrete perceptual information in cuing young children's memory, in another series of experiments, Perlmutter, Schork, and Lewis (1982) examined the cuing effects of less concrete information. They used twelve-item lists of drawings of common objects that included equal numbers of items of several colors and several categories. Free recall performance was assessed, as was cued recall with color and category cues. The results are shown in Fig. 11.16. Both color and category cues improved recall, although category cues were somewhat more helpful than color cues.

According to the encoding specificity hypothesis (see Tulving & Thomson, 1973), the effectiveness of cues provided during testing is dependent upon the encoding, during presentation, of the information contained in the cues. Therefore, to determine whether limitations in the category or color cues used in these studies could be attributed to children's failure to spontaneously encode the color or category membership of the items during presentation, cued recall of items for which these characteristics were specified during presentation was compared to cued recall of items for which the information was not specified during presentation. These data are shown in Table 11.5. As may be seen, there was a slight, but nonsignificant, advantage for cues that were specified during presentation; however, in general, cues were similarly effective, regardless of whether or not they were specified during encoding. Apparently, during presentation, preschool children spontaneously encode color and category membership of stimuli. Providing children with information about color or category membership, during testing, improves their memory, apparently facilitating their cognitive generation of the items.

The research just summarized provides some evidence that stimulus support can aid preschool children's memory. Furthermore, at least in a few instances, this stimulus support attenuated age differences (e.g., name cues for recall of colors; integrated unrelated picture cues for recall of names). The view that

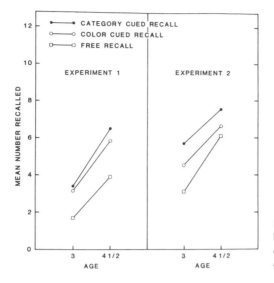

FIG. 11.16. Mean number recalled by younger and older preschool children with no cues, category cues, and color cues.

generative processing skill improves over the preschool years predicts just such effects, because reducing the generative demands of a task (by providing stimulus support) should reduce the effects of age difference in generative processing, and therefore, reduce age differences. However, in a number of instances there was no evidence of a facilitating effect of stimulus support (e.g., affective state; spatial memory aid; unintegrated unrelated pictures). Furthermore, in several instances stimulus support increased age differences (e.g., meaningful spatial aid; related pictures). Consideration of the types of information in the test environment that facilitate performance suggests that semantic support may be more potent than the degree of affect, spatial, or perceptual support used in these studies. Moreover, younger and older preschool children appear to differ in their use of semantic knowledge to aid the remembrance of specific information.

TABLE 11.5
Mean Number Cued Recall With Cue Information Provided at
Presentation and Test or Only at Test by Younger and Older
Preschool Children

Age Group	Experiment 1		Experiment 2	
	Presentation and Test	Only Test	Presentation and Test	Only Test
3	1.7	1.6	2.8	2.4
4½	3.4	2.8	3.8	3.4
Combined over age	2.6	2.2	3.3	2.9

Semantic Influences.   The influence of semantic knowledge on the memory performance of preschool children has been the focus of a number of studies. In several experiments, Perlmutter and Myers (1979) presented 3- and 4½-year-olds with nine-item lists of objects that were either from nine different conceptual categories (unrelated list) or from just three conceptual categories (related list). All children remembered more items from the related, than unrelated, lists (see Fig. 11.17). Moreover, this effect was stronger for the older, than younger, children. Thus, the age differences in free recall was greater for related, than unrelated, materials. Apparently, even by age 3, semantic knowledge influences memory performance, although this influence increases from 3 to 4½ years. Moreover, this increased influence of semantic knowledge on memory of specific information probably contributes importantly to age differences observed in memory over the preschool years.

In the first experiment of this series, the response time between recall of each item was also measured. Thus, for related lists, it was possible to compute response times between adjacent items that were conceptually related or unrelated. Response time between related items was shorter than was response time between unrelated items (see Fig. 11.18). Moreover, this difference between related and unrelated inter-item intervals was greater for the older, than younger, children, with the older children's response time between related items the shortest observed. Thus, these response time data are consistent with the recall data, indicating semantic influences on memory processing even in the younger group, but increased semantic influences over the age range studied.

Further evidence of semantic influences on preschool children's memory can be derived from clustering analyses of recall protocols of conceptually related lists. Perlmutter and Myers (1979), Perlmutter and Ricks (1979), and Todd and Perlmutter (1982) used RR clustering measures (see Bousfield & Bousfield, 1966) to determine whether preschool children's recall is semantically organized. In several experiments, significant semantic clustering has been obtained, even in young preschool children. Moreover, greater semantic clustering is ob-

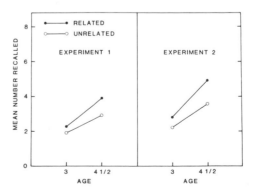

FIG. 11.17.   Mean number recalled by younger and older preschool children on related and unrelated lists.

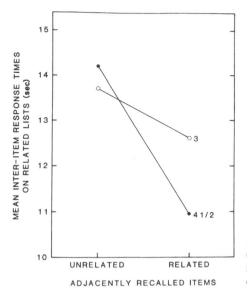

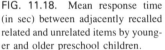

FIG. 11.18. Mean response time (in sec) between adjacently recalled related and unrelated items by younger and older preschool children.

served in the older children, although this age difference typically is not statistically significant. It may be that the lack of statistical significance of the age difference in semantic clustering reflect limitations in available methods of comparing clustering in recall protocols that differ in length (that is, where there is less recall from younger than older children), rather than to a lack of increase in semantic organization.

Further evidence of an age-related increase in semantic influences on the memory performance of preschool children comes from studies in which category cuing has been used (Perlmutter & Myers, 1979; Perlmutter & Ricks, 1979; Perlmutter, Schork, & Lewis, 1982). Category cues increased recall of both younger and older children, although this increase was greater for the older children (see Fig. 11.19).

Using a number of indices (differences in recall of related and unrelated lists, differences in related and unrelated inter-item response times, categorical clustering, and facilitation from categorical cuing), consistent evidence of semantic influences on memory performance has been obtained in even the youngest children included in these studies, that is, in 3-year-olds. Moreover, age-related increases in these semantic effects have been observed from 3 to 5 years. Unfortunately, it has been impossible to use these procedures with children under 3, and thus it has been difficult to obtain earlier evidence of semantic influences on memory. However, Goldberg, Perlmutter, and Myers (1974) developed a recall procedure to detect semantic influences on memory in even younger children. They presented 2-year-olds with a series of two-item lists, half of which were made up of unrelated objects, and the other half of semantically related objects.

Even 2-year-olds recalled more items from semantically related, than unrelated, lists (see Fig. 11.20).

Response times also were obtained. The first response always was more rapid than the second, and was not different for related and unrelated lists (see Fig. 11.21). Of greater import, response times for the second item were affected by semantic relation, with second responses from related lists produced more rapidly than were second responses from unrelated lists. Apparently meaning affects the memory processing of even 2-year-olds.

Metamemorial Influences.   Inherent in current discussions of metamemory (see Brown, 1978; Cavanaugh & Perlmutter, 1982; Flavell & Wellman, 1977) is the notion of deliberateness of self-regulation of remembering. Although much of what is experienced is encoded and retained quite incidentally (e.g., what one ate for dinner), in some circumstances, people intentionally try to remember (e.g., ingredients one wants to purchase for a future dinner). That is adults, at least, sometimes do things in an attempt to increase the effectiveness of their memory. Moreover, this metamemorially mediated ability to improve memory

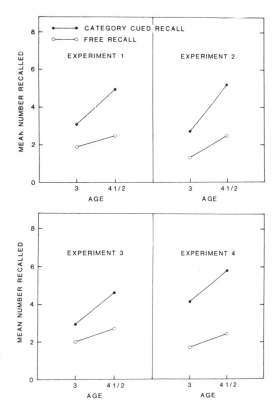

FIG. 11.19.   Mean number recalled by younger and older preschool children with no cues and with category cues.

performance has been found to increase during the grade school years. Older children perform better than younger children, and much of this age difference appears to be attributable to their greater deliberateness in approaching memory tasks (see Brown, 1978; Flavell, 1977).

In general, children less than 5 years of age appear nondeliberate in their performance of memory tasks (see Myers & Perlmutter, 1978). However, in some situations, it has been possible to demonstrate intentionality, even in children as young as 2. For example, Wellman, Ritter, and Flavell (1975) found that 2- and 3-year-olds exhibited strategylike behaviors (e.g., maintained visual fixation on a hiding location) during the delay portion of a delayed response task. Likewise, Wellman, Somerville, and Haake (1979) argued for logical search (e.g., first checking the last location of an object) in 3-year-olds.

When the goal of a memory task is particularly salient, or motivating, as it is in localization paradigms, strategic behaviors may be observed at an early age. However, in most situations, there is little evidence of strategy use in children under 3. While the rudiments of intentional memory apparently precede formal schooling, deliberateness of memory remains uncharacteristic of the preschool child. Moreover, another important point is that although there may be some intentional memory behavior prior to the grade school years, the overwhelming evidence of age-related improvement in memory performance during the preschool years seems unlikely to be accounted for by age-related increases in strategy use. The development of memory in the preschool years thus appears to

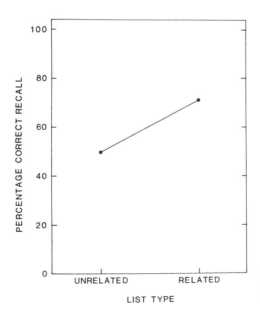

FIG. 11.20. Mean percentage correct recall on related and unrelated lists.

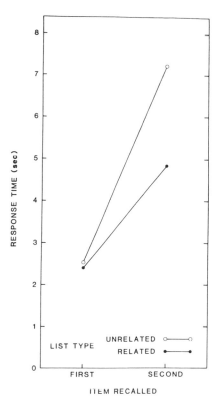

FIG. 11.21. Mean response time (in sec) for first and second items from related and unrelated lists.

reflect distinct processing changes, beyond the scope of those outlined to account for later memory improvement.

SUMMARY AND CONCLUSIONS

A general framework (see Fig. 11.1) for considering memory has been present-ed, and it has been shown that many paradigms used to study memory may be analyzed within this framework. Moreover, it was suggested that because of the discontinuities in the paradigms that have been used to study memory across phylogeny and ontogeny, such an analysis will be necessary to elucidate devel-opmental and species continuities and discontinuities in memory processes. By considering the task characteristics of each paradigm, the processing require-ments for demonstrating memory performance may be derived. Then it should be possible to integrate findings across age and animal.

This cross-paradigm task analytic approach to understanding memory devel-opment was illustrated with a program of research on memory during the preschool years. This research has demonstrated many basic processing competencies already established in young preschool children, as well as some of the ways in which these processes increase in proficiency between 2 and 5 years of age. In particular, the preschool years seem to cover a phase of development, prior to the refinement of intentional control over memory processes, when the meaning driven nature of human memory emerges. The child's accumulated knowledge comes to bear as events are experienced and reexperienced, and information in memory can increasingly be applied in contexts that are disassociated from original experience.

ACKNOWLEDGMENT

Much of the research reported in this chapter has been supported by grants from the Graduate School of the University of Minnesota, NICHHD, and NSF. The author gratefully acknowledges this support, as well as the contributions of many colleagues and students involved in the research.

REFERENCES

Anderson, J. R. *Cognitive psychology and its implications.* San Francisco: W. H. Freeman and Company, 1980.

Anderson, J. R., & Bower, G. H. *Human associative memory.* New York: John Wiley & Sons, 1973.

Blair, R., Perlmutter, M., & Myers, N. Effects of unlabeled and labeled picture cues on very young children's memory for location. *Bulletin of the Psychonomic Society,* 1978, *11,* 46–48.

Bousfield, A. K., & Bousfield, W. A. Measurement of clustering and of sequential constancies in repeated free recall. *Psychological Reports,* 1966, *19,* 935–942.

Brown, A. L. The development of memory: Knowing, knowing about knowing, and knowing how to know. In H. W. Reese (Ed.), *Advances in child development and behavior* (Vol. 10). New York: Academic Press, 1975.

Brown, A. L. Knowing when, where, and how to remember: A problem of metacognition. In R. Glaser (Ed.), *Advances in instructional psychology* (Vol. 1). Hillsdale, N.J.: Lawrence Erlbaum Associates, 1978.

Cavanaugh, J. C., & Perlmutter, M. Metamemory: A critical examination. *Child Development,* 1982, *53,* 11–28.

Cohen, E., Perlmutter, M., & Myers, N. A. *Reconstruction in preschool children.* Unpublished manuscript, University of Massachusetts, 1976.

Cohen, L. B., & Gelber, E. R. Infant visual memory. In L. B. Cohen & P. Salapatek (Eds.), *Infant perception: From sensation to cognition* (Vol. 1, *Basic visual processes*). New York: Academic Press, 1975.

Crowder, R. G. *Principles of learning and memory.* Hillsdale, N.J.: Lawrence Erlbaum Associates, 1976.

Duncan, S. W., Todd, C. M., Perlmutter, M., & Masters, J. *Affective state and memory in preschool children.* Unpublished manuscript, University of Minnesota, 1982.

Elkind, D. Developmental studies of figurative perception. In L. P. Lipsitt & H. W. Reese (Eds.), *Advances in child development and behavior* (Vol. 4). New York: Academic Press, 1969.

Flavell, J. H. *Cognitive development.* Englewood Cliffs, N.J.: Prentice Hall, 1977.

Flavell, J. H., & Wellman, H. M. Metamemory. In R. V. Kail, Jr., & J. W. Hagen (Eds.), *Perspectives on the development of memory and cognition.* Hillsdale, N.J.: Lawrence Erlbaum Associates, 1977.

Goldberg, S., Perlmutter, M., & Myers, N. Recall of related and unrelated lists by 2-year-olds. *Journal of Experimental Child Psychology,* 1974, *18,* 1–8.

Hasher, L., & Zacks, R. T. Automatic and effortful processes in memory. *Journal of Experimental Psychology: General,* 1979, *108,* 356–388.

Kail, R. V., Jr., & Hagen, J. W. (Eds.). *Perspectives on the development of memory and cognition.* Hillsdale, N.J.: Lawrence Erlbaum Associates, 1977.

Kintsch, W. *Learning, memory and conceptual processes.* New York: John Wiley & Sons, 1970.

Lachman, R., Lachman, J. L., & Butterfield, E. C. *Cognitive psychology and information processing: An introduction.* Hillsdale, N.J.: Lawrence Erlbaum Associates, 1979.

Metzer, R., & Perlmutter, M. *A developmental study of matching and recognition.* Paper presented at meeting of Psychonomics Society, 1980.

Myers, N. A., & Perlmutter, M. Memory in the years from two to five. In P. A. Ornstein (Ed.), *Memory development in children.* Hillsdale, N.J.: Lawrence Erlbaum Associates, 1978.

Neisser, U. *Memory observed: Remembering in natural contexts.* San Francisco: W. H. Freeman & Company, 1982.

Ornstein, P. A. *Memory development in children.* Hillsdale, N.J.: Lawrence Erlbaum Associates, 1978.

Perlmutter, J., & Perlmutter, M. *Some issues about recall and recognition.* Unpublished manuscript, 1979.

Perlmutter, M. Development of memory in the preschool years. In R. Greene & T. D. Yawkey (Eds.), *Early and middle childhood: Growth, abuse, and delinquency and its effects on individual, family, and community.* Westport, Conn.: Technomic Publishing, 1980. (a)

Perlmutter, M. (Ed.). *New directions in child development: Children's memory.* San Francisco: Jossey Bass, 1980. (b)

Perlmutter, M. Observational and experimental studies of preschool children's memory. In N. NirJaniv & B. Spodek (Eds.). *Early childhood education: International perspectives.* New York: Plenum Press, 1981.

Perlmutter, M. Memory development in young children. *Developmental Newsletter,* Spring, 1982, 28–30.

Perlmutter, M., Hazen, N., Mitchell, D. B., Grady, J., Cavanaugh, J., & Flook, J. Picture cues and exhaustive search facilitate very young children's memory for location. *Developmental Psychology,* 1981, *17,* 104–110.

Perlmutter, M., & Lange, G. A developmental analysis of recall-recognition distinctions. In P. A. Ornstein (Ed.), *Memory development in children.* Hillsdale, N.J.: Lawrence Erlbaum Associates, 1978.

Perlmutter, M., & Myers, N. Recognition memory development in two- to four-year-olds. *Developmental Psychology,* 1974, *10,* 447–450.

Perlmutter, M., & Myers, N. Recognition memory in preschool children. *Developmental Psychology,* 1976, *12,* 271–272.

Perlmutter, M., & Myers, N. A. Recall development in two- to four-year-olds. *Developmental Psychology,* 1979, *15,* 73–83.

Perlmutter, M., & Ricks, M. Recall in preschool children. *Journal of Experimental Child Psychology,* 1979, *27,* 423–437.

Perlmutter, M., Schork, E. J., & Lewis, D. Effects of semantic and perceptual orienting tasks on preschool children's memory. *Bulletin of the Psychonomic Society,* 1982, *19,* 65–68.

Perlmutter, M., Sophian, C., Mitchell, D. B., & Cavanaugh, J. Semantic and contextual cuing of preschool children's recall. *Child Development,* 1981, *52,* 873–881.

Spear, N. E. *The processing of memories: Forgetting and retention.* Hillsdale: N.J.: Lawrence Erlbaum Associates, 1978.

Todd, C. M., & Perlmutter, M. *Effects of prior experience on preschool children's recall.* Unpublished manuscript, University of Minnesota, 1982.

Tulving, E., & Thomson, D. A. Encoding specificity and retrieval processes in episodic memory. *Psychological Review,* 1973, *80,* 352–373.

Wellman, H. M., Ritter, K., & Flavell, J. H. Deliberate memory behavior in the delayed reactions of very young children. *Developmental Psychology,* 1975, *11,* 780–787.

Wellman, H. M., Somerville, S. C., & Haake, R. J. Development of search procedures in real-life spatial environments. *Developmental Psychology,* 1979, *15,* 530–542.

Werner, J. S., & Perlmutter, M. Development of visual memory in infants. In H. W. Reese & L. P. Lipsitt (Eds.), *Advances in child development and behavior* (Vol. 14). New York: Academic Press, 1979.

COMMENTARIES AND
PROSPECTS

12

Developmental Continuity of Memory Mechanisms: Suggestive Phenomena

Edward H. Cornell
University of Alberta

The notion of developmental continuity encompasses two very general ideas: commonalities of biological and psychological systems across different species, and within a species, commonalities across the lifespan. Historical analyses indicate that it is quite natural for comparative psychologists to note correspondences in the structures and functions of different living systems, but these observations are usually accompanied by debates (Beer, 1980; Harlow, Gluck, & Suomi, 1972). The debates have involved intricacies of method and interpretation, issues as old as experimental psychology itself. In the present chapter I consider recent evidence of laboratory animals and preverbal infants showing patterns of memory performance typical of adults in traditional verbal learning tasks. At least three classical effects can be demonstrated when paradigms are adjusted for the learning and response capabilities of animals and children. These effects—reinstatement effects, spacing effects, and serial position effects—were apparent in the results of Ebbinghaus's (1885/1913) tests of his own memory, and all are considered to be among the empirical phenomena that must be addressed in a complete theory of human cognition. In this chapter, I suggest the affinities in reactions by individuals of different species and ages when placed in situations structured to reveal these effects are due to a common mnemonic system.

Arguments based on similarities between phenomena are always tentative. Nevertheless, there may be advantages to summarizing these new demonstrations within the framework of developmental continuity. One possible advantage is parsimony, the quest for a small body of laws to account for the most general phenomena of learning and memory. Behavioral diversity may ultimately be the correct characterization of Mother Nature, but psychologists have periodically discovered enough relationships between events and behavior to make good applications and put the search for general laws on a schedule of intermittent veneration. In addition, there seem to be several historical instances in which novel methodologies have been developed or tangential phenomena have been discovered in attempts to elaborate or discredit notions of archetypal behavioral processes. I begin with a sketch of some of this history.

EARLY ORIENTING ATTITUDES

In the last quarter of the nineteenth century, students of animal behavior were exploring the implications of Darwinian theory of evolution. Romanes (1882) had put forward a provocative idea: Processes of associationism could be fundamental to animal as well as human behavior, hence mental life could show the same forms of ontological continuity found in studies of structural anatomy. Romanes's reports of animal behavior were too anecdotal and his inferences regarding their mental workings were too anthropomorphic for hard-nosed comparative psychologists such as Morgan (1894), but the issues were lively, and the next generation sought to assess the notion of psychological continuity with better methods.

Edward L. Thorndike had attended lectures by Morgan at Harvard and subsequently devised tests of the problem-solving abilities of cats, dogs, and monkeys. Thorndike gave an elegant account of this work in a monograph published in 1898 with a prefatory title identical to that of Romanes's book: *Animal Intelligence*. Thorndike's monograph set the standard for experimentation and descriptive language for comparative study. His approach was elementalism; he considered higher order mental phenomena such as intelligence to be derivable from the formation of simple habits. Curiously, he said little about how habits might be retained from trial to trial or from one situation to the next. Thorndike conceived of intelligence as the ability to use past experience to solve a problem when it reoccurred, yet he eschewed detailed discussion of memory in a general commitment to avoid mentalistic descriptions. Instead, he focused on observable determinants of performance. Practice alleviated forgetting, that could be seen. Learning was the measure of adaptive processes, and the avoidance of stress or the satisfaction of the appetite was obvious throughout the animal kingdom. Moreover, laws of learning were invariant with age and could be applied to the education of children and adults. Thus, Thorndike made substantial the continuity of associationism that had intrigued Romanes, yet did so by circumventing discussion of the processing of memories.

Two developments in 1913 served to stimulate study of these processes. Ebbinghaus's (1885/1913) book was translated, demonstrating systematic and powerful techniques for the analysis of verbal memories, and Walter S. Hunter (1913) published a *Behavior Monograph* entitled "The delayed reaction in animals and children.'' Hunter's (1913, 1917) work is summarized in the next section as a more detailed introduction to the pitfalls and benefits of search for developmental continuity in memory mechanisms. As we shall see, Hunter sought to scale memory performance of different organisms in a single task and became impressed by qualitative similarities in their reactions to the problem.

THE DELAYED REACTION PROBLEM

The subject in the delayed reaction problem has to remember the location of an event. In most of his experiments, Hunter took advantage of the subject's tendency to remember the whereabouts of food, thus the adaptive significance of performance was implicit. The chief independent variable was the duration of retention, or the delay between the subject's witnessing of an event and its release to react. In Hunter's initial studies, the event was the termination of a light marking a food location. Following the delay, there were usually three similar locations the subject could approach, and each of these served as the goal on different trials in a random manner. Different species and ages could be characterized by the maximal intervals of delay for correct choice.

Table 12.1 summarizes Hunter's (1913, 1917) findings when subjects were correct on 64% 70% of their choices in a series of trials. Because delay is expressed on a ratio scale (time), it is tempting to order the subjects in this regard. It is noteworthy that Hunter did not do so, nor did he suggest there was phylogenetic or ontogenetic continuity at this level of analysis. Instead, he focused on whether the subject reacted with an overt postural orientation, a much grosser index than delay. If subjects held an orientation to the goal during the

TABLE 12.1
Performance in the Three-Choice Delayed Reaction Problem[1]

Subject	Age	Number of Trials	Longest Delay	Fixed Orientation
Child, M.	8 yr	38	25 min	no
Child, Hd.	6 yr	47	25 min	no
Child, L.	6 yr	41	25 min	no
Child, H.	6 yr	15	25 min	no
Child, F.	2½ yr	507	50 sec	no
Child, T.	16 mo	264	20 sec	no
Raccoon, Bob	8 mo	720	20 sec	no
Dog, Blackie	7 mo	570	5 min	yes
Rat, #9	20 wk	575	10 sec	yes
Rat, #1	13 wk	345	1 sec	yes

[1] Entries are estimated from Hunter (1913, 1917).

retention interval, Hunter assumed they were incapable of representing the location mentally. This interpretation was in deference to Thorndike's (1898) work, which to Hunter indicated that the presence of ideas in an animal required vigorous proof.

Schoolchildren could know the correct location via the ideational function of language, but Hunter had to devise a hypothetical mechanism to account for the good performance of raccoons and his own preverbal daughter (T in Table 12.1). These subjects were held in neutral postures or distracted during the delay, yet continued to remember the goal. Hunter suggested that they solved the problem by the use of intraorganic cues, which he considered similar to ideas in terms of *function* and *mechanism* (emphases Hunter, 1913, p. 73). Specifically, he assumed that the activation of the light over one of the three locations aroused an approach response, which was represented internally as a kinesthetic cue. He further assumed that such kinesthetic cues become associated over trials with sensations the subject experienced at the time of release to approach the locations. His third assumption was that on any one trial, the release would revive all three kinesthetic cues, but the one most recently activated (by the light) would be strongest.

This reasoning preceded by decades two major theoretical approaches to the study of learning and memory. Central to mediation theory (e.g., Hull, 1930; Spence, 1956) was the similar notion that external stimuli become associated with internal responses, and these in turn serve as internal stimuli to direct overt behavior. Secondly, Spear (1978, p. 120) has noted the resemblance between Hunter's reasoning and current formulations of retention as a function of the cues available during study and test. That is, Hunter presented a preliminary description of contextual determinants of storage and retrieval processes.

Of the three explanations discussed by Hunter (1917) for solution of the delayed response problem—overt orienting, language, and revival of intraorganic associations—the first dominated the attention of comparative psychologists. There followed several reports of stimulus and procedural variations which allowed animals to perform at high levels without maintaining a fixed posture (see reviews by Fletcher, 1965; Ruggiero & Flagg, 1976). Yet there was very little discussion of how this performance might be mediated, and Hunter's notion of cued retrieval was neglected.

We have already noted that Hunter (1913, 1917) sought data specific to seconds of delay, yet he theorized on the basis of phenomenalistic observations. He pointed out several methodological idiosyncrasies preventing close comparative scaling. As indicated in Table 12.1, individuals were tested on the problem for a different number of trials, until several successive trials at a delay failed to exceed chance performance. Even though the tests were dispersed over days, weeks, or months, differences in the motivation to respond could underly tolerance of delay. For example, Hunter (1913) noted that one of the raccoons was tested near its period of hibernation, when its appetite would begin to fail. He also noted that one child's performance was affected by bouts of "ill humor" (Hunter, 1913, p. 57). There were large differences in perseveration of position preferences, so "that the regular tests had to be stopped until the habit could be broken up" (Hunter, 1913, p. 29). The apparati were different for different species, not only in size and layout, but different choice responses were required: entering an area, pushing a button, or opening a box. Finally, Hunter (1913) acknowledged that intraspecies differences preclude good interspecies comparisons:

> There is so much individual variation within the three groups of animals whose results have just been given that any exact correlation between length of delay and groups of animals is unwise. It is to be borne in mind moreover that it is not the length of delay but the methods of reaction after delay to which the greater importance attaches. (p. 37)

Thus, Hunter foresaw two general points that are now widely accepted by contemporary students of memory. First, it is probably futile to base phylogenetic comparisons, or analyses of individual differences in general, on the limits of an individual's capacity for retention, because these limits may shift drastically with changes in testing method (e.g., Spear, 1978, chap. 3; Weiskrantz, 1967, chap. 8). Second, parametric differences in performance are typically less informative than an analysis of the underlying processes used by subjects in reaction to specific task requirements (e.g., Dempster, 1981; Glaser, 1981; Medin, 1976).

As in Hunter's (1913) annotation of his subject's postural reactions, the first stage in the comparative study of processes is to describe a number of "apparently related" behavioral effects (Amsel & Stanton, 1980). In the next sections we consider three.

REINSTATEMENT EFFECTS

> By reinstatement we denote a small amount of partial practice or repetition of an experience over the developmental period which is enough to maintain an early learned response at a high level, but is not enough to produce any effect in animals which have not had the early experience (Campbell & Jaynes, 1966, p. 478).

The idea made explicit by Campbell and Jaynes was disarmingly simple: After learning and forgetting something, an abbreviated reminder can serve to reinstate the original learning. The construct seems to be related to the savings effect, Ebbinghaus's (1885/1913) observation that residual memories are indicated when relearning takes less time than learning. Much more functional, reinstatement refers to a broad class of procedures for alleviating forgetting. One of these is a brief reexposure of the test items in their entirety. Because the reexposure takes less time (or trials) than original learning, this reinstatement procedure taps the savings effect. Other reinstatement procedures involve techniques called "prior cueing" or "reactivation," in which stimulus, reinforcement, or contextual portions of the learning experience serve in isolation or combination to prime the retrieval of memories (e.g., Riccio & Ebner, 1981; Silvestri, Rohrbaugh, & Riccio, 1970; Spear & Parsons, 1976). These controlled studies with animals substantiate and elaborate conditions which are intuitive to our everyday mnemonics, situations in which fractional external events seem to be potent reminders. In addition, in line with the implications Campbell and Jaynes foresaw, it is clinically of interest that reinstatement can sometimes occur when internal states associated with original learning are simulated in the context of training cues (Riccio & Haroutunian, 1979). I will illustrate the general features of reinstatement with a more detailed discussion of this latter paradigm.

In a study conducted by Haroutunian and Riccio (1977), rats learned fear via Pavlovian conditioning. First, a rat was placed inside the black compartment of a two-compartment shuttlebox, where it received periodic mild footshocks. The rat was then placed for a comparable period in the adjoining white compartment, where it was not shocked. This brief acquisition phase was used to establish discriminative fear conditioning, aversive stimulation associated with the contextual stimuli of the black chamber, and safety associated with the adjacent white chamber. One week after this conditioning, the rat was injected with epinephrine and placed for 1 minute each in both compartments of the shuttlebox. The drug administration and brief reexposure to previously conditioned cues constituted one reinstatement treatment. One week after the reinstatement phase, a passive-avoidance procedure was used to assess retention of fear. In this final test phase, the rat was placed in the white chamber of the shuttlebox, a door was opened to the black chamber, and the latency to enter into the black chamber was recorded.

Before presenting the results of the experiment, I consider the rationale for this particular treatment and evidence necessary to infer reinstatement effects. The drug followed the postacquisition return to the shuttlebox because it was known that epinephrine is secreted endogenously when rats experience fear or stress. If the brief reexposure to the external cues was not enough to reinstate the association with shock, perhaps the additional induction of internal cues would be. Or, perhaps the injection of epinephrine alone would prime the memory of the aversive events. Thus, Haroutunian and Riccio (1977) included comparisons with these other treatments in order to isolate the necessary and sufficient conditions for reinstatement of fear. Because it was also possible that the aversive events would have been remembered regardless of any of the reinstatement procedures, they included a final comparison group. These rats received handling and a sham injection during what otherwise would have been the reinstatement phase.

The test results were straightforward. Rats who had not received reinstatement treatments seemed to forget what had occurred in the black compartment, crossing over to it within 3 minutes of being placed in the confines of the white compartment. Reinstatement groups receiving the drug alone or reexposure to the shuttlebox cues alone showed similar lack of fear. Only the treatment which included administration of epinephrine in the context of the apparatus maintained fear, because animals given these conjoint cues avoided the black compartment for up to 13 minutes.

When introducing the construct of reinstatement, Campbell and Jaynes (1966) had proposed that it was a mechanism by which the effects of early experiences could be perpetuated and incorporated into adult functioning. They noted that early traumatic events are considered pivotal in many clinical analyses of behavior disorders, but there was no systematic account of the forgetting or remembrance of fears. The work by Riccio and his colleagues represents one important approach, an attempt to determine the boundary conditions for reinstatement processes to maintain behavior. For example, the results of the epinephrine condition of the Haroutunian and Riccio (1977) study indicate that the occasional reactivation of internal consequences associated with stress would be insufficient by itself to revive memory of a specific trauma. It appears that other contemporary external cues are simultaneously reminiscent of early fear conditioning.

To return to the issues of the generality of memory phenomena, the study of reinstatement is a prime example of the interface of researchers who see men as rats and those who see rats as men (see Fig. 12.1, Bugelski & Alampay, 1961). Campbell and Jaynes (1969) also established that reinstatement applies to memory of appetitively motivated discriminations in these rodents. More recently, research by Rovee-Collier and her colleagues (see reviews by Rovee-Collier & Fagen, 1981; Chapter 5 of this volume) showed that reexposure to a crib mobile 4 weeks after learning could reinstate an amusing but otherwise forgotten operant: 3-month-old human infants had originally learned to kick their legs to make the mobile dance (Rovee-Collier, Sullivan, Enright, Lucas, & Fagen, 1980). Similarly, in a paradigm assessing infants' visual habituation, Cornell (1979)

FIG. 12.1.   An ambiguous subject. (From Bugelski & Alampay, 1961. Copyright Canadian Psychological Association, reprinted by permission.)

discovered that 6-month-old infants showed robust recognition of photographs of faces following a reinstatement exposure which by itself was too brief to instill familiarity.

The studies with preverbal human infants were anticipated by Campbell and Jaynes (1966), who suggested that reinstatement could be a mechanism to counteract early infantile amnesia, the failure of adults to remember events of the first few years of life. This memory deficit was seen as paradoxical in light of theory and evidence implicating the importance of early experience. As a determinant of forgetting, retrieval failure has more grounding than the Freudian construct of repression, especially in light of a considerable body of evidence suggesting that infantile amnesia is not unique to man (for recent reviews, see Campbell & Spear, 1972; Coulter, 1979). Again, investigators are beginning to programmatically explore the limits of reinstatement treatments, in this case as a mechanism for the alleviation of infantile amnesia (e.g., Fagen & Rovee-Collier, 1982; Spear & Parsons, 1976).

The reinstatement manipulation further applies to verbal learning by schoolchildren (Hoving & Choi, 1972; Hoving, Coates, Bertucci, & Riccio, 1972). This generalization is of interest because the technique could be exploited as an efficient reminder of lessons. The procedure used by Hoving et al. (1972) was quite natural for 7- and 10-year-old children. The items to be remembered were drawings of familiar objects that the children were required to name. The pictures were presented as paired associates, for example, cat and spoon, barn and watch. During learning, the children were shown one member of a pair and were asked to anticipate the second member. The training ended when the children responded correctly to 10 such pairs. The children were then tested in the same manner 8 weeks later. One group of children, however, was read a story 4 weeks after the paired associate learning; one group received no special intervention; and a third group received none of the original learning, only the reinstatement procedure followed 4 weeks later by the final training procedure. The story included drawings of both members of each pair presented on the same page. The children were shown these pictures during the story and the names were incorporated in the text, but the pairings themselves were not mentioned. Reinstatement clearly produced savings on the final training test. Children who had learned and then heard the story needed fewer trials to show complete anticipation of the pairs than children who had experienced only the original learning or the story in isolation.

In summary, reinstatement refers to a process by which retention can be facilitated without total repetition of original learning. The effect characterizes memory task performance of rats, human infants, children, and, of course, adults (Spear & Parsons, 1976). It has been demonstrated in paradigms involving classical and operant conditioning, habituation of orienting responses, and verbal learning.

SPACING EFFECTS

The spacing effect refers to an unexpected interaction between learning and memory: Retention is better when repetitions of learning are separated by time (or other events) than when the repetitions occur one immediately after the other. More specifically, distributed training typically facilitates performance on delayed memory tasks, whereas there may be no difference between massed and distributed training on immediate tests. Jost (1897) noted the spacing effect in Ebbinghaus's (1885/1913) data, and it has subsequently been established as one of the most ubiquitous phenomena in studies of human memory processing (for reviews, see Crowder, 1976, chap. 9; Hintzman, 1974, 1976). In verbal learning paradigms, the effect occurs when either nonsense syllables, words, or sentences are the items to be remembered (Hintzman, 1974). As we shall see, spacing effects also pervade performance by preverbal infants and infrahumans.

Operations to establish the spacing effect have been neatly outlined by Hintzman (1974). Suppose training is to occur twice. Let T_1 refer to its initial presentation and T_2 its second. Following the repetition of training, we can assess memories for the training events after a retention interval which is short or long compared to the T_1-T_2 interval. If the duration of the T_2-Test interval is held constant, we can vary the T_1-T_2 interval to determine interstudy intervals that affect test performance.

A variant of this procedure was used to demonstrate memorial processes in adult great apes (Robbins & Bush, 1973). The great apes, consisting of gorillas, orangutans, and chimpanzees, are the closest phylogenctic associates of man. Each ape had been pretrained to respond to two-choice discrimination problems presented on a panel mounted on the door of its cage. Subsequently, on the first learning trial (T_1) of one problem, two magazine pictures were presented side-by-side behind clear plexiglass panels. The ape received candy in a well above the panel after pressing the picture designated as correct. A correction procedure was used, so that on any trial the ape could press either panel until it discovered the correct choice. After T_1 a number of irrelevant pairings followed, each with different pictures. Then the original pairing was repeated, constituting the T_2 presentation. Again, various irrelevant trials followed, and a third pairing, T_3, formed the retention test. The number of interpolated trials between T_1 and T_2 (0, 2, or 10) and between T_2 and T_3 (2 or 10) was varied factorially over separate problems.

The proportion of correct choices on the retention test is represented in Fig. 12.2. The spacing effect is indicated because retention at the longest delay (10 trials intervening between T_2 and T_3) is best following distributed learning (10 trials intervening between T_1 and T_2).

Other features of these results occasionally occur in studies of human performance. For example, in the distributed condition there was a tendency that the

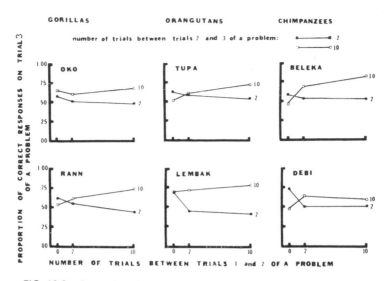

FIG. 12.2.   Proportion of correct responses on Trial 3, the retention measure, as a function of the number of intervening trials spacing Trials 1 and 2 for each ape. The curve denoted 10 represents long-term retention relative to the curve devoted 2. (From Robbins & Bush, 1973. Copyright American Psychological Association, reprinted by permission.)

proportion of correct response on T_3 increased as the T_1-T_2 lag increased. This so-called "lag effect" is sometimes observed in studies of free recall when the T_1-T_2 spacing exceeds 15 seconds or so (Bjork, 1970; Melton, 1970). In the study of memory in great apes (Robbins & Bush, 1973), there was 15-20 seconds between trials. The results of this study also indicated an occasional advantage of massed training at the shortest retention interval (note the crossover of functions in Fig. 12.2). This "massing" effect occurs in verbal paired associate learning (Peterson, Hillner, & Saltzman, 1962; Peterson, Wampler, Kirkpatrick, & Saltzman, 1963). Lag and massing effects are peripheral to our discussion, but are noted because investigators are beginning to be alert to their occurrence in other species. Theoretically, the massing effect has been taken as evidence for a refractory-like short-term memory; Wagner (1976) has suggested this interpretation to account for differential habituation by rats presented repetitions of events at short (2 sec) or long (16 sec) interstimulus intervals.

Distributed study similarly facilitates delayed recognition by human infants. To demonstrate this, Cornell (1980) took advantage of the baby's tendency to fixate novel visual events. When two photographs of faces were presented side-by-side, and one of these photos had just been seen, 5 and 6 month-old babies spent more time looking at the new one. This selective attention indicates visual recognition; it is assumed the previously exposed stimulus is less attractive because it is familiar (see reviews by Cohen & Gelber, 1975; Fagan, 1982;

Olson, 1976). In a within-subjects design, Cornell used two procedures to familiarize babies to photographs of faces. Massed familiarization consisted of four exposures of the photo to be remembered, separated by 3 seconds. The amount of visual study during each of these exposures was carefully monitored; the photo was withdrawn after an observer had recorded that the reflection of the photo had appeared over the center of the baby's pupil for a total of 5 seconds. The amount of study (four 5-second accumulations) was the same in a distributed procedure with a different face, except that the familiarization exposures were separated by 60 seconds. Recognition tests involving the aforementioned pairing of new and previously exposed pictures occurred either immediately (5 seconds) after the familiarization sequence or at one of three longer retention intervals (1 minute, 5 minutes, or 1 hour). The interaction indicating the spacing effect appears in Fig. 12.3. Note that, following 20 seconds of distributed study of a photo of a face, 5 and 6-month-old infants treat it as familiar 1 hour later. They prefer to look at a completely new photo. The familiarity obtained during massed study is less robust. The result is counter to the intuitions of pioneers in the study of infant memory, who thought that repetitions should be arranged in close succession to prevent any loss of memory from one exposure to the next (e.g., Jeffrey & Cohen, 1971, p. 81).

Positive effects of spacing on retention have additionally been established in studies of rats. The paradigms include delayed alternation problems (Roberts, 1974), habituation of startle reflexes (Davis, 1970), and suppression of appetitive responding due to classically conditioned fear (Coulter, 1979).

The spacing effect is sufficiently general that experiments that reveal limiting conditions are of interest. For example, in an initial study, 3-month-old human infants did not seem to benefit from distributed training as indexed by long-term retention (14 days) of operant footkicking (Enright, Rovee-Collier, Fagen, & Caniglia, 1982). The babies had learned to kick to activate a crib mobile that had been tied to their leg by a silk ribbon. A massed training episode (18 minutes of

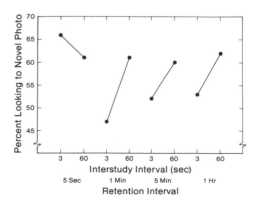

FIG. 12.3. Percentage of fixation to the novel photograph as a function of the distribution of study of the repeatedly exposed photograph. In massed study the familiarization episodes were separated by 3 seconds, in distributed study, 60 seconds. Each curve represents 24 infants receiving the recognition tests at the retention interval noted, either 5 seconds, 1 minute, 5 minutes, or 1 hour. (From Cornell, 1980)

the contingency) yielded immediate and 14-day delayed retention. Short training episodes (6 minutes of the contingency) separated by 24 hours were adequate to produce immediate retention but inadequate to produce the 14-day retention. Compared to the intertraining intervals used in most studies of spacing (cf. Hintzman, 1974), 24 hours seems long. Yet, in a second study, these same distributed episodes were quite effective for maintaining delayed performance if the baby received a reinstatement procedure prior to repetitions of training. In this case, reinstatement consisted of hanging the mobile over the crib so that the baby could visually examine it before the connecting ribbon was attached. Enright et al. suggest that the preliminary exposure served to prime the retrieval of memory of the contingency so that the brief training episodes proceeded without decrements in the initial rates of the operant.

Failures to obtain the spacing effect in animal preparations have potential theoretical importance. For example, Roberts and Grant (1976) reviewed several studies of short-term memory in the pigeon using the delayed matching to sample procedure. This procedure is a refinement of Hunter's (1913) delayed response problem. In general, the procedure begins with the presentation trial (T_1) of a sample stimulus; the center key of a row of three pecking keys is backlit by a color or pattern. The pigeon may acknowledge this event by pecking the sample key. The light behind the key is extinguished, and then, following an interval, the sample presentation is repeated (T_2). Following a delay, the two side keys are backlit, one with a pattern identical to the sample, one with a nonmatching pattern. This third presentation constitutes a two-choice retention test. A peck to the matching key produces reward, access to grain, whereas a peck to the foil turns off all the keys with no reward. A series of careful studies (Roberts, 1972; Roberts & Grant, 1974) failed to show any advantage of spacing repetitions of the sample stimulus. In fact, Roberts and Grant (1974, Experiment 2) observed a massing effect, more accurate matching on immediate tests following brief intervals between repetitions of the sample. This result is consistent with a simple model of accumulation of memory trace strength, and led Roberts and Grant (1976) to speculate that fundamentally different mechanisms of short-term memory are at work in birds and mammals.

We encounter this possibility again, when we discuss serial position effects. However, at this point we can note that spacing effects may be obviated in tasks in which the same stimulus serves as correct or as a foil on different problems. In the delayed response problem, the stimulus is a location. It is to be remembered on some hidings and ignored on others. To the extent tests of delayed responding are massed, opportunities for proactive interference are increased. Previous approaches to a location may be active memories and interfere with the memory of the most recently baited location. Thus, when testing rhesus monkeys, Gleitman, Wilson, Herman, and Rescorla (1963) found better long-term delayed reactions when 20 tests were given at the rate of 2 per day than when separated by 25 seconds and given on the same day.

In the delayed matching to sample problem, the stimulus to be remembered is a colored field or pattern on a key. If the sample has served on a previous problem as a foil, or vice versa (cf. Roberts, 1972; Roberts & Grant, 1974), the effects of spacing the interval between T_1 and T_2 on any one problem may be canceled by the massing of the problems. Thus, one way to avoid proactive interference in the delayed matching to sample task is to use a large pool of items, so that novel patterns occur on every problem (Wright, Santiago, Sands, & Urcuioli, 1982). Indeed, in a procedure which contrasted the performance of monkeys in problems with different numbers of test objects, Medin (1974) was able to affirm the spacing effect in a delayed matching-to-sample paradigm in which multiple stimuli were used.

It is interesting that issues concerned with the conditions for appearance of spacing effects in preverbal and nonverbal subjects have parallels in studies of verbal learning. One issue involves a possible tradeoff between forgetting during learning and retention after learning. Research with human infants suggested that learning occurring in an initial episode may become inaccessible if the duration of the interval prior to the next learning episode is long (e.g., Enright et al., 1982). Similarly, studies of verbal processing indicate an asymptote; performance on memory tests appears to improve as the spacing of two study episodes increases from 0 to about 15 seconds, while increases beyond 15 seconds may have no effect and in some conditions are inefficient (Hintzman, 1974). A second issue involves the attenuation of spacing effects in situations with opportunities for interference during the retention test. This limiting condition appears in studies of delayed choice by animals when the same stimuli are correct or incorrect on different trials within the same test session. Similarly, studies of paired associate learning have established that massed practice with a list produces marked interference when the same stimuli are subsequently used in a different list (e.g., Underwood & Ekstrand, 1967). In general, spacing effects are more apparent in verbal learning of individual items than in the successive acquisition of groups of items (Hintzman, 1974; Underwood, 1961).

In summary, the spacing effect is a facilitation of relatively long-term retention due to a relatively long interval between learning trials. The effect characterizes performance of rats, monkeys, apes, human infants, and adults on several memory tasks. There is some question whether birds such as pigeons can be included in this list. The spacing effect has been demonstrated in paradigms involving classical and operant conditioning, habituation of orienting responses and reflexes, and verbal learning.

SERIAL POSITION EFFECTS

Discussions of serial position effects inevitably address the context in which learning and retention occur. This is because serial position effects happen when an item (word, picture, or event) to be remembered appears in a sequence of other items (a list). Additionally, the list itself is in a context of extralist events, and the proximity of an item to this extralist context may be important. As noted by Ebbinghaus (1885/1917), acquisition and forgetting of an item are related to its serial position in the list—if the item occurred in the middle of the sequence, it is less likely to be remembered than if it occurred at the beginning or end. The benefit of position at the beginning of a list is termed "the primacy effect" and the benefit of position at the end of a list is termed "the recency effect." Like spacing effects, serial position effects are abundant in experimental and naturalistic studies of verbal mnemonics (see review by Crowder, 1976, chapter 12). The advantages for recall of the extreme positions in a list are so common as to be indicated in the time necessary to answer the following question: What day of the week is today? The response on Wednesday takes longest, and midweek names are also more prone to confusion than Sunday or Friday (Koriat & Fischoff, 1974). Those of us who live for the weekends may not be surprised at this result, even though recall of other semantic knowledge is not found to be attenuated when assessed at midweek (Koriat & Fischoff, 1974).

Serial position effects can be systematically revealed in a probe recognition memory test. The general features of this procedure are illustrated in a study of habituation of an orienting response in rabbits (Wagner & Pfautz, 1978). Five distinctive stimuli were ordered to make different lists for different subjects. The stimuli were short (1 second) sensory events: a tone, a click, a flashing light, a vibrating massage, or a faint electric current. The interstimulus interval was 2 seconds and, because 8 or 16 exposures of the list were necessary to produce habituation, the interlist intervals were 150 seconds. The orienting response was vasoconstriction, an autonomic reaction to reduce blood flow to the extremities prior to fright or fight. To the extent the animal is familiar with a harmless event, there is habituation of such vasomotor activity. Retention of habituation was probed after separate repetitions of an invariant sequence of sensory events. In this case, the probe followed the last list presentation by 15 minutes, a retention interval void of stimulus manipulations. The probe consisted of 12 presentations of one of the stimuli (the 1 second vibration) that had consistently occupied either the first, middle, or last position in the list. The probe indicated the amplitude of vasoconstrictive orienting was high if the vibration had occupied the middle position in the list, but appreciably lower if the vibration had occurred at the beginning or conclusion of the list. The analysis indicated retention of habituation was a nonmonotonic function of serial position; primacy and recency effects were apparent at the extremes of a bowed plot of peak response (see Fig. 12.4).

Similar functions have been obtained in serial probe recognition tests of human infants, adult monkeys, and pigeons. Figure 12.5 represents the test performance of 7-month-old babies who were repeatedly shown a fixed series of three photographs of adult female faces (Cornell & Bergstrom, in press). As with other studies within this paradigm, recognition is inferred from the baby's tendency to look more at a novel photograph when it appears side-by-side with one that had previously been exposed. In this case, the previously exposed face had

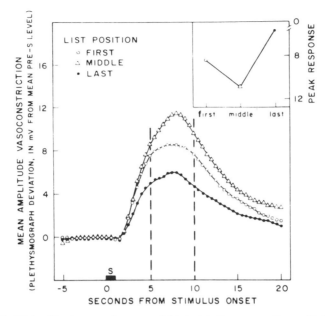

FIG. 12.4. The inset at the upper right depicts the mean peak amplitude of vasoconstrictive orienting response (5–10 seconds after probe stimulus onset) as a function of the serial position of the stimulus in a previous exposed list. The ordinate scale is inverted to suggest better retention is associated with less orienting. (From Wagner & Pfautz, 1978. Copyright The Psychonomic Society, reprinted by permission.)

appeared in a consistently ordered list repeated over multiple study periods. Separate groups of infants received probe recognition tests at 5 seconds, 1 minute, or 5 minutes following the last list presentation. Both primacy and recency effects appeared on the immediate (5 second) tests. The recency effect was significantly attenuated as a function of delay.

Figure 12.6 represents the test performance of monkeys in a variant of the delayed matching-to-sample task (Wright et al., 1982). An animal was shown a series of four pictures of various objects to constitute a single presentation of a list. The pictures were shown for 1 second with a 1-second interval between pictures. A (2 second) probe picture followed a retention interval after the list. The subject was rewarded for a response to the right if the probe matched one of the list items and received the same reward for a response to the left if the probe was novel. The notable result for both pigeons and monkeys is that at short probe delays retention of items increased with recency, at intermediate delays there were both primacy and recency effects (yielding the bowed-shaped serial position function), and at long delays retention of items decreased with recency (Wright et al., 1982).

These data encourage comparisons of immediate and delayed retention for items occurring in different serial positions in short lists. One of the most interesting results of research on verbal learning and memory is that primacy and recency effects may be differentially affected when a retention interval is long or interpolated materials occur between learning and free recall of a list (Crowder, 1976). The result is counterintuitive: Following a delay, memories of the most recent items are difficult to retrieve, whereas recollection of items at the beginning of the list appears to be unaffected. The selective effect of delay on recency has lent support to the notion that a separate process (such as rehearsal) underlies primacy (cf. Atkinson & Shiffrin, 1968, Waugh & Norman, 1965). The data from the studies of infants and infrahumans indicate this explanation may be inadequate. The latter research indicated primacy effects are not evident when probes occur immediately after a single list presentation, or at least within the time (1 second) that usually separates item presentations. In addition, if rehearsal is conceptualized as naming an item and covert repetition of the name, it seems likely that a different mechanism is responsible for the appearance of primacy effects in the intermediate and delayed retention of preverbal and nonverbal subjects. We consider alternative accounts later in the chapter, when common theoretical processes are proposed to accommodate most of the phenomena listed in these sections.

The forgetting of items embedded in the small lists employed in the preceding studies suggests phylogenetic and ontogenetic limits to memory processes. However, at this juncture it may be prudent to reinstate the lesson provided by Hunter's (1913, 1917) work: The quantitative implications of these limits are probably less important than the subjects' patterns of reaction to unique task requirements. Research with a dolphin (Thompson & Herman, 1977) and rhesus monkeys (Sands & Wright, 1980) illustrates this point with reference to the absence and appearance of serial position effects.

The dolphin was tested with the variant of the delayed matching-to-sample task previously described. An underwater speaker was used to present a list of six

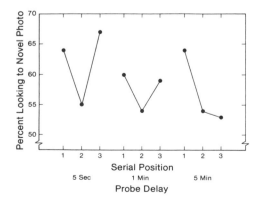

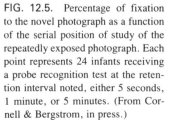

FIG. 12.5. Percentage of fixation to the novel photograph as a function of the serial position of study of the repeatedly exposed photograph. Each point represents 24 infants receiving a probe recognition test at the retention interval noted, either 5 seconds, 1 minute, or 5 minutes. (From Cornell & Bergstrom, in press.)

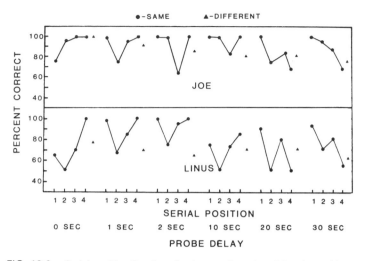

FIG. 12.6. Serial position functions for two monkeys in a delayed matching to sample task. The percentage of correct matching responses is graphed as a function of the serial position of the sample in a four-item list; probe matching tests followed different retention intervals in different problems. (From Wright, Santiago, Sands, & Urcuioli, 1982. Reprinted courtesy of Anthony Wright.)

discriminably different 2-second sounds separated by .5-second silent intervals. After a 1- or 4-second retention interval, a 2-second probe sound was broadcast. The dolphin responded by swimming either to a paddle on the left or right and pressing to classify the probe sound as old or new. The probability of recognizing a sound from the list was near perfect if the sound had been the most recently broadcast. Performance decreased successively to chance levels for earlier list sounds, with no indication whatsoever of a primacy effect. Thompson and Herman (1977) noted that the performance of the dolphin was remarkably similar, in both absolute and relative terms, to results for four human adults in a probe recognition task involving spoken lists of 3-digit numbers (Wickelgren & Norman, 1966). For six-item lists, the adults were almost perfect at recognizing the most recent numbers, but performance was near chance levels for numbers presented near the beginning of the list. Numbers, like sounds, may be discriminably different, yet difficult to encode rapidly as distinct for subsequent retrieval. A single number or sound in isolation may produce a memory which remains unaltered over long retention intervals, yet in the context of a list these same items may be confused with newly arriving items of a similar nature. In other words, the same forms of interference and retrieval failure may obviate primacy effects in serial list retention by mammals with environments as different as those of dolphins and man. Studies with preschool children indicate these sources of forgetting are dramatically reduced by repetitions of the to-be-remembered list or by increasing the discriminability of items (Rosner, 1972; see review by Hagen & Stanovich, 1977). It would be interesting to determine whether primacy effects in the auditory-probe recognition task could be established with identical treatments for adult humans and dolphins.

Quantitative estimates of serial retention have the same destiny as the measure of the length of delayed reaction. One procedure to expand the retention of lists has already been discovered (Sands & Wright, 1980). A rhesus monkey performed at high accuracy in a serial-probe recognition task employing 10- and 20-item lists. The monkey classified old items with 84% accuracy on the 10-item list and 81% accuracy on the 20-item list. An adult human was tested in the same apparatus and achieved 93% and 90% accuracy in the 10- and 20-item problems, respectively. The curves representing recognition performance as a function of the serial position of list items were nearly identical for the monkey and the human: bowed, with primacy and recency effects. The high accuracy and robust primacy effect shown by the monkey was determined to be due to the size of the test item pool (Sands & Wright, 1980, Experiment 3). Over 200 distinct photographs served uniquely as items to-be-remembered or foils. As in the facilitation of spacing effects, it is thought that this procedure minimizes proactive interference, providing conditions in which memories of earlier choices can be independent of the storage, retrieval, or response to the most recent items.

In summary, serial position effects refer to superior retention of events which occur at the extremes as opposed to the middle of a bounded sequence. A bowed serial position function indicates advantages due to both the primacy and recency of memories. This function characterizes memory task performance of pigeons, rabbits, monkeys, human infants, children, and adults. Serial position effects have been demonstrated in paradigms involving operant conditioning, habituation of orienting responses, and verbal learning. Further, there are correspondences in preparations in terms of the conditions for the appearance of primacy effects.

HOMOLOGIES, ANALOGIES, AND FUNCTIONAL RELATIONS

Up to this point, I have been compiling memory phenomena that appear to be the same across species, ages, and paradigms. Several other phenomena could be included as well: The effects of repetition, the effects of amnesic agents, and the postacquisition modification of memories. These topics are sufficiently broad and complex to warrant coverage by themselves and will not be reviewed here (see Crowder, 1976, chap. 9; Gordon, 1981; Hintzman, 1976; Riccio & Ebner, 1981; Spear, 1978, chaps. 7 & 8). Instead, I now consider issues encompassing all of these lines of inquiry. My concern is conceptualizing how demonstrations of effects can bear on questions of developmental continuity and theories of memory processing. Homology, analogy, and the determination of functional relations are ways to compare phenomena across subjects and situations.

Historically, detailed anatomical drawings highlighted the primary evidence for the continuity of lifeforms. By examining the position and dependencies of body parts of different species, comparative morphologists revealed shared patterns of structural organization. At issue was the source of these similarities. Homologies were indicated when the paleontological record showed continuity within a common ancestral line. Homologies were argued to be strong indices of phyletic affinities, and comparative ethologists saw advantages of the same analytical methods for description in the behavioral domain (Beer, 1980). However, because the structure of behavior does not leave a permanent environmental record, such as a fossil, there is no substantiation by ontological analysis. The notion of behavioral homology was perhaps most easily illustrated in reference to stereotyped or ritualistic patterns of behavior, in which the form and order of a component of a species-typical action sequence could be compared with that of a different species (e.g., Lorenz, 1974). The application of the construct appears to be limited presently with respect to memory phenomena. Similar patterns of retention and forgetting of items within a list appear in the serial position effects I have reviewed, but little else is known of the organization of memories of nonverbal and preverbal organisms. Studies of systematic foraging for items placed in multiple locations may prove informative in this regard (cf. Menzel's 1978 observations of chimpanzees with Cornell & Heth's 1983 observations of preschool children).

The comparative construct of analogy also developed from the early study of the forms of organisms. Again, the ontological source of similarities was pivotal. Analogies were indicated if the correspondences could be shown to be due to convergent evolution of originally dissimilar forms. A comparison based on analogy implied continuity from the similarity of function of body parts of different organisms, for example, the wings of a bird and the wings of a bat. The description of function involved observation of behavior in natural settings, so that the uses of body parts for locomotion, detection of events, or feeding could be ascertained for different species. The functions of many natural structures are masked or ambiguous, and it was not unusual for early field descriptions to be marred by anthropomorphism or teleology. Thus, judgments of phyletic affinity based on analogy were more contentious than those based on homology, at least until the experimental and mathematical methods of ecologists and population geneticists began to be deployed (Beer, 1980).

As with homology, the application of the comparative construct of analogy appears to be limited with respect to memory phenomena. Of the effects we have reviewed, only in the case of reinstatement was there any indication of the utility of mnemonics. Campbell and Jaynes (1966) suggested that the adaptive significance of reinstatement was in the retention and forgetting of fear. They pointed out that early memories of danger have survival value for the young organism, but adult activities must be more flexible and irrelevant fears must be forgotten. Only those experiences that are periodically reinstated by a particular habitat or culture are selectively retained to guide mature behaviors.

Such attention to the probable function of a memory phenomenon is rare. Currently there is little discussion of the utility of serial position effects or spacing effects, and theoretical reviews leave the impression that these phenomena, though pervasive, could be the result of limits on processing (e.g., Crowder, 1976). If this is correct, it would be difficult to argue continuity of memory systems by appeal to analogy. The purpose of a pattern of performance may not be obvious.

A more comprehensive and empirically based method for comparative analysis is the determination of functional relations (Bitterman, 1960, 1965, 1975). Essentially, the approach is to test whether the performance of two individuals is affected in the same way by the same variables. The individuals can be different species or different ages. The absolute values of the factors that determine their performance and the levels of their performance may be quite different. Comparison involves testing the relationship between these independent and dependent variables in a variety of situations. The choice of test situations is dictated by hypotheses as to the common processes underlying the performance of the two individuals. Thus, the comparison of functional relations systematically reveals similarities and differences in behavior and also provides information for refining process theories. Bitterman developed the approach for the phyletic study of learning, but its general utility can be appreciated in application to the memory phenomena we have reviewed.

Briefly, in the reinstatement procedure there is a functional relation between an initial learning experience and a later reminder. If only the first of these two experiences occurred, there would be ephemeral evidence of memory. If only the second of these two experiences occurred, there would be even less evidence of memory. When both are ordered with an interim, they accrue substantial delayed retention. It is not necessary to equate for different animals the absolute levels of learning, or the proportionality of the reminder, or the duration of the interval between original learning and the reminder, or the duration of the interval between the reminder and the retention test. It has been evident as early as the work of Hunter (1913) that such equalities are elusive given the variation in sensory, motor, or motivational differences between subjects. The basis for comparison is the pattern of retention and forgetting when events are systematically varied within the reinstatement paradigm (cf. Bitterman, 1965, p. 400).

In the spacing effect there is a functional relation between the temporal distribution of learning experiences and the duration of retention. As we have seen, the temporal parameters of study and test may vary across experimental preparations, but the spacing effect is clearly indicated by an interaction: Learning that is relatively spaced facilitates retention that is relatively delayed. The nature of the items to be remembered—words, sentences, pictures, painful events—does not seem to be as important as their occurrence over time. Again, continuity can be indicated by the pattern of retention and forgetting when events are arranged within the paradigm.

In the serial position effect there is a functional relation between the retention of an item and its position within a list. This relation is also revealed by an interaction, since items at the beginning or end of the list should have an advantage over those in the middle. The length of the list may be less important as a determinant of primacy effects than the relative distinctiveness of the items or the amount of experience with the list. Thus, we can estimate similarities in the processing of memories by different subjects by contrasting the conditions which produce or dissolve primacy or recency effects.

There is no set prescription for establishing the evolutionary relationships among species with the use of behavioral data. It is intriguing that functional relations are similar in the memory performance of the mammals we have discussed, but it could be that primates and rodents have independently developed memory mechanisms not present in any common ancestor. Such convergence would itself be interesting, suggesting that the demands of their respective lifestyles or environments were similar. An analysis along these lines would benefit from examination of the uses of memories as well as tests of functional relations in a wide variety of species. The appearance and order of appearance of effects can be charted in relation to what is known of the development and activities of the neural systems of these species (cf. Amsel & Stanton, 1980). Function and structure, purpose and substrate—it may indeed be impossible to prove phyletic continuity of memory mechanisms, but it seems inevitable that these will be the heuristics for our observations.

The same applies to the ontogenetic approach, which may provide unique information about the development of mnemonics. For example, a number of studies of short-term retention by children of 4 to 10 years of age have assessed recall of items at different serial positions in a list (reviewed by Hagen & Stanovich, 1977). Much of this research was stimulated by the theoretical emphasis on the development of strategic control of memory processing (Atkinson & Shiffrin, 1968; Flavell, 1970). It was assumed that age-related differences in the shape of the serial position curve reflect the acquisition of verbal strategies such as labeling and cumulative rehearsal. In the most frequently used paradigm (introduced by Atkinson, Hansen, & Bernbach, 1964), a child is shown five to eight pictures of common objects. The pictures are revealed one at a time, turned over, and placed face down left-to-right in a row. At the end of the sequence, the tester produces a probe picture and asks the child to turn over the picture in the array that matches it. Overall, recall of the location of the target picture is more likely with increasing age, and the performance of primary school children shows both primacy and recency effects.

Early explanations for these effects focused on the development of verbal strategies, suggesting two processes. The primacy effect was attributed to naming and the cumulative repetition of names for the pictures, with pictures occurring early in the sequence receiving more rehearsal than items near the end of the list. The recency effect, then, was usually attributed to the short-term persistence of a new name in an active state at the time of immediate recall.

The interpretation has not received consistent support, however. Hagen and Kingsley (1968) noted recall for initial items was not improved when young children were asked to name items out loud, and Allik and Siegel (1976) noted that the serial position curves of children who did not spontaneously rehearse nevertheless showed a primacy effect. Some other mnemonic seems to be available. Indeed, recent experiments indicate that the spatial context of the item to be remembered is a major factor in children's performance in this task (Berch, 1978; Siegel, Allik, & Herman, 1976). Children seem to note that the pictures on the far left and far right of the array are the only ones that have other pictures on just one side. The extralist context provides a unique cue for remembering these items.

The discovery that stimulus context is an active determinant of retention while children are acquiring strategic control of memory processes suggests a special form of developmental continuity. It is likely that basic mechanisms spontaneously represent the context in which a memory is stored and retrieved (Spear, 1978, chap. 2). The mechanisms may operate to produce serial position effects in the recognition performance of preverbal infants (Cornell & Bergstrom, in press) and incidental recall by adults (Crowder, 1976; chap. 12). Strategic mnemonics may function by activating, maintaining, or elaborating these more basic mechanisms, but the developmental research does not indicate that they are supplanted. At this time I can sketch the nascent skeleton of such basic mechanisms.

COMMON PRINCIPLES OF OPERATION

Theoretical and empirical insights on the processing of memories have been the result of cumulative scholarship. The present account borrows heavily from Spear (1978, 1981) and Wickelgren (1977, 1981), who synthesize and extend work by Underwood (1969), Estes (1955, 1972), and Anderson and Bower (1973), among others. The source of these latter contributions is a variegated lineage of research going back as far as Aristotle's *De Memoria et Reminiscentia* (Boring, 1961). The application here is a description of mechanisms which hypothetically can produce all of the effects in the memory task performance of the mammals we have discussed.

External and internal events are homomorphic. Episodes in the life of an organism are represented internally by nodes, consisting of a set of neural elements and their activities. A node serves to amalgamate several relatively independent attributes of a learning experience, including the processing of contiguous events via different modalities or codes: visual, auditory, olfactory, and so forth. The activation of a node produces a memory, hence a memory always consists of a collection of associated events.

Many stimuli are available during a learning episode, some exteroceptive, some interoceptive, and it is unlikely that any organism can register them all simultaneously. Some events may be salient for a species or an individual, while others constitute a context, and still others are ignored. There is fluctuation in the sampling of events that occur during acquisition. Concurrent processing of events strengthens the associations between them so that a subset of attributes common to different samples may be sufficient to define a memory node.

The retrieval of memories involves many of the same processes. A node may be reactivated by a processing of events yielding attributes which duplicate a subset of attributes encoded during learning. Memory nodes are extremely durable, and reactivation of a node arouses attributes represented during acquisition but not necessarily present to initiate retrieval. Forgetting occurs due to a lack of similarity of the events during acquisition and retrieval. Or, events sampled at the time of retrieval may reactivate several memory nodes, leading to associative interference in response production.

Retention is efficient when unique attributes of events are bound to a node. The node allows conjoint retrieval of associated attributes rather than separate retrieval of each. Similarly, retrieval of an attribute should be more likely the more other attributes are associated with it via the same node. The specificity of retention can be boosted by ensuring the contiguity of unique attributes (those not common to other events). These attributes should be represented in processing at the time of retrieval.

The explanation for reinstatement effects can easily be derived from these principles. In reinstatement, a partial reminder is presented to the organism, and the resultant processing of a subset of attributes of the original learning experience serves to revive it in its entirety. Reinstatement is therefore comparable to a complete (and usually spaced) repetition of learning.

The explanation for spacing effects includes the principle that sampling of events fluctuates. The same attributes of internal and external events are likely to be processed when a learning episode immediately follows the original learning episode. This redundancy strengthens the association of these events but may limit the attributes represented by a node. A wider variety of attributes can be sampled when learning episodes are distributed across different contexts, and some of these attributes may be present when retention is assessed in a context different from that of the original learning episode. In other words, encoding variability provides more avenues for retrieval of the same memory.

The explanation for serial position effects uses the principle that the same unique attributes should be represented in processing during acquisition and retrieval. Items near the beginning and the end of a list are distinctive because of their proximity to extralist events, whereas items embedded within a list are always preceded and followed by invariant events. Hence, items near the beginning and the end of a sequence are favored for associations to a wide variety of attributes. In addition, tests of serial retention may follow events which signal the end of the list, and items are typically probed in isolation, without prior cueing with a close list member. When retrieval is required, attributes of the retention test may be more similar to attributes of acquisition for extreme rather than intermediate items.

These principles characterize fundamental and automatic operations of memory. They invite more specific and formal extrapolation (e.g., Medin, 1976; Wagner, 1978). They are especially congenial to conceptualizations of innate and spontaneous mechanisms for processing basic information such as the spatial, temporal, and frequency of occurrence of events (e.g., Hasher & Zacks, 1979). Other more strategic and semantically organized systems may develop from such a prototype.

SUMMARY AND CONCLUSIONS

Early comparative theorists hesitated to argue that there is psychological continuity between humans and other animals. This posed several dilemmas for the interpretation of memory phenomena. It was difficult to reconcile the axiom that animals do not possess ideas with observations that they could benefit from past experience. One finesse was to concentrate research on empirical determinants of learning, limiting discussion of the mental representation of events. Animal memory was largely attributed to processes of sensory recognition, and investigators embraced the explanation that performance in the delayed reaction problem was mediated by mechanical response dispositions.

It was not long before evidence indicated these conceptions were inadequate. Research within the delayed reaction paradigm showed that several creatures remember locations without obvious postural dispositions. It was additionally reported that monkeys became agitated upon discovering that their bait was switched between the occasion of its hiding and the opportunity to retrieve it (Tinklepaugh, 1928). More recently, patterns of foraging have been observed in situations where mutiple food locations are simultaneously baited. Rats seldom return to a location where they have completely consumed the bait, even though there are no cues specifying its absence and obvious cues for recognizing the location (Olton, 1978).

The equation of animal retention with sensory recognition only deferred its explanation. There is no theory of recognition that does not include some form of representation and retrieval of the familiar. Conversely, there are few forms of recall that are not cued by some external context. Semon (1909) forecast the notion of correspondence of mechanisms of recognition and recall, but his ideas have only recently been appreciated (Schacter, Eich, & Tulving, 1978; Tulving, 1976).

As a rule, developmental theorists have adopted similar orienting attitudes, more impressed by the distinctiveness of behavioral adaptions at different ages than by evidence of invariance (Brainerd, 1978). This also leads to several interpretive difficulties, the most paradoxical that ontogeny, a course of change, is chiefly characterized as stable periods of unique abilities (Flavell, 1971). Piaget's (1968; Piaget & Inhelder, 1973) description of developmental stages of memory functioning is a major example. Piaget maintains that there is no evidence of symbolic thought in human infancy, the stage of sensorimotor intelligence. Preverbal infants rely on perceptual recognition and reproduction of motor schemes, and it is not until the age of 1½ or 2 years that children can evoke images of the past. According to this perspective, true mental representation is indicated when the child manifests memory of an object in the absence of its perception. This emphasis is problematic, since evocation of a memory independent of any contextual determinants constitutes autistic thought. Moreover, there is no evidence of changes in mnemonic processes (such as reconstruction) when children reproduce actions or recall images (Piaget & Inhelder, 1973, pp. 394–395).

It appears there can only be disputatious linkage of memory phenomena with questions of sentience, mental representation, and verbal abilities (Ruggiero & Flagg, 1976; Winograd, 1971). This does not preclude the establishment of the performance of different subjects in the same retention task, as Hunter (1913; 1917) set out to do. These attempts engendered new problems of comparison, however: The facile argument that situations can never be equated for two species, and the documentation of wide intraspecies variability in capacity. The interesting discovery was the spontaneous reaction to the delay that was qualitatively similar for different species, for example, pointing by rats and dogs. Performance in the absence of such a reaction indicated to Hunter the presence of a process parallel in function and mechanism to the memory of human experience. Thus, raccoons and young infants had ideational mnemonics by default.

There have since been many refinements of the methods for comparative psychology, but similarity of function and mechanism still retain central status in arguments for continuity. For example, comparative ethology has shown how the behavior of different organisms can be compared in terms of natural organization and purpose. These constructs seem compatible with emerging ecological approaches to the study of human memory (e.g., Baddeley, 1979; Neisser, 1982). At the present, however, there is a rich legacy of experimental analysis of the processing of memories, and it happens that patterns of forgetting and retention by animals and humans are functionally related. We have reviewed evidence for systematic correspondence in the determinants of reinstatement effects, spacing effects, and serial position effects. Moreover, these effects can be subsumed by a small body of explanatory principles recurring in basic associationistic theories. In sum, these phenomena may mark an archetypal system for processing fundamental events in the lives of a variety of organisms.

ACKNOWLEDGMENTS

Preparation of this chapter and the author's research reported herein was supported by Grant A0267 to E. Cornell from the Natural Sciences and Engineering Council of Canada. The Institute of Child Development at the University of Minnesota provided a pleasant and sustaining environment during the writing of this chapter.

REFERENCES

Allik, J. P., & Siegel, A. W. The use of the cumulative rehearsal strategy: A developmental study. *Journal of Experimental Child Psychology,* 1976, *21,* 316–327.

Amsel, A., & Stanton, M. Ontogeny and phylogeny of paradoxical reward effects. In J. Rosenblatt, R. Hinde, C. Beer, & M. Busnel (Eds.), *Advances in the study of behavior* (Vol. 11). New York: Academic Press, 1980.

Anderson, J. R., & Bower, G. H. *Human associative memory.* Washington, D.C.: Winston, 1973.

Atkinson, R. C., Hansen, D. N., & Bernbach, H. A. Short-term memory with young children. *Psychonomic Science,* 1964, *1,* 255–256.

Atkinson, R. C., & Shiffrin, R. M. Human memory: A proposed system and its control processes. In K. W. Spence & J. T. Spence (Eds.), *The psychology of learning and motivation* (Vol. 2). New York: Academic Press, 1968.

Baddeley, A. Applied cognitive and cognitive applied psychology: The case of face recognition. In L. Nilsson (Ed.), *Perspectives on memory research.* Hillsdale, N.J.: Lawrence Erlbaum Associates, 1979.

Beer, C. G. Perspectives on animal behavior comparisons. In M. Bornstein (Ed.), *Comparative methods in psychology.* Hillsdale, N.J.: Lawrence Erlbaum Associates, 1980.

Berch, D. B. The role of spatial cues in the probe-type serial memory task. *Child Development,* 1978, *49,* 749–754.

Bitterman, M. E. Toward a comparative psychology of learning. *American Psychologist,* 1960, *15,* 704–712.

Bitterman, M. E. Phyletic differences in learning. *American Psychologist,* 1965, *20,* 396–410.

Bitterman, M. E. The comparative analysis of learning. *Science,* 1975, *188,* 699–709.

Bjork, R. A. Repetitions and rehearsal mechanisms in models for short-term memory. In D. A. Norman (Ed.), *Models of human memory.* New York: Academic Press, 1970.

Boring, E. G. The beginning and growth of measurement in psychology. *Isis,* 1961, *52,* 238–257.

Brainerd, C. J. The stage question in cognitive-developmental theory. *Behavioral and Brain Sciences,* 1978, *2,* 173–213.

Bugelski, B. R., & Alampay, D. A. The role of frequency in developing perceptual sets. *Canadian Journal of Psychology,* 1961, *15,* 205–211.

Campbell, B. A., & Jaynes, J. Reinstatement. *Psychological Review,* 1966, *73,* 478–480.

Campbell, B. A., & Jaynes, J. Effect of duration of reinstatement on retention of a visual discrimination learned in infancy. *Developmental Psychology,* 1969, *1,* 71–74.

Campbell, B. A., & Spear, N. E. Ontogeny of memory. *Psychological Review,* 1972, *79,* 215–236.

Cohen, L. B., & Gelber, E. R. Infant visual memory. In L. B. Cohen & P. Salapatek (Eds.), *Infant perception: From sensation to cognition* (Vol. 1). New York: Academic Press, 1975.

Cornell, E. H. Infants' recognition memory, forgetting, and savings. *Journal of Experimental Child Psychology,* 1979, *28,* 359–374.

Cornell, E. H. Distributed study facilitates infants' delayed recognition memory. *Memory & Cognition,* 1980, *8,* 539–542.

Cornell, E. H., & Bergstrom, L. I. Serial position effects in infants' recognition memory. *Memory & Cognition*, in press.

Cornell, E. H., & Heth, C. D. Spatial cognition: Gathering strategies used by preschool children. *Journal of Experimental Child Psychology*, 1983, *35*, 93–110.

Coulter, X. The determinants of infantile amnesia. In N. E. Spear & B. A. Campbell (Eds.), *Ontogeny of learning and memory*. Hillsdale, N.J.: Lawrence Erlbaum Associates, 1979.

Crowder, R. G. *Principles of learning and memory*. Hillsdale, N.J.: Lawrence Erlbaum Associates, 1976.

Davis, M. Effects of interstimulus interval length and variability on startle-response habituation in the rat. *Journal of Comparative and Physiological Psychology*, 1970, *72*, 177–192.

Dempster, F. N. Memory span: Sources of individual and developmental differences. *Psychological Bulletin*, 1981, *89*, 63–100.

Ebbinghaus, H. E. *Memory: A contribution to experimental psychology*. New York: Dover, 1964 (Originally published 1885; translated 1913).

Enright, M. K., Rovee-Collier, C. K., Fagen, J. W., & Caniglia, K. *The effects of distributed training on retention of operant conditioning in human infants*. Manuscript under review, 1982.

Estes, W. K. Statistical theory of spontaneous recovery and regression. *Psychological Review*, 1955, *62*, 145–154.

Estes, W. K. An associative basis for coding and organization in memory. In A. W. Melton & E. Martin (Eds.), *Coding processes in human memory*. New York: Wiley, 1972.

Fagan, J. F. *Infant memory: History, current trends, and relations to cognitive psychology*. Paper presented at the Erindale Symposium on Infant Memory, May, 1982.

Fagen, J. W., & Rovee-Collier, C. K. A conditioning analysis of infant memory: How do we know that they know what we know they knew? In N. E. Spear & R. L. Isaacson (Eds.), *The expression of knowledge*. New York: Plenum, 1982.

Flavell, J. H. Developmental studies of mediated memory. In H. W. Reese & L. P. Lipsitt (Eds.), *Advances in child development and behavior* (Vol. 5). New York: Academic Press, 1970.

Flavell, J. H. Stage related properties of cognitive development. *Cognitive Psychology*, 1971, *2*, 421–453.

Fletcher, H. J. The delayed-response problem. In A. Schrier, H. Harlow, & F. Stollnitz (Eds.), *Behavior of nonhuman primates* (Vol. 1). New York: Academic Press, 1965.

Glaser, R. The future of testing: A research agenda for cognitive psychology and psychometrics. *American Psychologist*, 1981, *36*, 923–936.

Gleitman, H., Wilson, W. A., Herman, M. M., & Rescorla, R. A. Massing and within-delay position as factors in delayed-response performance. *Journal of Comparative & Physiological Psychology*, 1963, *56*, 445–451.

Gordon, W. C. Mechanisms of cue-induced retention enhancement. In N. E. Spear & R. R. Miller (Eds.), *Information processing in animals: Memory mechanisms*. Hillsdale, N.J.: Lawrence Erlbaum Associates, 1981.

Hagen, J. W., & Kingsley, P. R. Labeling effect in short-term memory. *Child Development*, 1968, *39*, 113–121.

Hagen, J. W., & Stanovich, K. G. Memory: Strategies of acquisition. In R. V. Kail & J. W. Hagen (Eds.), *Perspectives on the development of memory and cognition*. Hillsdale, N.J.: Lawrence Erlbaum Associates, 1977.

Harlow, H. F., Gluck, J. P., & Suomi, S. J. Generalization of behavioral data between nonhuman and human animals. *American Psychologist*, 1972, *27*, 709–716.

Haroutunian, V., Riccio, D. C. Effect of arousal conditions during reinstatement treatment upon learned fear in young rats. *Developmental Psychobiology*, 1977, *10*, 25–32.

Hasher, L., & Zacks, R. Automatic and effortful processes in memory. *Journal of Experimental Psychology: General*, 1979, *108*, 356–388.

Hintzman, D. L. Theoretical implications of the spacing effect. In P. L. Solso (Ed.), *Theories in cognitive psychology: The Loyola Symposium.* Hillsdale, N.J.: Lawrence Erlbaum Associates, 1974.

Hintzman, D. L. Repetition and memory. In G. Bower (Ed.) *The psychology of learning and motivation* (Vol. 10). New York: Academic Press, 1976.

Hoving, K. L., & Choi, K. Some necessary conditions for producing reinstatement effects in children. *Developmental Psychology,* 1972, *7,* 214–217.

Hoving, K. L., Coates, L., Bertucci, M., & Riccio, D. C. Reinstatement effects in children. *Developmental Psychology,* 1972, *6,* 426–429.

Hull, C. L. Knowledge and purpose as habit mechanisms. *Psychological Review,* 1930, *37,* 511–525.

Hunter, W. S. The delayed reaction in animals and children. *Behavior Monographs,* 1913, *2,* 1–86.

Hunter, W. S. The delayed reaction in a child. *Psychological Review,* 1917, *24,* 74–87.

Jeffrey, W. E., & Cohen, L. B. Habituation in the human infant. In H. Reese (Ed.), *Advances in child development and behavior* (Vol. 6). New York: Academic Press, 1971.

Jost, A. Die Assoziations festigkeit in Iher Abhangigheit von der verteilung der wiederholungen. *Zeitschrift fur Psychologie,* 1897, *14,* 436–472.

Koriat, A., & Fischoff, B. What day is today? An inquiry into the process of time orientation. *Memory & Cognition,* 1974, *2,* 201–205.

Lorenz, K. Z. Analogy as a source of knowledge. *Science,* 1974, *185,* 229–234.

Medin, D. L. The comparative study of memory. *Journal of Human Evolution.* 1974, *3,* 455–463.

Medin, D. L. Animal models and memory models. In D. L. Medin, W. A. Roberts, & R. T. Davis (Eds.), *Processes of animal memory.* Hillsdale, N.J.: Lawrence Erlbaum Associates, 1976.

Melton, A. W. The situation with respect to the spacing of repetitions and memory. *Journal of Verbal Learning and Verbal Behavior,* 1970, *9,* 596–606.

Menzel, E. W. Cognitive mapping in chimpanzees. In S. H. Hulse, H. Fowler, & W. K. Honig (Eds.), *Cognitive processes in animal behavior.* Hillsdale, N.J.: Lawrence Erlbaum Associates, 1978.

Morgan, C. L. *An introduction to comparative psychology.* London: Walter Scott, 1894.

Neisser, U. *Memory observed.* San Francisco: Freeman, 1982.

Olson, G. M. An information processing analysis of visual memory and habituation in infants. In T. Tighe & R. Leaton (Eds.), *Habituation: Perspectives from child development, animal behavior, and neurophysiology.* Hillsdale, N.J.: Lawrence Erlbaum Associates, 1976.

Olton, D. S. Characteristics of spatial memory. In S. H. Hulse, H. Fowler, & W. K. Honig (Eds.), *Cognitive processes in animal behavior.* Hillsdale, N.J.: Lawrence Erlbaum Associates, 1978.

Peterson, L. R., Hillner, K., & Saltzman, D. Time between pairings and short-term retention. *Journal of Experimental Psychology,* 1962, *64,* 550–551.

Peterson, L. R., Wampler, R., Kirkpatrick, M., & Saltzman, D. Effect of spacing presentations on retention of a paired-associate over short intervals. *Journal of Experimental Psychology,* 1963, *66,* 206–209.

Piaget, J. *On the development of memory and identity.* Barre, Mass.: Clarke University Press, 1968.

Piaget, J., & Inhelder, B. *Memory and intelligence.* New York: Basic Books, 1973.

Riccio, D. C., & Ebner, D. L. Post-acquisition modification of memory. In N. E. Spear & R. R. Miller (Eds.), *Information processing in animals: Memory mechanisms.* Hillsdale, N.J.: Lawrence Erlbaum Associates, 1981.

Riccio, D. C., & Haroutunian, V. Some approaches to the alleviation of ontogenetic memory deficits. In N. E. Spear & B. A. Campbell (Eds.), *Ontogeny of learning and memory.* Hillsdale, N.J.: Lawrence Erlbaum Associates, 1979.

Robbins, D., & Bush, C. T. Memory in great apes. *Journal of Experimental Psychology,* 1973, *97,* 344–348.

Roberts, W. A. Short-term memory in the pigeon: Effects of repetition and spacing. *Journal of Experimental Psychology,* 1972, *94,* 74–83.

Roberts, W. A. Spaced repetition facilitates short-term retention in the rat. *Journal of Comparative & Physiological Psychology,* 1974, *86,* 164–171.

Roberts, W. A., & Grant, D. S. Short-term memory in the pigeon with presentation time precisely controlled. *Learning & Motivation,* 1974, *5,* 393–408.

Roberts, W. A., & Grant, D. S. Studies of short-term memory in the pigeon using the delayed matching to sample procedure. In D. L. Medin, W. A. Roberts, & R. T. Davis (Eds.), *Processes of animal memory.* Hillsdale, N.J.: Lawrence Erlbaum Associates, 1976.

Romanes, G. *Animal intelligence.* London: Kegan Paul, 1882.

Rosner, S. R. Primacy in preschoolers' short-term memory: The effects of repeated tests and shift trials. *Journal of Experimental Child Psychology,* 1972, *13,* 220–230.

Rovee-Collier, C. K., & Fagen, J. W. The retrieval of memory in early infancy. In L. P. Lipsitt (Ed), *Advances in infancy research* (Vol. 1). Norwood, N.J.: Ablex, 1981.

Rovee-Collier, C. K., Sullivan, M. W., Enright, M., Lucas, D., & Fagen, J. W. Reactivation of infant memory. *Science,* 1980, *208,* 1159–1161.

Ruggiero, F. T., & Flagg, S. F. Do animals have memory? In D. Medin, W. Roberts, & R. Davis (Eds.), *Processes of animal memory.* Hillsdale, N.J.: Lawrence Erlbaum Associates, 1976.

Sands, S. F., & Wright, A. A. Serial probe recognition performance by a rhesus monkey and a human with 10- and 20-item lists. *Journal of Experimental Psychology: Animal Behavior Processes,* 1980, *6,* 386–396.

Schacter, D. L., Eich, J. E., & Tulving, E. Richard Semon's theory of memory. *Journal of Verbal Learning and Verbal Behavior,* 1978, *17,* 721–743.

Semon, R. *Die nmemischen Empfindungen.* Leipzig: Wilhelm Engelmann, 1909.

Siegel, A. W., Allik, J. P., & Herman, J. F. The primacy effect in young children: Verbal fact or spatial artifact? *Child Development,* 1976, *47,* 242–247.

Silvestri, R., Rohrbaugh, M. J., & Riccio, D. C. Conditions influencing the retention of learned fear in young rats. *Developmental Psychology,* 1970, *2,* 380–395.

Spear, N. E. *The processing of memories: Forgetting and retention.* Hillsdale, N.J.: Lawrence Erlbaum Associates, 1978.

Spear, N. E. Extending the domain of memory retrieval. In N. E. Spear & R. R. Miller (Eds.), *Information processing in animals: Memory mechanisms.* Hillsdale, N.J.: Lawrence Erlbaum Associates, 1981.

Spear, N. E., & Parsons, P. J. Analysis of a reactivation treatment: Ontogenetic determinants of alleviated forgetting. In D. L. Medin, W. A. Roberts, & R. T. Davis (Eds.), *Processes of animal memory.* Hillsdale, N.J.: Lawrence Erlbaum Associates, 1976.

Spence, K. W. *Behavior theory and conditioning.* New Haven: Yale University Press, 1956.

Thompson, R. K. R., & Herman, L. M. Memory for lists of sounds by the bottle-nosed dolphin: Convergence of memory processes with humans? *Science,* 1977, *195,* 501–503.

Thorndike, E. L. Animal intelligence: An experimental study of the associative processes in animals. *Psychological Review: Series of Monograph Supplements,* 1898, *2* (4, Whole No. 8).

Tinklepaugh, O. L. An experimental study of representative factors in monkeys. *Journal of Comparative Psychology,* 1928, *8,* 197.

Tulving, E. Ecphoric processes in recall and recognition. In J. Brown (Ed.), *Recall and recognition.* London: Wiley, 1976.

Underwood, B. J. Ten years of massed practice on distributed practice. *Psychological Review,* 1961, *68,* 229–247.

Underwood, B. J. Attributes of memory. *Psychological Review,* 1969, *76,* 559–573.

Underwood, B. J., & Ekstrand, B. R. Studies of distributed practice: XXIV, Differentiation and proactive inhibition. *Journal of Experimental Psychology,* 1967, *74,* 574–580.

Wagner, A. R. Priming in STM: An information-processing mechanism for self-generated or retrieval-generated depression in performance. In T. J. Tighe & R. N. Leaton (Eds.), *Habituation:*

Perspectives from child development, animal behavior, and neurophysiology. Hillsdale, N.J.: Lawrence Erlbaum Associates, 1976.

Wagner, A. R. Expectancies and the priming of STM. In S. H. Hulse, H. Fowler, & W. K. Honig (Eds.), *Cognitive processes in animal behavior.* Hillsdale, N.J.: Lawrence Erlbaum Associates, 1978.

Wagner, A. R., & Pfautz, P. L. A bowed serial-position function in habituation of sequential stimuli. *Animal Learning & Behavior,* 1978, *6,* 395–400.

Waugh, N. C., & Norman, D. A. Primary memory. *Psychological Review,* 1965, *72,* 89–104.

Weiskrantz, L. *Analysis of behavioral change.* New York: Harper & Row, 1967.

Wickelgren, W. A. *Learning and memory.* Englewood Cliffs, N.J.: Prentice-Hall, 1977.

Wickelgren, W. A. Human learning and memory. *Annual Review of Psychology,* 1981, *32,* 21–52.

Wickelgren, W. A., & Norman, D. A. Strength models and serial position in short-term recognition memory. *Journal of Mathematical Psychology,* 1966, *3,* 316–347.

Winograd, E. Some issues relating animal memory to human memory. In W. Honig & P. James (Ed.), *Animal memory.* New York: Academic Press, 1971.

Wright, A. A., Santiago, H. C., Sands, S. F., & Urcuioli, P. J. *Monkey and pigeon serial probe recognition performance: Effects of item pool size on proactive interference and item-specific associations.* Paper presented at the Harry Frank Guggenheim conference, Columbia University, June, 1982.

13 Infant Memory: Limitations and Future Directions

Mark S. Strauss
Philip Carter
University of Pittsburgh

The purpose of most of the chapters in this volume has been to explore the usefulness of studying the phenomena of memory development from a comparative perspective. In particular, an attempt has been made to explore commonalities that may exist between the learning and memory processes of rats and preverbal infants. Because the search for common psychological systems across different species has a long history, it is encouraging to note that current research from these two very different areas continues to support the idea that there are, indeed, a number of commonalities among the basic learning and memory processes of very different species. Perhaps this work is best summarized by Cornell (this volume) who illustrates how memorial phenomena such as reinstatement effects, spacing effects, and serial position effects, when "adjusted for the learning and response capabilities of animals and children," demonstrate an amazing degree of phylogenetic continuity. Similarly, James Gibson's (1979) ecological view of perception has recently had a considerable influence on research in infant perceptual development, and commonalities among the ways in which both infants and nonhuman animals pickup and abstract what appear to be highly structured, existing environmental information is striking (see, for example, Ruff, in press).

Yet, while it is important to explore and understand such comparative similarities, it is equally important to recognize that evolutionary development has led to many striking differences among organisms, differences that may ultimately limit the usefulness of emphasizing comparative similarities. Research on brain evolution using both comparative neuroanatomical studies and fossil records has shown that the human neocortex has increased in size by a factor of 156, in comparison to basal insectivores, and that most of this growth in the neocortex has occurred in the association areas of the temporal, parietal, and frontal lobes which mediate such functions as attention, memory, and language (Fishbein, 1976). To a large extent, these phylogenetic developments parallel the ontogenetic development of the human brain. The comprehensive work of Conel (1939–67) has shown that over the first year or two of life there are dramatic changes in the cerebral cortex, particularly in the frontal lobes, primary projection areas, and association areas.

The implications of this development are obvious—during the first years of life human infants undergo tremendous changes in their basic cognitive abilities. Consequently, although many similarities may exist between the memorial abilities of young infants and infrahuman animals, it is perhaps more important that researchers of infant memorial development recognize and explore how these underlying cortical changes result in the development of an organism that is very different from its infrahuman relatives.

There exist a number of excellent reviews of infant memorial development (e.g., Cohen & Gelber, 1975; Olson & Sherman, in press; Werner & Perlmutter, 1979; plus the chapters by Kail & Strauss, Cornell, Rovee-Collier, and Watson in this volume). From these reviews it can be seen that most current infant research has been concerned with relatively simple aspects of recognition memory. Indeed, to a large extent, the infant has been viewed as being a passive information processor whose memorial system is perhaps not very different from the typical "wax plate" metaphor. That is, there exists a plethora of studies where the infant is familiarized (either through habituation or conditioning) with some very simple, novel stimulus (e.g., a red circle) and then tested at some later point in time for his or her ability to remember the various aspects of this stimulus. Variations of this experiment include manipulations of the amount of familiarization the infant receives, the amount of delay before retesting, the degree of complexity of the original stimulus, whether interfering stimuli are shown between familiarization and retesting, the effects of spacing or reinstatement, and so on.

In general this research has demonstrated that, beginning at an early age, infants possess some relatively sophisticated recognitory abilities. For the most part, these abilities appear to be developmentally invariant and quite similar to the recognitory abilities of other infrahuman species. Yet, does this research truly reflect the developing memorial abilities of the infant? We suggest that research conducted thus far is still extremely limited and that the lack of any truly comprehensive theories of infant memorial development has resulted from these limitations. That is, although the number of studies is large, they have focused on several very limited issues at the expense of ignoring what may be other important aspects of infant memorial development.

Several general issues need to be explored in future infant memorial research. These issues stem from a consideration of current research with both older children and adults, which suggests that future infant research will benefit more

by focusing on issues common to the adult and developmental memory literatures than on current models of animal learning and memory. First is the issue of
the effect of knowledge on memory. It is well established that knowledge plays
an important role in the performance of memory tasks for both children and
adults. For example, Siegler (in press) described four types of phenomena that
have led developmental psychologists to reconsider the role of the child's knowledge base with respect to memory performance. First, prior knowledge is known
to influence memory for newly acquired material (Spilich, Vesonder, Chiesi, &
Voss, 1979). Second, performance on memory tasks may improve independently
of strategy development if knowledge of the content area increases (Chi, 1981).
Third, the developing knowledge base may underlie apparent age-related improvements in basic capacities and strategies (Huttenlocher & Burke, 1976).
Finally, in some cases the knowledge base may be both a necessary and a
sufficient condition for memory development (Lindberg, 1980). Yet the effects
of knowledge on memory have been virtually ignored in the infant memory
literature. This has been true despite the fact that infants by at least 6 months of
age are obviously beginning to accumulate a large knowledge base about their
environment. This knowledge base includes information about people, social
situations, the properties of objects, and the like. Consider, for example, recent
research on infant categorization. Several studies have demonstrated that by 7 to
12 months of age, infants appear to have some minimal knowledge of a number
of natural categories including human faces, dogs, food, and furniture (Cohen &
Caputo, 1978; Cohen & Strauss, 1979; Fagan, 1977; Ross, 1980). Similarly,
they appear to have some knowledge of numerical quantities including notions of
both cardinal (Starkey & Cooper, 1980; Strauss & Curtis, 1981) and ordinal
(Curtis & Strauss, 1982) properties. Unfortunately, the effect of such knowledge
on memory has been an unexplored issue with infants.

A second general issue that needs to be explored with respect to the development of infant memory is the use of schematic representations, prototypes, and
scripts. Again, it is clear from both the developmental and adult memory literatures that as a result of experiencing regularities in the environment humans often
form a type of central representation or summary of these regularities. For
example, research with both children (e.g., Nelson & Gruendel, 1981) and
adults (e.g., Schank & Abelson, 1977) has demonstrated that everyday temporal
events are often stored as generalized scripts. Scripts as they are described by
Nelson and Gruendel (1981) consist of temporal and causal sequences of actions
that form a "structural whole" and allow for variable elements or information to
be inserted in appropriate contexts. There is essentially no research on scripts
with infants, although it is conceivable that even young infants are beginning to
form such generalized representations of events. Consider, for example, the
social interactions in which infants participate. From a young age, infants and
parents have repetitive interactions in feeding situations, game situations (e.g.,
playing peek-a-boo), dressing situations, and so on. While these interactions

may consist of merely automatic routines, it may also be the case that infants are beginning to form some generalized representation of these events and of the roles which both the parent and the infant play in these activities. Obviously, if infants form such scripts, current conceptualizations of infant memory will have to be elaborated considerably to incorporate such constructive activity.

Similarly, much research has shown that categorical information is often represented in a summary fashion sometimes referred to as a prototype. This research by Rosch (1975), Posner and Keele (1968), Goldman and Homa (1977), and others has demonstrated that through experience with the exemplars of a category, subjects integrate the features that vary within the category into an internal representation which typifies the category. Categorization judgements can then be made by comparing unexperienced exemplars to this abstracted prototypical representation. More recently, it has been demonstrated that infants by at least 10 to 12 months of age are also capable of forming prototypic representations (Husaim & Cohen, 1980; Sherman, 1981; Strauss, 1979; Strauss & Carter, 1982).

Again, the ability to form prototypic representations would force a revision of current views on the nature of the infant's memorial system. Both scripts and prototypes allow for what Rosch has called "cognitive economy." By this she means that from an information-processing perspective it is economical to be able to categorize and thus represent information from a variety of stimuli in a summary fashion. That is, the ability to form central representations drastically reduces memory load. This ability may be especially important for the young infant who is constantly being confronted with novel environmental information. Hopefully, this ability will become a much more important area of focus in future infant memory research.

A third general area that requires considerably more research is the question of recognition versus recall memory. To date, infant memorial research has been restricted to recognition memory tasks or limited cued-recall tasks as required in operant conditioning paradigms. Perhaps it has been assumed that Piaget (1952) was correct in claiming that true recall memory is not possible until the emergence of a symbolic representational system at the end of the sensori-motor period. However, as Mandler (in press) has recently argued, while infants may not engage in deliberate or intentionally conscious memorial behaviors, they do appear to be able to retrieve information when they are given "reminders." For example:

> some of Piaget's observations on his own children in Stage III can be interpreted (although he did not) as instances of recall. The child reaching behind her to recover a toy with which she had been playing a minute before may be engaged in a deliberate retrieval process or merely being reminded, but it is hard to avoid the conclusion that some sort of recall is taking place. For present purposes it hardly matters whether or not an action scheme is the only kind of retrieval cue the child can use; it is still recall. (p. 6)

Similarly, recent research by Ashmead and Perlmutter (1980) which explored the memory abilities of 7- to 9-month-old infants in naturalistic contexts has suggested evidence of recall memory. For example, they describe a 9-month-old girl who usually played with ribbons that were kept in the bottom drawer of a dresser. When on a following day she opened the bottom drawer only to discover there were no ribbons, she proceeded to open all the drawers until the ribbons were found in the top drawer. On still the next day, the girl immediately proceeded to open the top drawer. As Mandler argues, it is easier and perhaps more parsimonious to "explain such performance by assuming that the information retrieved by the cue of the bureau was an explicit conceptualization of the location of the ribbons and not merely an attitude of expectation followed by recognition."

While certainly such evidence does not "prove" the existence of recall memory in infants, it is suggestive and obviously requires further research and questioning. To a large extent, our ignoring the issue of recall versus recognition memory may be the result of an over-reliance on limited set of methodological paradigms in infant memorial research. Because the experimental paradigms most widely used to study infant memory (i.e., novelty preference techniques) access operationally defined recognition memory (memory in the presence of the stimulus) there has been some concern that more important questions about the early development of memorial skills are not being addressed (Sophian, 1980). That is, if recognition memory is primitive and developmentally invariant, its study is of limited interest. Sophian (1980) has emphasized that varied methodologies are essential for a more complete understanding of infant memory. These methodologies would, among other things, measure more non-recognitory forms of memory.

Finally, there is the issue of episodic memory and the need for temporal markers and knowledge. Nelson (in press) has recently argued that without temporal markers such as *past, present,* and *future* it is likely that episodic events will become fused and confused. That is, without such temporal knowledge, memories may be considered "free-floating fragments." Nelson (in press) recorded and analyzed the spontaneous verbalizations of a very bright 21-month-old girl who was in the habit of talking to herself about significant events and activities of her day. Nelson noted that as the child began to use linguistic temporal markers more frequently (between the ages of 22 and 25 months) her memories began to be more definitely reconstructive and planful. They also began to become "more clearly thematic and episodic, focused on a particular happening or on the anticipation of a promised event with fewer apparently irrelevant intrusions from other experiences."

While Nelson's data come exclusively from a single verbal child, the issue of when temporal markers emerge conceptually and can be used as part of the child's memory base remains poorly understood. While they may not emerge until they are actively being used in a linguistic sense, the possibility exists that, prior to language, infants are beginning to acquire some minimal temporal knowledge. For example, an older infant who consistently experiences that he or she will be fed after waking up, or that after breakfast he or she is taken to a day-care center may begin to develop some type of minimal temporal knowledge of events. There is really no existing research that has explored such possibilities, yet it is quite likely that the use of temporal linguistic markers may be preceded by some prior conceptual realization of the temporal order of events, and that this temporal awareness may serve to organize experiences in the infant's memory.

The issues discussed here represent only a sampling of the many questions that remain to be explored with respect to the development of infant memorial processes. They suggest, however, that the research which has been done thus far remains quite limited and will have to be greatly expanded before any more general theories of development can be formulated. As can also be seen, it is our strong belief that the directions for such future research are more likely to come from existing conceptualizations of the mature human processor and not from existing comparative theories of memory.

REFERENCES

Ashmead, D. H., & Perlmutter, M. Infant memory in everyday life. In M. Perlmutter (Ed.), *New directions for child development: Children's memory* (Vol. 10). San Francisco: Jossey Bass, 1980.

Chi, M. T. H. Knowledge development and memory performance. In J. P. Das, M. P. Friedman, & N. O'Connor (Eds.), *Intelligence and learning*. New York: Plenum Press, 1981.

Cohen, L. B., & Caputo, N. *Instructing infants to respond to perceptual categories*. Paper presented at the Midwestern Psychological Association Convention. Chicago, Ill., 1978.

Cohen, L. B., & Gelber, E. Infant visual memory. In L. B. Cohen & P. Salapatek (Eds.), *Infant perception: From sensation to cognition* (Vol. 1). New York: Academic Press, 1975.

Cohen, L. B., & Strauss, M. S. Concept acquisition in the human infant. *Child Development*, 1979, *50*, 419–424.

Conel, J. L. *The postnatal development of the human cerebral cortex*. Cambridge: Harvard University Press, 1939–67.

Curtis, L. E., & Strauss, M. S. *Development of numerosity discrimination abilities*. Paper presented at the meeting of the International Conference on Infant Studies, Austin, March 1982.

Fagan, J. F. An attention model of infant recognition. *Child Development*, 1977, *48*, 345–359.

Fishbein, H. D. *Evolution, development, and children's learning*. Pacific Palisades, Calif.: Goodyear, 1976.

Gibson, J. J. *The ecological approach to visual perception*. Boston: Houghton Mifflin Company, 1979.

Goldman, D., & Homa, D. Integrative and metric properties of abstracted information as a function of category discriminability, instance variability, and experience. *Journal of Experimental Psychology: Human Learning and Memory*, 1977, *3*, 375–385.

Husaim, J. S., & Cohen, L. B. *Infant learning of ill-defined categories*. Paper presented at the International Conference on Infant Studies. New Haven, Conn., 1980.

Huttenlocher, J., & Burke, D. Why does memory span increase with age? *Cognitive Psychology*, 1976, *8*, 1–31.

Lindberg, M. A. Is knowledge base development a necessary and sufficient condition for memory development? *Journal of Experimental Child Psychology*, 1980, *30*, 401–410.

Mandler, J. M. Representation and retrieval in infancy. In M. Moscovitch (Ed.), *Infant memory*. New York: Plenum Press, in press.

Nelson, K. The transition from infant to child memory. In M. Moscovitch (Ed.), *Infant Memory*. New York: Plenum Press, in press.

Nelson, K., & Gruendel, J. Generalized event representations: Basic building blocks of cognitive development. In M. E. Lamb & A. L. Brown (Eds.), *Advances in developmental psychology* (Vol. 1). Hillsdale, N.J.: Lawrence Erlbaum Associates, 1981.

Olson, G. M., & Sherman, T. Attention, learning, and memory in infants. In P. Mussen (Ed.), *Handbook of child psychology* (Vol. 10). New York: John Wiley, in press.

Piaget, J. *The origins of intelligence in children*. New York: International Universities Press, 1952.

Posner, M. I., & Keele, S. W. On the genesis of abstract ideas. *Journal of Experimental Psychology,* 1968, *77*, 353–363.

Rosch, E. Cognitive representations of semantic categories. *Journal of Experimental Psychology: General,* 1975, *104*, 192–233.

Ross, G. S. Categorization in 1- to 2-year-olds. *Developmental Psychology,* 1980, *16*, 391–396.

Ruff, H. Infant memory from a Gibsonian point of view. In M. Moscovitch (Ed.), *Infant memory*. New York: Plenum Press, in press.

Schank, R. C., & Abelson, R. *Scripts, plans, goals, and understanding*. Hillsdale, N.J.: Lawrence Erlbaum Associates, 1977.

Sherman, T. *Categorization skills in infants*. Paper presented at the meetings of the Society for Research in Child Development. Boston, 1981.

Siegler, R. S. Information processing approaches to development. In P. Mussen (Ed.), *Manual of child psychology* (Vol. 1). New York: John Wiley, in press.

Sophian, C. Habituation is not enough: Novelty preferences, search and memory in infancy. *Merrill-Palmer Quarterly,* 1980, *26*, 239–237.

Spilich, G. J., Vesonder, G. T., Chiesi, H. L., & Voss, J. V. Text processing of domain-related information for individuals with high and low domain knowledge. *Journal of Verbal Learning and Verbal Behavior,* 1979, *18*, 275–290.

Starkey, P., & Cooper, R. G. Perception of numbers by infants. *Science,* 1980, *210*, 1033–1035.

Strauss, M. S. The abstraction of prototypical information by adults and 10-month-old infants. *Journal of Experimental Psychology: Human Learning and Memory,* 1979, *5*, 618–635.

Strauss, M. S., & Carter, P. Infant memory for prototypical information. *Child Development,* in press.

Strauss, M. S., & Curtis, L. E. Infant perception of numerosity. *Child Development,* 1981, *52*, 1146–1152.

Werner, J. S., & Perlmutter, M. Development of visual memory in infants. In H. W. Reese & L. P. Lipsitt (Eds.), *Advances in child development and behavior* (Vol. 14). New York: Academic Press, 1979.

14

Ecologically Determined Dispositions Control the Ontogeny of Learning and Memory

Norman E. Spear
State University of New York

Throughout this volume and related books (e.g., Kail & Hagen, 1977; Spear & Campbell, 1979) a common observation is that younger organisms show less learning or memory than do adults. It is often tempting to ascribe such differences to the immaturity of whatever fundamental neurophysiological features or events ("mechanisms") are responsible for recording permanently in the brain the residue of experience. This temptation should be resisted. Among the chapters of the present and related volumes one rarely or never sees reference to the maturation of such a basic neurophysiological mechanism. Those of us who observe daily the learning and memory of young animals or children think, or at least write and talk, in quite different terms. This is in my opinion a good thing, for several reasons: A separate neurophysiological mechanism that acts specifically to establish learning and memory has been "identified" only in terms of a number of potential candidates, at best; such a mechanism is unlikely to be fully verified at a general level for many years after it is identified in simple systems; and as I shall suggest later, it may very well not exist at all.

I take the view that the ontogenetic differences in learning and memory we observe are more likely due to age-related peculiarities of behavior at a variety of steps in the learning and memory process, than to differences in the "stamping-in" of the association designated by an experimenter. This makes our topic no less interesting in terms of learning and memory. The same processes and their modification by environmental pressures that lead immature animals to learn or remember less effectively than adults, can readily be applied toward understanding variance in learning and memory generally. So it is that topics such as ontogenetic differences in perceptual encoding, selective attention, "meta-memory" and rehearsal strategies, effectiveness of retrieval cues, and so forth, have become topics of central concern for us.

325

What seems to be implied in these topics is an orientation focusing on age-specific behaviors that are, generally speaking, a product of the ecological demands placed on a developing organism. In this chapter I focus on this orientation, which has become increasingly a topic of common interest among scientists working with animals and those working with children as subjects (valuable reviews within this orientation include those of (Rovee-Collier, 1983; Rovee-Collier & Gekoski, 1979; Rovee-Collier & Lipsitt, 1982). This chapter begins with a reconsideration of questions raised by some classical studies of early experience that lead, I believe, to specific ecological considerations. Focusing on experiments with the developing rat, I then provide some concrete examples of how the ontogeny of learning and memory depends on interactions between the rat's fundamental behavioral dispositions and the nature of the particular episode that is to be learned and remembered. Finally, a few implications of these interactions are suggested.

EARLY EXPERIENCE AND LATER LEARNING AND MEMORY

Throughout this chapter I maintain that an ontogenetic change in some neurophysiological mechanism responsible for all learning and memory seems unlikely. There may in fact be no "global learning mechanism" that is independent of the processing required for sensory detection of the contingency between events. Accordingly a great deal of the ontogenetic variance we observe in learning is a matter of what is selected to be learned or expressed, which may be due in part to age-related differences in perception. One predictable consequence could be opposite the benefits usually expected from special early experience, namely, impaired learning of certain episodes that include stimulus events experienced earlier in life. These issues require an initial look at some past research on early experience.

We all share a desire to provide developing members of our species those experiences that will best promote their success as an adult. Scientists in our field reap a special benefit in this: by identifying such experiences we also learn a great deal about what determines adult behavior and, possibly, what events of childhood are most likely learned and remembered. While the early environmental control afforded in studying animals make research on early experience more profitable than is possible with humans, the problem of what is learned and remembered is pertinent to both cases.

There are two parts to the early experience question. One is whether early experience makes any difference later on; the other is what should the early experience be, for the best outcome? Most studies of the ontogeny of learning and memory with animals have been influenced by these two questions and taken from either of two orientations. One orientation assumes the fundamental assumption of ontogenetic continuity, or wishes to challenge it, and so focuses on particular psychological processes—feeding, perception, sensation, and so forth—in these terms. The alternative orientation rests in consideration of how the developing organism's behavior is changed as a consequence of the new information it acquires and remembers later. Both orientations require some consideration of the ontogeny of learning and memory and both are represented in the present volume.

The question of whether early experience makes any difference is linked inevitably to the issue of infantile amnesia. The prospect of losing all infantile learning through amnesia does not augur for significant consequences of early experience—depending on what we mean by "amnesia." The question of what the early experience should be makes contact with practically everything, including religion and politics. Tests with animals that have historically illustrated some dramatic effects of relatively nonspecific early experience—by selective deprivation or enrichment of sensory experiences—are important but not directly relevant. It is instead the optimal early experience of a *specific* nature—the particular learning experiences that might be most adaptive for the growing organism—that has special importance for our topic. The general concept is most easily recognized in terms of a familiar prototypic exemplar, "learning readiness" ("reading readiness" is a version familiar to elementary school teachers), a parameter of childhood learning that has practical significance for education.

Both of these issues, infantile amnesia and learning readiness, have contributed importantly to the history and current activities of persons studying the ontogeny of learning and memory with animal subjects.

Infantile Amnesia

The background and importance of the general topic of infantile amnesia—the extreme forgetting of infancy among grownup people or animals—is well known (Campbell & Coulter, 1976; Campbell & Spear, 1972; Spear, 1978). These background aspects of infantile amnesia surely are realized more fully than are the fundamental empirical facts of the phenomenon. Infantile amnesia is a problem for which plausible theories far outnumber substantial facts. And because infantile amnesia is the topic of psychobiological theories that are of intrinsic interest in themselves, and because some of the psychoanalytic theories are also sort of interesting although at the same time so absurd, it is easy and fun to talk about. But it is hard to know when anything substantial is said.

Gathering solid facts about infantile amnesia—which belongs in the category of "intractable" or at least "too hard" if it is to be studied with human subjects, and is also no simple matter when studied with animal models—was given hope through the work of Byron Campbell. In a book with a purpose not unlike the present one several years ago, Campbell (1967) outlined the methodological problems that had to be solved to properly test infantile amnesia. More significantly, Campbell not only described the problems but also presented some solutions with solid and extensive data. These solutions both permitted and inspired a great deal of the research in our area. Prior to that, much of the published work was inadequate methodologically.

I would like to say that we now know a great deal about infantile amnesia. But of course we do not. We know that in comparison to adults, infants are more sensitive to common sources of forgetting, such as an interval of no activity or interfering associations. Most of the work on this topic has done little more than define the phenomenon, frequently telling us that infantile amnesia may not in fact represent a source of forgetting unique to young children or animals. A relatively few studies have tried to uncover a compelling singular reason for infantile amnesia but have failed; included are several of my own experiments. In my opinion there is still no substantial evidence that the causes of our "amnesia" for the events of infancy are any different from what causes forgetting of the events of our adulthood (cf. Spear, 1979a,b).

In retrospect, it should not be too surprising that we still know little about infantile amnesia. In the history of the psychology of memory it has been clear that before the basis of remembering or forgetting could be understood, it was necessary first to understand acquisition. And, we have so far learned very little about the uniqueness of infantile acquisition. This leads us to the other major feature of early experience effects, characterized as the problem of "learning readiness."

Learning Readiness

The issue of learning readiness arouses associations of related issues that are emotionally laden, linked to fundamental dispositions of a philosophical, cultural, or even political nature: the question of predeterminism; whether there is a general intelligence factor; whether such a factor is unperturbed by experience; and so forth. But leaving aside the philosophical and political associates of the term, the idea of "learning readiness" arose from consideration of the consequences of specific early experience—training on specific associative problems or learning skills prior to the age at which such skills or associative capacity might ordinarily emerge with relative spontaneity.

The empirical observations are classic. The work of Gesell indicated that for toddlers, specific training and practice on skills such as buttoning, climbing, and cutting with scissors led to very little advantage over untrained cohorts trained at an older age. For the latter, a week's worth of training brought them to the level of the toddlers that had been in practice for many weeks before. Gesell and Thompson (1929; see McGraw, 1943, p. 121) stated that "There is no conclusive evidence that practice and exercise even hasten the actual appearance of types of reactions like climbing and tower building. The time of appearance is fundamentally determined by the ripeness of the neural structures."

About the middle of World War II, two publications on our topic were both influential and representative of the argument. One was by Wayne Dennis in the *Psychological Review* (1943) who argued against the feasibility of any prenatal learning and the unlikely influence of neonatal learning. This was of course the same Dennis cited in practically all textbooks for his study with the Hopi Indians, comparing those permitted and those not permitted the opportunity to exercise walking (Dennis & Dennis, 1941; one item of a set of data that has been criticized effectively by Hunt, 1979, and others).

The other pertinent publication at that time, a small book by Myrtle McGraw entitled *The Neuromuscular Maturation of the Human Infant,* was reprinted in the mid-sixties and continues to be of value today because it describes so nicely the changes in specific reflex activity in the human infant. In the last chapter McGraw turned her attention to the influence of learning on the development of motor skills. She viewed learning as, in a word, *insignificant* for these basic behaviors. The implication was that the associative aspects of these behaviors, the learning that included these behaviors as a part, would emerge whenever the physiological system involved was ready. The learning might not occur even though sensory detection and perception of all elements of this learning were ready developmentally and even though learning of other kinds had already taken place. Some types of learning were viewed as just impossible pending development of the *physiological basis for that particular type*. She exemplified this point by her systematic work with a couple of sets of twins in which one member of each was given special toilet training. Training seemed to make no difference. Her conclusion from these and other data was that "training in any particular activity before the neuromechanisms have reached a certain state of readiness is futile" (p. 130).

Gesell and his insistence that even for humans, "training does not transcend maturation" had considerable influence. I think the influence was disproportionate to the substance of the evidence and largely an historical accident. Most of the best scientists interested in learning and memory were at that time focused on the development of all-encompassing learning theories. But rather than theoretical progress, it was some striking empirical effects of early experience in animals that provided the primary impetus for a view opposite to that of Gesell.

This opposing view has been represented well by J. McV. Hunt (e.g., 1979) whose arguments, even aside from the animal data, were that early learning can help. For instance, Hunt reminded us that the basis for attributing the growth curves of skills to nonlearning factors was by default because the nature of environmental factors that could account for them were neither appreciated nor closely documented. There were clear ceiling effects on measurement in the Gesell studies—that is, it was difficult to detect an advantage of early training because at the time of testing, performance was about as good as could be measured. And there was in fact some measured degree of retained superiority among the trained subjects; it was only that the effect was small relative to the expectation of a great deal of superiority. For instance, in spite of McGraw's conclusion that early toilet training had no effect at later ages, when tested at about 15 months of age the trained twin retained a 10% advantage over the untrained twin. And when training of roller-skating and swimming was timed for one twin so as to take advantage of particular neuromuscular dispositions, this little boy acquired a capacity to swim at 6 months of age and to roller-skate quite well at 16 months of age while the untrained twin brother could not learn to roller-skate at 22 months of age.

In more recent years research of this kind has revolved around the ontogeny of cognitive behaviors. One focus for this research has been within the Piagetian orientation. Another has dealt with the emergence of language as a skill for which, to theories such as Chomsky and Lenneberg, relatively hardwired dispositions are a critical part. But in spite of the influence of these theories, the problem of learning readiness has not seemed a burning issue for empirically oriented scientists working with human infants and toddlers. There are at least three reasons for this. First, the issue itself is hazy and becomes intermixed with the unproductive, always complicated and usually emotional issue of the nature/nurture distinction. Second, such work really does require special circumstances in which infants or toddlers are fairly continuously accessible for treatment and testing, and it requires either twins or large numbers of subjects that must be tested and retested frequently. This is not an easy state of affairs to accomplish, at least in the United States.

The third reason for empirical neglect of the learning readiness issue is that it has been customary for psychologists to think in terms of a learning or memory process that is essentially unitary in its capacity to alter behavior. Learning theorists have biased this kind of thinking by, for instance, applying a single learning rate parameter in mathematical models. It also is a tempting notion because it makes things simple (is "parsimonious"). And it would be feasible, too, if for instance a particular neurotransmitter were ubiquitous throughout the brain and also, somehow, the primary agent of learning. It would be especially pleasant for developmental psychologists if one could aim toward a conclusion of the form that capacity for a psychological process like memory emerges at 8 months, becomes better at 2 years, still better at 5, and adultlike at 12. But this is unlikely to be the form explanations will take. It now seems fairly certain that the brain is not, as Lashley had concluded, equipotential for learning capacity throughout all of its parts. And it is quite definitely true that the brain is not equipotential in rate of its neurophysiological maturation.

Other factors lead us to doubt that memory in general is the product of a unitary capacity. For instance, we have become better educated about apparently all-encompassing memory deficits that are associated with certain types of disease or brain damage. We now know that what were once termed "global amnesics"—persons who literally cannot read books or watch films or TV because they cannot learn and remember enough about the beginning of a story to appreciate the ending—are, however, capable of good learning and long-term remembering for selected sets of events. For instance, for "global amnesia" attributable to temporal lobe damage or advanced Korsakoff disease, the learning and memory of some 15 classes of episodes seems pretty effective for the behavior measured—episodes with tests of the pursuit rotor, mirror drawing, memory for simple paired associates, learned identification of Gollin figures (these are incomplete pictures that appear as if they were drawn in pencil and then partly erased), words treated the same way as the Gollin figures, classical eyelid conditioning, rapid reassembly of simple jigsaw puzzles, the solution to previously solved anagrams or jumbled sentences, reading inverted print, the McGill Picture Anomalies tests, solution to a small tactile maze, application of a mathematical rule learned and applied previously, or playing a tune on the piano learned just recently (cf. Moskowitch, 1982; Schacter & Tulving, 1982; Spear & Isaacson, 1982). To further illustrate the selectivity of this memory capacity it is notable that in none of these cases did the amnesics, upon questioning, give any indication they were aware that the training episode had in fact occurred.

It has similarly become apparent ontogenetically that we are not dealing with an elemental associative process that determines all learning and memory as it develops. Reference to an "emergence" of learning or memory at a particular age is to the learning and memory of a particular set of events. That an infant mouse may not show simple escape learning until 7 days of age and no long-term retention of that learning until 9 days of age should not be taken to imply that learning and memory of any type will not occur before those ages. But there is more to this issue than that.

The issue is the psychobiological version of "learning readiness" exemplified in the theory of the Soviet, Anohkin (1964), and now applied widely in our field. The essence of this orientation is the view that seemingly ineffective associative behaviors by infants do not primarily indicate that the animal is an incomplete, incompetent adult. For Anohkin, the major unit for developmental psychobiological analysis is the "functional system" by which is meant a ". . . functional combination of different organizations and processes on the basis of the achievement of the final effect . . ." (p. 56). Examples of such functional systems are those for alternative types of feeding or for sexual behavior, systems that most obviously emerge in mature fashion at quite different ages. An important point is that when a functional system becomes effective will depend on its adaptive value at that particular age. Anohkin's position is that a functional system is ". . . indissolubly connected with the final effect of adaptation" (p. 56). What might appear to be deficient learning from the perspective of the *adult's* adaptational needs is considered to be an indication of the immature animal's contrary solution to the different adaptational problems at its particular age. We are beginning to learn how different the ecological challenges and solutions are at different stages of development, and that if its genes are to survive, the organism must be capable of meeting the challenges of infancy as well as those of adulthood.

ECOLOGICAL CONSIDERATIONS

In recognizing the changing ecological challenges facing the animal at different points in its ontogeny, the emerging psychobiological orientation toward the ontogeny of learning and memory generally is in accord with Anohkin's approach. This orientation treats the infant animal as a quite capable, adaptive organism, but with a different set of problems to adapt to than is faced by an adult. When learning and memory are assessed for an immature animal in a test designed for adults and the young animal's response seems to indicate relative ineptness, this cannot be taken uncritically as an indication that the immature animal is cognitively less able than the adult. Behaviors by an infant that might seem to suggest ineffective learning or retention from the perspective of the adult's adaptational needs may instead indicate the infant's efforts to regulate its intake and expenditure of calories, for instance, in ways not required by the adult. Such "ineffective" behaviors might in other words be due to dispositions of the infant that are actually conducive to its survival under most situations, and the apparent cognitive failures of the infant could reflect a constraint or bias that has little to do with its capacity for learning and memory. Like the Piagetian approach, the developing animal is not viewed as becoming smarter or more capable but instead as "seeing" the world from a progressively changing perspective.

There is a compelling practicality in asserting that the ecological challenges of infancy, although different from those of adulthood in their greater emphasis on the pressures to achieve optimal growth, to maintain body temperature behaviorally, and so forth, are equally urgent if the genes of the species are to survive. The majority of the failures to see much associative capacity in immature animals probably can be attributed to the experimenter's insensitivity to the limitations and dispositions of the infant animal toward (1) events that signal contingencies and (2) responses in accord with these contingencies. Evidence for associative capacity seems more likely when experimenters recognize the infant animal's limitations on both the input and output sides and account methodologically for the young animal's probable reception to particular ways of "asking the question" and propensity to "answer" in the way anticipated by the experimenter.

Especially during the past 10 years, experimenters have increasingly accommodated the young animal's specific ecological niche and age-related stimulus and response dispositions in their tests of infantile associative capacities and characteristics (for examples, see chapters in Spear & Campbell, 1979). In the case of the immature rat, for instance, these studies have carefully taken such things into account: that during the first 2 weeks of life the world of the rat is dominated by tactile stimulation, temperature differences, tastes and odors with only suckling, mouthing, rolling, and crawling as instrumental behaviors that could be used to exert some control over its world; that thereafter, discrete visual stimuli add to the general sensation of brightness differences as important environmental events, together with noises of different frequencies than before; and that the gradually increasing, more coordinated mobility of the growing rat pup requires new mechanisms for its return to the nest, items of a familiar taste but probably new texture begin to be consumed, and littermates begin to be treated as something other than a source of heat.

It has become apparent during the past few years or so that for problems sensitively geared to the rat pups' ecological dispositions and capabilities, some evidence for learning and remembering can be seen essentially from the time of birth or even before. Whereas prior to about 1975 it seemed that the rat pup was so limited in its associative capacity that it could hardly learn or remember at all before the second or third week of life, one can now find a great deal of evidence to the contrary: (1) Rats a little less than 2 weeks of age not only can learn to traverse a straight alley runway, but they can also respond to subtle differences in the conditions of reinforcement in doing so, can learn when to run and when not to run, and will for some time thereafter continue to respond in accord with these different reinforcement conditions (e.g., Amsel, 1979); (2) rats only slightly older than a week can learn an active avoidance response and may remember it 24 hours later (Spear & Smith, 1978; Turns & Misanin, 1982); (3) 1-week-old rats trained in certain circumstances seem to learn a spatial discrimination about as rapidly as older rats (Kenny & Blass, 1977); (4) rats younger than 1 week show not only basic classical conditioning with either appetitive or aversive unconditioned stimuli, they also exhibit many of the conditioning phenomena of importance to general learning theories, including blocking, latent inhibition, and higher order conditioning (e.g., Johanson & Hall, this volume; Rudy & Cheatle, 1979); rats 1½ days old can learn to discriminate between two miniature switches that differ in location and odor and to move the switch that delivers a squirt of milk into the pup's mouth (and *not* to move the other switch; Johanson & Hall, 1979); (5) there is mounting evidence that the newborn rat applies its associative capacity to meet its newly encountered ecological challenges, such as how to obtain its first, and subsequent, meals (e.g., Pedersen & Blass, 1982); and there are suggestions that some of this associative capacity may perhaps be exerted prior to birth (Stickrod, Kimble, & Smotherman, 1982).

In part the above discoveries of infantile learning capabilities can be attributed to technical advances in the study of basic conditioning and learning irrespective of age of the subject. Harlow (1959) had thought it impossible to use nonprimates for ontogenetic studies because these animals "... learn so slowly . . . that they pass from infancy to maturity before their intellectual measurement can be completed" (p. 460). At that time the confirmation of learning in even adult rodents seemed to require many days for completion. But today it is common to test the learning of rats or mice with tasks that require only a few minutes or trials for learning and memory to be seen. With appropriate accommodation for ecological factors, these tasks have been used to test the infants of several altricial, nonprimate species. The results, as mentioned, show that they too can learn such things quite rapidly, although (perhaps) not as rapidly as adults.

But there are limits to the ultimate value of cataloging what is learnable at different stages of development. It has been known for some time that associative capacity does not depend on one's having a fully intact, adult brain. Conditioning can be quite effective even though animals or humans actually are missing significant parts of the brain, such as the hippocampus or cortex that have long been claimed as critical for learning and memory (e.g., Angermeier, 1982; Isaacson, 1982; Lewin, 1980). As a more extreme example, it is difficult to deny that the long-term potentiation widely seen *in vitro* with selected slabs of brain tissue constitutes a sort of memory (Bliss & Lomo, 1973). This is not to suggest that the neatly organized brain of the newborn is comparable to that of an adult brain with missing parts, but only to illustrate that the demonstration of some associative capacity at any age is in one sense quite underwhelming.

What may be more interesting is the probably systematic manner in which the manifestation of an associative capacity varies from one kind of event to another, from one ontogenetic stage to another. The evidence to date indicates that ontogenetic differences in the "capacity" to learn and remember depends on what is to be learned and remembered. This dependence is more than a matter of simple sensory deficiencies. For instance, infant rats during their first week of life can readily acquire a conditioned aversion to an odor paired with an illness or an electrical shock to the stomach, but under the same conditions they will not acquire an aversion to that odor if it is paired with footshock (Haroutunian & Campbell, 1979). Yet it is quite clear that the infant's aversion threshold for footshock is at least as sensitive as that of older animals which readily learn the odor-footshock association. Evidence of this sort implies that at each ontogenetic stage, the developing animal's behavioral focus may change so as to alter its selection of which events are learned about any particular episode.

Summary

I have tried to illustrate two ideas. The first is that to meet its particular, changing set of ecological challenges, the developing animal must change correspondingly in its behavioral dispositions as well as its physiological structures. The second point is that evidence for some associative capacity can be seen at least from birth throughout ontogeny, but drastic ontogenetic differences in this capacity may seem to occur depending on what is to be learned and expressed in behavior.

Emerging from these two points is the notion—simple, but of analytical value—that the special behavior dispositions and physiological structures applied to good effect by the developing animal in its particular ecological niche, *can act in other circumstances to constrain what the animal will or can learn at any particular age.*

ONTOGENETIC "CONSTRAINTS" ON WHAT IS LEARNED

We may now turn to what, specifically, differs between the infant and adult rat in terms of the attributes they store in memory to represent the same episode. Experimental analysis requires that infants and adults be tested in circumstances in which there is more than one learnable stimulus event (and the learning of each can be assessed) although only one is necessary, and may be sufficient, for the critical behavioral index of learning. This is simpler than it sounds in the general case: What is required is either a stimulus compound of two or more elements that predicts a reinforcer, or circumstances in which a redundant contextual stimulus as well as a CS or discriminative stimulus can be learned. The point of departure for analysis of such cases is appreciation that, again, those same physiological structures and behavioral dispositions the infant rat applies so well in adapting to its particular ecological niche can act in other circumstances as constraints on what the infant learns. These constraints determine not only what is learned, but how the stimulus selection actually takes place and, in natural circumstances, the ultimate cost or benefit of this selection in adapting to new environmental contingencies.

Four ontogenetically determined "constraints" may be used as illustrations: (1) those that arise from sensory limitations, (2) those that arise from systemic changes induced by particular contexts, (3) those potentially associated with what might be termed, for want of a better word, "memory capacity," and (4) those that may be characterized as naive encoding, or more generally, a cognitive constraint. This is only an illustrative, preliminary and certainly incomplete sample, selected because some data address it.

At this point I wish to disavow the term "constraints." Although having some communication value because of its common usage in this context, I do not like it because "constraint" connotes a general disadvantage in adaptation. Given the proven adaptiveness of the neonatal rat, it seems difficult to maintain that its lack of sight or vision, for instance, is so obviously a constraint. If this animal could be made to see and hear, it seems at least as likely that severely maladaptive behavior would result due to distraction from the more conventional events (e.g., odors) upon which its survival depends. I therefore prefer the term "disposition."

Sensory and Perceptual Dispositions

Sensory dispositions in infants are in some sense the most obvious and least interesting conditions that determine stimulus selection. The sensory systems reach adultlike levels at different rates in the developing rat, with the chemical systems emerging for use very early and the auditory, then visual systems last. The precise ontogeny of sensory detection is still uncertain for any system, but the ordering is established; Alberts (this volume) has reminded us of this and of the regularity of this ordering among all mammalian species. Aspects of the olfactory and taste systems are put to good use by the neonatal rat, and perhaps prenatally as well, and although the ears and eyes do not open physically until after the second week of life, there is evidence that the visual system (brightness differences), for instance, can determine behavior during the first week of life. The full development of all these systems is, however, incomplete for some time postnatally, including even the three olfactory systems that seem to reach full effectiveness at different times (Alberts, 1981).

Suppose an episode to be learned by infants includes a compound stimulus of two elements that requires the use of two separable sensory systems for processing. We may expect their stimulus selection to differ from that of adults if either the infant's detection and analysis of one of the elements were less probable without special effort than is the case for adults, or if the sensory information provided by one of the elements were of a kind for which the infant is perceptually naive relative to adults.

Several years ago a Ph.D. dissertation by James Wolz (1981) in our laboratory provided a point of departure for investigation of such possibilities. The information provided by this extensive study may be reduced considerably for our purposes by focusing on only the relative retention of 11- and 16-day old rats that had learned a discrimination task by using information about either the odor or the location of the correct alternative. The pertinent physical difference in these two age groups was that the eyes of the 11-day-olds had not yet opened whereas those of the 16-day-olds had been open for one or two days. We knew that animals of each age were capable of solving comparable discrimination problems on the basis of either location alone or when an odor difference was correlated with the location difference, although in either case the 16-day-olds seemed to solve the discrimination more readily than the 11-day-olds. In Wolz's study, odor and locations were combined as equally predictive and redundant indicators of the correct choice for escape from mild footshock, and a variety of conditions with the reversal of 0, 1, or 2 of the discriminative stimuli permitted an estimate of which of these stimuli were learned and remembered. A few minutes after learning of the discrimination, tests indicated that the 16-day-olds were a good deal more likely than the younger animals to use both kinds of information; the 11-day-olds learned about the odors but little or nothing about the locations. This provides an example of the class of stimulus-selection phenomena determined by sensory or perceptual dispositions.

Another example is provided by an unpublished experiment by Richard Bryan. Bryan developed for his Ph.D. dissertation a procedure for assessing a classically conditioned odor discrimination in the 7-day-old rat (Bryan, 1980). In the process of this development he found that if the CS+ consisted of a compound of a particular brightness and an odor and the CS− a compound with a different brightness and a different odor, or vice versa, 15-day-old animals tended to learn primarily about the odors, whereas animals a week or so older tended to learn primarily about the brightness differences. Overshadowing is indicated because comparable age-related differences in learning about only these odor differences or only these brightness differences are not nearly as large and sometimes negligible. The reason for this particular ontogenetic difference in stimulus selection is uncertain, but the visual naiveté of the 15-day-olds would seem an important factor; their eyes had been open for only about 24 hours whereas those of the 23-day-olds had been open for over a week. It is obvious that these sorts of age-related differences in overshadowing probably could differ depending on the relative salience of the elements of the compound. But the point to be illustrated, really quite a simple one, is that for any particular combination of stimuli there may be ontogenetic differences in which one is more likely learned, due to age-specific sensory or perceptual disposition.

Contextual Dispositions

Several theories of infantile amnesia have emphasized changes in redundant contextual events that occur between infancy and adulthood, and hence between learning and the "test" for retention. Quite aside from differences between the infant's and adult's cognitive processing of the critical events that are to be remembered, the infant's posture, hormonal state, social dominance, dependence relationships with those around him or her, and so forth, differ dramatically from those when, as an adult, the animal is asked to recall the events of infancy. The view of Tompkins (1970) is that if aspects of the infantile context were reestablished in adulthood—if adult humans were dressed in the clothes of an infant, placed in a crib scaled to their size and another adult reached down and tweaked their cheek—infantile memories would be more readily assessed. The main point of such theories is that the distinct differences in the contexts of learning (as an infant) and remembering (as an adult) preclude significant retention.

Special Salience of the Context for Testing the Infant Rat.   Tests of infantile learning and remembering in the rat conventionally have exposed the infant to a context involving isolation from its parents and siblings. For convenience in presenting the episode to be learned in such experiments, the infant is nearly always removed from its home and family. The experimental apparatus is no doubt a strikingly unique context for the infant rat and its response to such newness may differ perceptually from that of an adult rat. But beyond this, we now know that the mere act of removing the animal from its home and mother can have profound physiological and psychological consequences that alter drastically the infant's internal context, an effect that seems to differ from that of removing the adult animal from its home. This is not to say that the infant's response to isolation is maladaptive. In many ways these reactions seem geared to promote reunions with mother, at least for an animal existing in more natural circumstances (rather than in the lab). One important point here is that the infant's reactions to isolation are extreme and different from those of the adult; another is that this surely is not unique to the rat but must occur in other mammals as well, probably including the human.

The consequences of separation from parent and the home are particularly striking in the rat at about 2 weeks of age. This is about the youngest age at which its eyes and ears are fully open, so one might guess that this additional sensory input is an important factor in its response to separation from the home. It is not critical, however. The infant's response to separation or isolation increases gradually up to that point, and moreover, many of these same symptoms are found in a variety of species at ages when their eyes and ears have been open for some time. For instance, many of the effects we can cite for 2-week-old rats are seen in 6-month-old monkeys as well. It is notable that in the rat, infantile amnesia is readily seen for memories acquired at 15 days of age but is less apparent for memories acquired a week or so later. It may be significant that the response to isolation also decreases after the age of 15 days and is relatively small if at all noticeable a week later.

What happens when the 15-day-old rat is isolated from its parents and siblings? The work of Hofer (1981) and others provides some answers. Within a minute or so the infant rat's general activity triples; its vocalizations increase more than sixfold in number over 5 minutes, and over the same 5-minute period, heart rate increases 25% or so, from about 400 beats per minute to nearly 500. If it remains in isolation, the nature of the syndrome changes somewhat. After a few hours the infant's heart rate begins to drop and its "slouchy" posture makes it look depressed. After 18 hours or so of isolation, its heart rate decreases to only about 60% of its normal rate. The heart rate can be brought back to normal briefly by pinching the animal's tail or by injecting a sufficient load of milk into the stomach of the infant. The drop in heart rate seems to be independent of body temperature, thyroid activity and peripheral catecholamines from the adrenal medulla, but glucocorticoid release is necessary. Hofer believes that the heart rate is a reaction to vasoconstriction induced by adrenergic activity in the central nervous system, but perhaps most fundamentally due to being deprived of mother's milk.

After a period (12 hours or so) of separation in a warm nestlike environment, the infant shows considerable hyperactivity; locomotion, rearing, and grooming increase fourfold. Yet the infant rat shows rather severe hypoactivity if isolated in an environment only slightly colder than the nest, still warm (32° C) relative to typical room temperature.

Isolation from the home is also accompanied by severe insomnia in the infant. Infants take longer to fall asleep when isolated than when at home, and the sleep is more fragmented. Most of the loss is from the REM period and occurs even if littermates are present, suggesting that it is not related to a problem of regulating body temperature. The period of REM sleep is one that has been identified with the secretion of growth hormone. It is perhaps not too surprising, then, that the activity of growth hormone declines in the isolated infant (10 days of age). Yet it is striking that this drop in growth hormone begins within only 15 minutes of separation from the parents, and that within a period of only 2 hours it decreases to a mere 50% of its normal level (thyroid stimulating hormone, prolactin, and corticosterone are not affected). Growth hormone activity may depend on some physical aspects of maternal care eliminated by the isolation. The decrease in this hormone can be prevented if the isolated infant rat's back is brushed, perhaps simulating an aspect of maternal care (the decrease cannot be prevented by a tail-pinch). It is fairly certain that a similar drop in growth hormone occurs in human infants separated from their parents, and perhaps in separated older infants as well. There is a very common syndrome termed "deprivation dwarfism," referring to the common observation that abandoned children are smaller than would otherwise be expected. The differences in growth apparently are not entirely due to nutritional differences.

Finally, among the neurochemical changes that accompany isolation at 10 days of age is a rapid decline in an enzyme called "ornithine decarboxylase" that is known to regulate polyamine synthesis. Conceivably, this enzyme could be a vital step in the protein synthesis that might be important for learning and memory. (For a good review of the above aspects of the isolation syndrome, see Hofer, 1981).

How does the infant rat decide that it is isolated? In the normal nest life of the infant rat the mother is not always within touching distance. She actually goes away from the pups on about 17 occasions during a 24-hour period. She stays away for only 5–10 minutes at a time during the first day after birth. When the pups are 15 days old, this increases to separation periods of 45–60 minutes and contact, for each meal, of 15–20 minutes. By 21 days of age, the mother is absent for 2 hours at a time. If the 15-day-old is used to being away from its mother for an hour or so at a time, what sets off the alarm that says, in effect, "Help, I am isolated!"? Probably, *odors* of the mother and the nest ordinarily provide an important signal that the infant is safe at home.

The question I am leading up to is this: Does the infant's learning and memory differ for episodes presented when it is, or "feels," at home in comparison to when it is isolated? We thought the infant rat might learn different things in these two circumstances; and some strikingly adept learning reported for infant rats suggested they might learn more at "home" than elsewhere (this evidence is reviewed by Spear, 1979a).

Infantile Learning When in Isolation and When "at Home".   We have found that infants trained and tested in the context of odors from their home nest seem more mature than otherwise, for some learning tasks. In this sort of home environment, for example, rats in their second and third postnatal week behave as if they were several days older in their learning of an aversion to a particular location or in learning to withhold a punished response (older animals are un-affected by this context, e.g., Smith & Spear, 1978, 1981; Wigal, Smith, & Spear, 1980). I might note that analogous effects have begun to appear for human infants tested in the home rather than the laboratory (e.g., Acredolo, 1979; Durham & Black, 1978; Horner, 1980).

There are, however, some things that the infant rat learns more *slowly* in the home than when isolated in a novel place, such as a conditioned aversion to a taste that is paired with an illness (Infurna, Steinert & Spear, 1979; and here again, older rats are unaffected). This suggests that the presence of stimuli related to the infant's home determines what will be learned rather than the efficacy with which all things would be learned. A decision on this matter has been hampered by differences in the learning requirements in each case. Perhaps, for example, learning about novel tastes is simply especially difficult for the infant in the home nest. Until recently, no cases of facilitated learning in the presence of home odors involved the learning of relationships between tastes.

Stimulus Selection for Taste Events in the Home.   A paradigm recently ap-plied by David Kucharski, Tim Wigal and myself has begun to clarify this issue. We presented 18-day-old rats with two flavors (tastes) in a common solution. This was followed by an illness induced by LiCl, injected either immediately or 24 hours later (explicitly unpaired control condition). Some animals received this sequence of treatments in their home cage, while others received it while isolated in a relatively novel apparatus. As expected from the previous studies, those infants conditioned in the novel apparatus were thereafter more reluctant to consume the two-taste solution than were those conditioned in the home. In other words, conditioning an aversion to the compound taste was less effective in the home than in the novel apparatus.

We then asked about the relative learning of the association between the two tastes within the compound, when experienced in the home or the novel apparat-us. This was accomplished with a separate set of 18-day-old rats that also were presented the two-taste compound in either of these two locations. For these animals LiCl was not paired with the compound. Instead, they were later given a pairing of LiCl-induced illness with only one of the tastes that made up the compound. If the two tastes had been associated, the experimental inducement of an aversion to one of the tastes should have led to a decreased preference for the other taste as well (cf. Rescorla & Durlach, 1981). The results indicated that learning of the association between the two tastes did occur, but more important, this learning was stronger when the tastes were experienced in the home than when in the novel environment. This finding was established with two different sets of tastes, and in none of these experiments did the explicitly unpaired control conditions differ one from the other. In short, these experiments indicate that what is "selected" for learning by the infant may depend on whether the context is home or nonhome.

Disposition for General Memory Capacity

The notion of a general capacity for learning and memory that is unitary in its action, common to all circumstances and kinds of episodes, has not seemed a viable concept (Neisser, 1976; Spear, 1983). The reality of such general capacity differences among young and older human children has seemed in particular to be less likely than differences in the mnemonic preparation applied for remembering at each age (Kail & Hagen, 1977; Spear, 1978). Many theorists in fact argue pointedly against any age-related differences in capacity for learning and memory (e.g., Simon, 1974). There are, however, few or no data that directly address the problem, particularly in the case of infants, so the proposition of an ontogenetic increase in basic potential or capacity for learning and memory cannot be dismissed.

Quite aside from the effects of sensory or contextual dispositions, rats younger than about 10 days of age seem reliably to learn or remember less about odor-shock conditioning than those above 10 days of age. I refer to a conditioned odor discrimination in which a footshock is paired with odor A and in the same context, no footshock is paired with odor B. When the animal's relative preference for A or B is then compared against that of a third, neutral odor, C, learning about the presence of the footshock (CS+) is evidenced by less preference for A than C, and learning about the odor that predicted no footshock (CS−) may be seen most clearly when the animal prefers odor B to odor C. In an experiment reported by Kokot, Caza, Richter, and Spear (1982), such learning about the CS− seemed not be present in animals less than 9 days of age although learning about the CS+ seemed statistically present from age 6 days on.

Contrary to this finding, however, and also to our earlier expectations (Spear, 1979a,b), most of our data have indicated that infants learn as much and perhaps more about an episode than do adults. It is somewhat misleading to state it in this way, because the evidence I have in mind is probably better understood by the statement that younger animals are less *selective* in what they learn and remember about a particular episode.

Age-Related Differences in Response to Contextual Events. Solheim, Hensler and Spear (1980) compared infant (20-day-old) and adult rats in their response to a redundant novel odor present as context when they acquired an active avoidance (one-way avoidance cued by a flashing light compounded with a particular location). For this task, rates and final levels of learning were equal for the two ages. The animals were then given a nonshock test for retention of active avoidance in the context of either that same odor or a different odor. The basic assumption was that the disruption in retention observed when that odor was changed would be proportional to the amount learned about the redundant odor during initial training. Control animals in each condition were given equivalent familiarization with the footshocks, odors, and experimental handling. Two types of retention tests required that the animal exhibit its retention by either an active avoidance (running quickly) or a passive avoidance (withholding running) of the stimulus previously paired with footshock. By including both tests we could extract differences due to general activity.

The results clearly indicated that the younger animals were more affected by the change in redundant contextual odor, leading to the inference that they had been less selective than the adults in the memory attributes they had stored to represent the active avoidance episode. More recently, we have observed a similar effect of less-selective learning about redundant contextual odors among younger rats (25- and 35-day-olds compared to 45-day-olds) in the learning of a passive avoidance problem (Barrett, Rizzo, Spear, & Spear, 1982). Also, results leading to the same conclusion, although somewhat more problematic for present purposes, have been obtained in our laboratory by James Concannon and Gregory Smith (Concannon, Smith, Spear, & Scobie, 1979). In these experiments, injections of sodium pentobabitol seemed a more effective "contextual stimulus" for 16-day-old than for 23-day-old rats. The problem is that a limited number of doses were used, which further complicates the difficulty of interpreting ontogenetic differences in drug effects. Finally, a recent experiment by Newman, Caza, and Spear (1982) employed an experimental design similar to that of Solheim et al. but tested retention of classical conditioning to a location. In this experiment, change in the contextual odor significantly disrupted the retention of 16-day-old animals but had no disruptive effect on the retention of adults in the same situation.

Age-Related Differences in Response to Multiple-Element Conditioned Stimuli. Ontogenetic differences in capacity for memory processing may more likely be manifested the greater the number of stimulus events comprising the episode to be remembered. An analytically manageable paradigm for this circumstance is when in basic conditioning, the conditioned stimulus includes two or more separable events that predict the unconditioned stimulus. Examples would be two flavors that predict an illness when presented together in solution or when tasted in sequence, or other combinations such as two odors, an odor and a flavor, a light and a tone, and so forth. The fundamental question is whether, relative to adults, younger animals process fewer of the several elements in a conditioned stimulus, process them differently, or do not differ in either respect.

Our several experiments of this kind also have given little indication of an ontogenetic increase in memory capacity. The specific experiments and results are summarized by Spear and Kucharski (this volume). The fundamental observation in these studies is that when the conditioned stimulus consists of two or three elements that occur simultaneously, preweanling rats are less likely to focus their learning on a single one and hence are more likely to base their learning on all of the elements presented. In particular, the preweanling animals seem less likely than adults to show blocked or overshadowed conditioning of one CS element due to the presence of a more predictive or otherwise salient element, and they are more likely to show potentiated conditioning of a stimulus element by the presence of an alternative element. These phenomena seem to indicate that, relative to adults, the preweanlings either are more likely to form multiple associations among the elements of the CS and between those and the US, or they differ in how they perceive or encode the conditioned stimulus.

The conclusions are quite different, however, when separable elements of a conditioned stimulus are presented successively. In this case the younger animals show no less overshadowing than the adults and they may show more (see Spear & Kucharski, this volume). There have been other indications in our laboratory that what is learned by preweanlings about one element may especially detract, in these circumstances of successively presented elements of the CS, from learning of the other (Steinert, 1981). Perhaps whenever integration of temporally separate events is involved, a limitation in processing capacity is more likely to be manifested in immature animals. The serial presentation of CS elements presents a complex analytical situation, however, and it would be no simple matter to isolate experimentally the factor of temporal integration.

Limitation of Raw Memory Capacity or Perceptual/Cognitive Disposition?
By way of a brief summary, let me re-state my position so far. The several examples of learning being more effective the older the individual, reported throughout this volume and elsewhere, do not seem best explained by an ontogenetic increase in the animal's basic capacity to engage in the processes of memory storage and retrieval. They seem to reflect instead, age-related changes in dispositions that control what will be learned and expressed in behavior. So, for understanding ontogenetic change in learning and memory, the notion of variance in raw memory capacity does not seem at present to be of analytical value (cf. Spear, 1983). This is not to suggest that such a notion has no conceivable substance. The issue is real, not a "straw man," as evidenced by its potential value for theoretical synthesis in other circumstances (e.g., Isaacson & Spear, 1982). There is, moreover, no strong evidence opposing such an ontogenetic change in either "raw" capacity for processing or the effectiveness of

a hypothetical mechanism for establishing storage into memory (e.g., "consol-idation"). Yet there is no good evidence for either, and for the latter, some doubt exists about both its viability (Weingartner & Parker, in press) and its reality (e.g., Johnson, 1983). The data I reviewed did not directly address these issues, but do help establish that more parsimonious features of behavior could equally account for the ontogenetic differences in learning and memory.

This circumstance is of course familiar to persons studying children. A classi-cal example is seen when children between the ages of about 6 and 13 years read a list of 10–20 words and later recall as many as they can. One could confidently do a classroom demonstration with this, given access to enough subjects, and show that the number of words recalled progressively increases, with each age, from 6 to 7, 7 to 8, and so on. But, experimental analysis of this fact has not confirmed that children merely grow in their raw capacity to store and retrieve information. This effect seems instead to be accounted for by age-related dif-ferences in how the children treat the items to be learned, their use of the mnemonic-preparation devices of special encoding or rehearsal that might pro-mote later remembering. Similar to the approach of Piaget, the view is that as children become older they do not simply become more retentive in the sense of a more effective physiologically based mechanism for learning and remembering; instead, they change in the way they view and treat the events they are to learn and remember. They change in other words in cognition, how things to be remembered are perceived or thought about (for a review, see Kail & Hagen, 1982).

I suggest that some ontogenetic changes in learning by animals also are due to age-related changes in what might be termed "cognitive dispositions," perhaps more likely to be perceptual in nature for animals. This is, in my opinion, the implication of our recent data showing apparent ontogenetic changes in potentia-tion and sensory preconditioning in the rat, described in the chapter by Spear and Kucharski (this volume). I suggest also that the increasing variety of evidence indicating ontogenetic memory differences that depend on what is to be learned and remembered ultimately can be traced to the sort of age-specific dispositions mentioned above, including perceptual/cognitive dispositions, and for both ani-mals and humans.

Cognitive Dispositions for Age-Specific Perception, Categorization or Stimulus Selection

We observed in a variety of experiments that preweanling rats were more likely than adults to exhibit potentiation in the conditioning of one CS element by the simultaneous presence of another (Spear & Kucharski, this volume). For this effect it was necessary that the CS elements be presented simultaneously; as mentioned above, a quite different effect emerged with successive presentation of the CS elements. This difference was especially striking because "successive" meant being separated by no more than 30 seconds and the stimuli—tastes and odors—were such as to promote some sensory carryover from one element to the other.

With such successive presentation, mutual interference rather than potentiation tended to occur in the learning of CS elements, and preweanling rats tended to show more interference than adults, quite opposite to the relationship with simultaneous presentation. With CS elements presented successively, it was as if some processing limitation akin to the simple notion of raw attentional or memory capacity was manifested by the younger animals to limit the number of temporally separate elements they could learn. Yet, the complementary explanation for age-related differences in potentiation—that the simultaneous presence of another CS element somehow enhanced the younger animal's raw memory capacity—does not seem consistent with the experimental analysis.

Practically speaking, however, our experimental analysis has dealt relatively little with the case of the successive occurrence of CS elements. It is instead the unexpected effects of simultaneous pairing of two CS elements that has dominated our attention. The initial observation, "potentiation," was that especially for preweanling rats, a CS element becomes more strongly conditioned if presented together with another element. It was as if there was somehow more interaction between the elements in the younger rats' treatment of them whereas for adults, the tendency was toward independent processing of the elements, sometimes learning one at the expense of associative strength for the other ("overshadowing"). This seemed more than simply "less selection of stimuli among the preweanlings"; the younger animals' treatment of the compound stimuli seemed to differ from adults in kind as well.

While Spear and Kucharski (this volume) allowed the possibility that preweanlings might acquire more associations than adults, their experimental analysis seemed largely consistent with the hypothesis that the stimulus compound was perceived in configural ("integral") fashion by the younger animals but not by the adults. In other words, it was as if the younger animals perceived the simultaneous occurrence of the two elements as a distinctly unique event, different and quite apart from the separate presentation of each element, whereas the adults were more likely to treat the configuration as the combination of two separate elements.

The potentiation effect itself could be explained as either an associative or a perceptual phenomenon, in accord with the ideas of Rescorla and his colleagues (Rescorla & Durlach, 1981; Rescorla, 1981). In the associative case, more conditioned aversion to A when presented in an AB compound and paired with aversive stimulus C could be because not only is A associated with C, it is also associated with B which itself is aversive due to association with C. The greater potentiation among preweanlings than adults could be due to their stronger, or more probable, associations between A and C or B and C, or between A and B, the elements within the compound. Our data, however, did not support the former possibility and there is in general little precedent for stronger associative learning by preweanlings compared to adults. The alternative theory, the "Gestalt" or configural notion, accounts for potentiation on the grounds that the combining of A and B provides a more salient or intense CS than either A or B alone and this promotes stronger conditioning. Some generalization decrement would be expected when A alone is tested for its conditioning strength, because A is different from the compound CS that actually was conditioned, so this theory must expect that the benefit from the greater stimulus intensity of the compound CS more than compensates for the degree of generalization decrement.

It was the latter, Gestalt-like theory that seemed supported by our data. Compared to adults, preweanlings seemed more likely to have their conditioning strengthened by a more intense CS and less likely to suffer generalization decrement when the conditioning and testing CSs were different. Our further experiments (conducted primarily by David Kucharski) indicated that for preweanlings relative to adults, conditioning strength to a two-element compound was less affected by extinction of either or both of the elements presented in isolation. This indicated that at least under these circumstances, the younger animals were treating the compound as different from either element alone or the sum of the elements. They seemed, in effect, to treat the AB compound as a distinct "glob" whereas the adults treated it as a combination of A added to B. Within the conceptual framework of Garner (1970), which we will discuss shortly, it is as if the preweanling rats viewed a simultaneous combination of two CS elements as an integral compound while the adults viewed it as a separable compound.

A Classical Issue of Cognitive Dispositions.   Our recent experiments (Spear & Kucharski, this volume) have given us a little better idea of how infants and adults differ in response to the factors of CS intensity and generalization decrement that happen to be central to our form of the "Gestalt" theory of potentiation. We do not pretend that these experiments have led us to a decision between Gestalt and associative theories. Even in our restricted circumstances of classically conditioned aversions, it seems difficult to design a decisive experiment for which one can generate differential predictions for these two kinds of theories.

If these two theories are indistinguishable empirically, what good are they? I think it is useful to consider them because the substance of their differences is significant historically and also pertinent today. This apparently circumscribed problem of potentiation is in my opinion a subset of a much more general issue that has re-emerged in contemporary theories of perception and attention within cognitive psychology, represented importantly in developmental psychology by Eleanor Gibson's theory of perceptual learning (Gibson, 1969).

The continuing importance of the historical issue is nicely elaborated by Treisman and Gelade (1980) with regard to their "feature integration theory of attention":

The controversy between analytic and synthetic theories of perception goes back many years: the associationists asserted that the experience of complex wholes is built by combining more elementary sensations, while the Gestalt psychologist claimed that the whole precedes its parts, that we initially register unitary objects and relationships, and only later, if necessary, analyze these objects into their component parts or properties. This view is still active now (e.g., Monahan & Lockhead, 1977; Neisser, 1976). (p. 97)

To illustrate that their view differs from the latter, Treisman and Gelade continue:

It is logically possible that we become aware only of the final outcome of a complicated sequence of prior operations. Top down processing may describe what we consciously experience; as a theory about perceptual coding, it needs more objective support. (p. 97)

Treisman and Gelade's skepticism about this Gestalt view arises from their observation that ". . . the immediacy and directness of impression are no guarantee that it reflects an early state of information processing in the nervous system" (p. 98).

Dispositions Toward Integral Versus Separable Treatment of a Compound Stimulus.   One way to conceptualize the instances of cognitive disposition manifested in the work I described on stimulus selection is through the notions of integral and separable stimulus compounds (Garner, 1970, 1978). This distinction in how organisms treat compound stimuli is especially useful because there are specific rules for deciding whether any particular compound is treated as an integral or as a separable entity, behaviorally based rules applied readily to human subjects and in principle applicable to animals as well.

The distinction between integral and separable compounds may be shown in terms of simple cards. If the cards differ in size and also in shade of gray, they are treated by adults as separable compounds with two dimensions, size, and brightness. The integral case can be seen when the cards are all the same size but differ only in color, which also has two dimensions, hue and brightness. Ordinarily, however, persons do not "separate" hue and brightness when making a judgment about color. So such cards are treated as integral compounds, as if they differed in only one way. One consequence is that adults find it easier to categorize such cards if hue and brightness are correlated and harder to do so if they vary orthogonally. But if asked to categorize the set of different-sized cards in terms of brightness, it does not matter whether size is correlated with brightness or varies orthogonally with it, because adults "stimulus select" very effectively in this situation.

Garner (1970, 1974) outlined a firm set of such behavioral criteria for deciding when multidimensional stimuli are treated as integral and when separable, and Treisman and Gelade (1980) have added to it. The important point is that application of these criteria can reveal significant individual differences in perceptual/cognitive dispositions. For instance, the above illustration with the cards was based on normal adult subjects; children differ significantly in how they treat these same cards, and so might adults with special learning histories. Beyond the confining realm of card sorting, such dispositional differences are illustrated in my two favorite examples of integral and separable compounds:

(1) During the fifteenth century, a surprisingly advanced civilization developed in what is today central Mexico, stretching southward for some purposes into portions of Central America. Their ruling classes had migrated from the Northwest relatively recently, but the population drew its strength from a variety of cultures. They had a large, well-organized army and their men were skilled fighters. Yet it did not take long for a relatively small number of Spanish invaders to conquer and literally destroy this civilization, which the Spanish termed "Aztecs." These facts are of interest here because a legend about these native North Americans metaphorically attributes their defeat to a pertinent "error" in cognition. The core of the legend is a decisive battle between the greatest of Aztec warriors, fighting on foot, and a Spanish soldier, on horseback. This one-on-one battle continued for many hours, so the story goes, until finally, as the Spaniard charged, the Aztec sidestepped, lunged, and thrust his javelin into the horse, killing it instantly. With that, the Aztec laid down his weapons and walked away, chanting the Aztec victory song. The surprised Spaniard merely approached from behind and finished him with one blow of his sword.

The Aztec's fatal error was based on a cognitive disposition: Instead of viewing his opponent as a man on horseback, the Aztec had assumed the soldier and horse to be a single organism that he had stabbed and killed. The significant point is the difference in how the Spanish and the Aztecs represented the stimulus compound, "man on horse." The Spanish treated the compound in terms of separable components while the Aztecs saw it as an integral compound, and the consequences of this minor cognitive difference were substantial.

(2) In consideration of the ontogenetic development of object constancy in children, Bower (1979) described an instance that seems to characterize the human infant's treatment of stimulus components as an integral compound. A 6-month-old infant in reasonably good spirits will, when shown an attractive toy, reach for it. But if the toy is placed behind a barrier or covered with a bowl, the infant will stop reaching, as if that object had disappeared. Bower suggests that the characterization of "out of sight, out of mind" is not really appropriate for this behavior, because under other circumstances when a toy is placed behind a barrier, the infant acts as if it were there. In particular, if the toy is moved in space from right to left, the infant's eyes will continue to track it, as if it still existed, when the object passes behind a barrier and emerges from the other side.

Bower's point of special pertinence here is that infants also tend to behave as if the toy is gone when, rather than being placed behind a barrier, the toy is placed on top of it. In this case as well, the infant will cease reaching for the toy (even though in this case it clearly can be "seen," at least by adults). While this interpretation may in fact have little to do with object constancy, it does make contact with the present notion of age-dependent cognitive dispositions, because when an infant does reach for the toy atop the barrier, it does so in the direction of the "barrier-and-object." It is as if for the infant, the toy itself no longer exists and has been replaced by a new object consisting of a toy-barrier combination. Bower suggests that prior to 5 months of age, infants behave in accord with the rule, "Identical objects seen in different places are different objects" (p. 56). In other words, they may behave as if an object placed in a new location becomes part of that location. Some aspect of a differentiation process must occur if the infant is to treat the object otherwise. To say this another way, the young infant tends to treat an old object in a new location as an integral compound.

There is growing evidence that children and adults treat multidimensional events differently, in a manner reminiscent of the distinction between integral and separable processing. Such evidence may not imply a discrete ontogenetic shift between "integral" and "separable" processing in general. A principle has emerged to make the matter of stimulus processing more than an either-or circumstance for individuals or for particular classes of events. Lockhead (1972) illustrated that all integral combinations of stimulus dimensions are not necessarily viewed as such by all normal adult individuals, a matter agreed upon by Garner (1974). It is instead typical that a stimulus compound has the potential for integral processing, or ordinarily is processed in this wholistic manner, yet can in some circumstances be processed "separably," in terms of its dimensions (apparently, however, one can identify stimulus compounds that are manditorily processed as integrals).

Several experiments have verified that children about 5 years of age tend to treat as integral compounds, stimuli which children 4 to 6 years older treat as separable compounds, and that children in the intervening years tend sometimes to treat a particular stimulus as an integral and at other times as a separable compound (see for example, Kemler & Smith, 1978; Shepp, 1978; Smith & Kemler, 1977, 1978). Such transition stages indicate, as above, that we are not dealing with an either-or circumstance for processing. For instance, the studies by Kemler and Smith indicate that the 4- and 5-year-olds may treat the stimulus compounds as integrals when operating on them in terms of nonverbal sorting tasks but *speak* about the compounds as consisting of two different dimensions.

The generality of this tendency for younger children to view stimulus combinations in integral fashion is becoming impressive. This cognitive disposition seems to be an important determinant of age-related differences in, for example, the solution to discrimination problems involving explicit reinforcement. The regular ontogenetic change in how well children solve reversal-shift discriminations that are interdimensional compared to extradimensional has been shown by Tighe and Tighe (1979) to result in large part from age-related differences in integral and separable processing. For these experiments there are in effect four stimulus combinations of two dimensions. Preschool children tend to process all four of these combinations in terms of their associated contingencies, as if each combination were a separate and independent event; older children on the other hand treat the *dimension* as the more important predictor of the reinforcing event.

It is of course debatable whether these age-related effects with humans make any contact with what we believe to be ontogenetically determined cognitive dispositions in animals. But the omnipotent nature of the sorts of perceptual learning that would seem to be required by developing organisms, and the major psychological issues implicated in such consideration (see Gibson, 1969), argue that this is a promising area for further investigation.

SUMMARY AND FURTHER IMPLICATIONS OF ONTOGENETIC CHANGES IN ECOLOGICALLY DETERMINED DISPOSITIONS

This chapter has considered, in general fashion, two alternative interpretations of the common observation that the effectiveness of learning and memory seems to increase ontogenetically. One view is that the hypothetical "stamping in" mechanism of learning and memory simply is not fully mature (effective) at birth. In all fairness, I may not have given this alternative sufficient attention. Perhaps this was because I know so little about it, or maybe because the related issues are much too huge to deal with here. But regardless, I frankly suspect that such a mechanism does not exist.

I emphasized instead an alternative view derived from the equally common observation that for successful adaptation, the developing animal must alter the way it responds to its world, in accord with age-related changes in its principal ecological challenges.

These interpretations were considered in light of the general questions of whether early specific experiences really transfer positively to later learning, and other general issues pertinent to the ontogeny of learning and memory. I reviewed some of the ecological considerations and the related technical advances that have spurred the rapid growth of new information about the ontogeny of learning and memory. The principal observation, a simple one made in one form or another by many others, was that special behavioral dispositions and physiological structures may serve the developing animal well in solving its particular ecological problems within the environment expected for it in nature, but can act in other circumstances to constrain what the animal will or can learn at that particular age (also see chapters by Johanson & Hall and by Rudy et al., this volume).

Four classes of such "constraints" were discussed, with the proviso that the term "dispositions" seemed to better characterize the concept. One class arises from sensory limitations, another from systematic changes induced by particular contexts, and the third, from possible age-specific limitations on "memory capacity." The fourth class was characterized as age-specific "cognitive" dispositions. The bulk of the chapter dealt with verification and consequences of these hypothetical, ontogenetically determined dispositions.

I now turn, in closing, to three apparent implications of such dispositions.

(1) With increasing frequency, ontogenetic differences in learning have seemed dependent on what is to be learned and remembered, or in other words, on the "content" of the acquired memory (cf. Spear, 1978). Chapters in the present volume give some hint of this: Watson has developed with great care and ingenuity procedures for assessing separately the human infant's memories for the stimulus, the reinforcer, and the contingencies of reinforcement for the human infant. Rudy et al. have shown ontogenetic relationships in the rat's learning about flavor aversions that differ from those observed in its classical appetitive conditioning to tones. Furthermore, the ontogenetic function seen in the latter case differs if the CS is a series of clicks rather than a tone, or if both a CS+ tone and a CS− tone are conditioned. Although the differences in these functions relate ordinally to the maturation of the sensory systems involved, Rudy et al.'s data indicate that sensory detection may not be sufficient for the emergence of learning and remembering within that sensory system (also see Haroutunian & Campbell, 1981). Johanson and Hall (this volume) have discovered a great deal about ontogenetic determinants in the learning of an association between odor and the ingestion of milk, but these ontogenetic relationships seem quite different from those shown by Haroutunian and Campbell (1979) for the learning of an association between odor and a footshock. Rovee-Collier (this volume) has uncovered some remarkable capacities in instrumental learning and remembering in the two- and three-month-old human that seem very different, ontogenetically, from the feats of learning and memory observed with the habituation or selective-looking paradigms used to assess recognition in infants (see Strauss & Carter, this volume, and Werner & Perlmutter, 1979, for a review of the latter).

How can these particular differences in the ontogenetic relationships observed with different memory content be explained by special age-dependent dispositions? I have little idea. I have some confidence, however, that pursuing this type of explanation would provide a more profitable approach than suggesting an ontogenetic dependence on when a special neurophysiological mechanism for learning and memory becomes effective within a particular "functional system." It remains possible that there is a separate mechanism for learning—a specialized reinforcementlike device that "stamps in" contingency information or, in effect, issues a command to "print"—and that this either matures at different rates within different sensory (or "functional") systems or can be applied only when sensory efficacy is well beyond that needed for basic detention. But I think such a device is unlikely. Like Johnson (1983), it seems to me that a separate mechanism for learning and memory, beyond the basic processing needed for sensory detection, perception or further mnemonic preparation, is unnecessary and probably does not exist. I suspect that learning does in fact occur within a system from the moment sensory detection is present, but the events encoded by the infant's perception are so different from those expected by the experimenter or observed among adults that it is unlikely to be assessed by the sorts of tests we now apply.

(2) Return now to the general issue addressed at the beginning of this chapter: When does special early experience promote later performance that would seem to require learning, and when does it not? Changes in perception/cognition may help explain why in some circumstances early experience with the individual components of a skill or episode does not help learning of the skill or remembering of the episode. But I think we can expect a still further consequence from such ontogenetic changes, namely, explicit *impairment* of later learning or remembering as a consequence of certain early learning experience. When viewed as a matter of negative transfer between early training on an episode or skill perceived in integral fashion as a "glob" and performing the skill or remembering the episode at a later age when aspects of that same skill or episode are now perceived as separable elements, it would not be surprising if the transfer were negative. This addresses an important practical matter, namely, can we hinder a child's adaptation by either the wrong kind of early training or the "right" kind of training given too early? There is not a great deal of evidence for such negative consequences of early experiences, but perhaps much of it is not published. I will present a few examples for illustration.

Sameroff (1971) cites a comparison between two experiments by Papousek that illustrate how early experience with the "wrong" kind of information relevant to a discrimination task (or perhaps too much?) can retard acquisition of the discrimination solution at a later age. Papousek (1967) had cited data from human infants first presented the discrimination problem at 44 days of age. Previously, these infants had been given extensive experience with all components of the task. At various stages almost since birth the infants were practiced with the unconditioned response of headturning, the unconditioned stimulus of milk, and at one time or another, both stimuli that were to be differentiated according to the contingencies of the discrimination problem. This experience included actual conditioning and extinction with one of the conditioned stimuli. These subjects attained the criterion for differentiation performance when about 72 days of age, after 224 discrimination trials. Papousek (1969) later reported the results of a group of infants who had been presented the *complete* differentiation problem from the time they were neonates, too young to be given the prior experience with individual elements of the task. These subjects did not reach the criterion of differentiation performance until they were 128 days old; they required more than three times the number of differentiation trials (814) and four times as many days of practice as were required by the subjects that were not introduced to the complete task until 44 days of age. To say this another way, the infants who had begun practice at birth did not master the problem as well as those that began at 44 days postnatal, until they were twice as old.

Like the Papousek example with humans, evidence with animals for the negative consequences of early experiences for later learning has not been directly pursued but can be found as a by-product of other studies. For instance, Rudy et al. (this volume) report that rats given pairings of clicks and sucrose solution beginning at age 10 days lagged behind those begun at 12 days of age in terms of conditioning to the clicks. Also, we observed several years ago that in some circumstances rats that had learned an instrumental avoidance response at 15 days of age required more trials to "relearn" it in adulthood than were needed by comparable adult subjects introduced to the task for the first time.

More systematic evidence than this was reported by Harlow (1959). Four groups of rhesus monkeys began basic training on an object discrimination task at either 60, 90, 120, or 150 days of age. All monkeys achieved mastery over these problems, although this required somewhat longer for the younger monkeys. At the same time, these monkeys were tested for delayed responding (for which accuracy also was inversely related to age). For our purposes, though, the most interesting discovery occurred when the monkeys began a series of learning-set problems. For this series four discrimination problems were given each day, 5 days a week. By "learning set" is meant a progressive improvement in the solution to a class of discrimination problems, in this case discrimination problems with two alternatives. The achievement of a perfect "learning set" is attained to the extent that the animal becomes consistently correct in its discrimination performance for a particular problem after at most a single trial (which provides the information as to which alternative is correct).

Harlow found that the rate of acquiring a learning set in this situation also was inversely related to age. The more interesting statistic for our purposes, however, is how well the learning-set problems were solved later on by monkeys that had begun their problem-solving experiences at either 60, 90, 120, or 150 days of age. When the scores of each group were compared at a common age (8 months or older) it could be seen that the former two groups of monkeys never achieved the level of mastery shown by the latter two groups, in spite of the greater longevity of practice by the former monkeys. Harlow commented as follows:

> . . . these data suggest that the capacity of the two younger groups to form discrimination learning sets may have been impaired by their early intensive learning-set training, initiated before they possessed any effective learning-set capability. Certainly, their performance from 260 days onward is inferior to that of the earlier groups with less experience but matched for age. The problem which these data illustrate has received little attention among experimental psychologists. There is a tendency to think of learning or training as intrinsically good and necessarily valuable to the organism. It is entirely possible, however, that training can either be

helpful or harmful, depending upon the nature of the training and the organism's stage of development. (p. 472)

There are, of course, data with animal subjects indicating that gross overstimulation early in life can, perhaps like any set of stressful events, alter the behavior of subjects later on. But of interest here is the somewhat different case in which relatively innocuous and reasonable, information-bearing experience early in age can result in negative transfer to cognitive functions later. Potentially relevant are the studies of White and Held (1966), showing that specific early experiences can alter later attentional behaviors, and of Goldberg (1972, 1977), indicating that special tactual (carrying) experiences early in life, if continued too long, may alter object permanence later. These may be the sorts of more basic effects that could lead to negative transfer from early experience to later learning, or they may be quite unrelated. The point nevertheless is that the data of Papousek and Harlow illustrate a significant consequence of ecologically determined dispositions, dispositions that can lead an animal to respond very differently to an episode when presented as early experience than at a later age, when that same episode is again presented to be learned and remembered.

(3) Finally, suppose we accept the notion that what is reflected in ontogenetic increases in learning efficacy is not a change in raw memory capacity but instead, change in the animal's ecologically determined dispositions. If this were so, nonmonotonic functions relating ontogeny and learning efficacy should not be uncommon. In other words, one would expect frequent instances in which learning by animals of a particular age is poorer than that by either younger or older animals. So far there is not much indication of this in the literature, but the scope of applicable tests has been quite limited. Even so, a few nonmonotonic functions recently have emerged. (a) Beginning at about Postnatal Day 6, a conditioned aversion to an odor paired with a footshock can be acquired by the rat with relatively few pairings, and both the rapidity of acquisition and the strength of the aversion has seemed to increase monotonically with age. These facts hold when the odor is novel for the rat. But when the conditioned stimulus is the odor from the rat's home nest, the aversion acquired by 16-day-old rats is significantly weaker than that acquired by 12-day-old rats, independent of baseline preference for home odors (Corby, Caza, & Spear, 1982). (b) The periadolescent rat, defined as incorporating the 6th postnatal week plus or minus a few days, has been shown by L. Spear and Brake (1982) to have a variety of behavioral and psychopharmacological peculiarities; included among these is a tendency in certain circumstances to show less learning than younger or older animals. Perhaps when such nonmonotonic functions relating age and learning are viewed as not anomalous, more instances will appear in the literature.

Each of these three implications would appear to predict a specific set of ontogenetic phenomena of learning and memory that are equally relevant to animals or humans. Their potential significance suggests that I conclude this chapter and turn to the more pertinent task of testing them empirically.

ACKNOWLEDGMENT

Preparation of this chapter was supported by a grant from the National Institute of Mental Health (1 RO1 MH35219). I am grateful for the excellent secretarial assistance of Teri Tanenhaus and the technical assistance of Norman G. Richter with regard to data reported in this chapter.

REFERENCES

Acredolo, L. P. Laboratory versus home: The effect of environment on the 9-month-old infant's choice of spatial reference system. *Developmental Psychology,* 1979, *15,* 666–667.

Alberts, J. R. Ontogeny of olfaction: Reciprocal roles of sensation and behavior in the development of perception. In R. N. Aslin, J. R. Alberts, & M. R. Peterson (Eds.), *The development of perception: Psychobiological perspectives* (Vol. 1), *Audition, somatic perception and the chemical senses.* New York: Academic Press, 1981.

Amsel, A. The ontogeny of appetitive learning and persistence in the rat. In N. E. Spear & B. A. Campbell (Eds.), *Ontogeny of learning and memory.* Hillsdale, N.J.: Lawrence Erlbaum Associates, 1979.

Angermeier, W. F. *The evolution of learning.* Munich: Springer Verlag, 1982.

Anohkin, P. K. Systemogenesis as a general regulator of brain development. In W. A. Himwich & H. E. Himwich (Eds.), *The developing brain: Progress in brain research.* Amsterdam: Elsevier. 1964.

Barrett, B., Rizzo, T., Spear, L. P., & Spear, N. E. *Stimulus selection in passive avoidance learning and retention of weanling, periadolescent, and young adult rats.* Paper presented at meetings of Eastern Psychological Association, Baltimore, April 1982.

Bliss, T. V. P., & Lomo, T. Long-lasting potentiation of synaptic transmission in the dentate area of the anesthetized rabbit following stimulation of the perforant path. *Journal of Physiology* (London), 1973, 232, 331–343.

Bower, T. G. R. *Human development.* San Francisco: W. H. Freeman & Co., 1979.

Bryan, R. G. *Retention of odor-shock conditioning in neonatal rats: Effects of distribution of practice.* Unpublished Ph.D. Thesis, Rutgers University, 1980.

Campbell, B. A. Developmental studies of learning and motivation in infraprimate mammals. In H. W. Stevenson, E. H. Hess, & H. L. Rheingold (Eds.), *Early behavior: Comparative and developmental approaches.* New York: John Wiley & Sons, 1967.

Campbell, B. A. & Spear, N. E. Ontogeny of memory. *Psychological Review,* 1972, *79,* 215–236.

Campbell, B. A., & Coulter, X. The ontogenesis of learning and memory. In M. R. Rosenzweig & E. L. Bennett (Eds.), *Natural mechanisms of learning and memory.* Cambridge, Mass: MIT Press, 1976.

Concannon, J. T., Smith, G. J., Spear, N. E., & Scobie, S. R. Drug cues, drug states and infantile amnesia. In F. C. Colpaert & J. A. Rosencranz (Eds.), *First International Symposium on Drugs as Discriminative Stimuli.* Amsterdam: Elsevier/North Holland Biomedical Press, 1979.

Corby, J., Caza, P. A., & Spear, N. E. Ontogenetic changes in the effectiveness of home nest odor as a conditioned stimulus. *Behavioral and Neural Biology,* 1982, *35,* 354–367.

Dennis, W. Is the newborn infant's repertoire learned or instructive? *Psychological Review*, 1943, *50*, 330–337.

Dennis, W., & Dennis, M. G. Infant development under conditions of restricted practice and minimum social stimulation. *Genetic Psychological Monographs*, 1941, *23*, 149–155.

Durham, M., & Black, K. N. The test performance of 16- to 21-month olds in home and laboratory settings. *Infant Behavior & Development*, 1978, *1*, 216–223.

Garner, W. R. The stimulus in information processing. *American Psychologist*, 1970, *25*, 350–358.

Garner, W. R. *The processing of information as structure*. Hillsdale, N.J.: Lawrence Erlbaum Associates, 1974.

Garner, W. R. Aspects of a stimulus: Features, dimensions and configurations. In E. Rosch & B. B. Lloyd (Eds.), *Cognition and categorization*. Hillsdale, N.J.: Lawrence Erlbaum Associates, 1978.

Gesell, A., & Thompson, H. Learning and growth in identical twin infants. *Genetic Psychological Monographs*, 1929, *6*, 1–124.

Gibson, E. J. *Principles of perceptual learning and development*. New York: Appleton-Century-Crofts, 1969.

Goldberg, S. Infant care and growth in urban Zambia. *Human Development*, 1972, *15*, 77–89.

Goldberg, S. Infant development and mother-infant interaction in urban Zambia. In P. Leiderman, S. Tulkin, & A. Rosenfeld (Eds.), *Culture and infancy*. New York: Academic Press, 1977.

Harlow, H. F. The development of learning in the Rhesus monkey. *American Scientist*, 1959, *47*, 459–479.

Haroutunian, V., & Campbell, B. A. Emergence of interoceptive and exteroceptive control of behavior in rats. *Science*, 1979, *205*, 927–928.

Haroutunain, V., & Campbell, B. A. Development and habituation of the heartrate orienting response to auditory and visual stimuli in the rat. *Journal of Comparative and Physiological Psychology*, 1981, *95*, 166–174.

Hofer, M. A. Toward a developmental basis for disease predisposition: The effect of early maternal separation on brain, behavior, and cardiovascular system. In H. Weinder, M. A. Hofer & A. J. Stunkard (Eds.), *Brain, behavior and bodily disease*. New York: Raven Press, 1981.

Horner, T. M. Test-retest and home-clinical characteristics of the Bayley scales of infant development in 9- and 15-month old infants. *Child Development*, 1980, *51*, 751–758.

Hunt, J. M. Psychological development: Early experience. In M. R. Rosenzweig & L. W. Porter (Eds.), *Annual review of psychology* (Vol. 30). Palo Alto: Annual Reviews Inc., 1979.

Infurna, R. N., Steinert, P. A., & Spear, N. E. Ontogenetic changes in the modulation of taste aversion learning by home environmental cues in rats. *Journal of Comparative and Physiological Psychology*, 1979, *93*, 1097–1108.

Isaacson, R. L. *The Limbic System (Second ed.)*. New York: Plenum Press, 1982.

Isaacson, R. L., & Spear, N. E. *The expression of knowledge: Neurobehavioral transformations of information into action*. New York: Plenum Press, 1982.

Johanson, I. B., & Hall, W. G. Appetitive learning in 1-day old rat pups. *Science*, 1979, *205*, 419–421.

Johnson, M. K. A multiple-entry, modular memory system. In G. R. Bower (Ed.), *The psychology of learning and motivation*. New York: Academic Press, 1983.

Kail, R. V., & Hagen, J. W. (Eds.). *Perspectives on the development of memory and cognition*. Hillsdale, N.J.: Lawrence Erlbaum Associates, 1977.

Kail, R. V., & Hagen, J. W. Memory in childhood. In B. B. Wolman (Ed.), *Handbook of developmental psychology*. Englewood Cliffs, N.J.: Prentice Hall, 1982.

Kemler, D. G., & Smith, L. B. Is there a developmental trend from integrality to separability in perception? *Journal of Experimental Child Psychology*, 1978, *26*, 498–507.

Kenny, J. T., & Blass, E. M. Suckling as incentive to instrumental learning in preweanling rats. *Science*, 1977, *196*, 989–899.

Kokot, L., Caza, P., Richter, N., & Spear, N. E. *Ontogenetic changes in CS− and CS+ conditioning in infant rats.* Paper presented at meetings of Eastern Psychological Association, Baltimore, April 1982.

Lewin, R. Is your brain really necessary? *Science,* 1980, *210,* 1232–1234.

Lockhead, G. R. Processing dimensional stimuli: A note. *Psychological Review,* 1972, *79,* 410–419.

McGraw, M. B. *The neuromuscular maturation of the human infant.* New York: Columbia University Press, 1943.

Monahan, J. S., & Lockhead, G. R. Identification of integral stimuli. *Journal of Experimental Psychology: General,* 1977, *106,* 94–110.

Moskowitch, M. Multiple dissociations of function in amnesia. In L. S. Cermak (Ed.), *Human memory and amnesia.* Hillsdale, N.J.: Lawrence Erlbaum Associates, 1982.

Neisser, U. *Cognition and reality.* San Francisco: W. H. Freeman, 1976.

Newman, S., Caza, P. A., & Spear, N. E. *Ontogenetic differences in response to contextual stimuli.* Paper presented at meetings of the Eastern Psychological Association, Baltimore, April 1982.

Papousek, H. Experimental studies of appetitional behavior in human newborns and infants. In H. W. Stevenson, E. H. Hess, & H. L. Rheingold (Eds.), *Early behavior: Comparative and developmental approaches.* New York: Wiley, 1967.

Papousek, H. *Elaboration of conditioned head-turning.* Paper presented at meeting of XIX International Congress of Psychology, London, 1969.

Pedersen, P. E., & Blass, E. M. Prenatal and postnatal determinants of the first suckling episode in albino rats. *Developmental Psychobiology,* 1982, *15,* 349–356.

Rescorla, R. A., & Durlach, P. J. Within-event learning and Pavlovian conditioning. In N. E. Spear & R. R. Miller (Eds.), *Information processing in animals: Memory mechanisms.* Hillsdale, N.J.: Lawrence Erlbaum Associates, 1981.

Rovee-Collier, C. K. Infants as problem-solvers: A psychobiological perspective. In M. D. Zeiler & P. Harzen (Eds.), *Advances in analysis of behavior* (Vol. 3). *Biological factors in learning.* London: Wiley, 1983, in press.

Rovee-Collier, C. K., & Lipsitt, L. P. Learning, adaptation, and memory. In P. Stratton (Ed.), *Psychobiology of the newborn.* London: Wiley, 1982.

Rovee-Collier, C. K., & Gekoski, M. J. The economics of infancy: A review of conjugate reinforcement. In H. W. Reese & L. P. Lipsitt (Eds.), *Advances in child development and behavior* (Vol. 13). New York: Academic Press, 1979.

Rudy, J. W., & Cheatle, M. D. Ontogeny of associative learning: Acquisition of odor aversions by neonatal rats. In N. E. Spear & B. A. Campbell (Eds.), *Ontogeny of learning and memory.* Hillsdale: N.J.: Lawrence Erlbaum Associates, 1979.

Sameroff, A. J. Can conditioned responses be established in the newborn infant? *Developmental Psychology,* 1971, *5,* 1–12.

Schacter, D. L., & Tulving, E. Memory, amnesia and the episodic/semantic distinction. In R. L. Isaacson & N. E. Spear (Eds.), *The expression of knowledge: Neurobehavioral transformations of information into action.* New York: Plenum Press, 1982.

Shepp, B. E. From perceived similarity to dimensional structure: A new hypothesis about perspective development. In E. Rosch & B. B. Lloyd (Eds.), *Cognition and categorization.* Hillsdale, N.J.: Lawrence Erlbaum Associates, 1978.

Simon, H. A. How big is a chunk? *Science,* 1974, *183,* 482–488.

Smith, L. B., & Kemler, D. G. Developmental trends in free classification: Evidence for a new conceptualization of perceptual development. *Journal of Experimental Child Psychology,* 1977, *24,* 279–298.

Smith, L. B., & Kemler, D. G. Levels of experienced dimensionality in children and adults. *Cognitive Psychology,* 1978, *10,* 502–532.

Smith, G. J., & Spear, N. E. Home environmental effects on withholding behaviors in conditioning in infant and neonatal rats. *Science,* 1978, *202,* 327–329.

Smith, G. J., & Spear, N. E. Home environmental stimuli facilitate learning of shock-escape spatial discrimination in rats 7–11 days of age. *Behavioral and Neural Biology,* 1981, *31* 360–365.

Solheim, G. S., Hensler, J. G., & Spear, N. E. Age-dependent contextual effects on short-term active avoidance retention in rats. *Behavioral and Neural Biology,* 1980, *30,* 250–259.

Spear, L. P., & Brake, S. C. Periadolescence: Age-dependent behavior and psycho-pharmacological responsivity in rats. *Developmental Psychobiology,* 1983, *16,* 83–109.

Spear, N. E. *The processing of memories: Forgetting and retention.* Hillsdale, N.J.: Lawrence Erlbaum Associates, 1978.

Spear, N. E. Memory storage factors in infantile amnesia. In G. Bower (Ed.), *The psychology of learning and motivation* (Vol. 13). New York: Academic Press, 1979. (a)

Spear, N. E. Experimental analysis of infantile amnesia. In J. F. Kihlstrom & F. J. Evans (Eds.), *Functional disorders of memory.* Hillsdale, N.J.: Lawrence Erlbaum Associates, 1979b.

Spear, N. E. The future study of learning and memory from a psychobiological perspective. In V. Sarris & A. Parducci (Eds.), *Perspectives in psychological experimentation.* Hillsdale, N.J.: Lawrence Erlbaum Associates, 1983, in press.

Spear, N. E., & Campbell, B. A. (Eds.), *Ontogeny of learning and memory.* Hillsdale, N.J.: Lawrence Erlbaum Associates, 1979.

Spear, N. E. & Isaacson, R. L. The problem of expression. In R. L. Isaacson & N. E. Spear (Eds.), *The expression of knowledge: Neurobehavioral transformation of information into action.* New York: Plenum Press, 1982.

Spear, N. E., & Smith, G. J. Alleviation of forgetting in neonatal rats. *Developmental Psychobiology,* 1978, *11,* 513–520.

Steinert, P. A. *Stimulus selection among preweanling and adult rats as a function of CS amount and quality using a taste aversion paradigm.* Unpublished Ph.D. Thesis, State University of New York, Binghamton, 1981.

Stickrod, G., Kimble, D. P., & Smotherman, W. P. In utero taste/odor aversion and conditioning in the rat. *Physiology & Behavior,* 1982, *28,* 5–8.

Tighe, L. S., & Tighe, T. J. The unattended dimension in discrimination learning. In A. D. Pick (Ed.), *Perception and its development: A tribute to Eleanor J. Gibson.* Hillsdale, N.J.: Lawrence Erlbaum Associates, 1979.

Tompkins, S. S. A theory of memory. In J. S. Antrobus (Ed.), *Cognition and affect.* Boston: Little, Brown, 1970.

Treisman, A., & Gelade, G. A feature-integration theory of attention. *Cognitive Psychology,* 1980, *12,* 97–136.

Turns, L. E., & Misanin, J. R. *Retention of active avoidance behavior in infant rats.* Paper presented at meetings of Eastern Psychological Association in Baltimore, April 1982.

Weingartner, H., & Parker, E. S. (Eds.) *Memory consolidation: Towards a psychobiology of cognition.* Hillsdale, N.J.: Lawrence Erlbaum Associates, 1983, in press.

Werner, J. S., & Perlmutter, M. Development of visual memory in infants. In H. W. Reese & L. P. Lipsitt (Eds.), *Advances in child development and behavior* (Vol. 14). New York: Academic Press, 1979.

White, B. L., & Held, R. Plasticity of sensorimotor development in the human infant. In J. Rosenblatt & T. Allensmith (Eds.), *The causes of behavior* (Second ed.). Boston: Allen & Bacon, 1966.

Wigal, T., Smith, G. J., & Spear, N. E. *Effects of home environmental cues on retention of conditioned place aversion.* Paper presented at meetings of Eastern Psychological Association, Hartford, 1980.

Wolz, J. P. *Ontogeny of selection and retention of memory attributes by infant rats.* Unpublished Ph.D. Thesis, State University of New York, Binghamton, 1981.

Author Index

Numbers in italics indicate pages with complete bibliographic information.

Subject Index

369

218, 257, 259, 262–263, 273, 279, 303,
 309, 325, 335, 352
 specificity, 108, 109, 275
endo-choclear potential, 90
environment
 acoustic, 194
 enriched, 23
 reactivity to, 210
episode, 223, 230–232, 249, 335, 341
ethologists, 305
ethology, 23, 311
evoked potential, visual, 42–44
evoked response
 auditory, 91
 cortical, 94
evolution, 15, 66, 221, 288, 317
excitation, 4
expectation, violation of, 255, 258, 259
experience, 70, 103, 160, 194
 early, 23–24, 29, 130–135, 215, 293,
 326–327, 350, 352
exploration, 210
 visual, 123
extinction, 237, 240
eyeball, 40
 movement, 40, 51–55, 61

F

faces, 14, 48, 51, 159, 294, 296–297
 discrimination of, 49
failure-to-thrive syndrome, 214
family, 338
fatigue, 212
fever, 212
fixation, binocular, 40, 55
foraging, 305, 310
forgetting, 27, 96, 117, 119–122, 129, 190,
 230–231, 288, 306, 309
fovea, 40, 53
function, 305, 306
 developmental, 15, 16
fusion, 56, 57, 61

G

gaze, 124
generalization, 203, 240–241, 244, 346
 stimulus, 31
 response, 31
generation, 257–259, 262, 268
geotaxis, negative, 74
Gestalt, 240, 249

glomerular complex, 81
glossopharyngeal nerve, 86
goal, 280
gravity, 74
growth, 229
gustatory system, 182

H

habits, 288
habituation, 13–15, 32, 59, 93, 104–105,
 155, 171–173, 201, 211–214, 216–217,
 255–256, 258–259, 293–294, 297,
 299–300, 304, 318, 351
 patterns of, 218
 rate of, 218–219
heart rate, 92
helplessness, 176
heterochrony, 71–72, 81
hibernation, 290
hippocampus, 334
home, 338, 340–341
homology, 66, 305
hormone
 growth, 339
 thyroid, 32, 83
hyperactivity, 339
hyperopia, 46–47
hyperthyroidism, 94, 95
hypoactivity, 339
hue, 58–59
 discrimination of, 59

I

imitation, 256, 258
imprinting, 23–24
incentive, 26
individual differences, 209–210, 217
infancy, 3, 10, 11, 14, 17, 23
infantile amnesia, 23–24, 26–27, 31–32,
 104–105, 294, 327–328, 337–338
infants
 premature, 129, 213
 risk, 212, 220
inferior colliculus, 90
ingestion, 136–137, 141, 145–146, 150, 152,
 154
inhibition, 4
 latent, 155, 333
insomnia, 339
integration, 193–196, 204, 231, 245–247, 249
intelligence, 288